EIGHTH EDITION

Research Methods for Social Workers

Bonnie L. Yegidis
University of Central Florida

Robert W. Weinbach
University of South Carolina

Laura L. Myers
Florida A&M University

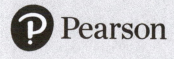

330 Hudson Street, NY, NY 10013

Director, Teacher Education & the Helping Professions: Kevin M. Davis

Portfolio Manager: Rebecca Fox-Gieg

Content Project Manager: Pamela D. Bennett

Media Project Manager: Lauren Carlson

Portfolio Management Assistant: Anne McAlpine

Executive Field Marketing Manager: Krista Clark

Executive Product Marketing Manager: Christopher Barry

Manufacturing Buyer: Deidra Smith

Cover Designer: Melissa Welch

Cover Photo: The Good Brigade/Offset.com

Full-Service Project Management: Srinivasan Sundararajan, Lumina Datamatics, Inc.

Composition: Lumina Datamatics, Inc.

Printer/Binder: LSC Communications

Cover Printer: LSC Communications

Text Font: Dante MT Pro 10.5 pt.

Library of Congress Cataloging-in-Publication Data

Names: Yegidis, Bonnie L., author. | Weinbach, Robert W., author. | Myers, Laura L., author.

Title: Research methods for social workers / Bonnie L. Yegidis, University of Central Florida, Robert W. Weinbach, University of South Carolina, Laura L. Myers, Florida A&M University.

Description: Eighth Edition. | New York : Pearson, [2018] | Revised edition of the authors' Research methods for social workers, c2012. | Includes bibliographical references and index.

Identifiers: LCCN 2016055316 | ISBN 9780134512563 (pbk. : alk. paper)

Subjects: LCSH: Social service—Research—Methodology.

Classification: LCC HV11.Y43 2018 | DDC 361.3/2072—dc23

LC record available at https://lccn.loc.gov/2016055316

13 2020

ISBN 10:   0-13-451256-1

ISBN 13: 978-0-13-451256-3

Preface

Social work practice continues to evolve. Research, now an integral part of practice, is changing along with it. In this edition of *Research Methods for Social Workers*, we have attempted to retain those features that faculty and students told us they liked. At the same time, we have added new material to address the needs of today's students of research and of those conscientious practitioners who aspire to be critical consumers of research reports.

What Can the Reader Expect to Find?

Like the previous editions, this book is designed for a one-semester or one-quarter course on research methods. It is well suited to either undergraduate or foundation-level graduate social work courses. Its content is consistent with both current Council on Social Work Education (CSWE) accreditation standards and curriculum policy guidelines. This book offers a brief conceptual overview of specialized topics such as statistical analysis and evaluation research and encourages its readers to seek a more in-depth coverage of them. The book is written for both current and future social work practitioners to assist them in becoming evidence-based practitioners. It presents research as a logical, non-intimidating activity that is inextricably linked to social work practice.

This book contains no unnecessary research terminology or references to obscure, rarely used methods of knowledge building. Necessary terminology is italicized and explained. Students, even those with no prior research background, should find the text interesting and easy to understand. It is written in a crisp, straightforward style and refers to contemporary social work practice on virtually every page. Examples are real—the kind of situations that social workers encounter every day.

Our belief that the knowledge, values, and skills of the social worker are much more of an asset than a liability in conducting research permeates the book. We do not take the approach that research is a "necessary evil" to be grudgingly studied and conducted. It is a logical extension of good practice and absolutely essential to it. Thus, the areas that are given a disproportional amount of attention (relative to other texts) reflect this orientation. For example, tasks such as problem identification and formulation, question selection, and use of existing knowledge receive extensive coverage. Are these not also important tasks in good social work practice intervention? Research design—the rich array of alternatives available to do the job of acquiring knowledge to inform our practice decision-making—is also discussed in detail.

We continue to believe that qualitative and quantitative research methodologies are mutually supportive and of equal importance in knowledge building for our profession.

New to This Edition

At the suggestion of reviewers, we have incorporated several major changes in this edition of the book.

- We combined the general discussion of literature reviews (what they are, their purposes, credibility issues, etc.) with the chapter on developing focused research questions and research hypotheses.
- We have expanded the section on writing the literature review into a complete chapter on writing the research report and disseminating research findings.
- We have made significant changes to the research design chapters. Over the years, we have come to believe that many research texts create a false dichotomy by describing research as either quantitative or qualitative. We have tried to emphasize that, while some research methods are clearly predominantly one type of research or the other, most research studies today have elements of both. Researchers conducting predominantly qualitative research now attempt to quantify their research data to the degree possible; those conducting more quantitative studies often attempt to verify and expand on their findings using qualitative methods.
- We have divided research methods and designs into four chapters in this new edition. Chapter 5 covers the group research methods generally associated with more quantitative research studies. Chapter 6 focuses on research methodologies used in predominantly qualitative research studies. Chapter 7 looks at program evaluation techniques. Chapter 8 focuses on evaluating individual practice effectiveness, with an emphasis on the single-system evaluation method used by social work practitioners to evaluate their practice with individuals, families, schools, communities, and so forth.
- We have added video examples in this edition. By clicking on the arrow icons in the Pearson enhanced etext, readers will be able to watch videos to enhance their understanding of the chapter concepts related to the videos.
- We have moved the Chapter Review sections to the Pearson enhanced etext. The Chapter Reviews are now interactive and provide immediate feedback to reader when the correct answer is selected.

Personalize Learning with MyLab®

MyLab is an online homework, tutorial, and assessment program designed to engage students and improve results. Within its structured environment, students see key concepts demonstrated, practice what they learn, test their understanding, and receive feedback to guide their learning and ensure they master key learning outcomes. The online resources in the MyLab with Pearson eText include:

- Practice applying research concepts and skills. Interactive Thinking Like a Researcher exercises allow the reader to practice specific research tasks.
- Practice reading research articles. Interactive Reading Research exercises provide readers with practice identifying key parts of research articles like purpose statements, research questions, descriptions of methods, and conclusions.

- Practice understanding research articles. Interactive Understanding Research exercises help readers not simply identify parts of articles but to use the concepts they have learned in the chapter to read articles with understanding.
- MyLab includes the Pearson eText version of the book, which integrates MyLab.

Acknowledgments

We would like to acknowledge and thank the following colleagues who critiqued the previous edition of this book and recommended many insightful and helpful changes for the current edition: Jennifer Hause Crowell, Belmont University; Andrew Fultz, Northwestern State University; Henry W. Kronner, Aurora University; Jina Sang, The University of Akron; and Leslie E. Tower, West Virginia University. We are also indebted to a number of colleagues who critiqued the earlier editions of this book and made many valuable suggestions. They are Sherry Edwards, Roselle Scagge, Makeba Green, Gordon Casebolt, Felix Rivera, Murray Newman, Ram Cnann, Miriam Johnson, James Stafford, Gail Leedy, Stephen M. Marson, Donald S. Pierson, Freddie Avant, John D. Clapp, Sophie Dziegielewski, Gary Widrick, and Bruce Thyer. We greatly appreciate their input and have responded to their helpful suggestions whenever possible. Students who used the previous edition and faculty who adopted it for classroom use were also generous with their comments and suggestions.

BONNIE L. YEGIDIS
University of Central Florida

ROBERT W. WEINBACH
University of South Carolina

LAURA L. MYERS
Florida A&M University

Brief Contents

Contents

             Structured Observation   *256*

                Advantages   *258*

                Limitations   *258*

     Surveys   259

         Potential for Distortion   *259*

         Identity of the Participant   *260*

         Return Rate   *261*

         Response Bias   *263*

     Interviews   265

         In-Person Interviews   *265*

         Group Interviews   *271*

         Telephone Interviews   *272*

     Electronic Communication   274

     Summary   275

12. Data Collection Instruments   277

     Fixed-Alternative and Open-Ended Items   278

     Composite Indexes and Scales   279

         Composite Indexes   *280*

         Scales   *280*

     Using Existing Data Collection Instruments   284

     Revising Existing Data Collection Instruments   286

     Constructing New Data Collection Instruments   287

         Issues in Development   *289*

     Use of Self-Administered Data Collection Instruments   293

         Advantages   *293*

         Supervised Administration   *293*

     Summary   294

13. Analyzing Data   295

     The Data in Perspective   295

     Preparing for Data Analysis   297

     Qualitative and Quantitative Data Analysis   298

         Qualitative Analysis   *298*

         Quantitative Analysis   *299*

     Uses of Statistical Analyses   300

         Designing Research   *301*

         Summarizing the Distribution of Variables   *301*

         Estimating the Characteristics of a Population   *306*

         Answering Questions and Testing Hypotheses   *306*

14. Writing the Research Report and Disseminating Research Findings   313

1

Toward Evidence-Based Practice

Social workers must make many decisions every day. Good, informed decisions require knowledge. What are the sources of our knowledge? Some is acquired through formal education in bachelors' and masters' programs in social work or from attending continuing education programs. It may come from reading articles in professional journals, textbooks, or through online searches. It may also be knowledge shared by senior-level practitioners based on their many years of practice experience. Historically, much of the knowledge derived from these sources has had one characteristic in common—it may not have been derived from research! However, this is changing.

The Council on Social Work Education (CSWE), the organization responsible for the accreditation of Bachelors of Social Work (BSW) and Masters of Social Work (MSW) programs, recognizes the importance of research content in social work curricula. The Educational Policy and Accreditation Standards (EPAS) (Council on Social Work Education, 2015) specify that research content and skills must be taught in both undergraduate and graduate social work education programs. Standard 4, *Engage in Practice-informed Research and Research-informed Practice*, maintains that:

> Social workers understand quantitative and qualitative research methods and their respective roles in advancing a science of social work and in evaluating their practice. Social workers understand the principles of logic, scientific inquiry, and culturally informed and ethical approaches to building knowledge. Social workers understand that evidence that informs practice derives from multi-disciplinary sources and multiple ways of knowing. They also understand the processes for translating research findings into effective practice. (p. 8)

In addition, CSWE (2015) defines three practice behaviors to exemplify this competency:

- Use practice experience and theory to inform scientific inquiry and research.
- Apply critical thinking to engage in analysis of quantitative and qualitative research methods and research findings.
- Use and translate research evidence to inform and improve practice, policy, and service delivery. (p. 8)

LEARNING OUTCOMES

- Summarize how social work practice and research have been developed and linked as the field of social work has progressed.
- Identify and describe the characteristics of evidence-based practice.
- Recognize various forms of alternative sources of knowledge (logic, tradition, and authority) and identify when decisions and opinions are being influenced by these sources.
- Describe why scientific knowledge is preferable to alternative sources of knowledge when making social work practice decisions.
- Define the types of knowledge derived from scientific research (descriptive, predictive, and prescriptive), and identify which type or types are being sought in a given research study.
- Differentiate research studies based on the study's general purpose or goal (basic versus applied research).
- Distinguish between qualitative and quantitative research methods and describe at least the basic characteristics of each.

CHAPTER OUTLINE

1

CSWE's Educational Policy and Accreditation Standards (2015) form the basis for what we have chosen to include in this book. By teaching students the best ways to conduct research, we hope that they will be equipped to acquire the knowledge needed for making good, informed decisions in whatever social system level they may work. However, understanding how research should be conducted has a second benefit—it enables social workers to critically and knowledgeably evaluate the research methods of others and, thus, assess the credibility of the findings and recommendations that they generate.

Knowledge of research makes possible a methodology that has been widely discussed and advocated: evidence-based practice (EBP). EBP is a process designed to help social workers make important decisions regarding the care they provide their clients. This model originated in the field of medicine in the early 1990s and has since been adopted in a wide array of health and human service disciplines. The primary source document for learning about EBP is a slim volume by Strauss, Richardson, Glasziou, and Haynes (2005), in which EBP is defined as "the integration of the best research evidence with our clinical expertise, and our patient's unique values and circumstances" (p. 1). A related definition is found in Guyatt and Rennie (2002): "The conscientious, explicit, and judicious use of current best evidence in making decisions about the care of individual patients. The practice of EBP requires integration of individual clinical expertise and patient preferences with the best available clinical evidence from systematic research" (p. 412). The National Association of Social Workers (2015) offers a definition of EBP that covers many of the important aspects of social work practice:

> EBP is a process in which the practitioner combines well-researched interventions with clinical experience and ethics, and client preferences and culture to guide and inform the delivery of treatments and services. The practitioner, researcher and client must work together in order to identify what works, for whom and under what conditions. This approach ensures that the treatments and services, when used as intended, will have the most effective outcomes as demonstrated by the research. It will also ensure that programs with proven success will be more widely disseminated and will benefit a greater number of people.

Thus, EBP entails a careful consideration of (1) what the best research on the question has suggested, (2) our own practice experience and expertise, and (3) the values and preferences of the clients we serve.

How might this work? Suppose a medical social worker is assigned to work with the parents of a 9-year-old boy who has a diagnosis of acute leukemia. The social worker knows (from medical knowledge acquired through research and the knowledge of the boy's specific situation) that he has a very small probability of surviving more than a few weeks without a bone marrow transplant. She also knows (from the same sources) that the likelihood of a successful transplant is quite low. Her practice experience reminds her that if the transplant is unsuccessful, his suffering is likely to be worse than if he never had the transplant. She has seen it happen before and it has been extremely stressful for all concerned. Ethically, she recognizes the need for the parents and the child (to the degree possible) to be involved in the decision to have or not have the transplant. She feels an ethical responsibility to inform the parents that the transplant could result in worse suffering and might even hasten death for their child. As a caring and concerned social worker, she feels compassion for the child and his parents. This will influence her behavior as well. She cannot and should not make the decision for them, but she understands that they will look to her for help in making it, and require her support for whatever decision they make. In EBP, how she ultimately presents the options to them (her intervention) will be determined by the combination of all of these factors.

> *EBP entails a careful consideration of (1) what the best research on the question has suggested, (2) our own practice experience and expertise, and (3) the values and preferences of the clients we serve.*

HISTORICAL ANTECEDENTS

Historically, social workers have not always emphasized the importance of research knowledge for practice decision making as much as have other professionals. In 1979, a sociologist, Simpson, shared his perceptions of social work practitioners and their relationship with research. He noted that practitioners tend to shun abstract knowledge and to rely instead on (1) humanitarian impulse, (2) occupational folklore, and (3) common sense. He also observed that most of the knowledge that is used for social work practice decision making was being drawn from the work of researchers in other fields. He went on to describe social work literature as permeated with faddism and lacking an empirical base.

During the late 1970s, both the CSWE and the National Association of Social Workers (NASW) devoted considerable effort to examining the problem of research knowledge utilization. They convened groups of leading practitioners and researchers to study it, and concluded that responsibility for the gap between practice and research must be shared by both practitioners and researchers, and that both groups must be involved in closing the gap.

Practitioners in the groups convened described their distrust of researchers and the lack of practical utility of much of the knowledge that their research generated. They viewed researchers, most of whom historically have been academicians, as people who did not really understand the realities of social work practice. The researchers, in turn, described their frustration with many practitioners' lack of understanding of research methods and general lack of interest in research. They cited a tendency of practitioners to reject those research findings that did not agree with what they "knew" to be true and to assume falsely that research knowledge was too abstract to be of value to them.

If social work practitioners are to rely heavily on the knowledge generated by scientific research methods, several conditions must exist. First, practitioners must have a knowledge and understanding of scientific methods, and must gain a respect and an appreciation for them. If they learn to appreciate the rigor that is built into well-designed research, practitioners are more likely to believe in and value the findings that are produced. They are also more likely to be critical of the conclusions and recommendations of the researcher whose methods are flawed (and that is a good thing).

Assessment

Behavior: Develop mutually agreed-on intervention goals and objectives based on the critical assessment of strengths, needs, and challenges within clients and constituencies)

Critical Thinking Question: What are three factors the social worker might consider when deciding how to discuss treatment options with the patient and his parents?

Second, social workers will rely more heavily on the findings of scientific research if there is support for it by their supervisors and peers. This can only occur when there is more reward (both tangible and intangible) for practice based upon scientific research findings than for simply doing things the way they have always been done. Will there be support for evaluating our individual practice effectiveness using scientific research methods, or will it be viewed by others as time that could be better spent in other ways? Will we be encouraged to attend professional conferences where research knowledge is disseminated or to read and discuss professional journal articles with colleagues, or will this be viewed as more time wasted?

Finally, social workers will be more likely to use their knowledge of scientific research methods if there is the expectation that any new knowledge that they generate will be used to improve client services. What is likely to happen when social workers employ scientific research methods to evaluate the effectiveness of programs of which they are a part? How will the findings be received? What if their evaluations suggest that current programs or some of their components are not effective or are even making a problem worse? Will the response of "higher ups" be to welcome this knowledge as a stimulus for change? Or will efforts be made to suppress it in order to maintain the status quo? Practitioners require support at all levels of human service organizations to effectively use research findings for decision making.

Practitioners require support at all levels of human service organizations to effectively use research findings for decision making.

Research-Informed Practice or Practice-Informed Research

Behavior: Use and translate research evidence to inform and improve practice, policy, and service delivery.

Critical Thinking Question: What are three things that administrators could do to encourage social work practitioners to use research findings in making their practice decisions?

Over the years, the need to bring social work practice and research closer together has produced a wide variety of conceptual models. Garvin (1981) conceptualized three overlapping research roles that the social work practitioner can play: (1) consumer of research, (2) creator and disseminator of knowledge, and (3) contributing partner. In performing the first role, the practitioner has a professional obligation to seek, evaluate, and use, when appropriate, the research knowledge that is generated by others. The second role implies an obligation to be directly involved in doing research and to share the results of one's own research with others. This role recognizes that there is a wealth of untapped knowledge that exists within the practice milieu that can be systematically collected, organized, and shared for the benefit of other practitioners. The third role, that of contributing partner, recognizes that not all social workers may have the knowledge, resources, or interest necessary to undertake large-scale research projects, but this does not preclude their making contributions to the research efforts of others, such as identifying researchable problems or providing data for evaluation of social programs.

The 1990s saw important refinements in our understanding of what should constitute the relationship between research and practice and thus moved us closer to our current understanding of EBP. The arrival of two professional journals—*Social Work Research* and *Research on Social Work Practice*—emphasized the publication of outcome research and encouraged social work's move to a more accountable era. The creation of the Institute for the Advancement of Social Work Research (IASWR) and the Society for Social Work Research (SSWR) was yet another indication that the gap between practice and research was narrowing. SSWR hosts a well-attended annual conference in which a wide variety of research findings have been disseminated.

At about the same time, there was a dramatic increase in the number of social work doctoral programs, which has increased the number of social workers educated and trained in advanced social work research methods.

These and other developments combined to move us to where we are today—to recognition of the importance of EBP. The demands for accountability that began several decades earlier continue to increase. Funding organizations, the general public, and individual stakeholders demand accountability, looking for proof that social programs and services demonstrate both effectiveness and efficiency.

EVIDENCE-BASED PRACTICE

We have looked at the current definitions of EBP and offered an example of how it might work in one setting. Now let us turn to a more detailed discussion of the five-step process of EBP (Strauss et al., 2005):

Step 1. Convert our need for information about the causes of the problem, and for possible interventions, into an answerable question.

Step 2. Track down the best evidence with which to answer that question.

Step 3. Critically appraise that evidence for its validity, impact, and applicability.

Step 4. Integrate the critical appraisal with our clinical expertise and the client's unique values and circumstances.

Step 5. Evaluate our effectiveness and efficiency in carrying out steps 1–4 and seek ways to improve our practice. (pp. 3–4)

Funding organizations, the general public, and individual stakeholders demand accountability, looking for proof that social programs and services demonstrate both effectiveness and efficiency.

A considerable literature, both within and outside the field of social work, is available that focuses on each of these steps. An excellent resource for understanding EBP is the *Social Worker's Desk Reference* (Roberts, 2009). Gambrill and Gibbs (2009) describe effective ways to develop well-structured questions (related to step 1 of EBP). These questions typically contain four parts, the *population* of clients (P), the *intervention* of concern (I), what the intervention may be *compared* to (C), and hoped for *outcomes* (O). Some examples of PICO questions include "How do persons with obsessive-compulsive disorder fare after being treated with exposure therapy and response prevention, compared to similar clients who are not treated at all?" or "How do clients receiving TANF benefits who also receive a job-finding club intervention fare compared to TANF recipients who did not receive this intervention?" or "Are people with alcoholism who regularly attend AA meetings more abstinent than similar individuals who do not attend AA?" The idea is when a social worker meets a client with a problem, one of the outcomes of the assessment process will be to formulate one or more such answerable questions, which might have a bearing on what options are presented to that particular client. Not all answerable questions bear on the topic of choosing interventions. Similar questions may be created to evaluate assessment methods, as in "Do children who are assessed for potential sexual abuse through the use of anatomically correct dolls more accurately report actual episodes of abuse compared to similar children who are assessed without the use of such dolls?" or "Does the use of the genogram to assess clients result in a more accurate understanding of the client's background than standard

6   Chapter 1

clinical interviews?" Other questions may be focused on issues such as the etiology of certain conditions, the cost-benefits of certain interventions, or questions related to the potentially harmful effects of a possible treatment (e.g., rebirthing therapy or facilitated communication). Chapter 3 will provide a more thorough discussion on creating research questions.

Once one or more answerable questions have been formulated, the next step is to track down credible information that may help answer it (Chapter 4). This process is addressed in Rubin and Parrish (2009) and may involve searching electronic databases, locating credible practice guidelines, or finding systematic reviews bearing on one's topic. Among the higher or more credible forms of evidence that EBP particularly seeks to locate are randomized controlled trials (see Montgomery & Mayo-Wilson, 2009), meta-analyses (Corcoran & Littell, 2009), systematic reviews (Littell & Corcoran, 2009), and practice guidelines (Howard, Perron, & Vaughn, 2009). The third step, critically appraising studies for EBP, is the focus of Bronson's (2009) study. Here, the social worker brings to bear his or her skills in reading and appraising research, paying attention to issues of internal and external validity, relevance, sampling, statistical analysis, and so forth.

The fourth step in EBP is integrating the information found from diverse sources with one's clinical expertise and the client's unique values and preferences. Of course, one's professional ethical standards are also a crucial consideration, as are available resources. This important topic is discussed by Gambrill (2009). The fifth step involves self-evaluating one's effectiveness and efficiency. This requires one's ability to not only conduct EBP but also evaluate the outcomes with one's client, which is actually the point of the entire exercise. Thyer and Myers's works (2007, 2009) are good resources to use in this regard. Portions of the preceding description of EBP are based on Thyer and Myers (2010).

In the twenty-first century, there still remain obstacles to the use of and objections to EBP (Rosen, 2003). However, most of the obstacles can be overcome and many of the objections reflect a misunderstanding of EBP. EBP is not intended to dictate to social workers what decisions they should make, only to get them to use all available data (including their practice expertise, professional values, and their knowledge of individual clients and their values and preferences) in making them. While EBP can result in cost savings for health insurance providers and other third parties, that is not its purpose—it is to offer services and programs with the greatest potential for success. Besides, what is wrong with cost cutting, as long as our clients are the ultimate beneficiaries? While there are still problems for which effective interventions have not been identified through research, these gaps do not negate the need for social work practitioners to know how to conduct research, locate and evaluate critically the research of others, and, when available, to use the findings of researchers as an important component of their practice decision making.

Research and Practice: More Similar Than Different

The *scientist-practitioner model,* developed as a training program for psychologists, encourages practitioners to adhere to scientific methods, procedures, and research to guide their practice. Gelso and Lent (2000) offer a synopsis of the scientist-practitioner model, stating that "ultimately, our science and practice will be enhanced by helping our students learn how scholarly work can be done in the context of practice and practice settings" (p. 135). A central premise of the model is that social work practice should closely resemble scientific research.

However, in 1996, Wakefield and Kirk cast doubt upon the model's value, suggesting that social work practitioners have not been (and probably cannot ever be) simultaneously both practitioners and researchers, regularly conducting research to make their practice more effective. The authors contend that there should continue to be a division of labor, with researchers continuing to take the major responsibility for determining which practice methods are most effective and practitioners conscientiously using the findings of research in making informed practice decisions—EBP. One type of scientist-practitioner relationship has emerged, the university-community research partnership, to encourage research collaboration between university researchers and community practitioners. Begun, Berger, Otto-Salaj, and Rose (2010) looked at the development of these partnerships and offered "a set of strategies for building and sustaining research collaborations between university and community-based social work professionals" (p. 54).

Although there is now a fair consensus that research and practice cannot be totally merged, they are not all that different. In fact, many of the attributes that are associated with good practitioners are the same ones that make for a good researcher. Even the tasks of practice and research are quite similar. Research entails a logical process not too unlike the steps involved in successful practice intervention. Grinnell and Siegel (1988) describe an early variation of the scientist-practitioner model that highlights the many ways in which research methods and the social work problem-solving process are alike. The authors note that, in its ideal form, problem-solving in social work practice follows a sequence of activities that is virtually identical to the traditional research process. Box 1.1 illustrates some parallels that can be drawn when one conceptualizes research and practice intervention as problem-solving processes.

Box 1.1   Research and Practice as Problem-Solving Methods: Related Activities

Research Tasks	Related Practice Tasks
1. Identify needed knowledge.	1. Identify broad problem.
2. Identify focus of the study.	2. Partialize the problem.
3. Specify question(s) for study.	3. Specify problem(s) for intervention.
4. Develop research design.	4. Develop action plan.
5. Collect data.	5. Implement action plan.
6. Organize, analyze, and interpret data.	6. Evaluate, summarize.
7. Disseminate knowledge, identify areas for more research.	7. Terminate intervention, identify other client needs.

Models for research utilization have consistently suggested that research should not be an activity that is foreign to social work practice or that draws precious resources away from it. On the contrary, social workers who wish to provide the best possible services to their clients can hardly afford not to be evidence-based practitioners. A research-oriented and research-involved practitioner is likely to be a better informed and a more effective and efficient practitioner than one who is not. In turn, a practice-oriented and practice-informed researcher is likely to produce research findings that will have value and be of benefit to those who deliver services to clients.

SOURCES OF KNOWLEDGE

Alternative Knowledge Sources

Social workers have always recognized the need for knowledge that would inform their practice with and on behalf of client groups. Often, they have had to rely on less "scientific" sources of information, such as the opinions of supervisors or peers, when stuck with a particularly difficult client problem or decision. These sources have limited utility and can be misleading. Is there still a need to use these sources of knowledge? Yes. When research-based knowledge is lacking or is not trustworthy, we still must turn to these alternative sources of knowledge. However, when we do so, we must use extreme caution.

Logic

Often, we assume that some things are self-evident and logical. They just "make sense." Unfortunately, this type of logic can sometimes lead to beliefs that are just plain wrong. For example, membership in a white supremacist group is generally a good indication of the presence of racist or anti-Semitic attitudes. But this logical assumption may break down in the case of an FBI infiltrator or a reporter seeking to understand the group firsthand. Similarly, we cannot depend on the self-evident truth that an individual who attends graduate school values an education, when he or she may have enrolled to appease a parent, to avoid having to work in the family business, or even to pursue a future partner.

Overreliance on logic has led to some costly errors among helping professionals. In the 1970s, a program called Scared Straight was promoted as a logical approach to reducing crime. It involved taking young people who had committed minor crimes, such as shoplifting, on a tour of prisons to see what might happen to them if they did not abide by the law. They experienced the booking procedure firsthand and talked with inmates who were serving long sentences. Logically, the experience should have turned the youths into better citizens. But it didn't. Petrosino, Turpin-Petrosino, and Buehler (2005) conducted a meta-analysis, a research method discussed in Chapter 7 and concluded that not only did the Scared Straight program not deter participants from future delinquency, participants were actually more likely to commit crimes than similar young people not participating in the program. The authors state, "despite the gloomy findings reported here and elsewhere, Scared Straight and its derivatives continue in use . . . when the negative results from the California SQUIRES study came out, the response was to end the evaluation, not the program" (p. 52). This is what can happen when there is not support for acquiring scientific knowledge!

Logic and common sense have produced other costly errors among helping professionals over the years. For example, many communities have implemented the Drug Abuse Resistance Education (DARE) program. Some of the readers of this text have undoubtedly participated in this program, even worn t-shirts! Its curriculum, designed to prevent young students from abusing legal and illegal substances, has been taught widely in public schools in the United States. It links local law enforcement agencies with middle school students and teaches students a range of refusal skills to use when confronted with offers of drugs and alcohol. DARE was initially presumed to be an effective program. However, Van Burgh, Redner, and Moon (1995) conducted a study of over 100 eighth graders that showed that the program was not effective in changing students' knowledge or improving their skills in refusing drugs and alcohol. Subsequently, other researchers reported similar findings (Lynam et al., 1999). Nevertheless, probably because it is so logical and is now so well established, many communities continue to use and support DARE. Following is a quote from Salt Lake City mayor, Rocky Anderson (2000), who questioned the efficacy of Project DARE:

> After I was elected Mayor, I examined Salt Lake City's participation in DARE, a substance-abuse prevention program with great popular appeal, but which has been demonstrated by study after study as being completely ineffective in reducing drug abuse over the long-term. Once my intent to terminate the DARE program in Salt Lake City became known, I was besieged by police officers, parents, and school officials who demanded that I retain DARE in our schools. Notwithstanding all the parents who have yelled at me during parades, I know it is my obligation to honestly and conscientiously examine the data and insist that our School Board put in place drug-prevention programs that have proven to be effective.

Tradition

Another dubious source of knowledge is tradition. We may believe something to be true simply because it has never really been challenged, at least not within our culture. This kind of knowledge is particularly dangerous. It can take the form of relatively innocuous misconceptions, such as the belief that retired military people are good leaders or bureaucrats. But it is more likely to result in destructive, negative stereotyping that promote the continued oppression of some members of our society. The persistence of erroneous stereotypes, such as that gay men and lesbians choose their sexual orientation and wish to convert others, that older people invariably suffer from intellectual deterioration, or that single-parent families are dysfunctional, have all helped to foster discrimination against members of specific groups.

People have a tendency to hold tenaciously to traditional beliefs, sometimes even in the face of scientific evidence to the contrary. We crave certainty in our lives, perhaps because so much of life is uncertain. Unfortunately, once we are convinced that something is correct, occasional observations that support our belief are all we need to confirm its correctness. Tenacious reliance on traditional beliefs can seriously affect our ability to provide competent services, thus we cannot afford to make practice decisions and undertake interventions on the basis of traditional beliefs alone.

Authority

Still another way we sometimes get our "knowledge" is through deference to authority. Social workers employed in medical and psychiatric settings are especially vulnerable to assuming that the physician always has a scientific basis for what, in actuality, may be little more than an opinion. We sometimes mistakenly conclude that "if she said it, it must be true" or "he ought to know, or he wouldn't be where he is today." Unfortunately, people in authority (e.g., our bosses, experts in the field), just like all of us, are subject to bias, limited experience, and perhaps the tendency to confuse reality with wishful thinking. Or they may simply be relying on logic or tradition!

Faulty Knowledge Can Promote Stereotypes

Logic, tradition, and authority can mislead us in many ways. They can affect our practice judgment, cause us to draw erroneous conclusions, or waste our time and energies looking for problems that don't exist. As mentioned earlier, they can promote unhealthy stereotypes and generalizations about people who are or may become our clients. What are some of these stereotypes?

Welfare Recipients

Who are the welfare recipients in our society? Most people believe they understand not only who our current welfare clients are but also the problems and issues surrounding the welfare system. Families receiving the old Aid to Families of Dependent Children (AFDC) benefits and, more recently, Temporary Assistance to Needy Families (TANF) have often been the subject of erroneous beliefs. The mothers of welfare families have been described as "welfare queens" (Levin, 2013). According to this stereotype, she has several children, lives extremely well on the welfare benefits, has no intention of finding work, and continues having more children to increase her benefits.

How accurate is this "knowledge" of welfare recipients? Rank (1994), a social work professor, published the following results of an eight-year study of 3,000 AFDC recipients:

- Most welfare recipients had no more than two children.
- During the previous twenty years, the value of welfare benefit levels had sharply declined when adjusted for inflation.
- States with the highest out-of-wedlock birthrates tended to have the lowest welfare benefit levels.
- Benefits to teenage mothers were lower in the United States than in European nations. (p. 6)

These findings clearly pointed out that AFDC was hardly a good deal in the United States. It would have been illogical, for example, for an AFDC mother to become pregnant just to receive a small increase in benefits that could not begin to cover the cost of another child.

People Who Are Homeless

Many people in our society, including some helping professionals, may feel comfortable with their "knowledge" of homelessness. What are some common beliefs about people who are homeless? They are older men. They are likely to suffer from mental illness and problems with alcohol and drugs. They are dropouts from mainstream society and prone to violence and public drunkenness. But what does research tell us about homeless people in the United States? There are some similarities to these common stereotypes but also some important differences. Data compiled in 2005 by The United States Conference of Mayors revealed that:

- A greater percentage of homeless men have served in the military than the general population.
- Approximately one-third of the homeless were families with children, the fastest growing homeless population.
- About 30 percent of the adult homeless population has an addiction to alcohol or other substances.
- While about 22 percent of the adult homeless population suffers from some severe, chronic mental illness, only a small percentage (5–7 percent) requires institutionalization.

We have offered just two examples of the disparity that often exists between what is generally believed to be true and what research has actually revealed. Reliance on knowledge from dubious sources can create problems for the social worker. Social workers or other helping professionals who make diagnostic or treatment decisions on the basis of false preconceptions about people might be misled into misdiagnosis, bad treatment planning, and/or ineffective intervention methods. This is exactly the opposite of what knowledge is supposed to do. Knowledge should inform our practice not mislead it. We will look more at the misuse of research data in the next chapter on ethics in social work.

Policy Practice

Behavior: Apply critical thinking to analyze, formulate, and advocate for policies that advance human rights and social, economic, and environmental justice.

Critical Thinking Question: Can you think of three examples when you have seen faulty knowledge promote stereotypes or prejudice?

The Scientific Alternative

Social work practitioners need many types of knowledge. Given the shortcomings of the alternative sources of knowledge we have discussed, aren't research findings still the best alternative? Yes. Knowledge derived from research, although certainly imperfect and still subject to unethical distortion and misuse, is the knowledge most likely to help us do our jobs effectively as social workers. Research relies on the use of the scientific method.

The *scientific method* (alternately referred to as *scientific thinking* or simply *science*) is a particular way of acquiring knowledge. It is a way of thinking about and investigating assumptions about the world. It differs from *scientific knowledge*, which is really only a collection of facts that were acquired through use of the scientific method. We could theoretically use scientific knowledge even if we did not know how to practice the scientific method. But that would be dangerous. Unless we engage in scientific thinking and understand and use the scientific method, we might have blind faith in scientific knowledge. That would be almost as bad as uncritically depending on logic, tradition, or authority. Scientific knowledge can be misleading or incorrect depending on the quality of research methods used, including sampling, data collection, measurement instruments, data analysis, and reporting. To correctly use the products of the scientific method (scientific knowledge), we must understand it. Certain characteristics of the scientific method set it apart from other ways of acquiring knowledge and, we believe, make it more likely to yield knowledge on which the social worker can depend:

- **Science is empirical.** *Empirical* means that knowledge derived from the scientific method is based on direct observations of the real world, not on someone's beliefs or theories. Scientific knowledge has undergone a rigorous evaluation and verification process to determine whether what was assumed to be true or what was believed to be true really is true.
- **Science strives for objectivity.** No conscientious and ethical scientist would deliberately introduce biases into research findings. Scientists take deliberate actions to avoid the possibility of their own preferences or beliefs influencing the results of their research. At the same time, there is recognition that total objectivity may be impossible and that a certain amount of subjectivity is inevitable, and these factors influence findings in all research to a greater or lesser degree. But the scientist attempts to assess how much subjectivity may have played a role and to evaluate its effects to arrive at the truth.
- **Science produces provisional knowledge.** As noted earlier, the possibility that research findings and conclusions may be wrong is always present. Science speaks, in effect, on the basis of what we think we know right now. It leaves open the possibility that subsequent scientific inquiry may lead to modified or even to totally contradictory conclusions. In this way, scientific knowledge is always regarded as tentative. Even the conclusions drawn from statistical tests of inference are based on a premise of *reasonable certainty*, usually greater than 95 percent.
- **Science employs a public way of knowing.** In science, it is not enough for a researcher to share findings with other scientists and the public. The research methods used to produce the findings should also be made available for critique so that other researchers can try to achieve similar results, a process called *replication*. If a researcher's findings can be verified by other researchers, they tend to have greater credibility.
- **Science employs certain rules, procedures, and techniques.** Although creativity and innovation are also characteristics of science, there are definitely acceptable and unacceptable ways to conduct scientific research. There are correct and incorrect sequences in which to perform research tasks, depending on the type of research that is undertaken. Even research that ventures into problem areas where we have very little knowledge attempts to go by the rules.

CATEGORIZATIONS OF RESEARCH

There are several ways to categorize a research study. One or more may apply to an individual study. Research studies can be categorized by the different types of scientific knowledge that are being accessed, the basic purpose of the research, or the primary

Box 1.2   Categorizations of Research

Types of Scientific Knowledge Sought

Descriptive knowledge	Seeks knowledge to describe how things were at some point in time or (less frequently) to describe change that occurred over time
Predictive knowledge	Seeks knowledge to predict how things will be in the future
Prescriptive knowledge	Seeks knowledge to suggest interventions to address an existing problem or prevent a possible future problem

General Purpose of the Research

Basic research	Research that contributes to our general body of knowledge for use in some future situation
Applied research	Research designed to produce knowledge that has immediate applicability to a problem or situation

Research Methods Used

Quantitative research	Research that uses deductive logic to arrive at conclusions; develops theories and/or hypotheses, then gathers and analyzes data to seek support for them. Focus is on events that occurred and can be verified.
Qualitative research	Research that uses inductive logic; data are collected and analyzed before theories and/or hypotheses are developed. Focus is on how individuals experienced or perceived events.

research methods being utilized. Box 1.2 offers an overview of three categorizations we will discuss here.

Types of Knowledge Derived from Scientific Research

If we are to become evidence-based practitioners, at least to the degree possible, we need access to different types of scientific knowledge. They are acquired in different ways using different research methods, a topic we will address in considerable detail in Chapters 5 through 8. While there is overlap among them, scientific knowledge tends to come in one of three forms.

Descriptive Knowledge

Descriptive knowledge gives us a reasonably accurate picture of the way things are, or, to be more precise, of how they were at the time the research took place. Descriptive knowledge is limited, but this does not mean that it is inferior to other types of knowledge. It is not any less valuable or, acquired correctly, any easier to achieve. In fact, descriptive knowledge often requires many months or even years of work and ingenious research methods. For example, Israel and Jozefowicz-Simbeni (2009) studied the strengths of homeless elementary-aged children as perceived by their mothers. Another study (Hamilton, Nelson Goff, Crow, & Reisbig, 2009) looked at the primary trauma and relationship satisfaction experienced by the wives of army soldiers who had recently returned from Iraq. Descriptive knowledge frequently forms the basis for desirable changes within our society. The accurate description of a problem (e.g., the statistical documentation of discriminatory employment practices or sexual harassment in the workplace) has been the basis both for bringing problems into public awareness and for subsequent social change.

Predictive Knowledge

Predictive knowledge is knowledge that helps us anticipate. It allows us to go a step beyond describing what is or was and to project into the future and predict with reasonable accuracy what will be. Predictive knowledge evolves from the accumulation of descriptive knowledge that reveals consistent reoccurring patterns. For example, suppose that several descriptive studies of gay adolescents reveal that a large percentage of them are victims of bullying. From this, we might evolve the predictive knowledge that a gay teenager is likely to experience bullying behavior. We can increase the likelihood of success in predicting a problem that he may face by observing what has tended to happen to others like him in the past.

Predictive knowledge can tell a social worker what is likely to occur. For example, one study (Prentky et al., 2010) looked at the ability of an instrument to assess the risk of future sexually abusive behaviors among a group of juvenile sexual offenders. A great deal of research has been conducted to determine if individuals who were victims of child sexual abuse are at a greater risk of later becoming perpetrators of such abuse (see Glasser et al., 2001). If we can identify who is most at risk for experiencing a problem in the future, we can anticipate who might require careful monitoring and/or intervention. But predictive knowledge stops short of telling a social worker exactly how to intervene to prevent a problem from occurring or how to treat one that already exists.

Prescriptive Knowledge

Prescriptive knowledge is knowledge that suggests the method of intervention that is most likely to be effective. In EBP, social workers use prescriptive knowledge, along with their experience, client preferences, and so forth, to decide what intervention should be used to address an existing problem or to prevent one that they predict will occur. Prescriptive knowledge is most frequently based on the findings of carefully designed research studies in which the researcher had considerable control over the ways in which the research was conducted.

When prescriptive knowledge exists, we know not only what is (descriptive knowledge) and what probably will be (predictive knowledge) but also what needs to be done to avoid something undesirable or to cause something desirable to occur (prescriptive knowledge). In fields such as sociology or anthropology, descriptive knowledge and, to a lesser degree, predictive knowledge are often the end product of research. In EBP, however, we seek to identify interventions with a high likelihood of success and to discount those that are less effective. Research studies that generate prescriptive knowledge aid us in this endeavor. For example, one study (Rotheram-Borus, Desmond, Comulada, Arnold, & Johnson, 2009) examined the efficacy of the Healthy

Living Program, a program designed to reduce risky sexual behavior and substance use among marginally housed adults with HIV infection. The authors reported that program participants showed significantly greater reductions than the control group members in unprotected risky sexual acts, the number of HIV negative sexual partners, alcohol and marijuana use, and hard drug use. Another study (Parish, Rose, & Andrews, 2010) assessed the success of TANF to reach its goals to increase employment, enhance family stability through marriage promotion, and reduce welfare reliance. The researchers concluded that the program had not led to an overall reduction in welfare reliance among low-income women raising children with disabilities. Mears, Yaffe, and Harris (2009) compared the outcomes of severely emotionally disturbed youth receiving wraparound services to youth receiving more traditional child welfare case management services and concluded that the youth receiving the wraparound services exhibited a higher level of functioning and experienced significantly fewer placements than the comparison group.

In terms of its value for decision making, it is clear how these and other prescriptive studies offer the social worker invaluable knowledge when developing interventions, as well as promoting policy changes that will help clients. Purely prescriptive knowledge is becoming increasingly available as more and more carefully designed research studies are conducted. The use of meta-analyses, in which the results from many different research studies are combined and contrasted, has also added more prescriptive knowledge to the social worker's professional knowledge base.

It should be emphasized again here that prescriptive knowledge alone should not dictate the choice of a method of intervention. That would not be consistent with EBP. There is also no guarantee that an intervention that has shown to be effective with a group of clients will be effective with a given client or client group. In all situations, our own experience, knowledge of ourselves and our client or client group, ethical practice issues, and client wishes and preferences must be factored into the decision as to how best to intervene.

It would also be inaccurate to say that prescriptive knowledge is the only type of knowledge that suggests how we might best intervene in a problem situation. Virtually all research findings can have some prescriptive potential. With thought, predictive and even descriptive knowledge can help to inform our practice decision making and thus increase the likelihood of successful intervention. For example, a descriptive study of youth gang activities and the social needs that gang membership appears to meet may suggest what other activities and programs might provide an attractive alternative to gang membership. Or, the findings of several studies of youth gangs might allow us to predict at what age pressure for membership is most likely to occur, thus helping us decide what age group to target in our intervention efforts.

In reality, most research studies generate a variety of knowledge, including some that does not fit cleanly into one of these three categories. The knowledge typology discussed here (like most typologies) is not perfect and clean. However, we discuss it primarily because it emphasizes the benefits that research can offer to the social work practitioner. Also, this discussion will prove useful in later chapters, when we examine different types of research designs and, especially, how they differ in their purpose, that is, the knowledge they seek to acquire.

Basic and Applied Research

Another way research studies can be categorized is on the basis of the study's general goal or purpose, specifically, when and how any knowledge derived from it is intended to be used. Research studies can be generally described as either *basic* or *applied*.

Basic Research

Basic research (sometimes called *pure research*) is designed to contribute to our general professional body of knowledge. Social workers conduct basic research and also rely on researchers from other fields to conduct basic research. For example, they benefit from the research of sociologists, anthropologists, economists, and psychologists to help them understand and predict human behavior. As social workers, we sometimes immediately apply findings from basic research in our practice. For example, information from Piaget's theory of cognitive development guides many human service workers when developing interventions for children and adolescents. The knowledge from basic research is sometimes tucked away, available for us to tap into at some future time for some as yet unknown purpose. We might not use it at all until a new social problem is identified or we conclude that we have misunderstood an old one. Then we might revisit the findings of basic research conducted years or even decades earlier to provide some insight into the problem. For example, some of the basic research conducted in the 1971 Stanford studies (Zimbardo, 2010), on the behaviors of college students when given power over others in a prison setting, were used to help us better understand the abusive treatment of prisoners in Iraq and Afghanistan by their American guards over forty years later.

Applied Research

In contrast to basic research, applied research is designed to produce knowledge that has immediate, and often narrower, applicability. Its findings are often used for answering a burning question or for making a decision that cannot wait, for example, whether an intervention should be terminated or whether a social program should be continued. Social workers identify the potential beneficiaries of applied research before it is conducted and design the research in a way that yields the data that will help answer the questions that must be answered.

Applied research is not inherently more valuable or more useful than basic research. Although its findings may appear to be more practical and more relevant to successful EBP, we could not be successful evidence-based practitioners without also having access to knowledge acquired through basic research. Sometimes, the practice benefits of basic research are quite indirect; we may even be unaware of their contribution to our current practice. As Proctor (2003) pointed out, "some research will have impact only over the long haul, shaping theory that in turn informs hypotheses for further study" (p. 195).

As we might suspect, not all research falls neatly into one of the two categories (basic or applied). In fact, some basic research studies produce findings that are of immediate use for practice decision making. Conversely, some applied research studies produce knowledge that represents a major contribution to our professional knowledge base. While some research studies have elements of both basic and applied research, the two terms are still widely used to communicate the broad characteristics of a given research study.

Quantitative and Qualitative Research

Another way to broadly categorize research, based largely on the primary objective of the research and the methods used to achieve it, is to describe it as *quantitative* or *qualitative*. This categorization is based on such factors as sources of data and how they are selected, the place of research hypotheses, and the methods of data analysis employed. As we shall see, as in the case of the basic and applied labels, the labels *quantitative* and *qualitative* can easily suggest a false dichotomy, since many research studies contain elements of both.

Quantitative Research

Quantitative research has often been incorrectly equated with the scientific method. It is sometimes even called *empirical research*, although it has no monopoly on either the scientific method or empiricism. Quantitative research emphasizes the building of knowledge through what is referred to as *logical positivism*. It stresses the use of deductive (linear) logic to arrive at conclusions.

Studies that employ quantitative methods are characterized by the following:

1. Careful measurement of variables
2. Relatively large, randomly selected case samples
3. Control of other variables through random assignment of cases to groups
4. Standardized data collection methods
5. Statistical analyses of data

Each of these concepts will be defined and discussed more fully in later chapters. The sequence of activities that occurs in quantitative research reflects the deductive logic of this approach to knowledge building. The steps generally used in quantitative methods are as follows:

1. **Problem identification.** The problem—that is, the condition or phenomenon that is unsatisfactory—must be clearly understood to the point that it can be specified precisely, along with its magnitude and consequences.

2. **Research question formulation.** After developing a number of broad questions, the answer to any one of which would have the potential to partially alleviate the problem (or at least to understand it better), the researcher selects one or more of these questions that will constitute the focus of inquiry for the research.

3. **Literature review.** The state of existing knowledge is assessed and assembled into a logical order to determine what is already known concerning answers to the research questions, to enable the researcher to specify the questions more precisely, and to formulate an appropriate research methodology for the current research.

4. **Construction of hypotheses and/or refinement of research questions.** Based on the literature review and the type of knowledge sought, the researcher formulates hypotheses and/or specific research questions that will provide the focus for research activities that follow.

5. **Design and planning.** A series of decisions are made as to how the research hypotheses are to be tested and/or answers to questions are to be sought. Tasks involved in this activity include the following:

   a. Selecting or formulating operational definitions of key terms
   b. Specification of what people or objects will be studied
   c. Development of a method for sampling (if the entire population of people or objects is not to be studied)
   d. Identification and definition of variables to be measured (conceptualization)
   e. Specification of exactly how variables will be measured (operationalization)
   f. Identification and/or development of instruments for measurement
   g. Specification and pretesting of methods for data collection
   h. Specification of methods for analysis of data

6. **Data collection.** Data are collected according to predetermined methods.

7. **Sorting and analysis of data.** The data are examined, summarized, and analyzed using appropriate statistical methods. If hypotheses have been formulated, tests of statistical significance are used to determine if the hypotheses will be supported.

8. **Specification of research findings.** Results of data analysis are displayed in tables, graphs, or other standard formats.

9. **Interpretation of research findings.** Results of data analysis are examined in order to draw conclusions relative to the research hypotheses and/or questions. The findings are examined in relation to the findings of other similar studies.

10. **Dissemination of research findings.** The researcher uses one or more vehicles to report the methods and findings of the research.

11. **Use of findings by the social worker.** Practitioners who have access to the research report critically evaluate both the findings and the methods that produced them, and adapt their practice methods accordingly.

This traditional sequence of tasks for performing research is described in most research methods texts. However, steps 1 and 11 are not universally included. By including them, we have emphasized our concern for the importance of research utilization by the social work practitioner as an integral part of EBP.

The knowledge generated by quantitative research that is supportive of EBP can take many forms. For example, quantitative research can provide evidence of a relationship between the incidence of child abuse and substance abuse, or it can compare the effectiveness of two approaches to the treatment of child abuse. The knowledge generated by quantitative research can be the results of an evaluation that measures how well a program to treat perpetrators of child abuse achieved its objectives or a social worker's systematic ongoing evaluation of his or her own practice effectiveness with an abusive parent.

For many years, quantitative methods were considered the best (if not the only) way to conduct research. They are still described as such in many high school science classes and in research courses in other disciplines. Indeed, the principles of quantitative research are ideal for obtaining certain types of knowledge. However, quantitative methods have their limitations and are not well-suited to studying certain subjective phenomena. We cannot always separate knowledge and values; they are hopelessly intertwined in human thought and behavior. For example, quantitative methods can provide reasonably accurate data about the incidence of date rape on college campuses or even which individuals are most at risk. However, it cannot provide much insight into how individuals perceive their experience or what the experience means to them. The limitations of quantitative research, along with the evolution of feminist research (discussed later), have taught us the importance of other, complementary approaches to knowledge building.

Qualitative Research

Qualitative research seeks to understand human experiences from the perspective of those who experience them. Qualitative research relies on inductive logic instead of deduction and emphasizes words such as *subjective, relative,* and *contextual.* Often, vast amounts of data are collected, sorted, and interpreted. A helpful definition of qualitative research is offered by Denzin and Lincoln (1994):

> Qualitative research is multimethod in focus, involving an interpretive, naturalistic approach to its subject matter. That means that qualitative researchers study things in their natural settings, attempting to make sense of or interpret phenomena in terms of the meanings people bring to them. Qualitative research involves the studied use and collection of a variety of empirical materials—case study, personal experience, introspective, life story, interview, observational, historical, interactional, and visual texts—that describe routine and problematic moments and meaning in individuals' lives. (p. 2)

Data collection often occurs through in-depth interviewing, conducting groups, or by participant observation (Chapter 6). In-person interviews, an important component of most qualitative studies, generally tend to be less structured and less standardized in qualitative research than in quantitative research. Often, what the researcher learns in conducting one interview results in adaptations for the next. Sample representativeness (Chapter 9) is often not a major concern.

In qualitative research, the researcher is really the primary instrument for data collection and analysis. The data are processed as they are received. There is no pretense that the researcher can collect data in an objective, value-free manner. In fact, when interviews are used, the relationships between the researcher and those being interviewed may be openly supportive and even therapeutic at times.

When using qualitative approaches to build knowledge, many of the same activities seen in quantitative studies take place. However, they often receive greater or lesser emphasis or may occur in a different sequence. There are two important differences that are especially common. First, research hypotheses are unlikely to be formulated in qualitative research prior to data collection as they are in quantitative studies. Instead, they may evolve from and be the final product of the research process. They generally appear late in the report of a qualitative study (if at all) as tentative conclusions drawn from the research study. Second, in qualitative studies, an extensive review of the literature generally does not occur prior to data collection. Vast amounts of data may be collected quite early in the research process. Some will be useful; others may be discarded. During and after data collection, the professional literature is used to either verify or question what the data seem to be suggesting, that is, to help in conceptualizing what has been observed.

The sequence of activities that occurs in qualitative research reflects the inductive logic used in this approach to knowledge building. In broad terms, the steps involve:

1. collecting a wide range of data.
2. observing patterns in the data.
3. formulating tentative explanations.
4. developing theories (and sometimes, hypotheses).

Results of quantitative studies are often reported using tables and graphs. Reports also contain the results of statistical tests and conclusions about support or nonsupport for research hypotheses. However, in reports of qualitative studies, findings are more often presented in narrative form or as case scenarios. There may be long descriptions of the researcher's interaction with individuals who provided data for the research, including direct quotations from them and speculation by the researcher on what their choice of words may suggest or imply. Increasingly, computer software is being used to perform a content analysis (see Chapter 6) of transcripts of interviews to attempt to quantify, for example, the presence of emotions in the subjects such as anger, despair, or anxiety. Results of such content analysis, if performed, are included in the findings.

The Quantitative versus Qualitative Debate

It is now generally agreed that both quantitative and qualitative methods are necessary to truly understand many problems or phenomena.

In the late twentieth century, the merits of qualitative versus quantitative research were the topic of lively debates among social work researchers. However, it is now generally agreed that both quantitative and qualitative methods are necessary to truly understand many problems or phenomena, and to provide a "complete picture." For example, how could we have a thorough understanding of posttraumatic stress disorder among returning war veterans if we focused only on its incidence, the forms it takes, and what experiences may be associated with it, and did not also explore how it is perceived by its victims or how they experience it emotionally?

Neither type of research is inherently superior to the other. Both quantitative and qualitative studies make valuable contributions to our knowledge base and help us to make better decisions as EBP social workers. Of course, there is good and not-so-good qualitative research, even as there is good and not-so-good quantitative research. Simply running a focus group and writing up a summary of what transpired is not good qualitative research, any more than mailing out a hastily constructed survey and compiling the findings is good quantitative research. Conducting good quantitative or qualitative research is not a haphazard process; there are rules that have been developed for both.

The findings of qualitative research and quantitative research often complement each other. It is not surprising, then, that research studies are often hybrids, frequently referred to as mixed-methods, containing features of both. Qualitative methods may be used to collect and analyze one type of data, while quantitative methods may be used to collect and analyze other type. Both methods may be used to attempt to provide a more complete answer to the same question, or one method may be used to see if there is support (or not) for the findings of the other method.

It is probably more accurate to describe many studies as *predominantly quantitative* or *predominantly qualitative*, rather than simply *quantitative* or *qualitative*. In the chapters that follow, when references are made to quantitative or qualitative research, it should be remembered that "pure" examples of either type of research are now probably more the exception than the rule. We will look more in depth at quantitative research designs (Chapter 5) and qualitative research methods (Chapter 6) later in this book.

THE CURRENT CLIMATE FOR SOCIAL WORK RESEARCH

Social work agencies and funding sources are requiring that practitioners and researchers involved in client interventions actually show that clients are getting better. Much of the research conducted by social workers today is some form of mandated evaluation research. Thus, it is becoming more and more important that social work practitioners, educators, and researchers at all levels of service be knowledgeable about basic research methods. Human service organizations routinely collect and compile excellent potential sources of research data, such as surveys and interviews with clients or organization staff, and agency data designating the number and characteristics of clients served. These data can provide evidence of the effectiveness of services and programs to program managers, administrators, funding agencies, and other stakeholders. However, analysis of program data may also have the potential to identify areas where individuals and programs have not met their responsibilities or have failed to achieve their objectives. Thus, a researcher conducting a mandated program evaluation may either receive excellent cooperation and assistance from organizational staff or encounter resistance and efforts to obstruct research activities that might reveal program deficiencies. Is it any wonder that administrators (and board members) are often fearful of research? On the surface, it would seem that they may have more to lose than to gain from research findings.

Still another concern relates to the protection of client and staff rights, especially their privacy rights. Recent changes in laws have made client record data off limits to researchers in many settings. Fears about the possibility of litigation (a major concern of administrators today) are likely to surface when a researcher, even an employee of the organization, asks to collect data from staff members or clients. Sometimes, permission to conduct research requires a series of compromises and accommodations that result in less than ideal research methods. This is an unfortunate reality, but, if done thoughtfully, these adjustments can be made in a way that will maintain the integrity of the research and its findings. As we shall discuss later, no research design is ever perfect, but there are ways to make less-than-perfect research acceptable and useful if social workers understand and apply the principles of scientific inquiry.

The professionalization of social work over the past few decades has influenced the ways in which social workers are able to conduct research. Leaders of organizations such as NASW have worked hard to ensure high-quality services to clients and greater public recognition for the contributions that social workers make to society. Professionalization has also been enhanced by the passing of state licensing bills that protect both social workers and their clients, and has been accompanied by the codification of certain values, ethical standards, and traditions. Overall, these developments undoubtedly have produced better services and served to protect clients from unqualified or incompetent service.

Generally, as we shall see in Chapter 2, professional values are highly consistent with research ethics. On occasion, however, a researcher will (and should) be constrained from using methods and designs that represent sound research, but are unacceptable to social workers and the values and ethics that guide their behavior. For example, in some circumstances, professional values will conflict with research practices, such as the random assignment of clients to two different types of treatment, direct observation of treatment, denial of services to some to see if treatment really makes a difference, or certain forms of deception. If allowed to occur, these practices might produce research findings that are more definitive and possess greater credibility. But, of course, research should serve practice; it should never be the other way around. Professional values and ethics must be adhered to, even if the quality of the research and the credibility of its findings suffer a little.

Professional values, such as a client's right to services, confidentiality, and the sanctity of a treatment relationship, will and should continue to present impediments to conducting scientific research. The welfare of individual clients cannot be sacrificed in the interest of knowledge building, sometimes even that which has the potential to produce improved services to clients. Frequently, an almost-as-good alternative exists and can be employed. The influence of professional values may make research in the social work practice milieu more challenging, and it may require special creativity on the part of the researcher. Fortunately, it rarely precludes conducting good research altogether. The experienced researcher knows that conflicts can often be resolved through compromise and trade-off.

Despite some of the obstacles and concerns that we have mentioned, the environment for social work research continues to improve in the twenty-first century. Social workers are becoming more aware that well-designed, credible research studies are essential if they are to provide the best possible services to their clients. They are also more aware that sound research is a necessity if they are to demonstrate that their efforts are worth their cost to government agencies, employers, and other funding sources that make decisions about which services will be supported and who should offer them (O'Neill, 2000). Without evidence of benefits through solid research findings, the profession faces the threats of financial cuts and the elimination of valuable and needed programs. Other disciplines and professions, with a longer history of research demonstrating practice effectiveness, could move in to fill roles that social workers have historically filled. Whether out of choice or necessity, the current climate for social work research, especially research that evaluates the effectiveness and efficiency of social work interventions, is very favorable.

SUMMARY

In this chapter, we looked at:

- The history of the relationship between research and social work practice. Many of the steps in the research process are quite similar to those of good practice intervention. Yet, in the past, social workers have tended to rely primarily on such unreliable sources as supervisors' opinions, logic and common sense, tradition, and authority to provide the knowledge they required for making practice decisions. They relied less frequently on the findings of research that employed scientific methods. However, this has gradually changed.

- Social workers now advocate and acknowledge the value of EBP, with its emphasis on the use of research findings as an important component of practice decision making. We need to understand the best ways to conduct research to (1) design and implement our own research findings and (2) evaluate critically the research methods and findings of others so that we can make informed practice decisions.

- We looked at several broad descriptions of different categorizations of research. Research methods focus on the production of different types of knowledge, classified as descriptive, predictive, and prescriptive. The primary purpose of basic research studies is to provide broad, generalized knowledge for future use, while the purpose of applied research is to provide knowledge for immediate use in decision making. The major differences between research that is primarily quantitative and research that is primarily qualitative were also described. They will be discussed in more detail in the chapters that follow.

- Finally, we looked at the current environment for social work research, its sources of support, and the obstacles it faces. Some of the obstacles result from misunderstandings that can be corrected, while others are likely to continue or even become more substantial. Such challenges will require social work researchers to be sensitive, diplomatic, and willing to learn new and creative ways to evaluate and improve social work interventions.

MyEducationLab® for Research

Try the Topic 1 Assignments: Introduction to Educational Research and the Topic 1 Study Plan.

Take the Chapter 1 Chapter Review Quiz.

2

Ethical Issues in Research

In the previous chapter, we described many similarities between research and social work practice. There is at least one other similarity and a very important one: both research and practice are shaped by ethical constraints.

In this chapter, we will examine (1) what is meant by research ethics; (2) some well-known research studies in which abuses of research participants contributed to the establishment of current ethical standards to ensure that individuals who allow social workers to collect research data from them are protected; (3) contemporary issues, such as research with vulnerable people who volunteer to become research participants, and the rights of individuals to participate in research even if it has the potential to harm them; and (4) the researcher's ethical obligations to others, including the sponsors of research, other researchers, colleagues, and the general public.

In some areas, research ethical standards have been clearly delineated. In others, there is a lack of clear-cut guidelines to assist decision making. In social work practice, ethical dilemmas and constraints are always with us. That is good, because they cause us to regularly question whether what we are doing is both justifiable and fair to others.

We have chosen to devote an entire chapter to the topic of research ethical issues because they play such an important part in the design and implementation of research studies. However, our intention is not to simply cover the topic and then dismiss it. Ethical issues impact all aspects of research; they can and do occur at any point in the research process. Thus, the reader will see reference to ethical issues throughout the book.

WHAT ARE ETHICS?

In some areas of both practice and research, ethics clearly dictate what is forbidden or required under certain circumstances. For example, in social work practice, sexual contact with current and former clients is universally regarded as unethical. Similarly, research that is likely to cause permanent harm to its research participants is unethical. More frequently, however, ethics fall into the category of *issues*. An issue is debatable—individuals can hold two opposing positions on the issue, and a good argument can be made for either position. In practice, an issue might be whether it is unethical to discontinue needed counselling with a client after his or her medical coverage has been exhausted. In research, an ethical issue might arise over whether deception is necessary to acquire certain types of knowledge or whether it might actually be harmful to research participants.

The term *ethics*, derived from the Greek word *ethos* (which comes closest to the English word *character*), refers to principles within a society that reflect what the society generally views as right or wrong behavior. Ethics are a little different from laws—they often fall into what is commonly called the *gray area*. Thus, we sometimes find ourselves asking the question, "It is not illegal, but is it ethical?" In the context of research, ethical issues generally revolve around three related questions:

1. Who should benefit or suffer from the actions of the researcher?

2. Whose rights should take priority over those of others?

3. Does the end (increased knowledge) justify the means (the methods used to acquire it and their potential for harm).

In the ideal world, all individuals and groups should benefit from the development of new knowledge. Potential beneficiaries include the researcher, those who provide research data, the institution sponsoring the research, the community, and other researchers whose efforts can build on the researcher's findings. But we know that, in the real world, the needs of one group are sometimes met at the expense of another. The Tuskegee Public Health Studies described later in this chapter is an example where the research methods used by researchers to acquire valuable knowledge were extremely harmful to the individuals who provided the data.

As social workers, most of our research depends on our fellow human beings providing the data needed to conduct research. They may be our clients, family members of clients, fellow professionals, or anyone else who can help us to better understand some problem and/or to intervene more effectively in solving it. Whoever they are, they generally have one characteristic in common—they are asked to give much more than they will ever receive from their participation. For this reason and others, we have an ethical obligation to safeguard their health and well-being.

People who provide data for research purposes are referred to by various terms within the professional literature. Three of the most common are *research subjects*, *research partners*, and *research participants*. All three refer to the same individuals, but the terms have different connotations. Some people use the most traditional term, *subjects*, because it is universally understood within research circles. Others contend that the term is condescending or dehumanizing and that it is not consistent with the way those who provide data relate to the researcher, especially in studies that use primarily qualitative research methods. They also suggest that it implies that these individuals are somehow subservient, and thus they may be susceptible to exploitation by the researcher. For a combination of these reasons, this term is being used less frequently now.

Researchers who conduct certain types of research (such as qualitative studies) prefer to use the term *research partner*. They contend that people who provide research data often share much of themselves, sometimes even very personal information. Thus, in building knowledge, they are just as important as the researcher; the relationship is one of equality. The word *partner* best reflects this relationship.

We have chosen to use the third term, *research participant*, throughout this book. *Participant* recognizes the importance of those who provide data for research purposes, while also recognizing that their objectives and degree of involvement in knowledge building generally differ from those of the researcher. The term is consistent with both the quantitative and qualitative approaches and conveys the awareness that these individuals are entitled to both respect and attention to their rights. It acknowledges that although they may sometimes choose to be involved in research that results in their discomfort, they should do so willingly.

EXAMPLES OF RESEARCH PARTICIPANT ABUSE

Researchers and those who sponsor or permit research have an ethical obligation to ensure that research participants are protected from harm. Unfortunately, this was not always the case. Many of the ethical issues that must be addressed by today's researchers were simply nonissues for researchers in the nineteenth and even the mid-twentieth centuries. Our history is replete with examples of research studies that seemed to value knowledge building more than the rights of research participants. The studies reflect a lack of concern for how the research might have negatively affected the physical and emotional health of those who provided the data that were sought. Research participants were often individuals who were either powerless or defenseless (e.g., the poor, minorities, children, the mentally ill, and prisoners of war).

The belated emergence of guidelines for conducting research with human participants occurred during the second half of the twentieth century. It came about because of a gradual recognition that, in a quest for scientific knowledge, the end cannot always justify the means. Our society has come to acknowledge that in some research studies done in the past, the cost to research participants was not justifiable, no matter how much knowledge was acquired.

Some widely publicized research studies are considered "milestones" in the development of today's research ethical standards. They are better known for their contribution to an increased concern for the protection of research participants than for the scientific knowledge that they produced. They employed methods that ranged from those that are now universally condemned to those that still continue to be defended by some people within the scientific community. Many examples of unethical treatment of human participants could be cited. We have chosen to describe a few of the better-known ones and have noted how each has contributed to one or more standards that are used to protect research participants today.

The Nazi and Japanese Medical Experiments

Following World War II, it was revealed that concentration camps in Europe and prisoner-of-war compounds in Asia had been the scenes of heinous and repugnant medical experiments conducted in the name of science (Annas, 1992). During the Nuremberg war crime trials in 1945 and 1946, many shocking stories were recounted that detailed how Jews, Gypsies, and other "undesirables" detained in German concentration camps were deliberately exposed to life-threatening diseases in order to study the course of the diseases, were exposed to severe cold, had injuries deliberately inflicted upon them to study the effects of new antibiotic treatments, were subjected to unnecessary surgery, or were placed in decompression chambers to study their tolerance for lack of oxygen and other effects of high altitude. Of course, viewed in retrospect, these experiments were little more than sadistic atrocities committed in the name of science.

Prior to the Nuremberg trials, little attention had been paid to the rights of prisoners and other vulnerable groups. All too often, they were regarded as having limited rights, and thus were convenient targets for experimentation. The shocking revelations that emerged at Nuremberg set about a process of questioning whether incarceration justifies the nonvoluntary participation of prisoners in medical and other research. A consensus emerged that it cannot. Research participation must be voluntary whether it involves a prisoner-of-war, a prisoner convicted of illegal activity, or other vulnerable individuals.

Interestingly, one ethical issue related to the medical experiments conducted on American prisoners in Japanese prison camps did not surface until the 1980s. Access to previously classified documents revealed that American authorities had apparently suppressed information about the experiments after the war in exchange for access to the medical knowledge acquired. As the news of the research became widely disseminated, current medical researchers sought access to data obtained in the prisoner-of-war camps. Newer and broader ethical questions were debated. Should research findings obtained through unethical methods be publicized or made available to other researchers for their use? Can suppression of valuable knowledge that has the potential to save lives be justified on the basis that the researchers' methods cannot be condoned? Who owns the data? Should the survivors of the experiments (who did not participate voluntarily) or the relatives of those who did not survive have the right to decide whether data from the experiments can be released or under what conditions it can be used? Like most research ethical issues, these are difficult questions with no easy answers.

The Tuskegee Public Health Studies

A second group of research studies that addressed some related ethical issues took place in the United States. In 1932, the American Public Health Service began its studies of the long-term effects of syphilis on men in the Tuskegee, Alabama, area (Jones, 1982). Ethical questions relate to whether these men were truly voluntary participants because of their vulnerability (health status, socioeconomic class, and race). The studies were influential in the development of today's ethical principle of *no unnecessary pain and suffering*.

The Tuskegee research was conducted on 625 African-American males. Most (425) had been diagnosed as having syphilis; the others were followed for comparison purposes. In 1937, penicillin was discovered and was shown to be an effective cure for syphilis. It became available to the general public several years later. Yet, for purposes of research, participants in the Tuskegee experiment, many of whom were illiterate, were not told about penicillin, and it was not given to them unless they somehow learned about it and requested it. Participants unaware of penicillin continued to be given painful regular medical examinations, including spinal taps, to chart the course of their disease. They received only a placebo, an inert substance that had no potential to cure their disease or alleviate their pain and suffering. In the interim, they experienced the long-term effects of syphilis, including skin disorders, insanity, heart disease, and even death. The study continued until 1957, at which time it was halted following public outcry.

Unlike many of the experiments conducted within Nazi concentration camps during World War II, the Tuskegee experiments were probably not the product of depraved minds. They were designed to gather data that would be accurate and would have the potential to benefit humanity. Prior to the availability of penicillin, there may have been a legitimate reason to study syphilis to learn more about the course of what was then an essentially incurable disease. But when the drug became available, there was no logical justification to continue the research, and there was a very good ethical reason to discontinue it immediately and treat participants with the effective drug. Looking back now, those who made the decision to not treat these men with penicillin appear no less insensitive in their lack of regard for the protection of research participants than the medical "researchers" of Dachau or Auschwitz. Some of the researchers later rationalized that the participants were fortunate in that they were given free regular medical examinations and did not have to pay for their burial expenses. Not until 1997 did the U.S. government offer a public apology for their treatment, and the participants and their families were awarded limited financial compensation for their suffering.

The Milgram Studies of Obedience to Authority

In 1963, Stanley Milgram conducted a series of ingeniously designed studies that sought to learn more about the phenomenon of human obedience to authority figures. His research evolved in part from the defenses of Nazi war criminals, who contended that they were just following orders and therefore could not be held responsible for their actions. (Similar defenses were subsequently used by American soldiers in Vietnam and by many others in military conflicts in Bosnia and Iraq where atrocities were committed.) Milgram hoped to learn what ordinary, civilized people are likely to do when ordered by a more powerful individual to do something that they would otherwise never do. He hoped to learn how far they would go in their obedience to authority figures.

The research used adult males as participants. They were told that they would participate in research on learning and would be assigned a partner for the research. In fact, the partner was a person working with the researcher; he was not another research participant. Through the use of a rigged drawing, the true participants always drew the role of the person assigned to reinforce learning through the administration of what they believed to be painful electric shocks to their partner. The participants sat in a room where they could hear but not see the alleged learner who was supposedly wired to receive electrical shocks. The participants read off pairs of words and asked their partner to match them. When the learner made a mistake, the participant was told to throw a switch placed in front of him to give a shock to the errant learner. The switches were labelled with phrases such as "Extreme-intensity shock" and "Danger—severe shock." As more mistakes were made, the participant was told to throw switches indicating increasingly severe electrical shocks. As higher and higher voltage switches were thrown, the learner began to beg for the experiment to end. When the switches continued to be thrown, he began to kick the wall and scream. Finally, as the highest voltage switches were thrown, the learner became silent, indicating that he might have lapsed into unconsciousness or perhaps died.

Many participants became emotionally upset by what they were doing and asked and even begged to be allowed to stop. However, when ordered to continue, only a third of the participants refused to complete the experiment. Nearly two-thirds continued to throw the switches as ordered, despite the fact that they had reason to believe that they might be administering disabling, if not fatal, shocks to another human being.

Of course, as was later explained to the research participants, they were only made to *think* they were causing pain to their partner. In reality, no electrical shock was ever administered. Following the conclusion of research, participants were told that their partners were only acting to their throwing the switches. So why did some researchers, and even the general public (subsequent to the showing of a 1975 made-for-TV movie called *The Tenth Level* depicting the research), object so strenuously to Milgram's methods? How did the Milgram studies come to be almost synonymous with unethical treatment of research participants? For one thing, people questioned whether the physical discomfort and anguish experienced by the research participants (unnecessary pain and suffering) could be justified in light of the knowledge acquired through the research. They experienced a great amount of stress. Critics asked if another method could not have been used to get the same results without causing so much duress for the participants. This question had already been asked about earlier research, for example, the Tuskegee studies.

A second ethical issue raised by the Milgram research was a relatively new one. People asked whether research should be conducted when the effects on the research participants are permanent. Had permanent harm been done to the research participants in the Milgram research? Apparently so. As a result of participating in the research, many of the men tended to view themselves in a different way than they had before. They now knew that, under the right circumstances, they were capable of causing severe physical harm to another person who represented no threat whatsoever to them. As we might anticipate, this was a disturbing revelation. No amount of debriefing to assure them that they had harmed no one while following orders could undo its effects.

The Milgram research helped us to formulate an ethical question: Does the researcher ever have a right to leave research participants in worse physical or emotional condition than the condition in which they were found? A consensus emerged that such a consequence is not justified if the researcher should have been able to anticipate it. Certainly, this had been the case in the Milgram research.

The Milgram research helped us to formulate an ethical question: Does the researcher ever have a right to leave research participants in worse physical or emotional condition than the condition in which they were found?

It is interesting to add that, despite the ethical questions raised by Milgram's original research, similar experiments have been carried out repeatedly since the original study results were released. At least some of these experiments were fashioned very closely after the original study. Most have added the use of female participants. The outcomes of these more recent experiments seem to be similar to the outcome of the original study, with a majority of the participants willing to inflict the highest level of shock to their partner. You can view portions of the documentaries created from these new studies on www.youtube.com by entering "Milgram's obedience to authority experiment in 2009" and "Milgram re-enactment 2002."

The Stanford Prison Experiment

Another research study, known as The Stanford Prison Experiment (Haney, Banks, & Zimbardo, 1973), examined the psychological effects of prison life by creating a mock prison in which 24 college students were selected as research participants to act as guards and prisoners. After only a few days, about one-third of the guards, armed with wooden batons, started to adopt abusive behaviors. The study was discontinued after only six days (the study was scheduled to last two weeks) due to the dangerous behaviors of some of the guards and reactions by some of the prisoners. Zimbardo concluded that situational forces can transform normally nonviolent people into violent perpetrators. There was no clear deception used in the study. However, one criticism of the Milgram studies can also be made against it—the research participants may have been negatively affected by their experiences after it was long over. A recent article by Griggs (2014) points out that despite the many criticisms made regarding the Stanford Prison Experiment (including that its findings may have limited validity because of design flaws), many introductory psychology textbooks present the experiment in a positive light and include little or no discussion of the many ethical questions that have been raised by critics. For more information, search for the Stanford Prison Experiment online.

The Laud Humphreys Studies of Homosexual Behavior

Laud Humphreys' studies (1970) of homosexual behavior in public restrooms sound quite dated today, but they were an important milestone in the development of ethical standards for the treatment of research participants. They also remain one of the most controversial research efforts in the human science professional literature. They have been defended and touted by some people as innovative, while being denounced by others as simply unethical snooping.

The special focus of Humphreys' research was casual homosexual sex acts between strangers who led otherwise heterosexual lives. He conducted observations of homosexual encounters between men in parks. Humphreys knew that the people he wished to study would be unlikely to agree to let him observe their behavior for research purposes. Even if they did, the data thus obtained would be of questionable value. So he engaged in a series of deceptions. He first gained the confidence of his intended research participants. He frequented the public restrooms and implied through his regular presence that he shared in their activities. He began to assume the role of *watch queen*, which entailed being a lookout for the police or other potentially threatening people. The payoff for being a watch queen was the opportunity to watch sexual acts being performed—exactly what he needed for his research. But the deception did not end there.

Because he believed he needed to know more about his research participants, especially about their public lives, Humphreys conducted follow-up interviews. When possible, he recorded the license plate numbers of his participants' vehicles and obtained their addresses through access to police records. Disguising himself so he would not be recognized as their watch queen, he interviewed them under the pretense of conducting a survey, and thus obtained additional descriptive data.

Many ethical questions were raised by the Humphreys study. Some of them continue to be debated. Had he violated the participants' right to privacy? Had their participation in the research been voluntary? They had granted permission for the researcher to watch, but he had misrepresented his real purpose for being there. Was there any other way he could have obtained the same knowledge without this elaborate deception? If he had informed the men of his real purpose, would he have been able to acquire the same amount and quality of data? How much would he have had to tell them about his research for them to be true voluntary participants? Some defenders of the research study contend that his deception caused no one any harm. After all, he conscientiously concealed the identities of his participants in his book that described the research.

The way in which Humphreys learned the identities of his participants and conducted his follow-up interviews was especially infuriating to some of his critics. They charged that the men's permission to be interviewed in their homes was not valid because he had been dishonest about the real reasons why he wished to interview them. He misrepresented both the real focus and the scope of his research. He also put participants at risk of someone making a connection between his survey in their homes and their activities in public restrooms. Although highly unlikely, a research participant's secret behavior could have come to light as a result of Humphreys pursuing them for a follow-up interview at home.

> ### Ethical and Professional Behavior
>
> **Behavior: Make ethical decisions by applying the standards of the NASW code of ethics, relevant laws and regulations, models for ethical decision making, ethical conduct of research, and additional codes of ethics as appropriate to context.**
>
> **Critical Thinking Question:** As a social worker, how do you feel about the fact that the Milgram experiment has been replicated several times since the original experiments? Do you feel social workers should be involved in this type of research? Why or why not?

The Willowbrook Hepatitis Study

The Willowbrook Hepatitis Studies (Education Development Center, Inc., 2009) were conducted from 1955 to 1970 at a residential facility that housed over 6,000 children with cognitive disabilities. Hepatitis was a major problem in the school, and many staff members and residents contracted the disease, a fact that was used as a rationalization for conducting a series of experiments. In one experiment, some children were given protective antibodies and others were not, and the immunity levels of the two groups were compared. In another experiment, newly admitted children were given experimental protective antibodies, then half of the children were purposely exposed to the hepatitis virus and the other half were not purposely exposed. The effects of the disease were then observed and recorded. It was noted that those children purposely exposed had milder symptoms than those who were naturally infected with the virus from the other children.

Some have argued that the benefits of the research conclusions gained by these studies outweighed the harm done to the research participants. These proponents contend that parents gave their consent for their children to participate in the study, most of the children would have contracted the virus even if they did not participate in the study, and the knowledge gained from the study was extremely valuable to the residents of this school as well as the general public. Opponents of the study, on the other hand, argued that the research participant students and their parents were not truly informed about the risks of the study. The school's recruitment methods were also considered questionable, because while the school was not accepting new residents in 1964 due to overcrowding, they were accepting students if they were willing to participate in this study. Critics asked why the researchers did not use adult staff members of the school, who also had a high incidence of hepatitis at the time, as the research participants. Also, why didn't the administrators deal immediately with the issues of overcrowding and unsanitary conditions to lower the incidence of the disease? The conclusion reached by researchers today is that it is unethical to use vulnerable, institutionalized populations, such as the population used in this study, as research participants. Clearly, regardless of the value of the information gleaned from the Willowbrook research study, it was unethical to deliberately infect cognitively disabled children with the hepatitis virus.

TODAY'S STANDARDS FOR PROTECTION OF RESEARCH PARTICIPANTS

Fortunately, today we need not operate in a vacuum in wrestling with ethical issues. As a result of public responses to abuses of research participants in earlier research studies, such as those we have just described, there now exists a list of generally agreed-on standards that govern the conduct of research.

Institutional Review Boards

In response to abuses in research, including those studies described above, ethical standards have now been developed for studies that use human beings as research participants. Many organizations now require review and approval of proposed research studies by a team of researchers and other concerned individuals. These groups are labelled an institutional review board (IRB), a human subjects review team, an ethics committee, or some similar title. Basic regulations governing the protection of human research participants were first published by the Department of Health and Human Services (HHS) in 1974. In 1978, the National Commission for the Protection of Human Subjects of Biomedical and Behavioral Research published "Ethical Principles and Guidelines for the Protection of Human Subjects of Research," also known as the Belmont Report. The Belmont Report identifies three basic ethical principles that should be applied to all human research participants: respect for persons, beneficence, and justice. The Office for Human Research Protections (OHRP, 2009) within HHS now publishes a booklet, "Protection of Human Subjects," in which they outline human subject protection regulations.

Any project that involves a systematic investigation with the intent to develop or contribute to generalizable knowledge is considered *research*. One way to determine if a project is research is to ask whether the investigators plan to publish the results of the project or present the results at an academic meeting. If the project is deemed research, the next step is to determine if human subjects are involved. The OHRP defines *human subject* as "a living individual about whom an investigator conducting research obtains 1) Data through intervention or interaction with the individual, or 2) Identifiable private information."

Research involving human subjects is reviewed and approved by an IRB before the subjects are recruited and data is collected. If the researcher does not work for an agency or institution that has its own IRB, the regulations developed by the U.S. Food and Drug Administration (2014) state, "FDA regulations permit an institution without an IRB to arrange for an outside IRB to be responsible for initial and continuing review of studies conducted at the non-IRB institutions."

Federal regulations have defined three categories into which human subject research can be divided. These categories are based on the level of risk posed to the research subjects:

- **Exempt.** Research in this category poses the least amount of risk to potential subjects. They generally involve either 1) the collection of anonymous or publically available data or 2) research that is deemed least harmful, such as research on normal educational practices.
- **Expedited review.** Research in this category involves the collection of data that is not anonymous but involves no more than minimal risks to the potential subjects.
- **Full committee review.** Research in this category involves greater than minimal risk or vulnerable populations, such as pregnant women or prisoners.

Individual IRBs define the policies and procedures they follow with regard to review of research proposals. For example, Florida State University (FSU, 2010) requires that all research proposals involving human subjects be submitted to its IRB. The researcher cannot make the decision on whether his or her proposal meets the federal criteria for the exempt category, so all proposals are submitted for either expedited or full committee review. Expedited reviews are completed by two members of the committee and the chairman of the committee and take approximately three weeks. The full committee review takes approximately six weeks. The FSU IRB also requires that all research involving vulnerable populations, such as children, prisoners, or pregnant women, be reviewed by the full committee. The members carefully review proposals for research to ensure that the rights of participants will not be threatened or violated and that protection measures are in place. Until the review team is convinced that this is the case, the research is not allowed to be initiated. We will look more closely at four of the major standards the IRB considers when reviewing a research proposal: voluntary informed consent, no unnecessary pain and suffering, anonymity/confidentiality, and the need to conduct the research.

Voluntary Informed Consent

We already know what is meant by the word *voluntary*. It refers to "by choice, not because of coercion or intimidation or because of promises of rewards." As we will discuss later in this chapter, it is often difficult to determine if this condition has been met.

When used in the context of research, *informed* relates to the following question: will the potential participants know what they need to know (at least in general terms) to determine if they wish to participate in the research? Prior to agreeing to participate, a person should have a fairly clear idea of what that participation will entail. This is designed to protect participants from unknowingly getting themselves into a situation that they never would have chosen had they been more fully informed from the outset. It also limits the researcher's ability to deceive research participants by grossly misrepresenting the purposes of their research or the nature and limits of the demands that will be made on research participants.

Consent refers to the fact that there is a clear, generally written, agreement to participate. A consent form, signed by the participant, provides a potential research participant with a description of what to expect. It also provides legal protection for the researcher, who may later need proof that participants willingly took part in the research. This principle is consistent with the social work practice value of self-determination, which upholds an individual's right to make decisions about matters that affect his or her life and well-being. Box 2.1 shows examples of a research participant request letter and an

---

Box 2.1   Research Participation Request and an Informed Consent Form

Dear Mr. or Ms. _____,

During October and November of 2017, students from the University of XYZ, School of Social Work, will be conducting a study to learn more about how support groups may be helpful to women who are HIV positive. Specifically, the study will identify the characteristics of these groups that have been found to be most helpful over time, as described by the group facilitators.

You have been selected to participate in this study because you facilitate such a support group in our state. Your participation would require that you complete a brief survey instrument that will be mailed to you, and also participate in a follow-up phone interview with a student researcher. Some biographic and demographic information about you (gender, age, religious affiliation, academic preparation, and work experience) will also be gathered. Any data that you provide would only be published or made public in the aggregate form.

Participation in this study is completely voluntary. Those who elect to take part in it may discontinue their participation at any time without prejudice or loss of benefits of any sort.

I hope you will agree to participate in this research. It has the potential to provide valuable knowledge to those in the helping professions who work closely with this population. If you agree to participate, please sign and date two copies of the attached consent form, keeping one copy for your records, and mail the other one back to me in the postage-paid envelope. After we receive your signed consent form, you will be contacted by a student to confirm a mailing address where we may send your survey form.

If you have any questions about the study, please contact me at 806-555-1234 or e-mail address: acharles@hotnet.com. Thank you.

Sincerely,

Alfred B. Charles

Professor, School of Social Work
Att.: Informed Consent Form

Informed Consent Form
I agree to participate voluntarily in a study from the University of XYZ, School of Social Work, examining support groups for women who are HIV positive. I understand that my participation in this study involves completing a survey form and participating in a phone interview with a social work research student. I may withdraw my participation in this study at any time without any prejudice or penalties of any sort.

Signature:

Printed Name:

Date:

informed consent form that could be used to acquire the voluntary informed consent of research participants. Note that it allows a participant to withdraw from the research at any time if for any reason he or she no longer wishes to participate.

In obtaining voluntary informed consent, special care needs to be taken in the case of persons from groups that are linguistically or culturally different from the majority population. Consent forms should be provided in the research respondent's native language, and clarifying comments and responses to questions should be addressed in the language most familiar to the respondent. Such situations may require using bilingual or native-speaking research assistants to ensure that participants understand the subtleties of the wording in the consent form.

Researchers also need to be sensitive to culturally determined patterns of deference to authority that may cause respondents to feel they cannot or do not have the right to refuse participation in the study. This may be a relevant issue when the researcher is from a dominant group and the respondent is from a historically less powerful group where there is a shared history. The issue may also exist with cultures that emphasize deference to age or social status, as in some Asian cultures. If a researcher is unfamiliar with the culture of the target population in a cross-cultural research situation, someone familiar with the culture should be consulted regarding issues in obtaining voluntary informed consent and protection of human participants within the specific cultural context. A perception of a power differential or an emphasis within the participants' culture on deference to people with more social status or educational credentials may lead participants to believe that they had little choice but to volunteer.

The principle of voluntary informed consent also recognizes that some vulnerable people—for example, very young children or people with a mental disability—may not be able to understand a description of their proposed participation in research and make an informed decision as to whether they wish to participate. In research that proposes to use people who may be considered incapable of giving voluntary informed consent, another responsible person may serve as an *advocate* to protect them and decide for them what should be permitted in the interest of scientific knowledge building. A parent, guardian, or, in some cases, a social worker or other helping professional, are logical choices to assume the advocate role.

Children, as they get older, should be allowed a greater role in deciding if they wish to participate in research. This is the ethical principle of *assent,* which entails involving older children in decision making, to the extent possible, based upon their developing capacity for rational thinking and their need for autonomy. The ultimate decision should result from an interactive process between the researcher, the child or adolescent, and the advocate.

No Unnecessary Pain and Suffering

Medical research and many research studies that social workers conduct have the potential to cause pain and suffering. In social work research, the pain is more likely

---

Diversity and Difference in Practice

Behavior: Apply and communicate understanding of the importance of diversity and difference in shaping life experiences in practice at the micro, mezzo, and macro levels.

Critical Thinking Question: What are some reasons why special care needs to be taken when obtaining consent from minority populations?

to be emotional than physical, although physical discomfort (symptoms of emotional distress) may occur as well. For example, studies that entail interviewing adult victims of child abuse are likely to require research participants to think about and react to events that they would prefer to repress. This can be very painful (or it may provide a healthy catharsis if the interviewer is sensitive and uses his or her social work skills appropriately).

The realities of science do not absolve the ethical researcher from protecting participants from unnecessary risk.

It is impossible to know all of the potential risks to participants posed by a proposed research study. By definition, science works in areas of inquiry in which cause-effect knowledge is fragmentary, if not totally absent. However, the realities of science do not absolve the ethical researcher from protecting participants from *unnecessary* risk. The researcher must ask, can the knowledge be derived in a way that has less potential to cause physical or emotional harm to the participant? Have protections been built into the research design that will minimize the risk of causing pain and suffering? If the research absolutely must cause some physical or emotional discomfort, will its severity and duration be the absolute minimum that is necessary to acquire data? What follow-up services will be available to participants that have experienced physical or emotional discomfort?

One study conducted by the University of California at Los Angeles (UCLA) during the 1980s and 1990s (Health and Medicine, 1994) illustrates the difficulty of balancing the need for knowledge and the principle of no unnecessary pain and suffering. It also shows how this principle can be related to another principle that we discussed earlier: voluntary informed consent. The researchers were attempting to learn if some people were unnecessarily taking antipsychotic drugs that may produce involuntary tremors. Fifty young patients being treated for schizophrenia had their medication abruptly discontinued. Of these fifty participants, twenty-three experienced severe relapses (including one suicide). Although their parents had signed consent forms for their children, they alleged that they were never told how severe the relapses might be or that it would be safer if the medication were continued.

The UCLA research was designed with good intentions. It sought to acquire knowledge that might help to alleviate a problem experienced by schizophrenic patients—unnecessary medication and its side effects. But in attempting to address the problem, some of the patients were harmed. Many ethical questions can be raised. Did the ends justify the means? Was the pain and suffering experienced by some of the participants in the research (and their families) necessary? Was there another way besides stopping their medication (perhaps gradually reducing it) to learn if the medication was necessary, while causing the patients less pain and suffering?

An important sub-issue that relates to pain and suffering is the presence of any negative aftereffects that people might experience from their roles as research participants. (Remember, this was a major issue in the Milgram studies.) A researcher is ethically obligated to leave research participants preferably in better condition than they were found, but at least in no worse condition. In recognition of the fact that virtually all research involving human participants has the potential to harm or change people in some way, human subject review teams generally pay careful attention to a researcher's plans for debriefing and restoration of participants' well-being after data have been collected. They may wish to ensure that, for example, counseling or other indicated follow-up services will be provided, if needed.

Anonymity/Confidentiality

As social workers, we need not be reminded of the importance of safeguarding the privacy and identity of our clients. The ethical principles of anonymity and confidentiality exist to safeguard research participants from the harm that can come to them if their identities are intentionally or inadvertently associated with any data that are collected. The two terms are used in research much as they are used in other areas of social work practice. The ideal condition under which participants provide data is anonymity. When it exists, even the researcher does not know the participants' names and cannot attribute to them any data that were provided. An example of anonymity might be a mailed questionnaire survey that does not use case numbers or other identification on the questionnaire or on the return envelope. The researcher cannot know who returned one and who did not or who said what in their replies. This protects the participants' anonymity, but it can have real logistical disadvantages for researchers. For example, what if researchers wish to send a follow-up questionnaire to those who did not respond or to acquire clarification about some data provided by those who did respond?

A more realistic and generally acceptable alternative involves protection of confidentiality. Especially when data are collected through in-person interviews, researchers are likely to know and recall who revealed what about themselves. Under principles of confidentiality, the researcher is ethically obligated not to reveal the participants' identities or in any way let others be able to associate any of the data provided with any one participant. However, even if nothing is ever revealed, sometimes the data themselves can disclose the identity of the participant. Anastas (2010) warns that inferred identification is a particular hazard in qualitative research. She states, "When case data are given in detail or verbatim quotations are used in the text, it is possible that certain readers of a research report will be able to identify a specific research participant even when no identifying data are given" (p. 60). Identification in quantitative research can also be inferred when there are very few participants in a particular minority category. For example, if a sample includes 240 Caucasians, 60 African Americans, 12 Asian Americans, and 1 Native American, all data reported for the Native-American category could be easily traced back to the one Native-American participant. Upholding confidentiality requires careful editing of the data before disseminating study findings to minimize the risk of participant identification. This may require that some potentially valuable data be excluded, unless it can be aggregated along with that of other participants in some way. Because these issues can be more complicated in qualitative research, Anastas (2010) calls for "a fuller discussion and articulation of consent, disguise, boundary issues, and other normative practices to protect participants in qualitative evaluation" (p. 61).

The principle of confidentiality often governs how social workers handle data about their clients. As researchers, it seems familiar and natural to protect participants from harm. However, people outside the social work academic and practice communities may attempt to convince a researcher to compromise the principle. What if, for example, a research report reveals that a participant is guilty of a crime such as fraud or has threatened the well-being of others? Does the public have the right to know the identity of that participant and to take appropriate legal action? It is a good idea to check out relevant laws and statutes when such issues arise or, better yet, before they do.

In the role of researchers, social workers may not enjoy the protection of privileged communication, as this varies from state to state. Research data can and have been subpoenaed and will continue to be subject to public scrutiny. For this reason, some researchers have chosen to destroy the names and other identifiable data from files about their research participants once the data have been coded and case numbers assigned.

For some behaviors we may learn about in the process of conducting research, we may have clear-cut solutions. In the presence of child abuse, for example, we have an ethical and a legal obligation to notify the proper authorities that transcends our role as researchers. However, in the presence of other behaviors, the appropriate course of action is not always that clear. Delva (2007) points out that researchers who conduct research on illicit behaviors, such as substance abuse or unsafe sexual practices among adolescents, often face an ethical dilemma. Should they respect the confidentiality of the research participants who have shared knowledge of their behaviors, or should they share the information with the participants' parents or other helping professionals since the behaviors are putting the participants at risk? What is the researcher's primary responsibility to participants—to protect confidentiality or to protect their health and welfare? Is the risk to participants less important than the knowledge that can be acquired (that can potentially help others in a similar situation) by adhering to promises of confidentiality? Such issues are not easily resolved. Whatever decisions are made, they can leave the researcher feeling a little uneasy.

Need to Conduct the Research

Ethically, research cannot be justified when it merely provides a research learning experience for the researcher, does not promise to significantly advance knowledge, or might provide knowledge that simply is not worth knowing.

Although sometimes not mentioned specifically among the criteria by which review panels evaluate a research proposal, there is a fourth ethical concern that should always be considered. Even if the proposed research represents no physical or emotional threat to research participants, the participants have a right to assume that the demands made on them (e.g., their time or other costs) are necessary for the advancement of knowledge. Ethically, research cannot be justified when it merely provides a research learning experience for the researcher, does not promise to significantly advance knowledge, or might provide knowledge that simply is not worth knowing. Thus, IRBs may question whether proposed research is justifiable, given the nature of the products that it promises to yield, or whether it represents an unnecessary imposition on its participants.

Research may not be approved if it seems designed only to advance a political or economic agenda. The issue of conducting research for purposes other than the advancement of knowledge came to the fore during the late 1980s as a result of people active in the antivivisection movement. A frequent argument against the use of animals for experimentation by the American cosmetics industry was that research on chimpanzees, rabbits, guinea pigs, dogs, and other laboratory animals was not conducted to learn anything new. Its primary purpose was to provide legal protection for manufacturers against charges that products had not undergone sufficient testing prior to their release in the market.

Is there a danger that social work researchers might conduct unnecessary research for purposes other than the advancement of knowledge? Yes. Even ethical researchers may inadvertently conduct unnecessary research. For example, a researcher may not conduct a thorough review of the literature to determine what knowledge is already available. Thus, researchers repeat the work of others and waste the time and energies of their research participants, as well as their own.

Research may also be conducted for purely educational purposes, that is, to give social workers supervised practice in conducting research. This can occur within colleges and universities, in high school science fair competitions, and even within human service organizations. Deriving new knowledge may not be a high priority. The same research questions may be studied year after year, and often nothing productive is ever done with the acquired data.

Learning to conduct research by actually designing and implementing a study can be a very effective way to become a good researcher. So what's wrong with this practice? Conducting research over and over on research questions whose answers are already available is ethically questionable, even if it does not represent a major imposition for research participants. It is a waste of scarce research resources and, what's more, it does not "model" good research. With a little extra effort, new questions (those begging answers) can always be found.

Concern over the ethics of unnecessary research is recognition that scientific inquiry involving human participants almost always represents an unequal trade. It offers less to the research participants than it takes from them. This "bad deal" can be justified only if some greater good can come out of the research, specifically, the advancement of knowledge that can help others.

Evaluation

Behavior: Apply knowledge of human behavior and the social environment, person-in-environment, and other multidisciplinary theoretical frameworks in the evaluation of outcomes.

Critical Thinking Question: Do you feel it is justified to require social work students to conduct research on their clients during their field placement experience? Why or why not?

CONTEMPORARY ISSUES RELATED TO RESEARCH "VOLUNTEERS"

By the latter part of the twentieth century, the standards for ethical protection of research participants had been developed. They have changed little since then. However, ethical issues are still with us and always will be.

Are Research Volunteers Truly Voluntary?

One important question relates to the standards of voluntary informed consent and no unnecessary pain and suffering. Some people choose, for a variety of reasons, to become research participants, even if they know that the research might result in some discomfort or suffering to them. If the researcher knows that the participant would probably choose not to participate if his or her situation were different, can the participant ethically be considered a volunteer?

What are some of the situations that cause us to question whether it is ethical to allow people to volunteer to participate in research? Perhaps they have little to lose (they may have a terminal illness and wish to make some contribution to knowledge before they die). Others find themselves in a situation (they may be homeless and/or struggling financially) where even small rewards for research participation (a few dollars, a meal, or the opportunity to get out of the heat or the cold) can provide a strong incentive to become research participants. Prisoners within correctional settings may volunteer to participate in research studies. However, we must ask, would they have agreed to be research participants had they not been incarcerated? Can we be absolutely certain that they are not being coerced by something or someone, or influenced by some implied promise of reward, such as more privileges or time off their sentences? How can we know if they are agreeing to do something that they would not do under other circumstances? And, what if they are? Is it their right to do so?

There is a similar ethical issue in research that involves new or experimental drugs. Efforts to find a cure for or to delay the course of AIDS and other serious illnesses, such as cancer, Parkinson's syndrome, and Alzheimer's disease have resulted in the experimental use of many unproven drugs. Some of them have painful and even potentially lethal side effects. Yet many people have willingly agreed to become research participants in medical research designed to test the efficacy of various medications and treatment regimens. Their "willing" participation, perhaps as a result of desperation or an inability to afford more proven medication (the cost is usually borne by the researchers), has caused us to ask a number of questions. Would they undergo the risks and discomfort if they had any alternative? Are researchers who conduct the research taking unfair advantage of their unfortunate situations? Similarly, people who have been convicted of the crime of pedophilia have agreed to undergo aversive therapy to attempt to cure a problem that many currently regard as incurable. Has their desperation (and, perhaps some pressure from prison authorities) caused them to undergo the considerable physical discomfort that they otherwise would not have selected? Probably. Is that necessarily unethical?

There are many other groups that are vulnerable to being unethically used as research participants. Their rights must be protected. However, that entails a difficult balancing act between (1) their right not to be exploited as a result of their vulnerability and (2) their right to participate in research that may be of benefit to them. Sieber (1992) lists different categories of people who are vulnerable:

People who lack resources or autonomy

People who are stigmatized by society

People who are in a weakened position, perhaps in an institutional setting

People who cannot speak for themselves and their best interests

People whose illegal activities might become known to law enforcement authorities

People associated with research participants who may be damaged by data revealed by the participants (p. 147)

Medical research provides some of the clearest and most dramatic examples of ethical issues relating to the vulnerability of people who might "volunteer" to become research participants, but these issues are just as prevalent in social work research. Naturally, most social work research focuses on people and the problems they experience rather than physical illness. Although these problems are not always life threatening, they can be serious obstacles to life quality.

Policy Practice

Behavior: Identify social policy at the local, state, and federal level that impacts well-being, service delivery, and access to social services.

Critical Thinking Question: Do you think people should be allowed to try unproven experimental treatments? Why or why not?

Dual-Role Relationships

Is it ethical to use our own clients or former clients as research participants? What about a colleague's clients, where the colleague serves as a *broker*, a person who asks potential participants if they would be willing to participate in research? Either group may readily agree to participate because of the relationship that is already established. What about the use of potential research participants who are not our clients but who share a problem or condition with us who we have met through a support group or in a social situation? Would any of these individuals be considered volunteers in the purest sense of the word? We might ask, would they agree to serve as research participants if we did not already have a previous relationship? Can we be certain that obligation, gratitude, or even fear of offending us is not influencing their decision?

What we have just described can be referred to as *dual-role relationships*. When researchers have a pre-existing relationship with potential participants, it is sometimes difficult to know if they are volunteer participants in the strictest sense. The presence of a dual-role relationship has often prevented good research from being conducted. However, IRBs have sometimes approved research studies despite the presence of a dual-role relationship. Why? This occurs most frequently when access to data would not have been possible had there not been a pre-existing relationship with the participants. Anyone else attempting the same research would have had much greater difficulty in establishing trust and may not have been able to get potential participants to agree to participate. For example, one social work researcher (Taylor, 1998) conducted in-depth interviews with parents who had lost an adult child to AIDS to better understand how different people cope with such a loss. She had gotten to know her research participants while providing social work services to their sons or daughters. Another researcher (Pryce, 1995) interviewed children whose parent had suffered a massive traumatic head injury and had survived, but at a much lower level of functioning. She had experienced the problem in her own family and was able to locate her participants because she was a member of an organization that consisted of persons in similar circumstances.

Was research participation in these two studies truly voluntary? Probably not. The IRB members who approved them also acknowledged that the interviews with participants were likely to be stressful for them. However, no one was likely to be seriously harmed. In fact, the researchers later concluded, it was probably psychologically beneficial to the participants to express some of their feelings about their losses to a caring professional who they already trusted. The fact that the potential benefits of the research for others in similar situations probably outweighed any discomfort to participants was another factor in the decision to allow the studies to be conducted.

When dual-role relationships exist, certain special precautions are required to protect research participants. Special effort must be made to assure potential participants that they will suffer no loss or disadvantage (including the respect of the researcher) if they decide not to participate. The pre-existing relationship should not be damaged in any way. A third, neutral person—not the researcher—should be provided to offer counseling, if needed, and to help at any time in deciding whether or not it is in the participant's best interest to continue participation. Finally, if feasible, participation should be anonymous, so the researcher cannot know who participated and who did not. Of course, in studies where the researchers themselves gather data using in-person interviews with participants who they already know (such as the two examples previously described), anonymous participation is impossible.

There is still another issue related to dual-role relationships and voluntary informed consent that we as social workers sometimes encounter when conducting research. Because of the nature of our work and the trust often placed in us by clients, we may have access to sensitive or private data not readily available to outside researchers. Clients often tend to become quite candid in what they say and do around social workers because they trust that the social worker is primarily concerned with helping them.

Should data (in the form of case records) gathered for the purpose of providing treatment to clients be used for a purpose for which they never were intended—research? In such cases, did clients and patients really give voluntary consent to be research participants? Sometimes, but not usually. Federal legislation, the 1996 Hospital Insurance Portability and Accountability Act (HIPAA), made access to medical records in many medical and psychiatric settings difficult, if not impossible, for use in research. In some settings, such as teaching hospitals, patients can still agree from the outset that data collected relative to their treatment can be used for research and teaching purposes. However, is this really voluntary informed consent, since it could be argued that consent may be granted under some duress? Undoubtedly, some participants want to provide information that might help others with the same problem. However, others may fear that not agreeing to participate may antagonize their social worker and thus affect their treatment.

Using Deception in Research

The social work researcher is perhaps less likely than researchers in other disciplines to conduct research that could result in irreparable physical or psychological damage to participants. We are sensitized to recognize the ways in which life experiences can negatively affect people's self-esteem or their ability to function. For example, we would not conduct or condone research that would involve telling clients that they should get out of a healthy marriage in order to study their emotional responses or lying to medical patients by telling them that they have a terminal illness in order to observe what changes they might make in their lives. We know the potentially negative consequences of any behavior designed to alter how we think of ourselves or others. The question remains, however, does deception in research always result in negative consequences for the research participants? Further, are all research designs that entail deception of any kind considered unethical? Not necessarily.

In some instances, deception may be necessary to study behavior or emotional responses that would be easily influenced if the participant had a complete understanding of the researcher's objective. In these cases, if the deception is deemed to be relatively harmless to the participant, it may be accepted as an ethical research technique. But deception can be an unnecessary and dangerous shortcut. It has been used when other, less potentially harmful methods, such as simulations, would have been equally effective. Before considering the use of deception, the ethical researcher should ask, is deception absolutely the only way that I can get the knowledge that I need? And if so, what will I do to be certain that I will not leave my research participants in worse physical or emotional condition than when the research began? Pittenger (2002) offers three recommendations to the researcher considering the use of deception: (1) A researcher who uses deception should provide, in their research report, a detailed account of the procedure used to minimize the harm created by the deception; (2) The American Psychological Association should develop a definition of deception that describes the techniques commonly used in research; and (3) The informed consent procedure should be revised to indicate that the researcher may use deception as part of the study (p. 117).

Withholding Treatment and Use of Placebos

Another old ethical dilemma is still with us and probably always will be. It is most often discussed in relation to recent medical research but is equally relevant for many forms of social work research. It relates to whether it is ethical to deny some research participants access to an intervention method that may prove helpful for them. For example, what is the best way to examine the effectiveness of one of the many experimental drugs being developed for the treatment of persons who suffer from Advanced Alzheimer's disease or have other serious or life-threatening illnesses? Or, how do we learn most definitively if a social program is really effective? Traditionally, the most rigorous research designs have used a control group, a group of people who are identified as having the problem of interest but are merely followed and evaluated and not offered the intervention. In medical research, members of the control group might instead be given a placebo (such as a sugar pill), but they would not know whether they received the experimental drug or the placebo. The use of a control group may be methodologically sound, but is it ethically defensible? What if the intervention is subsequently found to be effective? The quality of life of the people in the control group might have been higher or their lives even saved if they had received the intervention that they were denied. Or, suppose that early in the course of the research it became apparent that the drug was highly effective? Should the research have been stopped at that point and the drug offered to members of the control group as well? Or, what if it appeared to be making the condition of those people receiving the drug much worse? Shouldn't the research also have been terminated before it caused more harm? In either situation, ending the research study prematurely may be the only ethical response, even if it may compromise the credibility of the research findings.

Research in Third World countries has attempted to determine if HIV-infected mothers in a control group, who were given a placebo or low dosages of drugs known to be effective for delaying the onset of HIV symptoms, had a comparable or higher rate of passing the disease on to their babies than those given the full dosage of the drug (Associated Press Report, 1997). Critics have questioned whether such research, like the Tuskegee experiments, is unethical and exploitive of participants, in part because less vulnerable people may not have opted to participate in such research. Ellenberg (2009) presents the debate of the ethics involved in using placebos in research, stating that "the scientific considerations for using placebos in trials are complex and often poorly understood, thereby complicating the dialogue around the ethical issues" (p. 259). She summarizes the debate into two distinct questions: (1) Is it ethical to assign participants to a placebo when effective agents are available, as long as no irreversible harm will result from remaining untreated for the duration of the study? (2) Is it ethical to assign participants to a placebo when effective agents have been identified and are available in some regions but not where the study is taking place, even if the known effective agents have been shown to prevent irreversible harm in the regions where they have been evaluated?

Availability of Experimental Interventions

The pressure to find a way to prevent or cure serious chronic illnesses has spotlighted other common research ethical issues that are relevant to social work research. One of these might be described as *the right to be a research participant*. While some argue that it is unethical to deny people experimental drugs or treatment by placing them in a control group, others argue that such experimental interventions should not be made available at all. There are potentially life-saving experimental drugs that are currently not available to many who might benefit from them because they have not yet been cleared for use in the United States by the Food and Drug Administration (FDA). Most likely, some of these drugs remain in a warehouse awaiting further research into their efficacy and possible side effects. Should the usual seven- to ten-year testing process be waived on the basis of the urgency of a situation? How many studies of a program designed to prevent adolescents from experimenting with methamphetamines should we require before we include the program as part of our "best practices" and seek funding for its widespread use? If one well-designed program evaluation concludes that an intervention is effective when no other effective interventions are available, should that be enough for us to factor the results into our decision making (EBP)? Do we need two such studies? More?

Falit and Gross (2008) outline key themes for policy makers, advocates, and potential research participants to consider. One important ethical issue is discussed in light of a recent case, *Abigail Alliance v. Von Eschenbach*, in which the U.S. Court of Appeals ruled that the Fifth Amendment's due process does not include the fundamental right to access experimental treatments. Therefore, Congress and the FDA will continue to regulate access to such treatments as they see fit. Nevertheless, this will continue to be an ethical debate in social work and other research.

OTHER ETHICAL OBLIGATIONS OF RESEARCHERS

The ethical positions adopted by the National Association of Social Workers (NASW) provide guidelines for both professional practice and research. They limit one's behavior with clients and research participants. In the NASW (2008) *Code of Ethics*, it is evident that the unethical use of human participants for knowledge building is never condoned (see Box 2.2 for the NASW statement regarding social work research). However, the *Code of Ethics* and the professional literature suggest that the researcher has ethical obligations not only to the participants but also to the sponsors of research, other researchers, colleagues, and the general public. Most obligations relate to broad issues, such as the scientific integrity of researchers, the requirement that they adhere to certain standards in conducting research, and that they honestly report and interpret findings.

What do these position statements tell us about the general characteristics of ethical researchers? For one thing, they recognize the seriousness of scientific inquiry and the potential of research findings to influence the work and lives of others. Policy makers are aware that any research finding, no matter how unexpected or contrary to what they believe to be true, is potentially valuable. In addition, any misrepresentation of what is learned is potentially dangerous because, in an era of EBP, social workers rely more heavily than ever on research findings for their decision making. For example, ethical researchers

Box 2.2   NASW Code of Ethics (2008)—Section 5.02 Evaluation and Research

a. Social workers should monitor and evaluate policies, the implementation of programs, and practice interventions.

b. Social workers should promote and facilitate evaluation and research to contribute to the development of knowledge.

c. Social workers should critically examine and keep current with emerging knowledge relevant to social work and fully use evaluation and research evidence in their professional practice.

d. Social workers engaged in evaluation or research should carefully consider possible consequences and should follow guidelines developed for the protection of evaluation and research participants. Appropriate institutional review boards should be consulted.

e. Social workers engaged in evaluation or research should obtain voluntary and written informed consent from participants, when appropriate, without any implied or actual deprivation or penalty for refusal to participate; without undue inducement to participate; and with due regard for participants' well-being, privacy, and dignity. Informed consent should include information about the nature, extent, and duration of the participation requested and disclosure of the risks and benefits of participation in the research.

f. When evaluation or research participants are incapable of giving informed consent, social workers should provide an appropriate explanation to the participants, obtain the participants' assent to the extent they are able, and obtain written consent from an appropriate proxy.

g. Social workers should never design or conduct evaluation or research that does not use consent procedures, such as certain forms of naturalistic observation and archival research, unless rigorous and responsible review of the research has found it to be justified because of its prospective scientific, educational, or applied value and unless equally effective alternative procedures that do not involve waiver of consent are not feasible.

h. Social workers should inform participants of their right to withdraw from evaluation and research at any time without penalty.

i. Social workers should take appropriate steps to ensure that participants in evaluation and research have access to appropriate supportive services.

j. Social workers engaged in evaluation or research should protect participants from unwarranted physical or mental distress, harm, danger, or deprivation.

k. Social workers engaged in the evaluation of services should discuss collected information only for professional purposes and only with people professionally concerned with this information.

l. Social workers engaged in evaluation or research should ensure the anonymity or confidentiality of participants and of the data obtained from them. Social workers should inform participants of any limits of confidentiality, the measures that will be taken to ensure confidentiality, and when any records containing research data will be destroyed.

m. Social workers who report evaluation and research results should protect participants' confidentiality by omitting identifying information unless proper consent has been obtained authorizing disclosure.

n. Social workers should report evaluation and research findings accurately. They should not fabricate or falsify results and should take steps to correct any errors later found in published data using standard publication methods.

o. Social workers engaged in evaluation or research should be alert to and avoid conflicts of interest and dual relationships with participants, should inform participants when a real or potential conflict of interest arises, and should take steps to resolve the issue in a manner that makes participants' interests primary.

p. Social workers should educate themselves, their students, and their colleagues about responsible research practices.

Source: National Association of Social Workers (2008). *Code of Ethics*. Retrieved from http://www.socialworkers.org/pubs/code/code.asp

will honestly report *null findings*. In other words, they will report findings that demonstrate the ineffectiveness of a social program or the failure of an intervention as well as those that support the effectiveness of an intervention. They will place truth above the personal gain that can be attained through the manipulation of data to achieve desired results.

Ethical researchers function with neutrality and, to the degree possible, objectivity. They strive to keep an open mind to let empirical knowledge, not their own preferences, form the basis for any conclusions drawn from their research. When this is not totally possible—as it generally isn't—they candidly describe the amount and types of bias that they may have introduced.

Ethical researchers resist outside influences, such as political or economic pressures, that might influence either the results of the research or its dissemination. They give proper credit to funding organizations that provided support for their research, and, at the same time, do not allow these organizations to distort or suppress their findings.

Ethical researchers avoid research with which they have a conflict of interest. This includes any situation in which the researcher has the potential to benefit or lose depending on the outcome of the research. If research is going to provide social workers with scientific knowledge on which to base practice and policy decisions, they must be able to trust that the outcomes have been presented in a truthful and nonbiased way. If researchers have a personal investment in the findings of their research, the validity of the research findings may be compromised.

Ethical researchers are aware of the tentative nature of scientific knowledge and remain open to reinterpretation and even contradiction of their findings.

Ethical researchers are aware of the tentative nature of scientific knowledge and remain open to reinterpretation and even contradiction of their findings. They do not claim to have more definitive answers to research questions than are justifiable on the basis of their findings. They value constructive criticism and debate with their fellow researchers. They take responsibility for their research methods and findings, and they welcome legitimate critique.

Ethical researchers never attempt to take credit for work that they did not perform and always share the credit for collaborative efforts. They openly acknowledge the support and contributions of others to their research. They insist that appropriate credit be given to students and/or research assistants and consultants who contributed to the research effort. They will not allow their own names to appear as co-researchers on efforts where their own contributions were only minimal, or as the primary researcher when others did most of the work.

While recognizing the importance of building knowledge to promote better client services, ethical social work researchers resist any use of research that appears to represent a breach of professional ethics. Their activities are shaped by both research ethical standards and their professional ethics as social workers. They are social workers first, then researchers. When using clients as research participants, they acknowledge that their clients' best interests must take precedence over knowledge building. They will not allow confidentiality to be violated without permission, even if it requires them to suppress potentially valuable findings. They discontinue any research if it begins to threaten their participants' welfare.

Ethical researchers are also concerned about the ways that research findings are disseminated and used. They want the findings of research to help rather than degrade or contribute to the harassment of the people they serve. They will attempt to halt the use of their research data by others when it is taken out of context to embarrass others or otherwise create or contribute to a false public impression about them. They may insist that their findings be presented only in their entirety. They may seek to discredit interpretations of their research findings that they perceive to be self-serving or that otherwise misrepresent them.

Research studies have the potential to dispel myths and harmful stereotypes derived from less trustworthy sources. But research, especially when reported in the popular media, can also lend credence to myths and stereotypes. We would be remiss if we did not point out that one cannot always trust research findings, especially when they are selectively reported for "shock value" or to boost circulation or Neilson ratings. For example, during the 1980s, there was great concern about the use of crack cocaine by pregnant women and its long-term health effects on their babies. Logic, common sense, and early research studies suggested that these children suffer major physical and psychological damage from their mothers' chemical addiction. The newspapers and television channels picked up on it. The selective use of research findings made this "knowledge" more believable. However, a meta-analysis conducted by the Drug Policy Alliance (2004) revealed serious methodological flaws in the studies that led to numerous erroneous conclusions about the extent and severity of the potential problem. Subsequent research has shown that problems among babies of crack-addicted mothers could be attributed to other factors, such as poverty, violence, and demoralization (Day & Richardson, 1993). Unfortunately, the early, flawed studies have been used in at least one state, South Carolina, to assist in the successful prosecution of addicted women for child abuse, thus adding to their problem.

Wakefield et al. (1998) is an example of a research study in which the outcome data were purposely altered to support the presence of a link between the administration of the measles, mumps, and rubella (MMR) vaccination and the appearance of autism. When other researchers were unable to replicate Wakefield's findings, and the MMR vaccination took a downturn in England, Brian Deer launched an investigation that uncovered undisclosed financial conflicts of interest (Deer, 2004). In 2010, Wakefield was found guilty of charges of deliberately falsifying data and acting without ethical approval from an institutional review board, as well as several counts of maltreatment of developmentally challenged children (Deer, 2009; Deer, 2011). *The Lancet*, the journal in which the original study was published, subsequently fully retracted the article and Wakefield was barred from practicing medicine. Unfortunately, his original claim still affects many people's decisions today regarding the MMR vaccination. Many parents still choose not to vaccinate their infants for fear of the development of autism. Thus, this unethical researcher can be linked to a decrease in the use of the vaccination and an increase in the occurrence of measles and mumps, two serious illnesses. For more on the investigation conducted on the Wakefield study, go to the following http://briandeer.com/mmr-lancet.htm.

Much of what we have been describing falls under the heading of research integrity. It was discussed at a symposium devoted to the responsible conduct of research at CSWE's annual program meeting in Chicago in 2006. Subsequently, a subgroup of those in attendance began to meet to develop a statement that would continue and summarize the discussions. The members, with support from CSWE, produced a document, the National Statement on Research Integrity in Social Work (Council on Social Work Education, 2007), which is an excellent reference for social workers who wish to meet their ethical responsibilities to all parties likely to be impacted by their research efforts. Excerpts are included in Box 2.3.

Box 2.3   Excerpts from the CSWE's National Statement on Research Integrity in Social Work

To ensure the responsible conduct of research, social work researchers need to: (1) work to protect the people and communities whom they study; (2) ethically and effectively participate in mentoring relationships that are crucial to scientific activity; (3) manage apparent an implicit conflicts of interest and commitment; (4) collaborate ethically with researchers from other professions and disciplines; (5) ensure that research data issues are managed properly; (6) employ responsible publication and authorship practices; (7) responsibly conduct and contribute to the peer-review process; and (8) understand and prevent research misconduct (Office of Research Integrity, 2006). In the sections below we discuss each of these areas of concern and briefly discuss particular issues facing social work researchers.

1. Human Subjects and Communities

Social work researchers must strive not to harm the people or communities that they are studying. Research protocols should first ensure the protection of study participants, including consideration for the Basic Ethical Principles described in the Belmont Report. Respect for persons "incorporates at least two ethical convictions: first, that individuals should be treated as autonomous agents, and second, that persons with diminished autonomy are entitled to protection" (p. 4). Beneficence assures that persons are "treated in an ethical manner not only by respecting their decisions and protecting them from harm, but also by making efforts to secure their well-being" (pp. 4–5). Justice requires that the "selection of research subjects needs to be scrutinized in order to determine whether some classes (e.g., patients receiving government assistance, vulnerable racial and ethnic minorities, and institutionalized persons) are being systematically selected simply because of their easy availability, their compromised position, or their manipulability, rather than for reasons directly related to the problem being studied" (p. 6) (National Commission for the Protection of Human Subjects of Biomedical and Behavioral Research, 1979).

Research involving vulnerable populations needs to assure that risk of harm is minimized and benefits from the research are equitably distributed. While designing protocols to protect vulnerable people and communities can be extremely challenging, total or arbitrary exclusion of vulnerable populations from research is detrimental to the people the profession serves and can sometimes constitute research misconduct. Social work research in developing countries poses additional and specialized ethical problems in human protection that deserve special consideration. Rather than avoiding these difficulties, researchers should work with their colleagues and the appropriate IRBs to develop ways to ethically include vulnerable populations in research. Participation in research should be predicated on the potential participant's understanding of the project, including obtaining informed consent. Finally, social work researchers should keep in mind that students involved as research participants are to be afforded the same protections as any other population.

Before beginning any research investigation, researchers should receive all necessary approval from the organizational regulatory bodies. The organizational regulatory bodies, such as the researcher's Institutional Review Board, will provide another layer of protection for the participants and communities in research, by ensuring that pertinent laws and guidelines have been met by the protocol and that the research is ethical. Researchers should consult with colleagues and the Office of Research Integrity/IRB staffs in their institutions and universities if they have questions regarding regulatory bodies.

2. Mentor/Trainee Responsibility

Social work researchers have a responsibility to mentor trainees in a manner that enhances the professional development of the latter and advances the general progress of the profession. Mentoring junior researchers and trainees in social work research serves to instill the mentee with the ethics, techniques, and community of the profession (Vasgird & Hyman-Browne, n.d.). Social work's commitment to advancing the careers of traditionally underrepresented and marginalized groups indicates a special commitment to mentoring trainees who often experience isolation and exaggerated expectations in aca-

(continued)

Box 2.3   (continued)

demic and research settings. Senior researchers and mentors have a special responsibility to act ethically toward junior researchers and trainees by avoiding implicit and explicit exploitation. Mentoring relationships are complex; collaborative agreements that are developed early in the working relationship and that clearly delineate the rights and responsibilities of all parties can be very helpful in ensuring fair and just outcomes.

3. Conflicts of Interest and Commitment

Social work researchers are encouraged to develop relationships with public and private institutions. However, social work researchers should scrutinize their research endeavors and seek to avoid and eliminate any improper conflicts of interest that might result from their activities. These can involve tangible conflicts, such as untoward financial gain, but may also involve other and intangible forms of improper personal enhancement or advancement. Despite institutional pressures to attract high levels of external funding and to lead multiple projects, social work researchers should judiciously commit only to those projects and positions which they can reasonably undertake. The number and complexity of contemporary researchers' roles make this a challenging domain of responsible conduct.

4. Collaborative Science

Contemporary social work research is rarely an individual enterprise. Multidisciplinary and community-based research are often required, especially for significant research investigations. Social work researchers should engage in collaborative enterprises with other professions and disciplines to advance scientific knowledge. These efforts will require special attention and sensitivity to the ethos and cultures of those research partners. Social work researchers also should seek to clarify, and in many cases commit to a written agreement, issues pertaining to data ownership, authorship, project roles, and financial management.

As the growth of translational science continues, social work researchers will increasingly collaborate with communities. It is important that researchers work hard to understand and reasonably respond to local needs and expectations as research projects are designed, implemented, and published. This is especially challenging as social work researchers often collaborate with community members who come from very different backgrounds and have goals that are divergent from the researchers.

5. Data Acquisition, Management, Sharing, and Ownership

The rapid development of exciting technologies for data acquisition, analysis, and sharing create complex ethical challenges for social work researchers. Researchers need to consult and understand the regulations and obligations involved as they conduct research. The federal government and most other sponsors stipulate what these obligations shall be when a researcher is awarded a grant or contract. Universities also have policies and regulations in this domain which create obligations for researchers who are, in effect, agents of these academic institutions. The best strategy is to discuss the particular approaches the researcher will take with sponsors and their academic colleagues early in the life of the research project. It is important that the entire research team understands these issues as well, as they often intersect with more mundane personnel issues, for example, changing jobs or moving to a new institution.

6. Publication Practices and Responsible Authorship

An important part of social work research is the reporting of study results. Publication of research findings should include appropriate attribution of authorship. Authors and co-authors should be determined on the basis of the type and amount of work completed. There can be controversy over who should be included as an author, especially since being identified as an author or first author on a publication can have implications for tenure, funding, and other professional opportunities; beginning discussions of authorship earlier in the research process can reduce confusion. Many universities, departments, peer-reviewed journals, and professional organizations have specific policies outlining

(continued)

Box 2.3   (continued)

the criteria for who qualifies as an "author" for a publication (Eisner, Vasgird, & Hyman-Browne, n.d.).

Social work researchers must never fabricate data or publish data that are known to be fabricated or otherwise compromised in nature or engage in plagiarism. All ideas and phrasing not originating with the author or co-author should be appropriately acknowledged in publication of results. Researchers should respect ethical obligations, regulations, and laws pertaining to intellectual property, copyright, and patents. Complex developments in technologies and regulations regarding data acquisition, management, sharing, and ownership demand special consideration. The emergent quality of these areas requires social work researchers to regularly study pertinent issues, problems, and solutions as they develop.

7. Peer Review

Peer review is critical for the advancement of science. Journals and federal- and private-granting organizations are reliant upon reviewers to ensure the quality of their publications and awards. Social work researchers should participate in the peer-review process in a fair, constructive, and rigorous manner. Additionally, peer-review processes should be timely and protect the confidentiality of all participants. Social work researchers should identify all potential conflicts of interest and also strive to subordinate their personal preferences and biases to the higher purposes of advancing the profession, scientific activity, and the public welfare.

8. Research Misconduct

Consequences for engaging in research misconduct are varied but may include ineligibility for future grants, termination of positions, monetary penalties, or other penalties. Findings of research misconduct result in negative publicity for the researcher/research team and for the university. If the university is also implicated in misconduct (e.g., chronic nonresponsiveness of the IRB), sanctions may include the withdrawal of federal authorizations and funding for selected or for all federally-sponsored research. It is also important to note that local or state jurisdictions might impose criminal or civil penalties if such investigations reveal criminal misconduct or tortious behavior. Loss of personal integrity, moral authority, and community trust transcend the particular events associated with misconduct cases by destroying the relationships enjoyed by researchers and the wider community for years. In sum, research misconduct can be extraordinarily costly to all persons and organizations concerned. Consequences extend beyond issues of liability and damage to reputation, to include damage to: (1) relationships with the participating communities; (2) individuals involved in the work; and (3) professional integrity.

Undetected research misconduct can have even graver consequences, including the dissemination of practice technologies, programs, and social policies that have relied on unfounded or distorted scientific work. The result might be the waste of limited social resources, loss of life, or reduced personal well-being for clients and significant harm to the public welfare. Therefore, social work researchers have an obligation to work hard to prevent research misconduct, to report such misconduct when it occurs, and to support colleagues who attempt to do both despite the personal and professional risks involved.

Source: Reprinted with permission from the Council on Social Work Education © 2007. *National Statement on Research Integrity in Social Work*.

SUMMARY

In this chapter, we examined:

- The major ethical issues that social workers face when they conduct research.
- Past research that has helped to produce current ethical standards that are designed as general guidelines to protect the physical and psychological well-being of human research participants. However, as we discussed, there are many situations in which even highly ethical researchers and members of IRBs struggle with the specific meaning and application of these standards.
- Today's standards for the protection of the research participant, and some of the other major ethical responsibilities that researchers have toward the sponsors of research, other researchers, colleagues, and the general public. These standards are designed to ensure that, in the process of knowledge building, researchers respect the needs of others who may stand to benefit or lose from their activities.

MyEducationLab® for Research

Try Assignment 1.4: Ethics and Educational Research and Study Plan Quiz 1.5.

Take the Chapter 2 Chapter Review Quiz.

Developing Research Problems and Research Questions

Research should begin with the identification of a research problem and then move on to selecting research questions that relate to that problem. While this may seem self-evident, social workers are sometimes tempted to begin conducting research with insufficient articulation of the problem or the research questions that emanate from the problem. Rubin and Babbie (2008) note that "the impetus for selecting a topic should come from decisions that confront social service agencies or the information needed to solve practical problems in social welfare. . . A study is more likely to have value for the social work field [and to be considered social work research] . . . if the topic is selected because it addresses information needed to guide policy, planning, or practice decisions in social welfare" (p. 129).

Frankfort-Nachmias and Nachmias (1992) define a research problem as "an intellectual stimulus calling for an answer in the form of a scientific inquiry" (p. 51). Rothery (1993) describes research problems as "situations that are characterized by doubt and ignorance and that represent felt difficulties. There is something in the situation that is unknown, and there is a reason for wanting to reduce this doubtfulness" (p. 17).

What makes all research problems similar, yet different, from other kinds of problems? How are social work research problems different from personal problems, social problems, or even research problems in general? A social work research problem is an undesirable condition attributable (at least in part) to the nonexistence of some potentially useful knowledge. Not only is this knowledge gap felt by social workers, but there is a desire to fill it. For example, for some social work practitioners, a research problem may be the absence of knowledge that is needed to effectively influence pending legislation. For a social work manager, it may be the absence of evidence that a social program is effective, making the decision about whether to continue the program difficult. For the social work educator or trainer, it may be the absence of knowledge that could indicate which methods are most effective for inculcating certain values or teaching certain skills that students need. Note that the preceding examples describe problems faced by individuals and not caused by their own lack of awareness of existing knowledge. The knowledge that they require does not exist. It has not yet been generated.

WHY WE BEGIN WITH RESEARCH PROBLEMS

When designing and conducting research, it is important not to get ahead of ourselves. In both qualitative and quantitative research, there is a logical sequence of events; in both types of research, articulating a clear problem statement must precede all other tasks. Stating the research hypothesis, when appropriate, identifying the design for conducting the research, selecting an appropriate data collection instrument, and developing a plan for statistical analysis of data are all important tasks in research, but to perform these tasks without formulating the research problem is to ask for trouble later. We would inevitably waste time and resources trying to fit a research problem to the hypothesis, the research design, the data collection instrument, or the statistical analysis. A properly conducted project is an integrated whole from start to finish (Shontz, 1986). The start should always be research problem identification and specification, with all subsequent activities flowing from and clearly relating to the problem selected.

Identifying and then specifying research problems might seem like tasks that can be easily and quickly accomplished. Unfortunately, this is not always the case. Often, we know of research problems that we would like to study but have difficulty articulating them in a researchable form. This is true primarily because problems, by their very nature, are perceived in different ways by different people, often based on their individual life experience. If there were perfect consensus on exactly what the problems are, why they exist, and what should be done about them, most problems would have ceased to exist a long time ago!

IDENTIFYING POTENTIAL RESEARCH PROBLEMS

For the social work practitioner, the identification and specification of a problem is the first stage involved in developing intervention strategies. Thus, beginning the research process with a problem would seem to be a pretty natural thing for us to do. However, in social work research, *a problem* is a little different. It is not a problem of our client or client system, such as a group, organization, or community, as it is in other areas of social work practice. A research problem is *our* problem, a problem that *we* experience in our professional practice, specifically a knowledge gap that leaves us unsure about how best to intervene to address a problem of a client or a client system. We sometimes find ourselves thinking, "If only it were known if . . ." or "I wish there were more knowledge about . . ." If the missing knowledge existed, we believe that we would be able to intervene more effectively and with greater likelihood of success. Examples of such knowledge gaps are:

A research problem is our problem, a problem that we experience in our professional practice, specifically a knowledge gap that leaves us unsure about how best to intervene to address a problem of a client or a client system.

- A social work therapist might think, "If only I could know how others have experienced this loss and what it meant to them."
- A family counselor might think, "If only I could know if it would promote or decrease candid discussion of the family's problems if I were to include the mother's boyfriend in treatment sessions."

- A social worker running a support group might think, "If only I could know if providing name tags for members will result in better group participation."
- A social work administrator might think, "If only I could know if my staff would appreciate my reviewing some of their correspondence before it goes out or whether they would resent it as micro-managing."
- A social worker engaged in community organization might think, "If only I could know whether it would be better for me to personally chair a 'get-out the vote' campaign or attempt to encourage leadership from within the community."

Often, research problems are identified through interaction with others. A client may tell us about some phenomenon or behavior that is relatively new (at least to us) or that has not been studied for various reasons. It may be something we need to understand better if we are to intervene effectively with certain client groups. For example, as norms and practices continually change, our understanding of youth gangs and how to work with them is often hampered by our inability to understand their behaviors and the importance of gang membership to its members. A client who describes the behavior can cause us to want to learn more about it (who is most likely to engage in it, how it started, what police have done to prevent it, and so forth). We may identify one or several areas where knowledge is incomplete or missing altogether—potential research problems.

Other potential research problems emerge in case supervision. For example, a social worker, seeking assistance, may ask her supervisor a question about a client problem, its incidence (descriptive knowledge), what is most likely to happen if some intervention is attempted (predictive knowledge), or what intervention will produce the desired results (prescriptive knowledge). The supervisor, being candid, admits that she doesn't know, but will try to find out. She reports a week later that the answer to the social worker's question does not appear to be available within the professional body of knowledge. A potential research problem has just been identified.

Sometimes, just in casual conversation, two or more co-workers may recognize that they share the same sense of frustration because the knowledge that would help them be more effective in their practice seems unavailable. For example, a group of hospice social workers may feel frustrated in being unable to be as helpful to stressed-out family caregivers as they would like. So they first try to determine if the knowledge needed to assist them is already available. An Internet search and/or a brainstorming session may be used to articulate the problem better. They may discover that the knowledge they lack is indeed available, but they were just not aware of it. However, they may also conclude that there exists little knowledge about the need for certain types of self-care among caregivers and which type of caregiver support groups have been found to be most effective in addressing them. If so, another potential research problem has been identified.

Setting Problem Priorities

Not all knowledge gaps can be regarded as either equally important or equally well suited to social work research. In determining whether a particular problem justifies their attention and limited research resources, we must address certain issues and questions. In the ideal world of unlimited research resources, any knowledge gap that might be hindering social workers' capacity to help others would be a problem suitable for study. But in the real world, certain knowledge gaps must be regarded as higher priorities than others. Social workers must ask the basic question: Among those potential research problems that exist and that are of current concern, which are most in need of a solution?

Identifying a gap in knowledge as a higher or lower research priority can be a complicated process. It is not a task that comes naturally or comfortably to many social workers. The conclusion that certain knowledge gaps—although a source of frustration for some people—do not justify the use of limited research resources seems to go against social work practice values. However, we are not saying that research problems of lower priority are unimportant or should be ignored by social workers once and for all. As in any decision that employs EBP principles, social workers combine their knowledge of the problem (e.g., who is most affected by it, how severe it is) with factors such as practice experience, social work values and ethics, and even a little compassion, and decide, based on objective standards, whether the research should be conducted.

Research-Informed Practice or Practice-Informed Research

Behavior: Use and translate research evidence to inform and improve practice, policy, and service delivery.

Critical Thinking Question: Identify three specific social or psychological problems about which you would like to increase your knowledge by either studying the available literature or conducting your own research.

In attempting to set priorities, we acknowledge that in a world of limited research resources, we sometimes must opt to get the greatest possible benefit out of our time and efforts. Several questions can help us objectively assess the research priority of a potential research problem.

Is the problem really an important one? Sometime early in the research process, we need to demonstrate that the research problem selected for study ranks high in priority. This is especially important if a formal proposal must be written and submitted to a potential research sponsor or for review by an IRB (see Chapter 2). After the research has been conducted, we also would like to be able to demonstrate to potential critics, as well as to those favorable to the research, that the problem studied was important, more important than others that might have been studied. The question of what makes one research problem more important than another relates to a wide array of factors, such as the scope of the problem, which people are most affected by it, how badly knowledge is needed, and the potential value of the variety of products that can evolve from the research process.

The real importance of a research problem and the research that examined it may not be fully appreciated until years after the research has been completed. The fact that the findings of research are widely publicized, widely cited, or widely used seems to add importance retroactively to a research study. In some cases, a study's importance may relate less to its findings than to some other product of the research. For example, a standardized data collection instrument (see Chapter 12) developed to study a research problem may later gain widespread usage and may ultimately be considered that research project's greatest contribution to knowledge. The instrument may help to legitimize the researcher's efforts, even if the research findings themselves prove to be of limited value.

It is difficult to assess the ultimate importance of a proposed research problem. How can we envision all possible difficulties that could depreciate the value of the research? How can we accurately predict the final judgment of others as to whether the research effort was truly worthwhile? Fortunately, we can use certain guidelines to help us in wrestling with the issue of research priority. There are certain characteristics of research problems that seem to suggest that they are of higher priority than others. For example, a problem may be considered high priority if it (1) reflects a widely felt and critical knowledge gap; (2) relates to a difficulty that affects many people; (3) has the potential to generate specific recommendations rather than highly abstract knowledge; or (4) is likely to produce by-products that will benefit other researchers conducting scientific inquiry on a wide variety of topics.

Do we already have enough knowledge about the problem? Some human conditions have been thoroughly studied, often by people other than social workers, through major funding from government agencies or private foundations. Researchers review the social work literature as well as literature outside the social work field to learn what is already known about a potential research problem. (We will look more at the literature review in Chapter 4.) Many knowledge gaps have already been filled. For example, we know a great deal about the eating disorders, bulimia nervosa and anorexia nervosa, primarily based on research conducted in other fields. Studies have looked at diagnosis, prognosis, prevalence, risk factors, protective factors, group versus individual interventions, and inpatient versus outpatient interventions for these disorders. The existence of substantial knowledge regarding a problem area does not, however, mean that some aspect of the problem does not have potential for social work research. For example, Vrabel, Ro, Martinsen, Hoffart, and Rosenvinge (2010) conducted a five-year study of adults with eating disorders to determine the prevalence of personality disorders in this population. In addition to prevalence rates, they found that people who recovered from their eating disorder were less likely to have a comorbid personality disorder. Fennig and Hadas (2010) examined depression and suicidal behaviors in adolescents with eating disorders to identify risk factors associated with suicidal ideations and suicide attempts. Research studies like these generate new knowledge that will be of immediate use to social work practitioners working with people with eating disorders.

Are people in other disciplines better suited to conduct research on the problem? There may be a need for research on a potential research problem, but it might be better to let others with specialized expertise conduct it. For example, although social workers counseling children with attention deficit hyperactivity disorder (ADHD) could benefit from knowing the long-term physical effects of a child taking certain prescription medications designed to treat it, pharmacology or physiology professionals might be better suited to conduct research on the problem. Social workers, on the other hand, are better suited to conduct research designed to discover how use of medications may affect the need for certain parenting styles, or what patterns can be expected in a child's behavior in the evening hours after a medication's influence on behavior begins to wear off.

What is the potential for use of any findings and recommendations that would be generated by the research? Who will care, and what is the likelihood that anyone with the power to use the acquired knowledge will be inspired to take the recommended action? A study of a potential social work research problem that is not likely to result in needed change is of little value. People who might be able to use the findings may lack either the necessary resources or the value commitment necessary to do what research indicates is needed. Sometimes, both obstacles are present. For example, a community might have a problem of apathy among adolescents regarding the possibility of their contracting a sexually transmittable disease. A lack of understanding of the apathy and the lack of knowledge of how best to address it could be the impetus for good, worthwhile, methodologically sound research that would both identify the source of the apathy and generate recommendations as to how social workers could be effective in heightening adolescent awareness of the dangers involved. But because of certain conditions present within the community, research on the problem might be a waste of time. The research might recommend that school social workers provide education on sexuality or at least run needed information groups. However, it might already be known that a school board operating with a deficit budget might be unable to purchase the educational materials needed to successfully offer this service. Or it might be common knowledge that the powerful fundamentalist minister who chairs the school board would almost certainly intimidate other board members into blocking what he has already publicly described as "instruction in sinning." Therefore, the probability of implementation of research recommendations might be very small, even zero. Despite the need for research, it may have lower priority because research findings and recommendations would have little hope of being used.

Am I sufficiently interested in studying the problem? The development of knowledge to benefit social workers and their clients can be an exciting activity. But research is hard work. Certain tasks can become very tedious at times. Even a general interest in a research problem may not be sufficient to carry a researcher through times when necessary but less-than-exciting tasks must be performed. For example, entering research data collected from hundreds of participants into a computer program for statistical analysis, even when we are curious about the findings of our research, can be pretty boring. Is there a temptation for social workers to choose to study problems about which they have little interest? Unfortunately, yes. Pressures from supervisors and higher-level managers sometimes make it difficult to say no. On other occasions, the lure of grant money can help to convince social workers that they might be more interested in studying a research problem than they really are. If we conduct research without any real interest in it, we may be making a big mistake because it may negatively affect the quality of the research. It also can have a negative effect on our attitudes about future scientific inquiry. All other factors being equal, a problem about which a researcher is interested and concerned should have higher priority than one in which the researcher's interest results primarily from political or financial motives.

What logistical obstacles are present? Some potential social work research problems may face major logistical obstacles. Although it is probably correct to state that any problem can be studied, some problems by their very nature are so complicated, would require so many resources, or would require so many methodological compromises that it would be virtually impossible to do the job right. In determining if a problem is researchable on a practical and logistical basis, the following questions are worth asking:

- **Is the problem just too large?** Some problems are so widespread and pervasive that they would be totally unmanageable as the focus for a single research study. However, it might be possible to break off some small piece of the problem for study. For example, to attempt to understand the origin and extent of ageism within North American human service organizations would require a research study of such large scope that most social work researchers would lack the budget and other resources necessary to undertake it. (Research almost invariably ends up costing more than anticipated.) However, social work researchers with limited resources might be able to design research to study some aspect of the phenomenon, such as the discriminatory methods used for advertising supervisory job openings in not-for-profit organizations within their own state.

- **Can the needed measurement be accomplished?** As we shall discuss in more detail later, good measurement is absolutely essential to sound research. But some things are more easily measured than others. For example, behaviors, generally speaking, are more easily measured than attitudes or values. Although researchers have made great progress in the development of measurement of the latter in recent years, in many cases, measuring attitudes that might be of interest to us remains an imprecise art.

Which treatment interventions are effective and which ones are not provides special measurement difficulties. The success or failure rate in a job-training program can be fairly easily determined by counting how many people complete the program and successfully find and keep related jobs. However, the success or failure rate associated with a particular approach to marriage counseling can be much more difficult to ascertain. Was divorce indicative of success or failure? How should we interpret the fact that a couple voluntarily terminated counselling? They could have stopped seeing the social worker because most of their difficulties had disappeared, or because they perceived that they were getting no help! Indicators of successful or unsuccessful treatment in such instances may be limited to notations in a case record or follow-up phone calls.

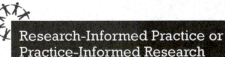

Research-Informed Practice or Practice-Informed Research

Behavior: Use practice experience and theory to inform scientific research and inquiry.

Critical Thinking Question: Identify two questions that are interesting to you but would probably be inappropriate for a scientific research study.

If studying a research problem would require the measurement of certain phenomena that seem to defy measurement, the entire problem may be regarded as not researchable, with no amount of research providing the needed answers. A classic example of a non-researchable problem is the debate that preoccupied some theologians several centuries ago. The problem of not knowing how many angels can dance on the head of a pin was not a candidate for scientific research then, and it would not be now either. Some contemporary social work problems—for example, a lack of understanding of why some physicians seem to undervalue the professional education of social workers—may be only slightly more researchable than medieval philosophical questions. Physicians' respect for social workers' education might be so difficult to measure that the problem, if it is indeed a real one, may not be able to be studied. Besides, it may not be a high research priority, given the other criteria that we suggested earlier.

- **Do I have the necessary skills and expertise to conduct research on the problem?** Specialization is characteristic of people who conduct scientific inquiry. Some researchers are especially adept at certain specialized research tasks, such as use of the Internet, interviewing, questionnaire construction, or statistical analysis of data, and less competent to perform other tasks. Although it is possible to learn to do what is required or to hire a consultant to do it, this can represent a costly use of limited research resources. If studying a research problem would require skill and expertise not currently possessed by a potential researcher—for example, the use of statistical analysis—the problem may as well be considered un-researchable.

Similarly, if the researcher's knowledge and skills lie in quantitative research methods, and studying the research problem would require a more qualitative approach, it might be best to let a researcher competent in the qualitative approach study it.

- **Will I have access to needed data?** Some research problems that would seem like excellent candidates for study by social workers may not be researchable because the data needed to study them are not accessible. For example, sealed court records and patients' medical records are safeguarded by law. Thus, it is generally impossible to access them for use in research. Knowledge that could be acquired only with access to data that is beyond reach should be regarded as unattainable. Unless other ways of addressing the research problem can be found that will produce findings of comparable credibility, it might be better to find another research problem to study.

In the past, some promising research studies have reached a costly dead end when researchers found out too late that they would not be allowed to, for example, conduct interviews with clients or staff, or review and record data from records that were assumed to be readily available. Similarly, some social workers have just assumed that it would be acceptable to record interviews with research participants, but found out belatedly that permission was denied. Today, most researchers understand the importance of inquiring into the availability of needed data prior to the selection of a problem for study and submission of a research proposal to an IRB. The IRB members will want to be assured that permission to access the data has been received prior to their granting approval to conduct the research.

Identifying and Specifying the Research Problem

As noted earlier, a careful identification and specification of a researchable problem has a way of keeping all the other steps in the research process on track. Any vagueness or ambiguity about the problem can haunt the researcher at many junctures in the research process, and can result in a considerable amount of wasted effort. In this way, research is similar to social work intervention with individuals, families, groups, organizations, or communities. Much valuable time has been wasted because social work practitioners failed to obtain a clear understanding of the problem or accepted at face value the presenting complaint of a client or client group. For a researcher, this barking-up-the-wrong-tree phenomenon can be especially costly.

One of the first things a researcher must determine is what individuals, groups, or organizations will be the target of the investigation. This is called defining the *unit of analysis*. Individuals are the most common unit of analysis for social science research. Individuals may be chosen based on some physical characteristic (e.g., age, race, gender), a mental health issue being experienced (e.g., depression, eating disorder), or group membership (e.g., high school student, gang membership), among others. Individuals may also be selected based on a combination of factors, such as single teenage mothers with depression or elderly homeless Hispanic people. It is important to note what unit of analysis is defined in a research study so we do not generalize to individuals that are not included in the sample. For example, if homeless Hispanic youth is defined as the unit of analysis, one should not generalize the findings to homeless Hispanic adults or to homeless non-Hispanic youth. Some studies define a unit of analysis other than individuals. These may include organizations, cities, families, social groups, neighborhoods, or universities, among others. In these cases, it is important not to generalize the findings of the study to the individuals that make up the group or organization being studied. This mistake is called the *ecological fallacy.*

Many years ago, one of the authors of this text was involved in an extended discussion that attempted to specify the research problem for a proposed project (Bellomy et al., 1989). The process that took place still provides a good example of the effort involved in identifying and specifying a research problem. It took several hours and produced a considerable amount of frustration. But the time was well spent. The process was absolutely essential prior to beginning other steps in the research process. Here is how it played out:

The director of a county agency had proposed that the researchers (a group of social work graduate students) might conduct research on a problem that he had identified in his organization to fulfill the requirements of their research practicum assignment. He had noticed that during the past year, child protection workers were receiving many more reports of possible child abuse by local professionals than in previous years. A large percentage of the cases were never opened for services because the worker assigned to investigate quickly determined that they were unfounded. From the director's perspective, this was an inefficient use of workers' time. They were spending much of their day dealing with reports where, apparently, no abuse had taken place, while not having enough time to devote to those cases where abuse was probable. Simply stated, from his perspective, there were too many unfounded cases. He didn't know why this was occurring, and thus did not know how to act to address it.

Further discussion with the administrator allowed the students to compile a list of five possible explanations for what was happening:

1. Social workers in the community were making too many inappropriate referrals.

2. Inappropriate referrals were the result of inadequate training of social workers.

3. Child protection workers were erroneously declaring cases to be unfounded because they were overworked.

4. Cases were being declared unfounded for fear that a determination of founded would result in more work for child protection workers.

5. Certain workers were contributing to the large number of unfounded cases by determining that all or most of their cases were unfounded.

Through additional discussion and further investigation of existing knowledge and available data, it is often possible to eliminate bogus explanations of a phenomenon and identify the real one that needs to be studied.

Each of these statements reflects what *might* have been occurring and, in some cases, even a possible reason for it. Each also suggests a different gap in knowledge that needed to be filled. Note that the unit of analysis involved in the first two problems are social workers in the community, while the unit of analysis for the third through fifth problems involve the child protection workers themselves. Once the researchers could identify what was happening, they could understand better why it was happening and what could be done to address it (the best intervention).

Through additional discussion and further investigation of existing knowledge and available data, it is often possible to eliminate bogus explanations of a phenomenon and identify the real one that needs to be studied. That is exactly what happened in our example. Following more inquiries and another meeting with the director, all but one of the preceding statements were eliminated. With respect to the first two explanations, it was decided that the great majority of the referrals were apparently quite appropriate, given what the literature suggested at the time about possible indicators of abuse. Their increased number was probably related to recent training that had emphasized recognition of conditions that suggest that abuse may have taken place and that a referral was in order.

As for the third explanation, although some instances of child abuse might have been missed, there was no evidence to suggest that this was the case, at least not any more so than in previous years. On the basis of recent data in the professional literature, it was impossible to know whether the current rate of founded versus unfounded cases among child protection workers was high, low, or about normal. It also would be difficult to measure accurately whether a case determination had been correct or incorrect, a measurement obstacle that was sufficient to preclude giving serious consideration to the third statement as the impetus for a research study. It was possible that the ratio of founded versus unfounded cases was about average, but that the cases were being categorized incorrectly; there was simply no way to know.

The fourth explanation was also unlikely, because a policy existed whereby a case with a determination of founded was referred for follow-up services by another worker in another division of the organization. Thus, it resulted in no additional work for the worker who made the determination.

On the basis of the director's observations and a quick count of records, the students found that some workers seemed to have a much higher rate of unfounded determinations than others over the previous three years. Given the random assignment of cases and the large number of cases seen, such a disparity should not have existed. The director speculated that the identity of the worker assigned to a referral might have more to do with the determination of founded or unfounded than the facts of the case. Consequently, the fifth explanation was seen as the most plausible explanation for what was occurring. Therefore, the research problem for the proposed study was stated, "Certain workers are contributing to the large number of unfounded cases by determining that all or most of their cases are unfounded."

To have used precipitously any of the first four explanations proposed by the research group as the research problem would have produced difficulties later on in the research. Much effort would have been wasted. The time spent in clarifying the exact nature of what was occurring was a productive and necessary exercise. It improved the overall efficiency of the scientific inquiry by saving much more time than it consumed.

DEVELOPING RESEARCH QUESTIONS

A concise, well-articulated problem statement is a good beginning. However, it is too broad to provide the needed focus for a research study and so the process of narrowing continues. Next, researchers generally select a group of broad research questions that relate to the problem, more than they could ever hope to address in a single study.

In predominantly quantitative studies, one or more of the questions may get answered during the extensive literature review that generally follows. The answers were there; the researcher was just not aware of them. Other questions may be eliminated as "un-researchable" or of relatively low priority. One or a few will be revised, usually made more specific, by what is learned from the literature review process (Chapter 4). A research design (Chapters 5–8) is then selected to attempt to arrive at tentative answers, and the research questions, along with a plan for answering them, are essentially "set." Changes are unlikely to occur.

In predominantly qualitative studies, the process of data collection often begins quite early, following a less extensive literature review. While some research questions may be answered or others revised by what is learned from the literature, the process of eliminating, revising, and even adding research questions is ongoing. It is not limited to and does not end with the literature review. It continues throughout the data collection process. New questions are often added as the data suggest other important areas of inquiry. Others may be dropped along the way if they prove unproductive for knowledge building. Creswell (1998) argues, however, that qualitative research should be guided by a clearly stated question that provides "a single focus" for the research study (p. 21).

Box 3.1 provides examples of some research problem statements and broad research questions that might relate to them. They are just examples; many other questions could be developed for each problem statement. Notice that the research problems are stated as declarative, descriptive statements of a condition – never as a question.

The broad research questions that are ultimately selected help to keep a researcher on track. For example, whether we are deciding what data must be collected, how to collect them, what statistical analysis to perform, or which research findings are most important to disseminate, the same question can be asked: How does it bear on the research question and contribute to its answer?

What is the connection between a research problem statement and a research question? How do they differ? Researchers choose to focus on certain research questions because they believe that, if answers can be found, they will help alleviate the research problem. Even if answers cannot be found, the knowledge obtained through the process of seeking answers generally provides increased insight into the problem itself. Unlike a research problem statement, a research question is always followed by a question mark.

There are many gaps in knowledge related to a research problem that could serve as the focus for the research. But they cannot all be studied. How many questions should a researcher attempt to study? What are the characteristics of a good research question? What makes one potential research question a better choice as the focus of research than another one? Selection of research questions, like the selection of a research problem, is often a matter of priorities.

As a general rule, it is better to do a good, thorough job of studying just a few research questions than do a more superficial job of inquiring into the answers to many.

We observed in Chapter 1 that all scientific knowledge is tentative by definition. But the researcher still hopes to generate knowledge that is as definitive as possible. Therefore, as a general rule, it is better to do a good, thorough job of studying just a few research questions than do a more superficial job of inquiring into the answers to many.

Box 3.1   Some Research Problem Statements and Related Research Questions

Problem: The parents of children who die while committing violent crimes are also victims. However, we know little about how the parents experience this tragedy.

Q1. How do these parents perceive potential sources of support in their time of loss?

Q2. What obstacles to their own grief process do they experience?

Q3. What feelings do they have toward the families of the victims of the violence?

Q4. How have their relationships with friends and relatives been affected?

Problem: Homicide by children 8 to 12 is increasing. Social workers working with children this age often hear them talk about wanting to kill someone. There is little available knowledge to help them decide how to respond.

Q1. What behaviors of children immediately prior to homicidal acts might have indicated that the acts might occur?

Q2. What common experiences exist in the social histories of homicidal children?

Q3. What common experiences exist in the current life situations of homicidal children?

Q4. What have been the experiences of social workers who notified authorities when their young clients talked about homicide?

Problem: Welfare reform has dramatically reduced the number of families receiving public financial assistance. However, we have little knowledge about the impact of welfare reform on those people who are no longer on welfare rolls.

Q1. Have those no longer receiving welfare assistance found good jobs, or are they now relying on other institutions for financial assistance?

Q2. What has been the effect on children of former TANF recipients who went to work after their benefits ran out?

Q3. Have day care facilities increased to adequately meet the needs of an increased number of working mothers?

Q4. How has the current economy and lower unemployment rates affected the numbers of welfare recipients?

Problem: High unemployment during the Great Recession was accompanied by a reduction in charitable giving. We have limited knowledge about how this affected not-for-profit agencies and their clients.

Q1. Has the reduction in funding lead to the deletion of some valuable programs that have never been re-implemented?

Q2. Did a lack of funding result in the more efficient use of resources in programs that survived?

Q3. Did the United Way's changes in priorities for allocating funding cause some agencies to redefine their mission in a way that some clients were no longer eligible for services?

Q4. Have social agencies become more cooperative and less competitive with each other since the economy has improved?

Many of the criteria that are applied in selecting broad research questions are the same ones that we examined in selecting a research problem. The following questions are often helpful, both for limiting the number of questions and producing a clearer understanding of just why the research is being conducted:

1. Which potential research questions would be most likely to contribute
   • new knowledge?
   • knowledge for more effective practice intervention?
   • knowledge that can be disseminated?
   • knowledge that will make a difference?
   • knowledge that other researchers will find useful?

2. Which potential research questions are most likely to have an answer that
   - is attainable?
   - would contribute the most to alleviation of the problem (the knowledge gap)?
3. Which potential research questions would require
   - measurement of phenomena that can be easily measured?
   - access to information that is likely to be available?
   - the use of research methods that are considered ethical?
   - the knowledge and expertise possessed by the researcher?

Each of the questions in Box 3.1 reflect an important issue in the selection of a research question. Let's return to our earlier example to see how the social work students selected their research question on the identified research problem. Having settled on what was apparently happening (i.e., some child protection workers had a much higher rate of unfounded cases than others), the students began to identify possible research questions, the answers to which might help to explain and/or alleviate the problem. Some of the many possible questions that were seriously considered were:

1. What laws and regulations govern child protection workers' decisions about whether a case is determined to be founded? Could ambiguity contained in them be producing different interpretations and thus reporting rates (founded versus unfounded) among workers? Could recent changes in reporting procedures somehow be affecting whether a case is regarded as founded?
2. Could different working conditions in some way help to explain the different rates?
3. Could differences in education and training of workers somehow relate to the different rates?
4. Do co-workers perceive that some workers are more conscientious in their investigations than others?
5. How great an influence does supervision have in worker determinations regarding reports of suspected abuse?
6. Are community professionals somehow influencing the decisions of some workers more than others? If so, how is this occurring?
7. Do some workers perceive rewards for either founded or unfounded cases that other workers do not perceive?
8. How might the work experience of the child protection worker affect the way that a case is perceived?
9. Does burnout somehow contribute to the different rates of founded cases among workers?
10. Are the different demographic characteristics of workers (e.g., age, race, gender, parenthood) related to their determinations?

What can we observe about the preceding questions? First, they all relate to the research problem in the same way. Each, if answered, could contribute to its alleviation. All the questions relate to factors that may influence the decision-making of child protection workers. However, each suggests a very different focus of inquiry. Note, too, that all of them are stated in a way that suggests that the cause for the different rates is unknown. This kind of noncommittal wording is appropriate for this stage of the research process. It suggests that the researchers were keeping an open mind and not beginning the research with any pre-existing biases.

All of the questions are quite broad. As we shall discuss later, the tasks of refining broad research questions to make them more specific, and, when possible, even proposing tentative answers to them in the form of research hypotheses, all come later in the process. In predominantly qualitative studies, this step often occurs much later.

Because researchers hope to acquire as much relevant knowledge as possible in a research study, they select questions that can be combined together in one study. As long as the research does not become unmanageable or lose focus, combining questions can be an efficient use of time. It is exactly what occurred in the research that we have been describing.

Most of the original questions (including many that are not in the preceding list) were rejected for reasons related to the issues discussed earlier. For example, question 1 was concluded to be too complex to study within the time available and with available resources. To study it would have required extensive interviews with the workers and the development of methods to test their job knowledge. The director stated that he could not permit his staff to take enough time off from their regular duties to participate in a series of extended interviews or other similar forms of data collection processes. Question 4 could not be examined because it was concluded that obtaining the required data would be difficult without damaging working relationships among staff members. All the caseworkers were found to share the same supervisor and work under virtually identical working conditions, so questions 2 and 5 were discarded. To answer question 6 would have entailed collecting data from more than 100 individuals in the community who frequently made referrals, a formidable and costly endeavor. In light of the small amount of knowledge related to the problem that would be generated, the effort involved did not seem justified. Question 8 was summarily answered without the need for further study: it was learned that another study had just examined this question and found no evidence of any such influence.

A variation of question 10 appeared to be the best choice. The answer to it seemed obtainable. No one in the group had ever seen it discussed within current professional literature. What's more, questions 3, 7, and 9 could easily be answered along with question 10 by adding a short personal interview designed to collect some of the needed data. The research question was restated as follows: Are characteristics of workers related to their determinations of whether a case is judged to be founded?

QUALITATIVE VERSUS QUANTITATIVE QUESTIONS

It is during the step of formulating and selecting potential research questions that the researcher will generally identify whether the research design will be predominantly quantitative or qualitative in nature. Qualitative research is generally exploratory in

It is during the step of formulating and selecting potential research questions that the researcher will generally identify whether the research design will be predominantly quantitative or qualitative in nature.

nature. It considers the underlying meanings, opinions, and reasons with regard to a given situation or phenomenon. It uses semi-structured or unstructured data collection techniques with individuals and sometimes with groups. Qualitative research can produce questions and hypotheses that are quantitative in nature and that will subsequently require more quantitative research methods for their study. Quantitative research is used to quantify opinions, attitudes, behaviors, thoughts, etc. It uses more structured data collection techniques, such as surveys, behavioral observation, and structured interviews. Sample sizes are generally larger in quantitative research studies, and findings, when appropriate research methods are used, can be generalized to the larger population.

Developing Quantitative Research Questions

In quantitative research, it is particularly important to develop research questions to guide the research process. The questions involve variables that are measured numerically, such as scores on a data collection instrument, number or severity of observed behaviors, absence or presence of some phenomenon, etc. The research question(s) and hypothesis(es) are established before the data are collected and they are not altered throughout the study.

Let us look at a couple of examples of quantitative research questions in the current research literature. Ramos-Lira, Gonzalez-Forteza, and Wagner (2006) defined their research study using the following research questions: (1) Is there an association between violence victimization and exposure to opportunities to use marijuana, inhalants, and cocaine? (2) Is there an association between violence victimization and actual drug use among youth with drug-using opportunities (p. 850). In this study, the presence of violence victimization, exposure to drugs, and drug use of the youth participants were measured using a cross-sectional (data collected at one point in time) survey of 767 middle school students.

Another study (Shields, Broome, Delaney, Fletcher, & Flynn, 2007) attempted to answer the following research questions: (1) What is the relationship between an individual's religiosity and retention in treatment and commitment to treatment? (2) How does the ecological context of treatment programs shape the individual-level relationships? (3) To what extent are program practices and characteristics directly linked to outcome level? (p. 355). To answer these questions, data were collected from a national study involving over 10,000 people participating in drug treatment programs nationwide. Quantitative research questions, once selected, guide the researchers in defining the literature review, research design, data collection methods, measurement instruments, data analysis techniques, and all other aspects of the research process.

Developing Qualitative Research Questions

Agee (2009) offers a process for developing effective qualitative research questions. She states that "the ongoing process of questioning is an integral part of understanding the unfolding lives and perspectives of others," and in her article addresses "both the developing of initial research questions and how the processes of generating and refining questions are critical to the shaping of a qualitative study" (p. 431). She describes the qualitative research question as a navigational tool that not only helps guide the researcher through the research process but also encourages the exploration into unexpected directions the research may take.

Agee (2009) further points out that some qualitative researchers prefer to begin the research process without a research question. However, this is often impractical in today's research arena. Since dissertations and most funded research must have a research question and a plan before the research begins, she has developed some suggestions for developing qualitative research questions. Social workers are often interested in how an individual is experiencing an event or condition. We try to understand what is happening in a particular situation with a particular person or group of people. A good example of a qualitative research question is from a study by Rortveit, Astrom, and Severinsson (2009). They asked, "How do women who suffer from eating disorders experience the bodily aspects related to their condition" (p. 91)? A research question that led to a mixed research method is presented by Smith (2007): "What are the needs of students with Asperger's Syndrome, and what are the services and accommodations available to them at the post-secondary level" (p. 515)?

Agee (2009) lists the following guidelines for developing good qualitative research questions: (1) The question should be clear enough to provide focus for the study. This allows the researcher to gather specific data that can add knowledge and potentially make a difference to the field of study; (2) The question should be framed in a way that either implicitly or explicitly makes a link with the theory being used by the researcher; (3) The question should be answerable. Will it be possible to answer the question with the time and resources available? (4) It is important not to phrase the question in such a way that it leads to presuppositions about the participants and events involved in the study; and (5) The question should be worded so that it is clear and avoids multiple sub-questions being included within the question.

Qualitative researchers, as we have already stated, do not necessarily start out with a clearly stated research question. Walsh and Tzelepis (2007), for example, developed a qualitative study to look at tobacco use among adolescents with an emphasis on three areas of interest: peer influences, access/sales issues, and dependence/addiction. There were no specific research questions developed at the beginning of their study. Other qualitative research studies may develop one or more research questions as part of the conclusions of the study. For example, Kartalova-O'Doherty and Doherty (2008) examined the experiences and needs of family caregivers for people with enduring mental illness. They suggested that the findings of their study raised the following research questions: In what ways and to what extent do contextual factors shape personal coping strategies? Are contextual factors more powerful predictors of coping styles than personal or developmental ones? To what extent and in what way are personal, developmental, and contextual factors related to individual coping (p. 26)? The hope is that these questions will lead to further research studies.

Qualitative versus Quantitative Research Process

In quantitative research, once the research question and hypothesis (when used) are defined, they are not altered or augmented in any way. On the contrary, research questions in qualitative research can (and often are) refined throughout the research process. Research questions are viewed as tools for giving a research study a primary focus, but it should be remembered the question will generally evolve throughout the research process. Creswell (2007) states, "Our questions change during the process of research to reflect an increased understanding of the problem" (p. 47).

If the research question selected lends itself to a predominantly quantitative design, the next step in the process is a thorough review of the literature to find out if the knowledge gap perceived by the researcher is real or if there is indeed information available to answer the question. In addition, the research may answer part of the question leading the researcher to another aspect of the problem, or research may be found that supports the need for research in this area and may give the researcher ideas about how to proceed.

In qualitative research, the step following formulation of the research question is not as clearly defined. Some qualitative researchers believe that completing a thorough literature review early in the process may bias the researcher as she begins to collect the data. Still others do not even emphasize the formulation of the research question early in the research process. Denzin (1989) offers a list of steps for conducting qualitative research, which starts out with "learn to prepare oneself, read the literature, and focus." There is, however, a school of thought among many qualitative researchers who believe the researcher should develop a research question, and then complete a literature review to become familiar with the current research on the topic. For example, Anastas (2010) states, "Qualitative or not, evaluation research should be informed by prior work—the theory that explains the nature of the problems to be addressed and the intervention to be used as well as prior research examining what has and has not worked in the past" (p. 59). Clearly the qualitative research process is more flexible than the quantitative process and depends to a large extent on the qualitative method and techniques chosen by the researcher.

Let us look at another example research problem and broad research questions to illustrate the process of determining whether research will be predominantly qualitative or quantitative. One of the authors is currently interested in an area where there seems to be a knowledge gap. Since African-American women have, in the past, had a lower prevalence of both anorexia nervosa and bulimia nervosa than Caucasian women, there seems to be little available research to explain, describe, and understand eating disorders among African-American women. Research has in the same way neglected studies on men and older women, instead focusing on young Caucasian women, the group most affected by eating disorders. When looking at this potential gap in the knowledge, there are many broad research questions that could be researched. The author came up with the following list of questions in which she was interested:

1. What is the current prevalence of anorexia nervosa and bulimia nervosa among African-American women?

2. How does the prevalence among African-American women compare to the prevalence among Caucasian women?

3. How do African-American women view their own bodies?

4. What societal pressures do African-American women experience to be thin?

5. For those African-American women who are suffering from disordered eating behaviors, what types of behaviors (i.e., binging, vomiting, diuretic use, laxative use) are they more likely to exhibit?

6. How do African-American women respond to various treatments for bulimia nervosa and anorexia nervosa?

7. What are the risk factors among African-American women for developing an eating disorder?

8. How is weight reflected in the African-American woman's concept of beauty?

Looking at these questions, it is fairly straightforward to assume that a research study looking at questions 1, 2, 5, 6, or 7 would be predominantly quantitative. Questions 1 and 2 look at prevalence statistics, questions 5 and 6 would use a measure of eating disordered behaviors, and question 7 would look at the prevalence of certain characteristics of women with eating disorders. If one were to select question 8, the resulting study would probably be predominantly qualitative as it looks at the concept of beauty among African-American women. Questions 3 and 4 could be studied using quantitative, qualitative, or a mixed research method. For example, question 3 could be studied using a survey to look at how African-American women view their body, or an unstructured interview to look more deeply at the question. Or a study might want to utilize both methods in order to gain a broader understanding of the question. It would depend on the specific research question developed and the measurement instruments and data collection methods the researcher selects. Therefore, in addition to the many factors we discussed earlier, the researcher will also be led by the type of research he or she is interested in conducting and in which area he or she feels most capable.

Diversity and Difference in Practice

Behavior: Apply and communicate understanding of the importance of diversity and difference in shaping life experiences in practice at the micro, mezzo, and macro levels.

Critical Thinking Question: Think of at least one other problem area in which a population has been understudied because they were less likely to suffer from the problem than another population.

SUMMARY

In this chapter, we examined:

- The earliest tasks in the research process: problem identification and selection of broad research questions. We devoted an entire chapter to these tasks because we regard them as critical to a thoughtful, organized approach to knowledge building. They are the first steps in all quantitative research and in most qualitative research.

- A distinction was made between problems in general (such as social problems or the problems of an individual social worker, client, or client system) and potential social work research problems. A research problem can be thought of as a gap in our professional knowledge base that interferes with our practice functioning and makes decision-making more difficult. Potential research problems are sometimes identified when we find ourselves thinking, "I wish knowledge was available to better inform my practice decision-making." Other times, our interaction with clients uncovers some phenomenon that we don't understand or, perhaps, didn't even know existed. A potential research problem may also emerge from discussion with our colleagues or with our supervisors.

- However, not all gaps in knowledge that are identified are necessarily good candidates for research. The needed knowledge may already exist, and, with a little effort (like an Internet search), can be easily acquired.

- Even if there really is an important knowledge gap, it may not be a good candidate for social work research because of priority issues, political or financial reasons, or its suitability for the application of scientific methods.

- Broad research questions evolve from and are closely related to a social work research problem. If answers can be found, they will help reduce the knowledge gap that constitutes the research problem and thus have potential to alleviate the problem.

- We offered guidelines to assist in selecting the best research questions to study from among those that might be studied. Examples illustrated the importance of identifying and articulating the *real problem* and how a long list of possible research questions can be reduced to a manageable number.

MyEducationLab® for Research

Try the Topic 2 Assignments: Selecting and Defining a Research Problem and the Topic 2 Study Plan.

Take the Chapter 3 Chapter Review Quiz.

Conducting the Literature Review and Developing Research Hypotheses

Reference to existing knowledge can occur at many points in the research process. Researchers often use it to select and specify a social work research problem, and they use it again to narrow their list of possible research questions (Chapter 3). Answering questions about, for example, how widespread a problem is or whether a phenomenon is easily measurable may require a quick trip to the library or an Internet search. However, the use of existing knowledge does not stop there. We use it to see if there are already full or partial answers to our research questions and, at least in predominantly quantitative studies, to help us formulate hypotheses about what we expect to learn through our research. It also helps us to make important decisions about how best to conduct our research. After data have been collected and analyzed, the literature can help us interpret our research findings in light of the knowledge accumulated by others.

WHAT IS A REVIEW OF LITERATURE?

In research, the term *review of literature* is used in two ways. It refers to both an activity and a written product. As we already noted, the activity of reviewing relevant literature occupies the attention of the researcher to a greater or lesser degree at many points in the research process. However, there is generally one time period when the researcher focuses intensely on the accumulated work of others who have studied and written about the research problem or some related topic. In studies that are predominantly qualitative, this is most likely to occur after some or all data have been collected—when the researcher is attempting to interpret them in relation to existing knowledge. In more traditional, quantitative studies, it generally occurs prior to data collection and is used to help plan the rest of the research process that is to follow. As we shall see, *literature* is also a somewhat generic term in research. It includes sources of knowledge that go far beyond the printed word, such as Internet websites, personal interviews, and sometimes even movies and television programs.

Eventually, what is learned from reviewing the literature is organized and written in summary form as a separate section of a research report or chapter of a book. This product is known as the *review of literature*, *relevant literature*, or something similar. It is written for the reader of the report and describes the existing knowledge that was considered most relevant to the current study, what the researcher learned from it, and how it influenced both the way the research was conducted and, ultimately, any conclusions drawn from its findings. We will look in more detail at writing the literature review in Chapter 14 along with writing other components of the research report.

When reviewing the literature, the researcher first looks for research that directly focuses on the research problem and the questions related to it that are of the most interest. In the absence of specific research on the topic, knowledge drawn from research on related topics can often be brought to bear on the current research problem. Even new problems or ones that have received little or no attention in the past can bear some similarity to other problems that have already been studied. For example, during the late 1980s and early 1990s, the problem of date rape belatedly received widespread attention in the media. There were conflicting opinions expressed about its incidence, the reasons for it, and how it should be addressed. This was a potential social work research problem because without a clear understanding of the dynamics surrounding date rape and how it was perceived by both perpetrators and victims, we could not know how best to provide successful intervention. When research on the problem began, there was limited knowledge about the problem. Yet, a review of the literature was extremely useful for acquiring both insight into date rape and how best to design research to study the problem. Research on this newly identified problem was greatly facilitated by an examination of previous studies on literally hundreds of diverse topics. Each made a valuable contribution that helped researchers focus their attention on the best ways to advance knowledge about date rape. Among the major topics examined were the following:

- History of violence against women
- Violence against women within different cultures
- Legal parameters defining *rape*
- Substance abuse and physical violence
- Law enforcement and judicial handling of rape accusations
- Sexual violence
- Anger expression and management

A problem identified in the late 1990s centered around our lack of understanding of the unwillingness of sexually active teenagers at risk for teen pregnancy to use free contraceptive injections. Because such injections (and contraceptive implants) were not even available until the mid-1990s, it would seem on the surface that a researcher wishing to study the problem would be in the dark. But there was plenty of literature on related topics that helped address the problem and questions that related to it:

- History of contraception
- Emerging pregnancy prevention methods
- Outcome studies of various methods of contraception
- Attitudes about contraception among adolescents
- Attitudes about pregnancy among adolescents
- Distrust of health care providers
- Obstacles to use of public health services

For every research problem and its related research questions, there is an existing body of knowledge that can guide a researcher. Whenever researchers report that little or nothing is known about the problem or that no relevant literature exists on the topic, it is an indication that (1) they probably do not understand the nature and purpose of the literature review or (2) they probably did not invest sufficient energy and time in this important step in the research process. There are no research problems and no research questions for which there is no existing relevant knowledge. Although it is conceivable that no one may have previously studied the exact research question or questions selected for study, there is always knowledge available that could help to enlighten and inform the researcher.

Research-informed Practice or Practice-informed Research

Behavior: Use and translate research evidence to inform and improve practice, policy, and service delivery.

Critical Thinking Question: Suppose you want to learn more about attention deficit disorder among adults. What are five major topics you might explore?

PURPOSES OF A REVIEW OF LITERATURE

Sowers, Ellis, and Dessel (2010) point out that a literature review can serve three important and distinct purposes: (1) It constitutes a reservoir of knowledge for understanding previous research and planning for future research. This allows the researcher to identify gaps in knowledge that may be addressed. (2) It affords a tool for conceptualization and operationalization of the variables of interest. (3) It provides an atlas of potential error, facilitating the identification of potential problems in the research process (p. 504). In addition, citing relevant literature fulfills three functions for the reader of the research report: (1) It helps to establish the credibility of the researcher and his or her background work. (2) It helps the reader to gain a basic understanding of the findings of other researchers as a foundation for evaluating the results of the current study. (3) It may form a source for additional information if the reader desires to learn more about the research (p. 505). Whenever it is conducted, a literature review is a recognition that knowledge building is a cumulative process that goes on over long periods of time and that each study has (or should have) a unique contribution to make to that process. The literature review has several complementary objectives that occur at different times in the research process. These are summarized in Box 4.1.

Box 4.1   How Researchers Make Use of the Literature

When a problem is first identified, to
- specify the problem;
- determine its suitability for study;
- select broad research questions related to it.

Prior to data collection, to
- learn more about the history, origin, and scope of the research problem;
- learn what methodologies have been applied successfully (and unsuccessfully) to study-related research problems;
- learn what answers or partial answers already exist for their broad research questions;
- decide what is the best way to acquire needed data, who or what might best provide them, and how best to analyze them;
- refine and better specify their research questions;

- identify variables that will need to be measured and learn what methods are already available to measure them (quantitative studies);
- construct operational definitions of key variables (quantitative studies);
- propose answers to their research questions in the form of hypotheses (quantitative studies).

After data collection, to
- attempt to explain differences between current findings and existing knowledge;
- identify ways in which current findings are consistent with and support existing knowledge;
- interpret the data in light of existing knowledge;
- specify how current findings advance knowledge;
- develop additional theories and formulate hypotheses for future research studies to test.

POTENTIAL SOURCES FOR THE LITERATURE REVIEW

Several important steps are involved in conducting a literature review. The first step is identifying what sources of literature will be included in the review. There are many potential sources, such as books, journals, the Internet, electronic databases, and governmental reports. For researchers, the term *literature* really means relevant knowledge. This knowledge can be found in many places and forms.

Popular Sources

What qualifies a source of information for inclusion in what we have called the product known as the *review of literature*? It should enlighten and inform the researcher and the reader of the research report. It should also be credible. The issue of credibility is often debatable. Even the best of sources are sometimes vulnerable to political or economic influences. The most common sources (some of them clearly more credible than others) for a review of the literature include the following:

- Professional journal articles
- Internet websites
- Books
- Personal interviews with authorities
- Research reports and monographs
- Research presentations at conferences
- Standard reference materials

Professional Journal Articles

Articles in the major social work professional journals, such as *Social Work Research*, *Social Work*, *Research on Social Work Practice*, and *Journal of Social Work Education*, usually represent a sizable and important portion of the knowledge available relevant to a social work research question. Generally, they undergo an anonymous peer review process involving two or more reviewers. While this gives no guarantee of scholarliness, it at least suggests that others independently believe that they are worthy of publication.

Journals in social work and related fields have proliferated in recent years. Some publications that purport to be professional journals are not always refereed; that is, their publishers do not use a blind review process, which ensures that a friendship, the name of the author, or the author's prestigious affiliation will not influence publication decisions. Also, some of those that do use a blind review process receive so few submissions that they publish the majority of all submissions that are received, sometimes despite the recommendations of their reviewers. A reference book published by National Association of Social Workers (2009) reports on the percentage of article submissions that were accepted for publication among nearly 200 social work and social work-related journals. The high rate of acceptance (a rate of over 50 percent) of some refereed journals was enlightening. Are they simply receiving mostly good, publishable submissions? Or are they "taking what they can get" in order to have enough articles to publish an issue? Box 4.2 offers additional guidelines for evaluating professional journals as a potential source of trustworthy literature.

Box 4.2   Evaluating Professional Journals as a Literature Source

- Does the journal disseminate important knowledge that social workers can use to help them be better practitioners? Does it sometimes publish articles containing null research findings that can help to inform practice?

- Are any research methods described in sufficient detail that the reader is able to judge whether they were methodologically sound and ethical?

- Is the journal published by a professional organization, respected university, or teaching institution? Is it widely cited in the professional literature?

- Is the journal more *serious looking* than other, less scholarly publications? Does it contain tables, graphs, and the results of statistical analyses rather than pictures or colorful graphics?

- Do articles consist of mostly reports of primary research (original research conducted for the first time) and far fewer compilations of research results previously published elsewhere? If the journal contains any replications of previous studies, is the justification for the replication clearly articulated and convincing?

- Do articles contain technical terminology that is specific to the discipline for which it was written, since there is the assumption that anyone interested enough to read them has some scholarly background in the area?

- Do the authors of articles have credentials (advanced degrees, but also work experience, reputations, and/or previous publications in the topic area) that qualify them as scholars or authorities? (An Internet search by the author's name can help to confirm this.)

- Does the style of the writing of articles reflect objectivity, rather than an effort to try to win over the reader to the author's position?

- Do the articles contain references and footnotes that suggest the authors did not just present their own beliefs or theories but tied it to the work of others?

Libraries have limited budgets for purchasing journal subscriptions, either in print or online. Since journals are expensive (many journals actually charge libraries more for subscriptions than they do individual subscribers), difficult choices must be made. Librarians have shown a special interest in the scholarliness of professional journals and devoted whole reference books to the evaluation of the quality of these journals (see LaGuardia, 2003). Such books are frequently available in the reference section of university and public libraries.

It sometimes seems as if the topic of a journal article (maybe it was a hot topic at the time of publication), its use of a particular research method, or a newly developed statistical procedure may have had more to do with its publication than the quality of the study. The findings of research may also be a major factor in the decision to publish. Undoubtedly, some findings are more popular than others, especially if they are consistent with popular opinion or seem to be supportive of the social work profession rather than critical of it. For example, suppose the researchers in one research study reported that a new, experimental program designed to address the problem of urban homelessness had twice the success rate as a traditional program. Yet another, equally well-designed study that examined the effectiveness of the same program found that the difference in success rate between it and the traditional program was negligible (a *"null finding"*). Which study is more likely to be published? Probably the first one. Which is more valuable? They are potentially of equal value. In fact, null research findings—those that report that variables believed to be related or just logically assumed to be related were found to be unrelated—can be an extremely valuable contribution to our professional body of knowledge. They can help to prevent us from continuing to spend limited resources on programs or services that just don't work! A question we might ask ourselves is, "Is it possible that the topic of the article, the research methods used, or the research findings themselves, rather than the quality of the research, resulted in publication of the article?"

Relevant literature can be found in professional journals in many other fields besides social work (e.g., psychology, nursing, sociology, criminal justice, education, health, anthropology, public administration, public health). The journal may have been published anywhere in the world. If an article has been written in a foreign language and is considered critical to understanding the problem being investigated, English translations will need to be found or undertaken. Bilingual and bicultural students in the helping professions at nearby universities may be a good resource for both identifying relevant literature and translation. When a researcher is conducting a study with a different ethnic or cultural group or within a cross-cultural context, literature that helps the researcher to better understand the manifestation of the target problem or research issue within that particular cultural framework is especially useful. Additional effort may be required to locate journal articles written by either indigenous social scientists or social work researchers and practitioners who possess special expertise in conducting research within a specific culture.

Additional effort may be required to locate journal articles written by either indigenous social scientists or social work researchers and practitioners who possess special expertise in conducting research within a specific culture.

Internet Websites

The Internet is a popular source for existing knowledge. For many people, it is now the first place to look when they want information about most anything. Its easy accessibility and the breadth of information available can greatly expedite a literature search. Unlike books, journal articles, or other commonly used reference materials, which are often out of date before they are available in print, data on the Internet can be updated as frequently as is necessary. The ease with which knowledge can be put on the Internet is, at the same time, its greatest weakness. Individuals can put anything they want on it—no verification is required. Freedom of speech also permits individuals to play loosely with facts or just plain fabricate information.

If the Internet is so vulnerable to misinformation, why do we include it as a popular source of literature? Along with websites that we would never want to quote from in a review of literature, there are also some very useful ones for the social work researcher. The challenge is to learn to identify the trustworthy websites. Many of the sources of literature described throughout this chapter (including journal articles) are now accessible via the Internet; more will undoubtedly follow. Websites come and go, addresses are subject to change, and even the content and credibility of specific sites tend to vary based upon the preferences and biases of their current webmaster. Therefore, it is important that we learn to distinguish trustworthy information obtained from the Internet from that which cannot be trusted and should not be cited in a review of literature. The question of what constitutes a trustworthy website is itself widely discussed on the Internet. Box 4.3 contains some of the more commonly mentioned indicators that reflect on a website's credibility.

Box 4.3   Evaluating Websites as a Literature Source

- What does the URL tell you? Does it contain a personal name, often an indicator that it is a personal Web page, rather than the name of an institution or organization? If it does not appear to be a personal Web page, what is the domain? Is it where you would expect to find the knowledge that you are seeking, for example, .gov or .us for data collected by governmental organizations; .org for information relating to problems addressed by not-for-profit organizations; .edu for research conducted in colleges or universities; and so forth.

- Are there links that would allow you to verify the credibility of the site and the author of the material it contains? More reputable sites will contain links that, for example, take us to a description of the organization that sponsors it and its mission, goals, and philosophy or the author's professional vitae or biography. If there are links to other websites, such as "additional sites," they should not just be those that reflect the same positions as those of the current one. Their credibility should also be examined. The links should work. When was the site last updated?

- What are the author's (or the organization's) claims to expertise in the area? Credentials are important, but look at the content of the Web page. Is it what we should expect from a true scholar? Does the content seem to be little more than an opinion, a diatribe, or an attempt to sound off about some issue? A rambling discourse is not characteristic of scholarly writing. Scholars are well organized and concise; they rarely repeat themselves unless it is for emphasis.

- Does the page seem to have been put there as a service to the scientific community or to other professionals? Or does it seem like it was put there to try to influence others to adopt the author's ideas or sell them on his or her way of viewing things? Is it possible that it contains deliberate exaggerations and misstatements or was just meant to be funny or outrageous or to shock others in order to get some reaction?

- How well documented were statements that were made? How credible are they? Could citations have been taken out of context or the position of articles cited otherwise distorted or altered in order to make a point?

Books

Books remain a popular source for literature reviews. The reports of some major research studies are published in book form. Other books contain scholarly presentations of carefully researched theories, research designs, and statistical methods. Of course, books also may contain material that falls far short of the standard of scholarliness that is expected for citation in a literature review. Just because something is in print is no guarantee of its trustworthiness. Much of what is published in book form has not undergone rigorous review and scrutiny. Some textbook publishers consider potential sales along with quality issues and other factors when they make the decision to publish (or not to publish) a book. Checks on the accuracy of the content are often delegated to a few academicians who receive only minimal compensation for their reviews and who may be less than thorough in their efforts. There are also "vanity publishers," who will publish virtually any material in book form (including a professor's course notes and other writings) if the author is willing to pay enough to become a published author.

In deciding whether to use what is in a book to influence one's own research or include a citation from it in the literature review section of a report, it is desirable to ask certain "credibility" questions. We have listed them in Box 4.4.

Personal Interviews with Authorities

Some of the other usual sources of information should be approached with even greater caution. When conducting personal interviews, unless the information is examined critically, researchers can be misled by assertions that are questionable, possibly damaging the credibility of their own research efforts. The following questions should be asked: Where do I draw the line? What constitutes usable knowledge and what does not?

The reader will recall that authority is one of the non-scientific sources of knowledge that we described as untrustworthy in Chapter 1. So why would we include it here as a possible source of knowledge? Because sometimes people in authority do know something important! The problem surrounding content drawn from interviews with authorities is lack of consensus regarding who is an authority. Unfortunately, in some

---

Box 4.4   Evaluating Books as a Literature Source

- Does the author have a reputation for scholarly integrity? What are his or her credentials? With what professional institution is he or she affiliated? Is it considered reputable? Does it have any unusual beliefs, values, or commitments? Is the author frequently cited by others as an expert on the topic?
- Does the author's position in the book seem to be based on well-designed research, either original or a scholarly review of the work of others?
- Does the author seem intent on the advancement of knowledge, not on pursuing some personal or political agenda?

- Was the book published by a reputable, well-established publisher with a reputation for quality and selectivity, such as a major university press or widely used publisher of textbooks in the field?
- Is the book a recently revised edition? If it was published some years ago, is it considered a classic in its field that contains material of historical significance?
- Are reviews of the book generally positive? What strengths do reviewers identify, and do they relate to those parts of the book that you plan to cite?

parts of Western society, authority has frequently been assumed to reside in all individuals with certain academic credentials or job titles. For the social work researcher, an authority whose comments are worth quoting in a literature review is someone who has in-depth knowledge of some aspect of the research problem or who has arrived at answers (or at least partial answers) to certain research questions, preferably through the use of scientific methods. This greatly limits the number of authorities who should be quoted in a review of literature.

Today's researcher should not make any assumptions about an individual's claims to knowledge based solely on academic or other formal credentials. It would be erroneous to assume that, for example, a quotation from any physician is appropriate on a medical question or one from a lawyer will provide needed knowledge on a legal topic. The physician may see primarily older patients; thus, her position on a problem related to child rearing may have no basis other than her experiences as a child or as a mother and may even be distorted through interaction with a biased sample of patients. The lawyer may specialize in contract law and may speak more out of personal opinion than out of knowledge in discussing needed changes in child abuse reporting laws. This is not an indictment of these or other professions; it is only a recognition that the base of knowledge within most professional fields (including social work) and even their subspecialties has grown dramatically during the past century, to the point where no one can possibly know it all.

Use of a few, carefully chosen quotations from interviews with authorities in the literature review section of a research report will usually not harm the credibility of the researcher's efforts. On the contrary, it may suggest balance and thoroughness in the final product. However, it might be wise to prevent any possible challenges to the credibility of authorities by including brief descriptions of the source of their expertise in the narrative. For example, a descriptive statement such as "one medical researcher, who has conducted research funded by the National Institute of Mental Health on the possible relationship between the use of party drugs and suicide among young men, has concluded that . . ." would help to justify why that particular physician was cited in the literature review section of a research study on adolescent suicide.

Research Reports and Monographs

Research reports and monographs are generally intended to be honest communications of a researcher's methods and findings. Although the findings are only as good as the methods used to produce them, the fact that a researcher's methods are open to public critique and to replication increases the likelihood that a report or monograph will be credible. Of course, if the research was funded by an organization or special interest group that may have exerted undue influence over what was reported, the findings may not be trustworthy. For example, the credibility of findings about the benefits to society of payday loans or title loans by research sponsored by companies that have much to gain by their continued legality would be highly suspect. They would not be suitable to cite.

Research Presentations at Conferences

While there is a great amount of knowledge disseminated at conferences and symposia, there is also a good amount of unsubstantiated opinion and misinformation shared. A presentation may not be selected using a blind review process. Often, the reputation of the presenter or the topic (if it is a popular one) is a major factor in its selection.

Frequently, a conference presentation may have no basis in research at all. It may be little more than a show-and-tell description of what the presenter has done and why he or she thinks it was good.

Most presentations at annual conferences, such as those sponsored by the NASW, the SSWR, the CSWE, or the Child Welfare League of America, have undergone a fairly rigorous screening procedure. Only a small percentage of proposals submitted are accepted for presentation. These gatherings also give program space to invited speakers whose past expertise in a subject area has been recognized by one or more members of their planning committee but who may not have been active in the field for years. Personal friendships, quid pro quos, or other political concerns sometimes influence the decision to invite these individuals. Information acquired at regional, state, and local conferences also varies widely in its credibility. Before placing too much credence in what is presented, inquiries should be made as to the selection process for presentations and the credentials of the presenters. Of course, a critical assessment of the research methods used should also be made.

Many other professional gatherings that call themselves national and international conferences and symposia have far less credibility. (After all, any group can describe its conference as "national" or "international" if it chooses.) Some of the most suspect of these consist of a small group of individuals who share some specialized interest. They get together annually to present to each other (sometimes even on the same topic as the previous year) at geographically desirable locations. Participants take turns hosting the annual gathering and inviting each other to present their work. Although some knowledge is undoubtedly shared, there is also a liberal amount of networking, rest and recreation, and sight-seeing. The conference is viewed as more of a "perk" than the fulfillment of a professional responsibility to remain knowledgeable in one's field of specialization.

Standard Reference Materials

For relevant knowledge that is available in written form, publications of abstracts (e.g., Social Work Abstracts, Sociological Abstracts, Psychological Abstracts, Dissertation Abstracts International, SAGE Urban Studies Abstracts) are always a good place to start a literature search. Listed by topic area as well as by author, they provide a good overview of where recent publications on various topics can be found. However, quotations from abstracts publications should not be used in the report of a review. They are not meant to be a substitute for the original source, just a convenient way to learn about the existence of a publication that may (or may not) prove to be helpful.

Historically, standard reference materials, such as almanacs, encyclopedias, atlases, statistical abstracts, directories, annuals, and yearbooks, have contained verified facts that can be cited in a review of literature. They have tended to possess higher credibility than, for example, data obtained from unverified sources on the Internet, because they have undergone a more thorough review and verification process. However, the publishers of many standard reference materials are increasingly replacing printed material with material available electronically, where they can be kept up to date much better than in print. There is no need for a periodic new edition or supplement—just make the needed changes as they are required and they are immediately available to the researcher.

The Internet has also produced another phenomenon related to standard reference materials. In the past, volumes such as encyclopedias and almanacs were compiled and published by specialists who worked full time, year after year, carefully verifying and re-verifying the content that went into them. In recent years, websites have emerged that also claim to be standard reference materials and are regarded as such by many people. Yet they lack the quality controls that we expect in a standard reference. Whether or not they possess the knowledge or expertise, anyone can contribute to them and can even edit the contributions of others. Currently Wikipedia, "the people's encyclopedia," is the best known example of this trend. It is now one of the first links that appears when we do almost any Web search. Can it be trusted? Like most of the other sources of knowledge described in this chapter, it undoubtedly contains many useful facts, submitted by knowledgeable people. However, it also undoubtedly contains misinformation and falsehoods, at least until a more knowledgeable contributor comes along and corrects them. At some point in time, it may become a trusted resource. However, that time has not come yet. For now, its primary usefulness is to locate links to other, more trustworthy sources, such as research monographs or professional journal articles.

Other, More Questionable Sources

What we have just described are those sources that, if used selectively, tend to be among the more credible sources of literature. However, there are others that, while they possess less credibility, appear in literature reviews from time to time. We mention them here not to encourage their use but to caution why they should be used only when better sources are unavailable or cannot be found, and then only after a careful check of their credibility.

Content of Workshops

Workshop content may be based on empirical findings; often it is not. Frequently, workshop leaders have been contracted with and paid to deliver content in a way consistent with the wishes of the individual or organization paying for it. This leaves the knowledge contained in the workshop vulnerable to influence and distortion. The researcher may need to explore whether the material was based on the best knowledge available or simply reflective of what the workshop's sponsoring organization wanted its participants to hear. If it is the former, workshop content may be appropriate for inclusion in a research literature review. However, it would still be better to go to the original sources that the presenter may have relied on in putting together the presentation.

Newspaper Articles

Newspapers, either in print or online, can be a valuable source of knowledge. Some of the better ones (e.g., the *Christian Science Monitor, New York Times*) are frequently cited in a literature review. They provide news of general interest and are written for educated readers. However, it should be remembered that even the better newspapers depend on commercial success for their continued existence. Newspaper sales and a large number of Internet hits at their websites are good for newspapers. Utilization data can be used to help sell print advertisements and online links, which can generate the needed cash to survive. Thus, what will *sell* sometimes has higher priority than carefully researched contributions to knowledge.

Newspapers acquire some of what they publish from generally credible sources, such as reports of government-sponsored research. But they also publish findings (sometimes selectively) from research of questionable quality. They regularly publish guest editorials written by invited "experts" who may have more name recognition than expertise. When a topic is believed to be of widespread interest, it sometimes seems that getting the facts is less important than producing a timely piece that will be widely read.

Unless an article can be determined to possess a carefully researched origin and contains only first-hand information, it is probably best to use it with extreme caution. Often, newspapers are best used to learn about the existence of the knowledge-building work of others. It is then possible to seek out the original source, obtain a full report, and evaluate its merits on the basis of the description of the researcher's methods.

Radio and Television Broadcasts

There is a great amount of knowledge and advice shared gratuitously by network radio and television talk show hosts and their "authority" guests. Occasionally, news specials and documentaries on major networks and public radio and television are well researched and present excellent sources of information. However, the proliferation of certain types of television journalism and pseudo–news specials in recent years, along with the revelation that some of what was reported on documentaries was falsified or staged, has cast increasing doubt on the credibility of television news broadcasts. Frequently, they appear to be designed to entertain and appeal to the lower interests of viewers and listeners. Special care and discretion should be used in separating knowledge from content that, if cited, would only weaken the researcher's scientific credibility.

Magazines and Periodicals

Magazines and periodicals vary widely in how much credible knowledge they publish, as opposed to how much pure fiction they include to sell subscriptions and single copies in supermarkets and other outlets. They run the gamut from informative and generally trustworthy (e.g., the *Scientific American*, *Economist*, *National Geographic*) to popular but unscientific (e.g., *Reader's Digest*, *Parents*, *Cosmopolitan*) to sensational (e.g., *Star*, *Globe*, or *National Enquirer*). Only the first group is occasionally cited in a scholarly literature review without jeopardizing the researcher's credibility. Some newsmagazines and pop science periodicals seem to walk a thin line, attempting to appear scholarly and scientific while selecting topics and presentation formats (e.g., short, topical articles featuring provocative pictures) that clearly reflect an eye on sales figures rather than the knowledge needs of their readers. They may even reflect a pragmatic mixture within a single issue; for example, a fairly scholarly article written by a respected researcher juxtaposed with a bit of fluff that would be an intellectual insult to anyone with more than a superficial knowledge of the topic. The message to the social work researcher should be obvious—think very carefully before you rely on such publications for knowledge. You may subscribe to it, read it religiously, learn some things that are helpful to you in your work, and even display it on your coffee table without embarrassment. But that does not mean it is a potential source of knowledge that can be cited with confidence.

USING INTERNET SEARCHES TO LOCATE INFORMATION SOURCES

Regardless of what sources of information the researcher is looking for, he or she will eventually turn to Internet searches to locate information. Internet search engines have made the task of finding relevant data for literature reviews much easier than it was in years past. But there is a certain finesse involved in performing an effective search, regardless of the type of search engine you are using. Once you have learned some of these skills, they can be transferred (with slight variations) to many search engines, electronic databases, and virtual library systems.

For example, returning to the example used in the preceding chapter, suppose a researcher is interested in studying the disordered eating behaviors among African-American women. The researcher could start with one of the many electronic library systems available through universities and state governments. Once you have logged onto a virtual library system, you can generally search through a long list of licensed commercial databases as well as other free Internet resources. These resources offer access to thousands of full textbooks, journals, magazines, and encyclopedias. There are many electronic databases that may be relevant to research completed in the social work field, and it is wise to select the database(s) that most closely matches the general topic area of the literature review. In the case of eating disorders, for example, it is likely that psychological databases will include the most relevant research. Some psychology databases that are available through virtual library systems include PsychINFO, PsycARTICLES, and Psychology and Behavioral Sciences Collection.

Once the database has been selected, you are ready to enter the search parameters to locate research studies in the area of interest. To continue with the eating disorders example, you might enter "eating disorders and African American women." Using the connector *and* in the search parameter returns only those publications that include both phrases; using *or* returns publications that include either phrase. Most search engines will automatically search for the phrase or phrases entered anywhere in the title, abstract, body, or reference list of the publications included in the selected database. If you want only those documents that include these phrases in their title or abstract, you can complete what is often called an *advanced search*, in which more specific search criteria are entered. In an advanced search, other parameters can be used to further delineate the search, including type of research (e.g., quantitative, qualitative, meta-analysis), year of publication, author's name, and type of publication.

Suppose this search returns several thousand articles. After looking at the titles of the first several, you may find that the majority of the articles are looking at African-American women and obesity, and, while an interesting topic, is not what you are interested in. You can then return to the search parameters and narrow the search by entering "bulimia nervosa and African American women" and subsequently "anorexia nervosa and African American women." The search will now return publications that are more closely related to the problem selected by the researcher.

Once you have narrowed the search to his area of interest, you can then begin to look at each publication listed. You can often tell by the publication's title and abstract if the material might be helpful. If you are lucky, the full text of the article will be immediately available. Journal articles can sometimes be found on other websites, such as the journal's website or publisher's site. If you still fail to locate the full text, you can visit your university's library and find a hard copy of the journal or book. If the library does not have the needed publication, there is usually an

Research-informed Practice or Practice-informed Research

Behavior: Apply critical thinking to engage in analysis of quantitative and qualitative research methods and research findings.

Critical Thinking Question: What are three ways you could limit an Internet search that has returned too many journal articles?

inter-library loan system in place, which would allow you to get a copy of an article or book from another library that does have the needed publication.

FOCUSED RESEARCH QUESTIONS

Researchers rely heavily on existing knowledge to assist them in developing all aspects of the research design. The next step in the research process is to specify more clearly the research questions that will be examined in the research. Depending on the knowledge acquired through the literature review, the researcher may be able to predict what answers will be found. The rest of this chapter will focus on these two products of the literature review: the focused research question and the research hypothesis.

Selecting broad research questions reduces the study of a research problem to a manageable size and guides us in conducting the review of the literature. However, broad questions, such as those in the examples in Chapter 3, do not provide a specific-enough focus to guide the researcher in performing such necessary tasks as identifying the most appropriate people or objects to study, determining what needs to be observed and/or measured, or selecting the methods to sort and analyze data. Before these tasks can be undertaken, further refinement and specification of the research questions are required.

What is the difference between a broad research question and the more specific questions that are likely to be formulated following a literature review? How does a review of existing knowledge help the researcher to move from the former to the latter? To illustrate the difference between broad and focused research questions, we will return to the old example used in Chapter 3 (Bellomy et al., 1989). The reader will recall that after eliminating other options, the student researchers, looking into the problem of large numbers of unfounded child abuse determinations, settled on one broad question, "Are the different demographic characteristics of workers (e.g., age, race, sex, or parenthood) related to their determinations?" This was a good start. The question provided a beginning focus for the study and helped to narrow the literature review to a manageable number of topics. It provided a research focus—the exploration of a possible relationship between various social worker characteristics and those decisions. But the question was still too general to provide any real direction to the researchers as to the best way to go about seeking an answer.

Before the literature review was completed, the researchers did not know to what degree answers to the question already existed, what methods had been used to study it, or what other researchers had learned in the process of conducting their research. For example, without reviewing the literature, it was not possible to know which worker characteristics would or would not be promising to examine.

When the researchers began to search the literature, they soon confirmed what they had suspected—they were not attempting to build knowledge in a vacuum. For example, it was learned that even back then other researchers had been studying professionals' decision making for many years; some had even used human service workers as research participants. The researchers found one article that was especially helpful in suggesting how to study their research question. It described the relative merits of different research methods to identify factors that seem to influence social workers' decision making in a variety of settings other than child protection. Other literature confirmed their hunch that there was a lack of consistent, clear federal procedural guidelines, and that the definitions of what constitutes child abuse were vague. A review of state policy manuals suggested that state guidelines were no less ambiguous.

As they continued to search the literature and speak with child welfare administrators, the researchers began to compile a list of personal characteristics that, on the basis of past research, might be related to the decisions that the workers make. Several characteristics were found to be related to social workers' decision making, including level of educational achievement, discipline methods used in the workers' homes of origin, feelings about their jobs, and whether they were parents themselves. The researchers decided to collect data on each of these characteristics. Just as importantly, they decided not to gather data on certain other worker characteristics (e.g., age, health status, or gender) that, on the basis of past research, probably would not be related to social workers' decision making.

The literature review produced focused research questions that would have been impossible to formulate without finding out what was already known about the problem, what related questions had been studied, and what answers had been found. Because of the review, the researchers were able to take their broad research question and reformulate it into two more focused or specific questions:

- Is there a relationship between disciplinary practices in child protection workers' families of origin and their decision making about cases referred for suspected child abuse or neglect?
- To what degree do workers perceive that their formal education and training in child protection services has influenced their decision making about cases referred for suspected child abuse or neglect?

With these more focused questions to work with, the research took on a clearer focus. As a result of conducting the literature review, it was now possible to know what data about workers and their decisions should be gathered, and, by learning from the experiences of other researchers, the best ways to go about gathering it. Box 4.5 provides additional examples of broad research questions and corresponding focused research questions that might be produced through reviewing relevant scientific literature.

Box 4.5 Examples of Broad Research Questions and Focused Research Questions	
Broad Research Questions	**Focused Research Questions**
A. Are people with developmental disabilities unhappy working in sheltered workshops?	A. Does the style of supervision in sheltered workshops affect the job satisfaction of people with developmental disabilities?
B. How do value conflicts affect client services when social workers are supervised by nurses?	B. When nurses supervise social workers, are patients less likely to refuse painful life-extending treatment?
C. Why do social work students dislike courses in research and statistics?	C. Is the rate of math phobia higher among social work students than in the general population?
D. What obstacles to the grief process do parents of children who die while committing violent crimes perceive?	D. Do parents of children who die while committing violent crimes withdraw from contact with friends and families more often than parents of children who die in other circumstances?

RESEARCH HYPOTHESES

A *research hypothesis* is a tentative answer to a research question. It is based on existing knowledge (and sometimes, to a lesser degree, on practice experience) and is a prediction of what the researcher will find. It generally takes the form of a statement of a relationship between certain variables. As previously noted, in predominantly qualitative studies, researchers usually do not formulate research hypotheses prior to data collection. Relevant variables are often not even identified when data collection begins, so it would be impossible to predict a relationship between them. In most qualitative research, a brief search of available literature prior to data collection helps to formulate a plan or design for conducting the research and to narrow and refine the research question or questions. But it goes no further. The literature does not suggest answers to the questions. Thus, data collection begins without the researcher being able to predict what will be found. However, the final product of a qualitative study may be one or more theories or *hypothesis statements*. Other researchers may adopt them as the research hypotheses for subsequent, often more quantitative, research studies.

In predominantly quantitative studies, the research problem or a similar one may have been studied extensively; a considerable amount of related knowledge may have accumulated. Data may also have been analyzed to determine whether support for the research hypotheses exists. If the literature review suggests what will be found after data are collected and analyzed, it may be possible to formulate one or more research hypotheses. See Box 4.6 for example research hypotheses based on the research questions shown in Box 4.5.

Box 4.6   Examples of Focused Research Questions and Research Hypotheses

Focused Research Questions	Research Hypotheses
A. Does the style of supervision in sheltered workshops affect the job satisfaction of people with developmental disabilities?	A. The job satisfaction of people with developmental disabilities in sheltered workshops will be higher when supervisors reflect a supportive management style than when they use more autocratic methods of supervision.
B. When nurses supervise social workers, are patients less likely to refuse painful life-extending treatment?	B. Patients are less likely to refuse painful life-extending treatment when social workers are being supervised by nurses rather than by other social workers.
C. Is the rate of math phobia higher among social work students than in the general population?	C. The rate of math phobia is higher among social work students than among students in the "hard sciences."
D. Do parents of children who die while committing violent crimes withdraw from contact with friends and families more often than parents of children who die in other circumstances?	D. Parents of children who die while committing violent crimes are more likely to withdraw from contact with their friends and families than parents of children who die in other circumstances.

Research hypotheses are generally stated in either the present or the future tense. In rare instances, such as in the case of historical research (Chapter 6), the past tense is used. They are stated in the form of declarative statements, never as questions, because they are tentative answers to the research questions.

Related Definitions

To understand fully just what research hypotheses are and how a literature review can help in formulating them, we will first need to define certain key research terms.

Variable and Constant

We have already used the term *variable* several times, because the study of variables is essential to research. A variable is an attribute or characteristic that differs in quantity or quality among different persons, objects, times, places, and so on. In our earlier example, the different parenting experiences of child protection workers within their homes of origin would be a variable. A *constant* is a characteristic or attribute that does not differ either in quantity or in quality among the cases involved in the research study. For example, the employment position of all the research participants in the example that we have been using in the past two chapters did not differ—they were all child protection workers. Therefore, employment position is a constant in this study. In research, constants are usually of less interest than variables.

Demographic Variable

The term *demographic variable* is a generic term that refers to those commonly measured variables that give researchers and the readers of research reports a clearer understanding of the general characteristics of the research participants. Some of the variables generally referred to as demographic are age, gender, income, religious affiliation, education, and marital status.

Although certain demographic variables are frequently included in questionnaires and other research data collection instruments, there is no rule that they must be. Demographic data should be collected if the researchers have reason to believe that the information is related in some way to the research question (as determined through the literature review), or if the readers of the research report will require the information in order to determine if individuals or groups with whom they are working are similar to the research participants. Unless one of these justifications exists, there may be ethical and practical reasons not to measure it. Some demographic variables (e.g., age, religious affiliation, marital status, or income) may be considered sensitive and personal. Collecting data about them when the researcher has no practical use for them is an unnecessary invasion of the participants' right to privacy. Besides, requesting unnecessary data from participants who are less than eager to provide them can jeopardize the collection of other data that are really needed.

Value Label or Value

The terms value label and value are the name (value label) or number (value) assigned to a specific measurement of a variable. A value label (some people prefer the term attribute) is a word or words used to denote the form or category that a variable can

Diversity and Difference in Practice

Behavior: Apply and communicate understanding of the importance of diversity and difference in shaping life experiences in practice at the micro, mezzo, and macro levels.

Critical Thinking Question: What are some possible problems with creating the attributes for such variables as "race" and "sexual orientation?"

assume. For example, for the variable "Parenting Style in Home of Origin," different value labels might be "autocratic," "democratic," "laissez-faire," or some other categories that reflect the differences in parenting style that existed within child protection workers' homes of origin. Note that the differences reflect different kinds or qualities (rather than quantities) of the variable. A value is a specific measurement of a variable and is expressed as a number reflecting the quantity of the variable. For the variable "Number of Siblings," for example, possible values would include 0, 1, 2, 3, 4, and so on, indicating the number of siblings present in the home.

Whether we use the term value label or value is a function of how precisely a variable can be measured (see Chapter 10) and whether its different measurements reflect a difference in just kind or quality or a difference in quantity. Thus, the variable "Children" might use the value labels "Yes" or "No" to denote whether each worker is a parent. However, if we were to ask how many children under age 18 reside with the worker, the variable "Children" could indicate the number of children in the home, taking on the values 0, 1, 2, 3, and so forth.

Frequency

Frequency refers to the number of times a given value label or value was found to exist among the persons or cases that were studied. If five workers were found to have been reared in homes that used autocratic parenting styles, we would say that the value label "autocratic" had a frequency of 5. If democratic styles existed in the homes of nine workers, the value label "democratic" would have a frequency of 9, and so forth.

Dependent Variable and Independent Variable

Researchers often use one of two pairs of terms while communicating their predictions within a hypothesis. The terms dependent variable and independent variable form one such pair. Dependent variable refers to the variable whose variation the researcher is most interested in understanding and explaining. In social work research, the degree of treatment success that occurs among clients is a common dependent variable, but a dependent variable can be any variable that the researcher has declared to be the one whose variations are of primary interest.

The label dependent variable is not applied to a variable unless at least one other variable, an independent variable, has been hypothesized to be at least a contributor to its variations. The term *independent variable* is applied to the variable or variables that the researcher believes may produce at least some of the variation that exists within the dependent variable. If, for example, the variable "degree of treatment success among clients" in a hypothesis is labeled the dependent variable, the independent variable might be "method of treatment," "degree of family involvement," or "frequency of treatment sessions."

Ideally, an independent variable is introduced and/or manipulated in some way by the researcher so that its effects on the dependent variable can be monitored and recorded. As long as the researcher is asserting that one variable is believed to influence the values of a second variable (and not vice versa), it is appropriate to refer to the first

---

Box 4.7   Examples of Independent and Dependent Variables

Independent Variable	Dependent Variable
A. Group (Experimental group receives the cognitive therapy and the Control group does not receive the intervention)	A. Score on a clinical depression scale
B. Group (Group 1 receives Behavior Therapy plus medications and Group 2 receives Behavior Therapy alone)	B. Score on an eating disorder scale
C. Group (Group 1 receives individual therapy sessions and Group 2 receives group therapy sessions)	C. Score on an anger management scale

---

variable as the independent variable and to the second as the dependent variable. The terms independent variable and dependent variable are used together or not at all. See Box 4.7 for example pairs of independent and dependent variables.

Predictor Variable and Outcome Variable

The term *predictor variable* is used in place of independent variable when the researcher has no control over or is unable to manipulate the independent variable. In this case, the term *outcome variable* is used in place of dependent variable, and, like the dependent variable, generally refers to the variable of primary interest to the researcher. These terms are used when previous research has hypothesized that the variables are either associated or correlated (discussed later in this chapter) and that the values of one variable (the predictor variable) can be used to predict the values of the second variable (the outcome variable). For example, Townsend, Floersch, and Findling (2009) conducted a study to determine to what extent scores on the Drug Attitudes Inventory (DAI) (Hogan, Awad, & Eastwood, 1983) would predict the rate of adherence to psychotropic medication among adolescents. They concluded that there was a low but significant correlation between DAI scores (the predictor variable) and adherence rate (outcome variable). To use the terms *independent variable* and *dependent variable* to refer to the variables in this study would be misleading, since the researchers did not manipulate either of the variables. See Box 4.8 for example pairs of predictor and outcome variables.

Box 4.8   Examples of Predictor and Outcome Variables

Predictor Variable	Outcome Variable
A. Gender	A. Score on Statistics exam
B. Ethnicity	B. Measure of Parenting Style
C. Education level	C. Score on Job Satisfaction questionnaire

The terms *dependent variable* or *outcome variable* and *independent variable* or *predictor variable* are specific to a given piece of research. That is, they describe the focus of one researcher's investigation and the nature of a relationship between variables believed to exist within it. Another researcher is likely to have a different focus and suggest a different relationship. Thus, a variable may be defined as the independent or predictor variable in one research study and the dependent or outcome variable in another study. For example, one study may use scores on the Beck Depression Inventory (Beck, Steer, Ball, & Ranier, 1996) as the dependent variable to determine the effectiveness of a cognitive intervention. In another study that looks at the influence of depression level on the severity of disordered eating behaviors (such as binging or purging), scores on the same depression inventory may be defined as the predictor variable.

Sometimes, neither pair of labels is appropriate. In some research that predicts the existence of a relationship between variables, it may not be possible or appropriate to identify one variable in a hypothesis as clearly dependent (or outcome) and another as independent (or predictor). For example, the literature may suggest that alcoholism and unemployment are related, but in a study of the relationship between the two social problems, it may not be possible to make a case for applying the label *outcome* (or *dependent*) to one variable any more than to the other. The researcher may be more interested in studying their interaction than in examining to what degree (if any) one may influence or predict the other. Or the research goal may be simply to learn the extent to which one problem tends to be found with the other, the degree with which they co-vary. In this case, the hypothesis should be stated so that it is clear that the researcher is not communicating that one variable is contributing to or causing the values of the other, only that they vary together in a certain pattern. As we noted earlier in this chapter, null findings can be a valuable contribution to our knowledge base, especially when variables are generally believed to be related. A finding of no co-variance can be useful, especially in dispelling stereotypes. For example, Bonewell (2009) compared intrinsic and extrinsic religious beliefs to the extent of sexual compulsivity among Christian males and found no relevant association between these two variables.

Confounding Variable

We know from our knowledge of human behavior that the relationship between two variables is rarely a simple one. For example, the decision to join or not join a youth gang is not solely a function of whether or not there is a father figure in the home. Many other variables come into play that can easily confuse researchers about the true relationship between these two variables. Researchers have labels to describe these other variables as well.

The terms confounding variable *or* extraneous variable *refer to any variable that can mislead the researcher about the true relationship between the dependent and independent variables.*

The terms *confounding variable* or *extraneous variable* refer to any variable that can mislead the researcher about the true relationship between the dependent and independent variables. The term *intervening variable* relates to the time when the variable's influence on the relationship between an independent variable and a dependent variable was believed to occur. A variable is considered an intervening variable when it influenced the dependent variable after the effects of the independent variable have been experienced. For example, sexual experiences during adolescence may be an intervening variable in the relationship between the presence or absence of sexual abuse as a child (predictor variable) and current sexual satisfaction of adults (outcome variable). The predictor variable (the presence or absence of sexual abuse as a child) may have influenced the intervening variable (sexual experiences during adolescence), which in turn influenced the outcome variable (current sexual satisfaction).

An *antecedent variable* is a variable that preceded both the dependent and the independent variables and influenced both. Leung (2007) studied how peer relations and perceived social self-worth affect the level of shyness among a group of young adults. She identified two variables, temperament and parental characteristics, as antecedent variables that had an effect on all three of the variables of interest in her study: peer relations, perceived social self-worth, and the level of shyness. An *obscuring variable* is a variable that interacts with the dependent and independent variables in such a way as to make the two variables appear <u>less</u> closely related than they really are. It hides their true relationship.

In an introductory book like this one, these distinctions are not too important. We will use the term *confounding variable* to refer to any variable that has the potential to distort or misrepresent the true relationship between the dependent (or outcome) and independent (or predictor) variables, no matter how it does this or in which direction it may potentially mislead the researcher.

Control Variable

Social work practitioners are aware of and work with confounding variables all the time, although the label may be an unfamiliar one. In practice, as in research, we hope to control confounding variables and minimize or eliminate their influence, but this is often not possible. For example, as practitioners, we might wish to know to what degree our treatment is influencing a client's social functioning. But we may be concerned about how the attitude or behavior of a spouse or an employer (potentially confounding variables) might influence the level of treatment success that our client may achieve. The spouse's and the employer's behaviors and attitudes and any number of other possible confounding variables can muddy the water as we attempt to determine the relationship between our treatment and the client's level of social functioning.

Fortunately, researchers have devised ways to minimize or at least help sort out the influence of variables potentially confounding the relationship between the dependent and independent variables. In such cases, we no longer refer to a variable as a confounding or extraneous variable. We instead refer to it as a *control variable* (sometimes called a *moderating variable*), a potentially confounding variable whose influence has been recognized and controlled. This can be done using one of several statistical tests that employ mathematical formulas designed for this purpose.

If the apparent relationship between the independent and the dependent variables disappears following introduction of the measurements of the control variable into the formula, researchers describe the original relationship as *spurious*. In research, a spurious relationship is one in which there is actually no relationship between two variables, but a relationship has been inferred

Evaluation

Behavior: Apply knowledge of human behavior and the social environment, person-in-environment, and other multidisciplinary theoretical frameworks in the evaluation of outcomes.

Critical Thinking Question: In evaluating the improvement in a client's functioning after completing a treatment for depression, identify some potential confounding variables that could also have affected the client's depression level.

because of the influence of a confounding variable that has not yet been identified and controlled. Of course, the introduction of the control variable can also have the opposite effect—an obscuring variable (discussed earlier) can reveal an apparent relationship between the independent and dependent variables that was not previously in evidence.

Types of Relationships between Variables

A research hypothesis states that researchers believe (on the basis of practice experience and existing knowledge revealed through the literature review) that certain variables are related. A research hypothesis generally goes a little further, stating the nature of the relationship between the variables. The three types of relationships that are most commonly stated in research hypotheses are association, correlation, and causation. See Box 4.9 for a brief description of each along with an example hypothesis for each type of relationship.

Association

A research hypothesis that states a belief in an association between variables asserts that certain value categories of one variable tend to be found with certain value categories of another variable. A research hypothesis is likely to be stated so as to reflect an association between variables (and nothing more) if:

- the variables can be measured so that their values reflect only qualitative differences (differences of kind) and not the precise quantity of the variable present;
- the statistical analysis produces only an indication of degree of association; and
- the researcher was unable to introduce or manipulate either variable in any way or to exert control over potentially confounding variables.

Research hypotheses that state beliefs about association between or among variables are quite common in social work research. Although an association between variables

---

Box 4.9	Relationships between Variables Expressed in Hypotheses
Association	Certain value categories of X are found with certain value categories of Y.
	Example hypothesis: Among adolescent psychiatric patients, those who receive group treatment are more likely to be rehospitalized than those who receive individual treatment.
Correlation	Higher values of X are found with higher values of Y and vice versa, or, higher values of X are found with lower values of Y and vice versa.
	Example hypothesis: Among adolescent psychiatric patients, there is a negative correlation between number of group treatment sessions attended per week and the length of time a patient remained in the hospital.
Causation	Values or value categories of X cause values or value categories of Y.
	Example hypothesis: Adolescent psychiatric patients receiving cognitive therapy and medication will score lower on the depression inventory than those who received medication alone.

gives researchers less information about the relationship than they might like to have, knowledge of an association between variables can still be useful to the social worker. For example, Donate-Lopez et al. (2010) looked at the association of age, gender, and helmet use with the risk of death for occupants of two-wheeled motor vehicles involved in crashes. In another study, Marmorstein (2010) examined the longitudinal associations between depression and alcohol problems, while accounting for the potential interaction effects of delinquent behaviors during adolescence.

Correlation

If a research hypothesis predicts a *correlation* between variables, it implies a little more about their relationship than just a simple association. A prediction that variables will be found to be correlated predicts that the values of the variables co-vary, that is, the values of the two variables tend to move either in the same direction or in opposite directions. It does not, however, predict that the values of one variable will be shown to have caused the values of the other. As in the case of association, inadequately controlled confounding variables may be producing the apparent relationship between the variables. A hypothesis is likely to be stated so as to reflect a correlation between or among variables if:

- the variables can be measured so that their values reflect precise and measurable quantities of the variables;
- certain statistical analyses designed to determine the strength and direction of the relationship will be used; and
- the researcher was unable to introduce or manipulate either variable in any way or exert control over potentially confounding variables.

Unless specifically stated otherwise, when a correlation between variables is predicted in a research hypothesis, it refers to a linear correlation (see Weinbach & Grinnell [2015] for a description of other types of correlation). A linear correlation between two variables is a relationship in which one of two patterns exists: (1) high values (indicating large, quantitative measurements) of one variable are found (disproportionately) with high values of the other variable and low values of the first are found with low values of the second (described as a positive correlation); or (2) high values of one variable are found with low values of the other variable and vice versa (described as a negative or inverse correlation). These patterns can be seen in a graph called a *scattergram*, with values of one variable shown along the x-axis and the values of the second variable shown along the y-axis. In a scattergram, strong correlations will be reflected in a pattern of dots that approximate a straight line, hence the term *linear correlation*.

Like association, correlation does not prove causation. Many variables are highly correlated, yet the different values of one variable do not cause the different values of the other. In a research hypothesis that predicts a relationship of correlation, researchers may use the labels predictor variable and outcome variable (rather than *independent variable* and *dependent variable*) to describe the relationship between variables. Such a hypothesis is used when it is believed that values of one variable (the predictor variable) are a better predictor of values of the other (the outcome variable) than the other way around. If neither variable is seen as predicting the other, only that the variables co-vary, these terms would not be used.

One example of a correlational study, by Smith (2009), explored the relationships between levels of job burnout, intrinsic spirituality, and social support among perinatal social workers. Another correlational study (Acker, 2010) explored the relationships between the level of conflict that social workers experience when interfacing with managed care organizations and the worker's job satisfaction, organizational commitment, emotional exhaustion, and turnover intentions.

Causation

A research hypothesis that states a belief in *causation* goes out on a limb. It states that the values or value categories of the independent variable produce different values or value categories of the dependent variable. It leaves no room for the possibility that one or more confounding variables or any other phenomenon (such as a biased sample or chance) may have produced this apparent relationship within the cases studied. An example of a hypothesis that states a relationship of causation between variables is as follows: "Among adolescent psychiatric patients, group treatment produces lower rates of re-hospitalization than individual treatment." To demonstrate support for this relationship, three conditions would have to be present:

- The treatment must have occurred before the rehospitalization/ non-rehospitalization.
- There must be an association between the independent and dependent variables.
- All other explanations for rehospitalization or non-rehospitalization (besides the type of treatment given) must have been ruled out.

The first two conditions can be easily computed with statistical methods (discussed in Chapter 13). The third condition is more problematic. To rule out all other explanations for an outcome requires a research design that can be logistically difficult and may, perhaps, be unethical. The requirements of such a design will be discussed in Chapter 5.

Research hypotheses suggesting a relationship of causation between variables (also known as a cause-effect relationship) have historically been relatively rare in social work research. If the dependent variable is a human behavior (which is often the case), it is difficult to conclude that it is caused by the influence of any one variable, since social systems theory maintains that behavior or conditions have many interrelated causes. Because of ethical (see Chapter 2) and logistical reasons, it is sometimes difficult to identify, let alone control, potentially confounding variables that are likely to influence the relationship between the dependent and the independent variables.

Types of Research Hypotheses

If a researcher predicts that variables will be found to be related (association, correlation, or causation), it is possible to express that relationship in one of two ways within a research hypothesis: either a directional or a nondirectional hypothesis may be appropriate, depending on what was learned from the literature review.

In a directional (also called one-tailed) research hypothesis, the researcher not only asserts that the variables will be found to be related, but also predicts the direction of their relationship. In contrast, in a nondirectional (or two-tailed) research hypothesis, the researcher asserts that the variables will be found to be related, but does not wish to hazard a guess as to the direction in which they will be found to be related (Weinbach & Grinnell, 2015). An example of a directional hypothesis is as follows: "Among adolescent psychiatric patients, those who received group treatment will reflect a higher rate of rehospitalization than those who received individual treatment." An example of a nondirectional hypothesis using the same two variables is as follows: "Among adolescent psychiatric patients, there will be a difference in rehospitalization rate between those who received group counseling and those who received individual counseling."

Sometimes, variables are commonly believed to be related, but the researcher, on the basis of the literature review and practice experience, is convinced that they really are unrelated. In this case, a research hypothesis would predict that the variables will be found to be unrelated. An example of a hypothesis that predicts no relationship between variables is as follows: "Among adolescent psychiatric patients, those who received group treatment will have the same rate of rehospitalization as those who received individual treatment." In this example, the two variables were described as having no association. A research hypothesis that predicts there will be no relationship between the two variables is not the same as the null hypothesis. The null hypothesis is a theoretical construct that is supported when there is not enough statistical evidence to support the research hypothesis. We will discuss the null hypothesis and how it relates to the research hypothesis more in Chapter 13. Box 4.10 provides another example of the differences between these three forms of research hypotheses.

When Are Research Hypotheses Appropriate?

In some cases, there may not be enough known about an area to justify creating a hypothesis about how certain variables might be related or even which variables are relevant to the research problem, as in the case of many qualitative studies. Or, if there is enough information on which to base a hypothesis, the literature, research ethics, and/or researchers' knowledge of social work practice may reveal that it would be impossible to test the hypothesis. If either of these is the case, a testable hypothesis might not be appropriate.

Box 4.10	Three Types of Research Hypotheses
1. Directional	"Clients who receive individual therapy will score higher on the self-esteem inventory than clients who receive group therapy."
2. Nondirectional	"Clients who receive individual therapy will score differently on the self-esteem inventory than clients who receive group therapy."
3. No relationship	"Clients who receive individual therapy will score the same on the self-esteem inventory as clients who receive group therapy."

However, if previous efforts have been made to study the research question, if at least a tentative statement about the relationship between variables seems justified, if finding or not finding support for such a relationship would be a valuable contribution to knowledge, and if it appears that a method can be devised to test that relationship, one or more hypotheses may be in order. Whether a research hypothesis should suggest a belief in causation, correlation, association, or no relationship between or among variables is a judgment call based on the researcher's assessment of how much is already known about the answer to the research question, and what type of measurement of variables, control of potentially confounding variables, and data analysis is believed to be possible. Existing knowledge (and the researcher's belief in its credibility), as well as personal observations, would be used in deciding whether the research hypothesis should be stated in a directional or nondirectional form.

There is one additional guideline that should be used in formulating a research hypothesis. At this point, it should be obvious that when a hypothesis is tested, the results should produce a reasonable extension of existing knowledge as found in the literature. If it simply confirms what we already know, as in a replication study, it should be overtly recognized as a replication of a previous study. It is rare, however, that the knowledge generated by hypothesis testing represents a quantum leap from what we already know. The findings of most research make a relatively small contribution to filling a knowledge gap.

Although, as social work researchers, we might like to formulate and demonstrate support for research hypotheses, it is not essential to the goal of advancing our understanding of a research problem. One of the beauties of research is that, if it is conducted according to principles of scientific inquiry, which justifies our confidence in the research findings, we stand to advance knowledge by demonstrating either that the variables of interest are probably related or that they are probably not. For example, a researcher might hypothesize that one treatment intervention designed to reduce clinical depression is more effective than another. But if it is learned that both methods are really about equally effective (nonsupport for a directional research hypothesis), this null finding can still inform practice decision making. A manager might decide to discontinue the more expensive program and expand the less expensive one, thus improving organizational efficiency.

Wording of Research Hypotheses

It should be obvious by now that the way a research hypothesis is stated is important. Researchers should communicate exactly what they are predicting and nothing else. Goldstein (1969) offers some guidelines that continue to be used within the scientific community.

Consistency of Conceptualization

The variables within the hypothesis, the dependent (outcome) and independent (predictor) variables, should be stated at approximately the same level of abstraction or concreteness. For example, the research hypothesis, "People who hold college degrees have a high level of self-awareness," fails to meet this criterion of a good hypothesis. The first variable, "education level," is easily measured and would fall on the concrete end of the continuum of conceptualization. The other variable, "self-awareness," is far more abstract and difficult to measure with precision. A restatement of the research hypothesis that reflects greater consistency of conceptualization would be "People who hold college degrees will be more likely to receive a score of more than 80 on the Smith and Jones Scale of Self-Awareness than those who do not hold a college degree." Or, by moving education to a more abstract level, we could state "People with high achievement will have a higher level of self-awareness than those with low achievement."

Relevance to the Problem

Good hypotheses, when tested, will generate knowledge that has the potential to contribute to the alleviation of the research problem. This criterion seems obvious. Why would a researcher ever state and test a research hypothesis that is unrelated to the problem? It can happen, usually unintentionally. Sometimes, in the process of reviewing the literature, researchers can get sidetracked, losing sight of why they wanted to study the problem in the first place. They emerge with some very justifiable and logical research hypotheses that unfortunately have little or no relationship to the problem or its solution. This generally occurs because the broad research questions were not well formulated and did not provide enough focus. With good, broad questions, this problem is less likely to occur.

Completeness

A research hypothesis should be stated as completely as possible. The person reading it should not wonder about the researcher's meaning. A sure indicator that a hypothesis is incomplete is the use of words that suggest comparison without the presence of a reference point. For example, the research hypothesis, "Women under age thirty are more assertive," lacks completeness. It leaves the reader in doubt about what exactly the researcher believes to be true about the assertiveness of women under thirty. Are they more assertive than women over thirty, than men under thirty, than all men, or than whom? A research hypothesis that would be considered more complete is, "Women under age thirty are more assertive than women thirty and older." Phrases like "faster," "more frequently," and so on are useless in communicating the researcher's beliefs unless a reference point (for example, a comparison group) is included in the hypothesis.

Specificity

Specificity requires that the words chosen to describe the variables in the research hypothesis and the relationship believed to exist between them should suggest only one meaning to the reader of the hypothesis. The researcher has the responsibility to ensure that a research hypothesis is stated so that no misunderstanding can result. For example, the hypothesis, "Poorly timed marital counseling will reflect a low success rate," lacks specificity (in addition to having other problems). The expression "poorly timed marital counseling" probably refers to the time within a couple's relationship history that they have chosen to seek marital counseling. But we cannot be sure. It may also refer to social workers' tendency to let their appointments run over the time scheduled, or the time of day the appointments were scheduled.

Specificity requires that the words chosen to describe the variables in the research hypothesis and the relationship believed to exist between them should suggest only one meaning to the reader of the hypothesis.

Potential for Testing

In order to examine a possible relationship between or among variables, it is necessary to measure those variables with reasonable precision. Different cases must be able to be sorted into different groups (assigned value labels or values) in such a way that each case clearly falls into one and only one group. Some variables seem almost to defy objective measurement and therefore are inappropriate for inclusion within research hypotheses. For example, teachers and students continue to disagree on what constitutes effective teaching or on what the characteristics of good leadership are. A research hypothesis, "Good teachers will exhibit leadership within the classroom," would be a difficult one to test until we can achieve better agreement on how to measure both good teaching and leadership. Like beauty or a good personality, they remain a little too subjective to be able to measure objectively. However, another research hypothesis, "Teachers who post office hours are more likely to receive higher teaching evaluations than those who do not post office hours" is more testable. Here both variables are easily measurable.

SUMMARY

In this chapter, we looked at:

- The term *literature review* refers to both a process of referring to existing knowledge at different points in the research process and to a product, namely, a section of a report or chapter of a book. The process of reviewing existing knowledge about a research question can shape our thinking about the question and its possible answer. We discussed the purposes and objectives of completing a literature review.
- The pros and cons of including various potential sources of knowledge in the review of the literature section of a research report were discussed, with special focus on how the selection of a source can affect the credibility of the researcher and the research findings.
- Two of the important products that may emerge from completing the literature search of existing knowledge: focused research questions and hypotheses. In both primarily qualitative and primarily quantitative studies, the researcher may use the knowledge gained from the literature review to state the research question or questions more precisely, reflecting a more specific focus of the research.
- Existing knowledge sometimes suggests a possible answer to one or more focused research questions. The researcher then goes even further and draws conclusions from the literature in the form of one or more research hypotheses that will be tested.
- Terms were defined that are essential to the understanding of hypotheses: *variable, demographic variable, value label* or *value, frequency, dependent variable, independent variable, outcome variable, predictor variable, confounding variable, and control variable.*

- Terms used to describe the nature of a relationship between variables (*association*, *correlation*, and *causation*) were differentiated, and the forms that a research hypothesis can take (*directional, nondirectional,* or *no relationship*) were explained.
- Finally, the importance of wording in hypothesis construction was emphasized throughout this chapter.

MyEducationLab® for Research

Try the Topic 3 Assignments: Reviewing the Literature and the Topic 3 Study Plan.

Take the Chapter 4 Chapter Review Quiz.

5

Quantitative Research

In both qualitative and quantitative research, the review of existing knowledge is used to develop well-articulated, focused research questions. In quantitative studies, it often allows the researcher to develop research hypotheses as well. In all types of research, existing knowledge helps the researcher make decisions about how the research should be conducted, what is generally referred to as the *research design*. Chapters 5 through 8 will look at various research designs and methods. This chapter is devoted to research designs used in quantitative research studies. Chapter 6 will turn to various methods that are used primarily to conduct qualitative research studies. Chapter 7 focuses on techniques used to evaluate social work programs, and Chapter 8 looks at how social workers can evaluate their own social work practice using single-system evaluation.

WHAT IS A RESEARCH DESIGN?

A review of existing knowledge reveals what is already known about the research problem and the methods that have been used to study it. It thus suggests to us what specific research methods and strategies are best suited to conduct further inquiry. A *research design* is a plan to find answers to our research questions and/or to test any hypotheses that were formulated. The design of a research study is a response to a series of questions:

- Where and when should the research be conducted?
- What data should be collected?
- From whom can the data best be obtained?
- What would be the best way to collect the data?
- How will research participants be located or selected?
- What information will be sought?
- What variables will need to be measured?
- How and when should they be measured?
- Are there other variables that will need to be controlled?
- If so, how should this be accomplished?
- What unavoidable methodological limitations will exist, and how can their effects be minimized?
- How should the data be organized and analyzed?
- How should research findings be disseminated?

The research design serves as a plan for the latter stages of the research. The answers to the preceding questions are not arrived at independently of each other. The decision making process is made easier because these questions and their answers are interrelated. Having determined the answer to one or more of them, the answers to other questions often become quite obvious. For example, the selection of certain individuals to provide research data is likely to influence the general method of data collection used. Similarly, the way variables are measured and the way research participants are selected generally suggest the most appropriate type of statistical analysis to use. If one examines the ways that research has been conducted in the past, the interrelatedness of the preceding questions becomes readily apparent, and certain patterns emerge.

CATEGORIZATIONS OF RESEARCH DESIGNS

The terminology used to describe the design of a research study can be confusing, because the design of a given research study can be (and often is) described in a number of ways and at several levels. We discussed two of the most general of these characterizations back in Chapter 1. Describing research as either *basic* or *applied* communicates how and when the knowledge derived from a study is intended to be used. The findings of a study are designed to either (1) contribute to our professional knowledge base (basic) or (2) be of immediate use for addressing a problem, answering a question, or making a pending decision (applied). We also described predominantly *quantitative* and predominantly *qualitative* research. These terms suggest reliance on certain research methods, the nature of the data that are collected, and the method of analysis used, as well as other distinguishing characteristics (see Box 5.1).

In this chapter, we will look at three additional ways research studies can be categorized: 1) cross-sectional, pretest–posttest, and longitudinal designs; 2) exploratory, descriptive, and explanatory studies, and 3) pre-experimental, experimental, and quasi-experimental designs. These different terms suggest how and why research is conducted, how many times key variables are measured, what general methods for acquiring data are used, and what type of knowledge is sought. In the last of these categorizations, we will look at specific research designs within each of the categories that have been developed and used effectively in past research. They have become standards or models for answering certain types of research questions. These designs are displayed graphically to reflect certain key features of the design, such as the number of research samples that are used, whether participants were randomly assigned to groups, and the order in which interventions and observations are introduced during the study. However, these graphic representations of the research design do not provide a detailed description of how a given research study should be conducted. They merely offer a general framework on which to build the specifics needed to conduct the research. We would still need to supply the specifics, and make sure they are properly executed.

Box 5.1 Qualitative and Quantitative Research	
Qualitative Research	**Quantitative Research**
• Is admittedly subjective	• Seeks to be objective
• Seeks to understand	• Seeks to explain, predict
• Uses inductive logic	• Uses deductive logic
• Produces hypotheses	• Tests hypotheses
• Data analyzed as collected	• Data analyzed after it is collected
• Researcher is the instrument	• Reliance on standardized instruments for measurement

CROSS-SECTIONAL, PRETEST–POSTTEST, AND LONGITUDINAL DESIGNS

One way to describe a research design in general terms is to state the number of times observations or personal contacts will occur or key variables will be measured and, to a lesser degree, the length of time over which the research is conducted. Three terms are frequently used for this purpose: cross-sectional, pretest–posttest, and longitudinal research.

Cross-Sectional Designs

In *cross-sectional designs*, observations are made at one point in time, with all variables measured as simultaneously as possible. We would seek to acquire *a snapshot in time*, and then to draw conclusions about what has been observed. Conclusions may include a description of the distribution of certain variables, such as how many people experience one problem as opposed to another one or how severe a problem is. They may also answer questions or test hypotheses about the relationships between variables. For example, one group of social work researchers (Schwinn, Schinke, & Trent, 2010) analyzed cross-sectional data to explore gender and mental health influences on urban adolescents' use of alcohol, tobacco, and illicit drugs. While they found that substance use did not differ by gender, they found that it was associated with greater symptoms of depression, anxiety, and hostility.

Pretest–Posttest Designs

In *pretest–posttest designs* (sometimes called *before and after designs*), we would conduct observations or interviews or measure key variables twice, generally before and after an event. In evaluation research, the event is likely to be a social service or intervention that is offered to clients or some other life experience to which people are exposed. A pretest measurement is used to determine just how much change occurred in the interim between the first and second measurements. That can be important information in helping determine the effectiveness of a social work intervention. For example, social work researchers (Gonzales-Prendes & Jozefowicz-Simbeni, 2009) evaluated the effect of cognitive-behavioral treatment on anger and paranoid ideation for a group of men being treated for anger issues. By comparing pretest and posttest scores, they found that both anger and paranoid ideation were reduced after the treatment was completed.

Longitudinal Designs

A *longitudinal design* involves conducting observations or interviews or measuring key variables more than twice, often many more times, and sometimes over a long period of time. All longitudinal research designs share a single characteristic—they entail the repeated study and/or measurement over time at predetermined intervals. Longitudinal studies are designed to study change, but they try to find out more than simply whether or how much change occurred. They seek to identify exactly when change occurred and what phenomena were associated with the change. Only longitudinal research can provide this type of valuable knowledge. For example, in one longitudinal study, social workers McMillen and Raghaven (2009) interviewed foster care youth a total of nine times between their 17th and 19th birthdays to determine if their use of mental health services changed after they "aged out" of the foster care system at age 18. They found that all types of mental health service use dropped dramatically after these youth left foster care.

Three additional adjectives are often used in describing longitudinal research. They reflect differences in the way that a sample of research participants is selected for a longitudinal study. The *trend study* entails drawing a sample of participants at different points in time from a pool of potential participants that tends to change over time. For example, a group of students may be selected at random from a social work program each year to participate in a study to assess changes in attitudes toward research. Although some students may appear in the sample selected in two or more years, the sample of students will be different each year. The overall trend in changes in attitude within the program, but not within individual students, thus can be observed.

In the *cohort study*, the pool of potential research participants does not change, but the specific cases selected for study differ during the different stages of data collection. For example, a class of full-time students might be measured regarding their attitudes toward research over an academic year. Assuming that the class suffered no attrition or added no new members during the year, the class would be known as a cohort. Participants would be selected at random from the class at different points in time. No two groups selected for study would likely be identical in terms of which students would be included, but each group selected would represent the class at the various points of data collection.

In the *panel study*, the same group of research participants are studied over time. In our example of a study to examine changes in student attitudes toward research, a randomly selected sample of students would be selected and then they would be studied over their student careers to monitor any changes in their attitudes. Only attrition would result in any change in the composition of

Research-informed Practice or Practice-informed Research

Behavior: Apply critical thinking to engage in analysis of quantitative and qualitative research methods and research findings.

Critical Thinking Question: Using middle-school students as the sample, describe how a trend study, a cohort study, and a panel study would differ in how research participants are selected.

the group. The infamous Tuskegee studies, described in Chapter 2, provide an example of a longitudinal study that used the panel method.

Most longitudinal studies are designed to document change over a long period of time. Longitudinal studies can last for a few days or a few weeks, but more typically they are conducted over a period of years. Some have gone on past the lifetime of the researchers who originally designed them and have been carried on by others. They are well suited to document and learn more about the existence of certain patterns of behaviors over time. Good examples of longitudinal research are the studies of a large number of terminally ill patients conducted by Elisabeth Kübler-Ross (1989) and her associates over several decades. The researchers were able to identify five predictable stages in the dying process and describe them in detail. As a result, hospice social workers and others who work with people who have a terminal illness now possess greater insight into their clients' behaviors and are better able to help them come to successful resolutions relating to their impending death.

The findings of other longitudinal studies in the area of grief and loss (Benoliel, 1985) have similarly proven invaluable to the social work practitioner. For example, we now know that the time around the first anniversary of the death of a loved one is often accompanied by depression and that anger at a deceased loved one is a very predictable phenomenon at certain stages of the grieving process. Consequently, counseling now can focus on helping clients anticipate and deal with anniversary depression, and to verbalize, better understand, accept, and work through their anger toward the deceased.

Longitudinal designs can yield knowledge not readily accessible using other designs. Slowly developing changes and up-and-down fluctuations in behaviors and phenomena, which can be identified and plotted by repeated measurements over long periods of time, would be missed using cross-sectional or pretest–posttest designs. Longitudinal

---

Box 5.2 Examples of Cross-sectional, Pretest–Posttest, and Longitudinal Designs

Design	Example
Cross-sectional	All students at a university are anonymously surveyed in April 2017 to ascertain the prevalence of marijuana use.
Pretest–Posttest	Students who participate in an 8-week marijuana addiction group complete a questionnaire on drug use and attitudes toward it before and after the group.
Longitudinal	
• Trend study	A random sample of students at the university is selected and surveyed in May of each year for 10 years to analyze the trend in marijuana use.
• Cohort study	Each year, for the four years that they are at the university, a random sample of students is selected from the freshman class of 2017 to see how attitudes and use of marijuana changed while they were in college.
• Panel study	A random sample of students from the freshman class of 2017 is selected. They are then surveyed in May of each year over the four years they are at the university to see how their attitudes and use of marijuana changed while they were in college.

designs alone tell us when changes occur and help us predict their occurrence with reasonable accuracy.

The major drawback to using longitudinal designs is cost. Researchers are often unwilling or unable to make the expensive, long-term commitment that is necessary to properly conduct them. Because they take so long to complete, researchers who hope to build an academic or scientific career around publication of numerous research papers tend to shy away from them since one can spend a decade or longer on a longitudinal study that may result in a single published scientific paper. However, such studies may be more substantive and often produce more definitive answers to research questions than cross-sectional or pretest–posttest studies. See Box 5.2 for examples of cross-sectional, pretest–posttest, and longitudinal designs.

EXPLORATORY, DESCRIPTIVE, AND EXPLANATORY STUDIES

Another way to characterize a research design in general terms is to describe it as exploratory, descriptive, or explanatory. The terms describe the primary type of knowledge that the study seeks to acquire and the primary methods used for acquiring the knowledge. Knowledge building in a given problem area is a cumulative process. As we suggested in Chapter 1, uncovering and disseminating knowledge is a systematic process that occurs over time. It is rarely (if ever) the work of one individual. That's why social work researchers review the past literature in order to tie their research to existing knowledge. They want to build on the work of others, and their findings will in turn help to facilitate the work of subsequent researchers. Sometimes the process occurs relatively rapidly, but more typically, progress in knowledge building is slow work. It entails the use of a variety of methods (designs) that occur most often in a certain logical sequence. When very little is known about a problem and there are many more questions than answers, *exploratory* research designs are indicated. These designs are used when a researcher is exploring a subject area that is relatively new and unstudied. They can be either qualitative or quantitative, and are often a mixture of both. As knowledge in an area accumulates, *descriptive* designs are both possible and indicated. These studies attempt to describe situations and events. Once the general characteristics of a problem are understood, descriptive studies are in turn replaced by *explanatory* designs, which have the potential to provide more definitive answers to certain types of questions. Because there is a logical sequence in which different designs are employed in the study of a research problem, they can be placed on a continuum such as that shown in Box 5.3. Some writers (see Rubin & Babbie, 2012) add *evaluative research as* a fourth type of research that seeks to evaluate social policies, programs, and interventions. Others place evaluative studies in the category of explanatory research.

An important task for us when reviewing existing knowledge is locating just where on the continuum our own research should fall, that is, what type of research should we undertake? For example, if a review of professional literature reveals that virtually all of the past research on a problem has been of an exploratory nature, explanatory research may be premature. Descriptive research designed to expand the current description of the problem and the conditions that surround it would be more appropriate. Conversely,

---

Box 5.3   The Knowledge-Building Continuum

Exploratory → Descriptive → Explanatory

Example Using Cyber-Bullying as Our Research Problem:

An *exploratory study* might interview 20-30 adolescents in the local high schools and middle schools that have reported cyber-bullying to the school counselor or teachers in order to learn which forms of bullying occurred.

A *descriptive study* might send out a survey to all students in middle and high schools in the school district to determine the prevalence of the problem

of cyber-bullying and the specific behaviors that the adolescents have experienced.

An *explanatory study* might bring in an expert on cyber-bullying to conduct a 2-day workshop for adolescents who have experienced cyber-bullying. The workshop could focus on how to respond to cyber-bullying and prevent it from re-occurring in the future, and a brief questionnaire could be completed by the adolescents before and after the workshop to determine if the workshop improved their self-confidence in dealing with the cyber-bullying problem.

---

if the professional literature contains reports of explanatory research that have begun to isolate the cause of the problem, exploratory or descriptive research would not seem appropriate. The existing level of knowledge would suggest that such research would be unnecessary and redundant and that, perhaps, it is time to conduct evaluation research designed to test the effectiveness of interventions (prevention or treatment) in order to make a contribution to evidence-based practice.

Exploratory Research

In exploratory research, we often don't even know what it is we need to know!

Exploratory research is appropriate when problems have been identified but our understanding of them is quite limited. It is conducted to lay the groundwork for other knowledge building that will follow. Exploratory designs are predicated on the assumption that we need to know more about something before we can begin to understand it or attempt to confront it using intervention methods with high potential for success. In exploratory research, we often don't even know what it is we need to know!

In an exploratory study, the researcher begins his or her inquiry without much insight into the research problem, as is often the case in predominantly qualitative studies. Because the relevant variables cannot yet be specified, there can be no hypotheses to test. However, a frequent goal of exploratory research is to derive hypotheses for future research endeavors.

Similarly, selection of research participants or cases for study is usually not a rigorous or exacting procedure when exploratory research designs are used. There may be few cases studied (sometimes the only ones that we can identify or to whom we have access), or a large number may be selected to learn as much as possible about the problem. In either instance, because the population is often not clearly defined yet, there are usually no legitimate claims to the sample being representative of the overall population. We do not wish to imply that persons who conduct exploratory research employ a more haphazard approach to knowledge building than those who use other designs. Good exploratory research is always carefully planned and conducted using specific methods and according to established guidelines. But researchers who conduct exploratory research must work with less "pre-knowledge" than those who use other research designs.

Thus, exploratory designs are employed to begin the process of knowledge building about a problem or focused question. For example, prior to the 1960s, exploratory research was used to study child abuse. In the early 1980s, it was used for studying spouse abuse and the problems of people with HIV infection. In the 1990s, it was used to study the phenomenon of bullying within school settings. Early in the twenty-first century, exploratory research was used to study cyber-bullying, as we were just beginning to recognize the existence of a problem that did not exist before the widespread availability of electronic communication. Exploratory studies try to conceptualize exactly what a problem is, the degree to which it is recognized as a problem, what forms it takes, and what variables might relate to it.

Descriptive Research

The accumulation of the findings derived from exploratory research makes it possible to design studies that allow us to gather *descriptive* knowledge. In predominantly qualitative descriptive studies, the researcher often seeks to describe the variety of ways that people experience or perceive something. In descriptive research that is predominantly quantitative, measurement and description of relevant variables (those identified using exploratory research designs) and the distribution of their values is usually the goal. For example, research on the problem of child abuse moved beyond exploration and into description by the late 1960s and early 1970s. Studies sought to measure its patterns of incidence and severity and chronicle its different forms. The major relevant variables had already been identified through exploratory research; it was now possible and desirable for researchers to measure how the variables were distributed and to see if there were any patterns of relationships (associations or correlations) between and among them.

Quantitative descriptive research seeks to better understand and measure how variables are naturally distributed. It does not entail introducing or manipulating variables to see how other variables are affected. Thus, support for a relationship of causation between variables would not be possible using descriptive methods. Although seeking support for relationships between variables is not a major objective of most descriptive research, we sometimes see hypotheses tested in quantitative descriptive research designs. When we do, they predict a relationship of association or correlation, rather than causation. In one common type of descriptive study, the census, it is often possible to detect apparent associations or correlations that appear promising and worthy of additional study.

In quantitative descriptive research, we hope to generalize from cases that were part of the research study to the whole population. Thus, it is critical that we select and study cases that are typical or representative of the entire group (see Chapter 9 for sampling techniques). Accuracy of the measurement of variables also takes on great importance (see Chapter 10). Quantitative descriptive research is only as good or as bad as the representativeness of the sample of cases that are studied and the accuracy of the description that it produces.

In predominantly qualitative descriptive studies, acquiring a representative sample of research participants is less important than in predominantly quantitative studies. What is often sought instead is diversity, for example, the widest possible variety in the way participants experienced some event such as family violence, how they perceived it, the range of meanings they attributed to it, and so forth. We again want to emphasize that studies are often a combination of both qualitative and quantitative methods. Exploratory, descriptive, and explanatory research can all include both qualitative and quantitative components.

Explanatory Research

Exploratory and descriptive designs seek primarily to understand a problem and the factors that are associated with it. Although some design variations of exploratory and descriptive studies may give hints as to which solutions might be effective, it is explanatory research that yields more definitive answers as to what might cause the problem and what intervention methods are effective in treating or preventing it.

At some point, the knowledge about a problem may have advanced sufficiently to justify the use of *explanatory designs*. Exploratory and descriptive designs seek primarily to understand a problem and the factors that are associated with it. Although some design variations of exploratory and descriptive studies may give hints as to which solutions might be effective, it is explanatory research that yields more definitive answers as to what might cause the problem and what intervention methods might be effective in treating or even preventing it.

In quantitative explanatory research designs, the researcher uses hypothesis testing to try to verify possible relationships between variables. The dependent and independent variables have already been identified through exploratory research, and their distribution has been described through descriptive research. Cases are selected for study with the goal of making them as representative as possible of all cases in the population, including those not studied. We hope to verify the presence of important relationships (cause-effect ones) between or among variables. Whenever possible, confounding variables, which might misrepresent the true relationship between dependent and independent variables, are controlled. This is accomplished through randomization, manipulation of variables, or through statistical methods. If they cannot be controlled, every effort is made to determine the degree to which they may have obfuscated the relationship between the independent and dependent variables.

Explanatory designs seek to uncover causal relationships between variables. As we indicated in the previous chapter, causality is a special kind of relationship. It goes beyond association and even simple correlation. In a causal relationship, exposure to an independent variable (and to its different quantities or qualities) actually brings about changes in the dependent variable. As noted previously, there are three conditions that must be present in relationships in order to conclude that one variable (x) causes the changes in the other (y). These conditions are that

1. x must actually precede y in time order.
2. x and y must consistently co-vary.
3. All other explanations for changes in y must be ruled out.

All three of these conditions must be present in order to conclude that the value categories or values of x caused or produced the value categories or values of y.

PRE-EXPERIMENTAL, EXPERIMENTAL, AND QUASI-EXPERIMENTAL DESIGNS

Next, we will look at specific research designs that have been widely used in social work research. These designs are categorized as either *pre-experimental*, *experimental*, or *quasi-experimental*, on the basis of the number of measurements taken and the type of comparison group, if any, that is used. Pre-experimental designs are those designs that do not attempt to control threats to the internal validity of the research study (see discussion of internal validity later in this chapter). These designs generally do not use a comparison group, and when they do, only one measure of the dependent variable is taken. Experimental designs are more rigorous designs and do attempt to control threats to the study's internal validity. Quasi-experimental designs attempt to control threats to internal validity but are different from true experiments in that they do not randomly assign participants in the study to either the experimental or comparison group.

We will use the following standard notations to describe these research designs:

X = Exposure to the independent variable or treatment condition

O = Measurement of the dependent variable

O_n = nth measurement of the dependent variable in case of multiple measurements

R = Random assignment of participants to a group

Pre-Experimental Designs

1. Cross-sectional survey design. The cross-sectional survey design entails measurement of a characteristic in a defined sample or group at a given point in time. It is diagrammed rather simply as

$$O$$

where O represents one measurement of the dependent variable. For example, let's say the associate dean of a school of social work wishes to know what particular social work electives students might wish to take during the summer semester. A brief survey instrument describing proposed elective courses is developed and mailed to students. The associate dean determines from their responses which courses should be offered during the summer semester.

The cross-sectional survey design, as used here, provides information about what individuals may want, feel, or believe at a given time. This is its primary usefulness. The alternative would be to guess what students might want for summer course work and run the risk of offering courses that no one is interested in taking or not offering courses that students may want or need.

2. One-shot case study or one-group, posttest-only design. The one-shot case study design, is schematically noted as

$$X \quad O$$

where X represents exposure to a variable (such as a program or intervention) and O represents measurement of a dependent variable. Suppose a social worker in a neighborhood community center wishes to determine if eight weeks of English classes are helpful for teaching the English language to a group of Spanish-speaking residents who are seeking employment in an industry where a certain level of English fluency is required. The social worker identifies interested participants and arranges for them to receive the instruction. When the course is completed (eight weeks later), the group takes a brief paper-and-pencil test that measures proficiency in the English language. The social worker scores the tests and calculates the percentage of people who pass it. The major advantage of this design is simplicity. However, it does not provide any comparisons between how much the participants were already proficient in English before exposure to the class and how proficient they were following the eight-week course. Thus, one cannot conclude from this design that the program brought about any improvement in the participants' English proficiency. It does, however, suggest whether the participants will have enough English proficiency to meet the job requirements.

3. Longitudinal case study design. In the longitudinal case study design, research participants are exposed to an event or are introduced to an independent variable (e.g., an intervention) followed by several repeated observations, interviews, or measurements. It may be diagrammed as follows:

$$X \ O_1 \ O_2 \ O_3$$

Using our previous example, suppose the social worker wanted to determine if the proficiency in English language possessed by participants declines, is retained, or continues to grow over a six-month period. X represents participants' exposure to the eight-week language course. O_1 is the first measurement of their proficiency in English taken immediately following the course. O_2 is the second measurement of their proficiency in English taken three months later, and O_3, the third measurement, is taken after six months. From this design, the social worker is able to determine (1) the level of English proficiency after completion of the course, (2) if proficiency in English continued to improve over time, and (3) what (for example, employment) may have been associated with any continued improvement. We still cannot determine if participants' proficiency in English improved following completion of the course. For that, we must turn to the next design.

4. One-group pretest–posttest design. The one-group pretest–posttest design represents an improvement over the preceding designs, as it adds an opportunity to compare pretest and posttest measures of the dependent variable. It is symbolized as follows:

$$O_1 \ X \ O_2$$

where O_1 represents the first measurement of the dependent variable, prior to exposure of participants to the independent variable (X). Afterward, the dependent variable is again measured, O_2, and participants' pretest and posttest scores are compared. Using the previous example, the social worker asks the participants to complete the English proficiency test before the first session of the eight-week class (O_1). Following completion of this course (X), the participants complete the measure again (O_2). Because of the pretest measurement (O_1), it is possible to know how much change in the dependent variable actually occurred over the course of the intervention. This is the major advantage of the one-group pretest–posttest design. We still cannot, however, make the leap to conclude that the intervention caused any improvements found. For this, an experimental design, discussed in the next section, would be required.

5. Static group comparison design or posttest-only design with nonequivalent groups. The static group comparison design allows the researcher to compare two groups on their measurements of a dependent variable following exposure of one group to the independent variable. It is symbolized as follows:

$$X \ O \ O$$

where X is the independent variable and O is the only measurement, in this case, a posttest. For example, a social worker wishes to compare two groups on their levels of anxiety following a behavioral treatment program designed to reduce the anxiety symptoms in otherwise healthy adults. The experimental group consists of those people who are selected for inclusion in the treatment program, a cognitive-behavioral approach to treatment that lasts three months. Following completion of the program, the participants are measured on their level of anxiety using a standardized measuring instrument designed for this purpose. For comparison purposes, a group of similar adults who did not complete this program (perhaps they are on a wait list for receiving this service) is measured using the same instrument. Then a comparison is made between those who completed the treatment and those who did not. If the group receiving the treatment shows a lower level of anxiety than the comparison group, it is possible that the treatment had the desired effect. The major limitation of this design is that, because there was no pretest for either group, we really do not know if the two groups were equivalent on their anxiety levels before treatment began.

Experimental Designs

Experimental designs seek to explain the variations of a dependent variable in relation to one or more independent variables. When reputable researchers use the word *experiment* to characterize their research, they are stating that their research design has specific features that justify use of this word. An experimental research design is very rigorous, and its requirements make it the ideal design for generating cause-effect knowledge. In a true experiment, the following three requirements must be met:

- **The independent variable or variables are introduced or manipulated by the researcher.** For example, the researcher studying the relationship between enrollment in a specific job-training program and clients' success in finding employment must control who is enrolled in the program and who is not. Another researcher studying the effect of hours of treatment time on recovery in an inpatient psychiatric facility should control the exact number of treatment hours given to patients participating in the study.
- **There are one or more control groups, which are not exposed to the independent variable.** Using the previous example, the control group would consist of individuals who would not enroll in the job-training program. They would be identified, but not given the training. Their success rate in finding employment (the dependent variable) would be compared to the success rate of those selected for the program and given training. In the second example, individuals assigned to the control group might have their hours of treatment time set to the usual treatment time, while the treatment hours of the experimental group might be increased.
- **Research participants are randomly <u>assigned</u> to experimental and control groups.** *Random assignment* to groups, probably the key requirement of an experimental design that sets it apart from other designs, means that participants are assigned to the experimental and control groups in a completely random manner. In other words, each participant selected has an equal chance of being assigned to the control or experimental group. *Why is random assignment so important in an experiment?* When experimental research designs are used, random assignment

of research participants to experimental and control groups is the primary vehicle used for control of confounding variables. Random assignment relies on the laws of probability and what is likely to occur in the long run. It depends on the equalization effect that occurs naturally within groups (subsamples) when they are randomly drawn from the same pool. In our first example, if the researcher assigned cases to the experimental and control groups randomly and if the two groups were sufficiently large (see Chapter 9 for further discussion of sample size), the groups should be similar in all respects. This means that characteristics the researcher has reason to believe may affect participants' success in finding employment, such as motivation level, work experience, health, intelligence, physical appearance, or verbal skills, will tend to be similar in the two groups.

A highly desirable effect of random assignment is that, if performed correctly (and a reasonably large sample size is used), it will control for the effects of all confounding variables, even those whose existence we have no reason to suspect!

But what if the literature review failed to reveal one or more other confounding variables that might affect participants' success in finding employment? They may be neither logical nor obvious, something that we might not have guessed to be potentially confounding variables (e.g., number of siblings or birth order). Can these variables also be controlled through random assignment of cases to relatively large experimental and control groups? Yes. A highly desirable effect of random assignment is that, if performed correctly (and a reasonably large sample size is used), it will control for the effects of all confounding variables, even those whose existence we have no reason to suspect! This is why random assignment is such an important feature of experimental designs.

The process of randomization is so useful a method for controlling for confounding variables that researchers frequently use it in other ways within experimental designs. In our example of an experiment designed to measure the effectiveness of a job-training program, the researcher might randomly select trainers (from among those available) to facilitate the program. The researcher might also randomly select times of day to offer the training, rooms to be used, or any other potentially confounding variable that can be randomized without affecting the nature of the program being evaluated. This prevents the researcher from selecting trainers or times of day, for example, which could potentially bias the outcome of the research.

Experiments are the only research designs that possess the three characteristics listed above. True experimental designs help us rule out the possible effects of any other factors (besides the independent variable) that may be affecting the dependent variable. Consequently, among the basic designs we have described, experimental designs do the most convincing job of providing evidence that a cause-effect relationship between variables exists. They can help us conclude with reasonable certainty that the presence of a certain value of the independent variable caused a certain value of the dependent variable to occur.

Because all true experimental designs require rigorous control over certain conditions (assignment of people to groups, exposure to the independent variable, and so on), it can sometimes be difficult to implement them because of ethical concerns. In human services, social work researchers are committed to delivering the best possible services to each individual client, regardless of what a research design may indicate as desirable. Research must be of lower priority than service. However, with careful planning, experiments can be designed and implemented within human service organizations.

1. **Classic experimental design or pretest–posttest control group design.** The classic experimental design, also called the pretest–posttest control group design, does a good job of controlling for the possible effects of confounding variables. It is portrayed as follows:

$$R \quad O_1 \quad X \quad O_2$$
$$R \quad O_1 \qquad O_2$$

In this design, individuals are randomly assigned to one of two groups: an experimental group or a control group (the R denotes random assignment). The first line in the notation above denotes the experimental group and the second line denotes the control group. The dependent variable is measured for both groups (O_1). The experimental group is exposed to the independent variable (X), such as participation in a treatment program. Following completion of the program, the dependent variable is again measured for both groups (O_2). Then the following comparisons are made:

- **Comparison 1.** We would examine the O_1 scores for both groups, anticipating that these measures will be essentially equivalent since the research participants were randomly assigned to the two groups. In addition, these measurements can be used to compute changes between O_1 and O_2 in each group.
- **Comparison 2.** We would examine the O_2 scores for both groups, anticipating that O_2 for the experimental group will have changed in a predicted direction, whereas O_2 for the control group will not, or will change much less, because this group was not exposed to the treatment program. Assuming we find the expected change in O_2 for the experimental group, with no or much less change in the control group, it can be concluded with some degree of certainty that the change is due to exposure to the independent variable rather than to some other factor.

The classic experimental design requires that we have the authority to randomly assign research participants to one of two treatment conditions. It also requires that both groups are pretested and posttested. Finally, the design requires that individuals in the control group not receive the intervention being tested—a requirement that might be regarded as professionally unethical and therefore unacceptable. Given that we may not know the effectiveness of the intervention being tested, however, it may not be regarded as unethical to either withhold treatment from the control group, wait list the control group or, in some cases, offer the control group "treatment as usual."

2. **Posttest-only control group design.** The posttest-only control group design uses random assignment of participants to either an experimental or a control group to equalize the groups. This design is used when we believe that taking the pretest may have an effect on the posttest measurement; therefore, neither group is pretested. For example, suppose the measurement involves timing how long it takes the participant to create a pattern using different colored blocks. Even if there are several weeks between the pretest and posttest, the participants might reduce the time it takes to complete the

---

Ethical and Professional Behavior

Behavior: Make ethical decisions by applying the standards of the NASW Code of Ethics, relevant laws and regulations, models for ethical decision-making, ethical conduct of research, and additional codes of ethics as appropriate for context.

Critical Thinking Question: If you worked in a counseling center, what would be an ethical concern with regard to randomly assigning participants to either the control or the experimental group? Would the ethical concern change if you worked in a psychiatric hospital?

task the second time simply because they are familiar with the task. We may, therefore, choose a posttest-only design symbolized as follows:

$$R \quad X \quad O$$
$$R \qquad O$$

Where O is the only measurement of the dependent variable, which in this design is a posttest. Using this design, only one comparison can be made:

- **Comparison 1.** We would compare posttest measurements of the dependent variable between the two groups. If the posttest measurement for the experimental group is either significantly higher or lower than for the control group, then the intervention had an effect.

Even though there is no pretest to ensure equivalence of the groups prior to exposure to the independent variable, random assignment theoretically takes care of this. Pretests are required, however, when the measurement of the amount of change between pretest and posttest is important for the purpose of the study.

3. Solomon four-group design. The Solomon four-group design combines the classic experimental design and the posttest-only control group design. The two groups from the classic experimental design are used so changes between pretest and posttest can be examined. In addition, the two groups from the posttest-only control group design are used to determine if the use of a pretest may have contributed to changes in the dependent variable. The design is symbolized as follows:

$$R \; O_1 \; X \; O_2 \qquad \text{(Experimental group 1)}$$
$$R \; O_1 \quad\; O_2 \qquad \text{(Control group 1)}$$
$$R \quad\; X \; O_2 \qquad \text{(Experimental group 2)}$$
$$R \qquad\; O_2 \qquad \text{(Control group 2)}$$

Although the design may appear complicated, it is actually quite simple. Both of the experimental groups receive exposure to the intervention, while the two control groups do not. The experimental group 1 and control group 1 are pretested and posttested, while the experimental group 2 and control group 2 are posttested but are not pretested. At least four comparisons can be made using this design:

- **Comparison 1: O_1 and O_2 for both experimental groups.** We generally hope to find a significant positive change in both experimental groups. If there is a difference, it might indicate the effect of the pretest measurement on the posttest measurement.
- **Comparison 2: O_2 for both control groups.** These measures ought to be similar, because neither group received the intervention. Differences here could also indicate that the pretest measurement has had an effect on the posttest measurement.
- **Comparison 3: O_1 for all groups.** These measures ought to be similar, because random assignment has been used to assign participants to groups, and no one at this point had received the intervention, that is, the independent variable.
- **Comparison 4: O_2 for all four groups.** If the intervention was successful, posttest scores for experimental group 1 should be better than posttest scores for

control group 1, and posttest scores for experimental group 2 should be better than posttest scores for control group 2.

Quasi-Experimental Designs

Quasi-experimental research designs differ from true experiments primarily because they fail to randomly assign participants to either the experimental or control groups. Groups that are used for comparison purposes, but are not randomly assigned, are referred to as *nonequivalent control groups* or *comparison groups*. At times, there are compelling ethical reasons for not using random assignment to create true control groups. Practitioners may need to assign clients to the experimental or control group based on their judgment as to who will likely benefit from and not be harmed by the intervention. Whole books have been written on various experimental and quasi-experimental research designs. The classic remains a 1963 work by Campbell and Stanley and its subsequent revisions. We will look at two quasi-experimental research designs.

1. Nonequivalent comparison groups design or pretest–posttest comparison group design. When random assignment is not possible for ethical or logistical reasons, the nonequivalent comparison groups design is an alternative. It is portrayed as follows:

$$O_1 \quad X \quad O_2$$
$$O_1 \qquad O_2$$

In this design, individuals are assigned either to the experimental group or the comparison group. The dependent variable is measured for both groups (O_1). The experimental group is exposed to the independent variable, such as participation in a treatment program. Following completion of the program, the dependent variable is again measured for both groups (O_2). Then the following comparisons can be made:

- **Comparison 1.** We would examine the O_1 scores for both groups. We would hope that these two measures will be equivalent. However, without use of random assignment, these measurements may be different. Any differences found between the pretests must be considered when evaluating the outcomes of the posttests. Pretest measurements will also be useful to compute changes in each group from O_1 to O_2.
- **Comparison 2.** We would examine the O_2 scores for both groups, anticipating that O_2 for the experimental group will have changed in a predicted direction, whereas O_2 for the comparison group will not, or will change much less, because this group was not exposed to the treatment program. Assuming that we find the expected change in O_2 for the experimental group, with no or much less change in the comparison group, it can be tentatively concluded that the change is due to exposure to the independent variable. A further study using an experimental design could then be used to verify the outcome.

2. Time series design. In the time series design, several measurements are taken on a dependent variable over time, typically before and after exposure to the independent variable (another longitudinal approach). A typical time series design looks like this:

$$O_1 \quad O_2 \quad O_3 \quad X \quad O_4 \quad O_5 \quad O_6$$

These symbols indicate that three measurements of the dependent variable were taken prior to exposure of the group to the intervention. Following intervention, three more measures (over time) were taken of the dependent variable. An example will help illustrate the usefulness of this design in social work research.

A group of men meet weekly at a local mental health center to work on issues related to anger expression. During week 1, week 2, and week 3, the level of expressed anger is measured using a standardized measuring instrument designed for this purpose. The social worker introduces a new model of treatment at week 4. The model requires several weeks of group process. When enough time has lapsed for the new treatment to have taken effect, the men's expressed anger is again measured for three consecutive weeks.

Several comparisons are possible using a time series design. First of all, the three pretest measures allow the researcher to establish a baseline measurement of the dependent variable. The baseline measurement would be the average expressed anger score of the group over the three-week period prior to the introduction of the intervention in week 4, which would probably be more accurate than a single score measured on one day because the variable is likely to fluctuate naturally over time.

In cases where a control group is not possible, a time series design can help evaluate the effectiveness of a program. By repeatedly measuring the outcome or dependent variable, trends in the data can be identified. If these trends change significantly when the intervention is introduced, support exists for the possibility that changes in the dependent variable were caused by the independent variable. We will look at this concept more in our discussion of single-system evaluation research in Chapter 8.

The time series research design allows us to make at least two comparisons:

- **Comparison 1.** We can compare the average pretest measure to the average posttest measure to see if the intervention has possibly produced changes in expressed anger in the desired direction.
- **Comparison 2.** We can compare changes between O_4, O_5, and O_6 to see if any changes that occurred in the desired direction endured over time.

We have to remember that these are just example designs that have been used successfully in social work research. Many other designs can be found in the research literature. For example, a multiple time series design is created by adding a comparison group to the times series design. It would look like this:

$$O_1 \ O_2 \ O_3 \ X \ O_4 \ O_5 \ O_6$$
$$O_1 \ O_2 \ O_3 \quad O_4 \ O_5 \ O_6$$

The time series design can be easily transformed into an experimental design by adding a randomly assigned control group rather than the comparison group in the multiple times series design. The control group would have the same pretest measurements and the same posttest measurements taken as the experimental group, but without the intervention. Another variation would be two experimental groups randomly assigned to compare two different interventions (X and Y). This design would look like this:

$$R \ O_1 \ O_2 \ O_3 \ X \ O_4 \ O_5 \ O_6$$
$$R \ O_1 \ O_2 \ O_3 \ Y \ O_4 \ O_5 \ O_6$$

Design	Example
Box 5.4	**Examples of Pre-experimental, Experimental, and Quasi-experimental Designs**
Design	**Example**
Pre-experimental	A group of middle school girls completes a self-esteem inventory, participates in an 8-week program offered by the school counselor on building self-esteem, and then completes the inventory again after the program is completed (one-group pretest–posttest design)
Experimental	A group of middle schools girls are selected and half are randomly assigned to the experimental group and the other half to the control group. All the girls complete a self-esteem inventory, then the experimental group participates in an 8-week program offered by the school counselor, then both groups complete the self-esteem inventory again (classic experimental design)
Quasi-experimental	A group of middle school girls are selected and girls from two homeroom classrooms are assigned to the experimental group while girls from two other homeroom classrooms are assigned to the comparison group. All the girls complete a self-esteem inventory, then the experimental group participates in an 8-week program offered by the school counselor, then both groups complete the self-esteem inventory again (pretest–posttest comparison group design)

Such a study, completed by Plow, Mathiowetz, and Lowe (2009), compared two interventions designed to promote health and physical activity among clients with multiple sclerosis. Research participants were randomly assigned to either individualized physical rehabilitation or group wellness intervention. Two pre-intervention measurements were taken and two post-intervention measurements were taken on all of the participants. They concluded that the clients benefited more physically from the individualized rehabilitation and more mentally from the group wellness intervention.

The reader should not look at the designs described here as a definitive list of research designs. Designs are created to fit the needs of the researcher and the research study, not the other way around. These designs are just some of the more commonly used designs in the social work literature. See Box 5.4 for examples of pre-experimental, experimental, and quasi-experimental research designs.

CHARACTERISTICS OF A GOOD RESEARCH DESIGN

The fact that experimental research is characterized by rigorous hypothesis testing and methods that attempt to control for the effects of confounding variables has often led to the erroneous conclusion that they are always appropriate or are a standard by which to judge other research. Historically, there has been a pronounced bias in this direction. High school science teachers still sometimes denigrate any student research proposals that lack a control group when they are entered in science fairs. The knowledge sought may suggest the need for an exploratory or descriptive study or for a more qual-itative approach to knowledge building, but the student may pay the price for using a design that is still regarded by some as "unscientific" or otherwise inferior. Similarly, social workers seeking funding for their research from private foundations and gov-ernment institutions have struggled to compete with others who submit research pro-posals describing experimental or quasi-experimental designs. Qualitative studies, even though they may be exactly what are needed to address a research problem, face espe-cially difficult odds when grants are awarded. It is important to remember that designs should be selected based on the purpose and goals of each individual research study. It does a disservice to the field to assume that one research design is always preferable to another. Sometimes, the ideal research design is one that is most appropriate for the knowledge that is being sought and/or the only one possible, given ethical and logistical constraints.

Although no design is ever perfect (compromises are inevitable), we should strive to come up with the best design, given unavoidable limitations. The advantages of differ-ent design features must be considered. Generally, the selection of an appropriate design should be guided by the following conditions:

- **It is based on a review of existing knowledge.** It should be obvious why the design was selected, and the design selected should suggest that we have learned from the methodological successes and failures of others. A design may have come directly from a recommendation of the suggestions for future research sec-tion of another recent study, or it may represent a needed replication of research conducted years earlier.
- **It is appropriate for the level of knowledge that exists.** The design should promise to advance knowledge about a problem or question. It should not threaten to reinvent the wheel, such as attempting a descriptive study on a prob-lem that has been widely researched using experimental designs. Nor should it represent a quantum leap by, for example, attempting experimental research on a problem that has barely been explored and adequately described.
- **It is internally consistent in each of its components.** As suggested earlier, cer-tain design types can be recognized by groupings of characteristics. A design or design component should contain features that belong together, not a little bit of one and a little bit of another. For example, if a design claims to be both quan-titative and descriptive and attempts to generalize from research participants to the larger population, it should reflect careful attention to selection of a research sample that will represent the group being studied. The use of a group of partic-ipants selected less rigorously (as they might be in more qualitative, exploratory research) would not be appropriate. An experimental or quasi-experimental design would be expected to test hypotheses and contain methods for control of confounding variables. Once the researcher settles on a design type, the decision provides help in resolving such issues as the importance of obtaining a represen-tative sample or the degree to which control of potentially confounding variables is critical to the credibility of the research study's findings.
- **It is feasible.** The ideal research design may be impossible to implement because of economic, political, ethical, or logistical obstacles. It may have to be

compromised to deal with the realities that exist within the context of social work research. For example, descriptive research on gang members' initiation rites that is otherwise well designed will probably have to rely on sources of data other than firsthand observation. A feasible alternative might be to use interviews with community leaders or police officers who are closely affiliated with gang members. Such secondary sources, although probably not as good, would reflect a reasonable compromise. The research design would be *doable*.

Internal Validity

Internal validity refers to the amount of confidence the researcher has that only exposure to the independent variable produced changes in the dependent variable and that there are no other factors that accounted for these changes. Obviously then, internal validity is critical to any conclusions about causation drawn from experimental (or explanatory) research (but not for exploratory or descriptive studies). For example, suppose that a researcher asserts that, on the basis of research findings, "when counseling victims of rape, counseling method A produces a higher rate of success than counseling method B." Peers will agree with this conclusion only if they are convinced that, on the basis of the research design used, it seems to have internal validity; that is, if the differences in success rate observed appear to have been caused by the two counseling methods and nothing else. It was not client age, marital status, varying skill level of the social workers who counseled the clients, or any of the multitude of other potentially confounding variables that could affect the different rates of success. The research should have been designed so that these variables were all controlled in some way.

There are many factors that are generally acknowledged to threaten internal validity. Singleton and Straits (2005) offer a description of the most common ones.

- **Testing effects.** As we suggested in one of our earlier examples, the use of a pretest to measure the dependent variable may actually result in a change in measurements of the variable. Participants can learn from or be otherwise influenced by the process of completing a questionnaire or other measurement procedures. If feasible, the use of two or more experimental and control groups (as in the Solomon four-group design described earlier) can help us to assess the extent to which testing effects might represent a threat to internal validity.

- **Maturation or passage of time.** Some behaviors and problems seem to have a logical life cycle, or change naturally over time. For example, grief over the death of a loved one tends to subside over time, with or without counseling. Any conclusion that the presence of long-term bereavement counseling may have resulted in improved survivor functioning would thus have to be tempered with an assessment of the degree to which time (the threat to internal validity) might have contributed to apparent treatment success.

- **History.** An event sometimes occurs during the course of a research study that might have a major effect on the dependent variable, possibly a much greater effect than the intervention. Such a historical event may never make the newspapers. For example, it may be the firing of a popular coworker or the implementation of a new personnel policy that affects the job satisfaction of a group of clerical workers much more than the presence or absence of a new longer lunch break (the independent variable). Or the event may be truly historical in scope, such as a tsunami or a terrorist bombing. We could sympathize with researchers who, for example, might have been attempting to prove that "type of counseling affects anxiety level of clients" if one of these disasters occurred in the community during the course of treatment. The internal validity of their findings would almost certainly be questioned.

- **Statistical regression to the mean.** Sometimes it is desirable to select research participants who exhibit only the most extreme measurements of some variable. We might do this to be certain that our participants are those currently most in need of intervention and/or that they truly possess certain characteristics the researcher wants to try to affect (e.g., low assertiveness or a high level of hostility). Such participants will score very low or very high (respectively) on pretest measurements of the dependent variable. The second, posttest measurement of the dependent variable is likely to be less extreme than the first one. Would that mean that the intervention was successful? Maybe, but maybe not. Even if the intervention had no effect whatsoever, a less extreme measurement of the dependent variable might have occurred simply because participants were unlikely to repeat their extremely high or low measurement of the variable. There would be little room for the measurement of the variable to become more extreme, but plenty of room for it to moderate as part of its normal fluctuations. If feasible, a control group consisting of other individuals possessing equally extreme measurements can be used to determine whether statistical regression threatened the internal validity of research findings. If changes in the control group are found to parallel those in the experimental group, it was probably statistical regression and not the independent variable that caused the improvement in the dependent variable.

- **Instruments used.** If a pretest was completed using one version of an instrument and the posttest using another version (in an attempt to avoid the threat of testing effect), we must be certain that any differences observed between the experimental and control groups did not result from differences in the instruments used rather than the intervention. Were the pretest and posttest measurements equal in difficulty or otherwise comparable? Were the experimental and control groups given different versions, and were the two versions comparable? If two observers were used to measure behaviors, were the measurement procedures clearly operationalized so the same behaviors were consistently measured the same by the two observers?

- **Lack of sample comparability.** No comparisons between an experimental group and a comparison group following the introduction or manipulation of an independent variable are valid if the two groups are not comparable to begin with. As noted, ideally we would use random assignment in true experiments to improve comparability. But we often must use experimental and comparison groups in which participants are not randomly assigned. The samples may deliberately or unintentionally have been constituted in such a way that one group might have a higher likelihood of success. For example, what if we compare clients who attend a substance abuse counseling program with those who do not choose to participate after being referred for counseling? The counseling offered (the independent variable) may not be the reason that the people in counseling had a lower rate of recidivism. Perhaps the participants who chose to participate were just more highly motivated to get better than those who chose not to participate. Their recidivism may have been lower even if they had not participated in the counseling. In designs where random assignment is not used to create true control groups (quasi-experimental ones), we cannot be sure that the two groups were comparable in relation to important variables.

- **Experimental mortality.** The fact that we can (an often do) lose research participants or objects over the course of research can offer a threat to internal validity. This is particularly true in longitudinal research, but it can occur in other types of research as well. If the reasons why cases are lost are related to the dependent variable, the results can be misinterpreted and the findings may lack internal validity. For example, in a study of the effectiveness of a new method of addiction counseling, a control group may be used that receives the usual treatment. Clients could be randomly assigned to either the usual treatment or the experimental intervention. At the time of the posttest interview, the experimental group (those who received the new treatment) might reflect a much higher rate of success. But what if the experimental group lost 40 percent of its clients (and those clients are no longer available to be interviewed), whereas all clients in the control group agree to participate in the posttest interview. The lost 40 percent may reflect the same rate of treatment success as the remaining 60 percent in the experimental group that was interviewed. But, of course, they also may not. They may have dropped out of treatment because the treatment was so successful that they perceived it as no longer necessary, although that would probably be an overly optimistic interpretation of their behavior. It is also possible that they left because they concluded that their treatment was doing them no good, and they decided to devote the time they had been "wasting" to better pursuit of their addiction! If so, the conclusion that the experimental treatment was more successful than the usual treatment would be lacking in internal validity because of experimental mortality.

- **Ambiguity about direction of causation.** Sometimes in pre-experimental research designs, it could be argued that it was really the dependent variable that produced different values of the independent variable, rather than the other way around. For example, we might conclude in a study of a random sample of women who are homeless that inadequacy of diet (our independent variable) causes severe, untreated dental problems (our dependent variable). However, it may really be the other way around. Perhaps, the dental problems may make it difficult to eat certain nutritionally rich foods, thus resulting in an improper diet.

- **Diffusion or overlap of intervention methods.** If we hope to compare the effectiveness of two intervention methods, it is best if the methods are discrete and bear little or no similarity to each other. Unfortunately, this is not always the case. In the real world, blurring takes place over time, often because features of one intervention become imitated by practitioners of the other intervention method. Thus, any comparison is not a clean one. For example, suppose we wanted to find out whether support or confrontation is more effective in counseling spouse-abusing clients. Would the social workers assigned to use confrontation methods be able to stick to the method assigned to them? Would their treatment have elements of support? Would those assigned to be only supportive of clients occasionally lapse into a little confrontation? Perhaps both groups of social workers offering treatment will have learned over the years that certain elements of the opposite treatment method can be helpful on occasion and, consciously or unconsciously, they infuse them into their interventions. Then how will we be able to say that it was the treatment intervention (support or confrontation) that produced the different treatment success rates of the two groups of clients? Or if no difference in success rates were to be found, how do we know that the similarity between the two intervention methods used did not hide a real difference in the effectiveness of the methods?

These threats to internal validity should be regarded as the most common problems to be aware of, rather than a complete list. Experimental designs are more likely than other designs to produce findings with acceptable internal validity because they use true control groups consisting of participants who are randomly assigned to groups.

When findings in an experimental research study appear to have a high level of internal validity, it is possible to conclude that the values of the independent variable (and not something else) caused the values of the dependent variable among cases studied. But how far can the researcher generalize this relationship between variables? To all cases that were not selected for study? To all persons within the state who are similar to those studied? To all persons everywhere who are similar? These are issues of external, rather than internal, validity.

External Validity

External validity refers to the extent to which findings are believed to apply beyond cases that were actually studied to their population. External validity relates directly to the number and characteristics of the cases that were studied and to what degree they can be assumed to be representative of other cases in the population that were not studied. The keys to increasing external validity are *sample size* and *random sampling* (see Chapter 9). Random sampling means that we have randomly selected the research sample from the total population. For true random sampling to take place, every person in the population must have an equal chance of being selected as a participant in the research sample. In addition, having a large sample size increases the chance that the sample will be representative of the population. If the sample size is small, the chance of there being differences between the sample and the population (referred to as *sampling error*) increases. Therefore, randomly sampling a large sample from the population is one way to increase a study's external validity.

We want to emphasize here that external validity is not an either-or proposition. It is incorrect to say that a study either *has external validity* or *has no external validity*. The

Randomly sampling a large sample from the population is the way to maximize a study's external validity.

goal is to maximize the external validity by making sure the sample is large and as much like the population as possible. Suppose we want students at a university to complete a survey regarding their views on the economy. A method that would create very low external validity would be to interview the students in one section of the Introduction to Social Work class. Obviously, this sample would be small and would not, in any way, represent the university student population. Students in this class, for example, might be older and more likely to be female, have children, and be employed than the average university student. Therefore, their views on the economy would not be representative of the larger population. If we randomly selected ten courses across the university and surveyed the students in those classes, the sample would be more representative, and any findings would, therefore, be expected to have greater external validity. The sampling method that would maximize external validity would be to get a complete list of all students from the university (population) and select a large, random sample from the list. By using true random sampling and having a sufficiently large sample size, we can be reasonably confident that the views held by the students in the sample are representative of the views held by the student population.

Assessment

Behavior: Collect and organize data and apply critical thinking to interpret information from clients and constituents.

Critical Thinking Question: In obtaining a sample of high school teachers in Florida, describe one method of sampling that would have extremely poor external validity and another that would have very good external validity.

Obviously, good external validity (also referred to as broad generalizability) is important in explanatory research, which attempts to identify relationships between variables within research samples and provide evidence that the same relationships exist beyond those samples. If the external validity is considered limited, research findings lose value. However, external validity is also often important to researchers conducting quantitative descriptive research studies, because they often study a representative sample of people or objects in hopes of learning something about the larger population. In a descriptive study, a sample that is different from the population can tell us little or nothing (or even mislead us) about the characteristics of people not actually studied. A descriptive study with good external validity, on the other hand, can be useful to the social worker, providing tentative knowledge about clients or other people who may never themselves have been studied by researchers.

External validity is not nearly as important in exploratory studies as it is in explanatory or descriptive studies. In fact, many exploratory studies make no pretense of studying a representative sample of people or objects, often because one is simply not available. Internal validity, of course, is also a nonissue, because exploratory studies generally do not seek to find support for relationships between variables.

Research studies involving racial and ethnic groups raise some special concerns with regard to external validity. One issue is the use of generic labels when describing racial and ethnic groups in the United States. As the diversity of the American population continues to increase, the use of such labels in social work research is and will increasingly become problematic. For example, the term *Hispanic* is essentially a linguistic designation that refers to people from countries where Spanish is the dominant language and where cultural aspects, such as religion, music, art, dance, and food, are influenced by traditions emanating from Spain. However, findings from studies on one Hispanic group may not be generalizable to other nationalities or ethnic groups that are included in the

Hispanic population. There are distinct idiomatic differences, belief systems, and cultural patterns among and between groups, such as Cubans, Puerto Ricans, Dominicans, and Mexican Americans, who are part of the Hispanic mosaic in the United States. The failure to recognize these differences may lead to overgeneralizations from one group to another.

Differences within groups, such as in the Hispanic population, related to variables, such as nationality, social class, education, religion, language, immigration patterns, and degree of acculturation, influence responses in research and thereby determine the degree of external validity of a given research study. A similar issue must be addressed when using the term *black non-Hispanic*, which refers to people of African descent in the United States, South America, Africa, and the English-speaking Caribbean. The terms *American Indian* or *Native American* are generally used to describe 512 federally recognized tribes, who speak more than 200 dialects. *Asian, Pacific Islander* refers to more than 60 separate racial and ethnic groups. The desire of demographers and researchers to reduce this vast complexity into a few easily applicable labels can lead to a false sense of security in generalizing findings across and within racial and ethnic subgroups. In the research report, a detailed description should be provided of one's research participants and exactly how they were selected so the readers can assess the external validity of the research findings. We will look in detail at sampling techniques used to increase external validity in Chapter 9.

Any conclusions about the degree to which the findings of a research study possess both internal validity and external validity are always a bit subjective. Ultimately, they are based on one's individual judgment of the quality of the research design and the limitations that it contains. Our responsibility as researchers is to describe a research

Engagement

Behavior: Apply knowledge of human behavior and the social environment, person-in-environment, and other multi-disciplinary theoretical frameworks to engage with clients and constituencies.

Critical Thinking Question: If you wanted to obtain a sample of Native Americans in the United States, what would be some of the challenges of trying to make your sample representative?

Box 5.5   General Terms Used to Describe Research

Term	Major Differences	Decision Criteria
Basic/Applied	Purpose, application of findings	Knowledge requirements
Qualitative/Quantitative	Methods used; data and its analysis	Knowledge sought
Cross-sectional/ Pretest–Posttest/ Longitudinal	Number and time of measurements	Knowledge sought
Exploratory/ Descriptive/ Explanatory	General nature of the research	Current knowledge level
Pre-Experimental/ Experimental/ Quasi-Experimental	Use of control/comparison groups; number and time of measurements	Resources; feasibility of random assignment

design honestly and completely and let the readers of the research report draw their own conclusions.

SUMMARY

In this chapter we looked at:

- Various categorizations of research designs. The general characteristics of a research design can be conveyed in a number of ways. As noted in Chapter 1, research can be described as 1) basic or applied or 2) predominantly qualitative or predominantly quantitative.
- Research studies can also be described as cross-sectional, pretest–posttest, or longitudinal, suggesting (among other things) how many times participants were observed or interviewed or certain key variables were measured and what questions the researcher was attempting to answer.
- Research can be described as exploratory, descriptive, or explanatory, suggesting (among other things) the kind of knowledge that was sought and how the researcher went about seeking it.
- Finally, specific research designs can be labelled as pre-experimental, experimental, or quasi-experimental. We examined a number of the designs within each of these categories, including the best known—the classic experimental design. Of course, even when using a commonly used design, it must still be "fleshed out" to meet the specific requirements of a given research study. Thus, every research design is different, tailored to answer the questions that are unique to the study. Box 5.5 summarizes some of what was discussed here and in Chapter 1.
- Research designs are never perfect. They are limited by logistical, ethical, legal, monetary, political, time, and other factors. However, given these constraints, some designs are better than others. We examined the most common criteria used in evaluating the quality of research designs—the degree to which they produce findings that possess internal validity and external validity.

MyEducationLab® for Research

Start with the Topic 1 Assignments: Introduction to Educational Research and the Topic 1 Study Plan and then try the Topic 6 Assignments: Selecting Measuring Instruments and the Topic 6 Study Plan.

For specific quantitative designs, try:
Topic 7 Assignments: Survey Research and the Topic 7 Study Plan.
Topic 8 Assignments: Correlational Research and the Topic 8 Study Plan.
Topic 9 Assignments: Causal Comparative Research and the Topic 9 Study Plan.
Topic 10 Assignments: Experimental Research and the Topic 10 Study Plan.

Chapter 5 Chapter Review Quiz.

6

Qualitative Research

In this chapter, we will present an overview of qualitative research, describing those methods that it frequently employs. We will also suggest criteria for evaluating qualitative research studies.

KEY CHARACTERISTICS OF QUALITATIVE RESEARCH

Most qualitative researchers agree that there is no specific definition of qualitative research. It can be viewed more as a group of methods that often contain certain key characteristics, such as studying research participants in their natural settings, interpreting events through the meaning ascribed to them, and interpreting the data with an open-minded viewpoint. Anastas (2004) defines the key characteristics of qualitative research:

1. Flexibility of method and procedure during the conduct of the study, often in response to findings as they emerge.

2. The collection of relatively unstructured data to describe the phenomena of interest in the words or actions of those who live them.

3. A scope of study that includes the observational context of the study, usually the one in which the phenomena of interest naturally occurs, as well as the decisions made during the conduct of the study.

4. A scope of study that includes the subjective experiences of the researcher and the research participant as data while also describing and analyzing them. (p. 58)

5. Many qualitative researchers advise locating a qualitative study within a specific epistemological tradition because there are significant differences among them. Five epistemological frameworks found in qualitative evaluation are postpositivism, pragmatism, phenomenology, interpretivism or constructivism, and critical, normative science. (p. 59)

These frameworks share certain features that make them particularly useful in qualitative research. *Postpositivism* is a scientific framework that recognizes that the researcher's values and biases, as well as the theories and background knowledge involved in the research study, will affect what is observed throughout the study. *Pragmatism* emphasizes the practical uses and successes of ideas, theories, and knowledge, and thus believes in acting on these theories to test them in real situations. *Phenomenology* recognizes that all experiences are subjective, and depend on the values, life experiences, and biases of the person having the experience. *Constructivists* go one step further and assert that our knowledge and experience of the world is our own creation, and *interpretivism* guides researchers to analyze *why* people behave the way they do, as well as *why* and *how* they make the decisions that they make.

As we discussed in earlier chapters, qualitative research studies generally do not include research hypotheses to be tested. Pure qualitative research is often interested in an ongoing process, event, or problem about which little is known; therefore, findings cannot be predicted. The researcher attempts to maintain a broad perspective in order to develop a comprehensive understanding of the phenomenon being studied, and the study is generally carried out in the setting where the phenomenon naturally exists. Holosko (2010) lists the following reasons why a researcher may select a qualitative approach to research: (1) one wishes to explore a topic or phenomenon of which little is actually known; (2) one wishes to study something that is sensitive and has emotional depth; (3) one may wish to capture an experience from the perspectives of those who live it and create meaning from it; (4) one may wish to delve inside a program and/or intervention; (5) one is a quantitative social work researcher who has reached an impasse in data collection, interpretation of data, and/or findings; and (6) one wishes to give voice to a group and merge social activism with research (pp. 345–346).

> The researcher attempts to maintain a broad perspective in order to develop a comprehensive understanding of the phenomenon being studied, and the study is generally carried out in the setting where the phenomenon naturally exists.

OBSERVER-PARTICIPANT ROLE

In qualitative research, we must decide what role we will play as observer, and how we will relate to the other participants in the study. Unlike in quantitative research, a qualitative researcher is free to act as a full participant, living fully within the setting of interest, at the other end of the continuum as an observer looking at the participants as a total outsider, or anywhere in between. Four distinct observer-participant roles have been defined (Gold, 1969): 1) *Complete participant*. In this role, we would actually become a full participant in the activity, program, or community that is being observed; 2) *Participant-as-observer*. In this role, we would act as a full participant of the group being studied, but we would not deceive the research participants in the group. They would be fully aware that we are conducting research; 3) *Observer-as-participant*. In this role, we would clearly identify ourselves as researchers, and although we would interact with other participants and perhaps even participate in certain group activities, we would not become full participants in the group being studied; and 4) *Complete observer*. In this role, we would not become part of the group being studied at all. In some cases, the research participants in the study are not even aware they are being observed. In other cases, they are aware of the observer's presence, but they do not interact with the observer at all.

Relationships between the observer and participant can be more complex in qualitative research than in quantitative research. When acting as a complete participant in a group being studied or even as a participant-as-observer, it is especially challenging to maintain one's objectivity. The qualitative researcher wants to understand the deeper meanings and experiences of the group members, but may, in some cases, still want to maintain the ability to see the phenomenon from a perspective that is different from the perspectives of the participants. Some qualitative researchers learn the ability to closely relate to other participants in some activities, then be able to step away and become the observer for the next activity. Others acquire the ability to simply maintain both perspectives simultaneously, acting as a full participant in the group and at the same time observing the activities from the perspective of researcher. See Chapter 11 for a more thorough discussion of the researcher-participant role as it relates to research in general.

QUALITATIVE RESEARCH TECHNIQUES

Many of the specific research methods used in qualitative research are also used in quantitative research. We will mention some of these methods here, but will describe them more fully in the appropriate chapters through the rest of the book. A few that are almost exclusively found in qualitative research will be discussed more fully here.

Sampling Techniques

Sampling techniques used in qualitative research are described in detail in Chapter 9. However, it seems appropriate here to point out the techniques that are particularly well-suited to qualitative research. Non-probability sampling, sampling that does not require sampling randomly from the larger population, is generally used in qualitative research. Often, the population has not even been clearly defined yet as qualitative research is often interested in areas of research that have received little attention. Therefore, the following non-probability sampling techniques are utilized most often:

- **Snowball sampling.** A sampling technique in which the researcher identifies a few participants who are willing to participate in data gathering. The researcher then asks these participants if they can refer any other people who also share the same problem or issue. Thus, using the snowball effect, more and more people can participate in the study.
- **Quota sampling.** This technique involves setting a quota for how many participants will be in each of a set of categories (e.g., male, female; older adults, younger adults; etc.) and then finding and interviewing participants until the quota for each category has been met.
- **Purposive sampling.** This technique involves selecting a sample of participants that will offer you the most complete and unbiased understanding of the phenomenon being studied. One example of purposive sampling is *deviant case sampling*. This technique is sometimes used in qualitative research and involves deliberately identifying cases that fall outside the norm with regard to some problem or characteristic. Because qualitative researchers acknowledge that they often know very little about the topic of interest, they study these deviant cases to ensure they haven't biased the outcome of the study with preconceived notions of what the outcome data will look like. *Maximum variation sampling* looks at participants that offer the most diversity on characteristics of interest,

and *homogeneous sampling* only looks at participants who share a very specific characteristic (e.g., an extreme score on a scale of disordered eating) of particular interest to the researcher.

In some cases, qualitative researchers do not even draw a sample. They simply select one person, group, or phenomenon and observe and record the events that occur. This is a form of the case study, described in more detail later in this chapter. Case studies often lead to other research studies, qualitative or quantitative, in which a sample of the newly conceptualized population is selected and studied.

Data Collection Techniques

A variety of data collection techniques have been developed to help us accomplish the goals of qualitative research. Qualitative data may include words from an interview, field journals, minutes from meetings, television shows, newspaper or journal articles, or other historical documents. Some of the more commonly used techniques for gathering qualitative data are:

- **In-person interviews.** Structured, semi-structured, or unstructured interviews are often used to collect qualitative data. Sometimes, data collection instruments are developed to assist in this process.
- **Focus groups and key informant interviews.** Discussion groups are often held in which a small group of people discuss the topic of interest. These can be structured or unstructured, and can allow the researcher to interview several people simultaneously.
- **Systematic observations.** Observations, structured and unstructured, are made and may be recorded on logs, in field journals, using audio/visual recordings, and so forth. Techniques such as *memoing* and *concept mapping* are used to record observations during interviews and informal meetings.
- **Secondary data.** Information that has already been gathered, including recordings or written materials, can be analyzed as qualitative data.
- **Client logs.** Client logs are used to gather both quantitative and qualitative information on specific events, feelings, and thoughts that are relevant to the problem being studied. Logs are particularly helpful to record detailed events that may be difficult for clients to remember at a later time.

As each of these data collection techniques may be used in quantitative research as well as qualitative research, they are described in greater detail in Chapter 11 in which we discuss methods for acquiring research data.

In qualitative research, data from personal interviews, focus groups, and informant interviews are often recorded in order to transcribe the participants' comments word for word after the interview is completed. The interview process itself is generally much more unstructured than interviews in quantitative research, allowing for changes to the interview format throughout the data collection process. Qualitative interviews are often very flexible, with only an overall plan rather than a list of detailed questions. There are even *informal conversational interviews* that are simply unplanned conversations that occur between the observer and the research participants during routine daily activities. If the conversations are not recorded, it becomes important to remember the exact words that the participant used so we can later record them accurately.

Data Analysis Techniques

Content analysis uses both qualitative and quantitative methods to analyze the content included in literature, interview transcripts, client logs, and many other types of information on a selected topic. In qualitative research, content analysis looks for patterns in the data, then for contradictions to the patterns in order to redefine the patterns or identify new patterns. Content analysis can be used to transform qualitative data into quantitative data by identifying, categorizing, and counting certain responses, ideas, etc.

Content analysis is a versatile form of secondary analysis, analyzing various types of pre-existing data sets. It can be used in predominantly qualitative studies, for example, in analyzing CD or DVD recordings of interviews in studies that use grounded theory methods (described below). Content analysis is cross-sectional, since the data are examined at one point in time. Yet, if those data were accumulated over a long period of time, they can be used to identify changes that occurred during the time that they were being accumulated, a feature associated with longitudinal research. Data sources may include:

- DVD or CD recordings of in-person interviews or focus groups
- client logs
- personal journals
- oral histories
- documents such as newspaper articles, professional journals, or congressional records
- movies or television programs
- minutes of meetings
- films or DVD recordings of social gatherings
- photographs
- recorded phone conversations
- e-mail or text messages

Content analysis generally entails a categorization and counting process, something that used to be a tedious process. The development of computer programs that can quickly scan various forms of human communication and, for example, count how often certain words or phrases appear, has made it much easier. As the technology for doing this continues to expand so that more and more types of communication can be examined by a computer, content analysis is likely to continue to gain in popularity.

One example of a study that used content analysis (Dauz Williams et al., 2010) examined the experiences of siblings of children with developmental disabilities. Interviews were completed with 151 parents of children with developmental disabilities, in which they were asked their perceptions of how other siblings in the home were affected by living with their brother or sister with a developmental disability. Researchers identified 363 themes, and found that over 60 percent of the parents felt that their children who were not suffering from the developmental disability nevertheless experienced increased risks for adjustment problems because of their home environment. The researchers were thus able to recommend additional intervention with this vulnerable population. Another content analysis (Bengtsson-Tops, Saveman, & Tops, 2009) examined interviews with thirteen staff members working with abused women suffering from mental illness. The aim of the qualitative study was to attempt to describe how these workers experience and understand their work with this vulnerable population. Findings suggested that workers experience their work as ambiguous and painful and as a result tend to act pragmatically to achieve concrete results through their interventions. Still another study (Timmerman, 2006) used content analysis to examine food journals to compare the restaurant-eating behaviors of women diagnosed as binge eaters to women who were dieting but did not report a history of binge eating.

The need for another type of content analysis has emerged during a time in which many people turn to the Internet for information on everything from recipes and movie reviews to medical diagnoses and medication choices. New studies are using content analysis to examine information found on the Internet to both learn from this information as well as evaluate its validity. For example, Moncrieff, Cohen, and Mason (2009) conducted a content analysis on a database of comments made by people about prescribed medications. They analyzed over 400 comments on five antipsychotic medications to understand the subjective experiences of people taking these prescribed medications. The researchers were able to learn a great deal about the desired benefits as well as the undesirable side effects of taking these drugs.

The main data analysis technique used in content analysis is called *coding*. Variables or concepts must be clearly conceptualized and operationalized so the data can be correctly identified and classified. Coding can focus on the surface content of data, such as the actual words included in the manuscript, or it can focus on the deeper meaning of the material. Coding that is more interested in classifying the underlying meaning of the participants' comments is most often found in predominantly qualitative research. Often, both levels of coding are used to add to the depth of understanding of the material being analyzed.

Qualitative researchers use the technique of *memoing* during the coding process to record notes to oneself and to others involved in the research process. These notes can be used to explain the meaning of the various codes defined throughout the coding process as well as ideas for future data collection, operationalization and conceptualization of research variables, additional questions to be added to interviews, new ways to categorize data, etc. Another technique, *concept mapping*, is used to help qualitative researchers map out the thoughts and ideas they formulate while coding the data. This may be in the form of a flowchart or in whatever graphic form is meaningful to the researcher. For a more detailed description of coding and other techniques used in content analysis, the reader can turn to thorough discussions provided by Krippendorf (2004) and Neuendorf (2002).

QUALITATIVE RESEARCH PARADIGMS

There are many different areas in research that have utilized predominantly qualitative approaches. In the next section, we will discuss some of the paradigms in which social work researchers have often selected qualitative research methods to study issues and problems. Box 6.1 summarizes the general purpose, the data sources each rely on most frequently, and the primary research activity this is employed by each of these methods.

Box 6.1   Qualitative Research Methods

Label	Purpose	Major Data Source(s)	Major Activities
Case study	Gain beginning insights	In-person interviews	Speaking, listening
Grounded theory	Develop theories, hypotheses	In-person interviews	Conceptualizing, verifying
Ethnographic	Understanding of a culture	Interviews, observation	Field research methods
Cross-cultural	Identify cultural differences	Interviews, observation	Field research methods
Feminist	Empowerment/advocacy	Widely varying	Widely varying
Participatory action	Social action/change	Interviews, focus groups	Suggesting new policies and guidelines

The Case Study

A case study is descriptive and generally more qualitative than quantitative. It combines observations of behavior with observations of attitudes and perceptions of research participants. The case study employs methods of data collection that rely heavily on the interviewing skills of researchers and their capacity to establish relationships of trust. As we shall see, there are some good reasons for the case study's continued popularity among social work researchers.

A case study is appropriate for situations where

The case study employs methods of data collection that rely heavily on the interviewing skills of researchers and their capacity to establish relationships of trust.

- **little is known about the area being studied.** Topics for which there already exists a substantive body of relevant knowledge are better studied using other research designs.
- **it is impossible to draw a representative sample of participants.** Participants are selected on the basis of their availability and willingness to participate in the research. There is no way of knowing if they are typical of others who are involved in the same behavior.

Researchers conducting case studies collect their data from just one or a few cases. Usually the number does not exceed four or five. A case need not be an individual person; it can also be a family, a group, an organization, a community, or virtually any other system or entity that can be readily defined.

In a case study, interviewers must be receptive and nonjudgmental, and must be able to observe and interpret a wide variety of verbal (responses to preselected questions) and nonverbal (interviewer's observations of participants) communication. The topic area being studied may involve illegal behavior or at least behaviors that are not socially acceptable. Participants may be fearful of being "found out" and may be very concerned about the confidentiality of what they reveal about themselves or their situation. Thus, acquiring the trust of participants is absolutely essential. Relationships of trust are not easily developed and nurtured, because participants naturally tend to be guarded in what they say and to whom they say it. Participants may have learned how to give evasive answers to sensitive questions and may find it difficult to be candid. Social workers are ideally suited to conduct case studies. Their interviewing skills, nonjudgmental attitudes, and other professional values and ethics help to foster trust.

Case studies have often been misunderstood and sometimes maligned, sometimes leading to a belief that the case study is a less-than-scientific method for knowledge building. Part of this misunderstanding may be attributable to misapplication of the label to research that is poorly designed and implemented. For example, sometimes, researchers have conducted group research using a very small sample of research participants. In order to deflect criticism of their work and the credibility of their findings, they have incorrectly applied the case study label to their research design. But case studies, when conducted properly, are an excellent method of gathering important information on a new area of interest to social work researchers.

Suitable Topics

There are many problem areas that are well suited to a case study design. Currently, they might include new forms of substance abuse, sexual deviance, white-collar crime, or any problem area about which little is known. It should be remembered that the list of problems suitable for a case study is constantly changing. Once more is known about a problem, or once a problem is no longer considered socially unacceptable, researchers would be able to move to a different type of research to gather data from a larger sample.

An example of this is a study by one of the authors (Weinbach, 1989), in which he conducted a case study on "secret survivors," people who had experienced the sudden death of a partner with whom they were involved in a long-term extramarital affair. At that time, the case study was appropriate for studying this problem because extramarital affairs were not a topic that people freely discussed. A great deal of trust had to be developed between the researcher and participants before they would share feelings of grief over the death of their loved one. But less than a decade later, changing societal values and the accumulation of other exploratory studies of the problem had moved our understanding of the problem beyond the point where a case study would be appropriate. Another example is a study by Harding and Hamilton (2009), who used the case study design to determine the extent to which abuse and coercion influenced the decision of homeless women to engage in sex work. Another case study (Bergen & Ezzy, 2009) looked at the influence of mass media on the recent growth of interest in the Wiccan religion. Every year, problems emerge that are appropriate for research using a case study design as others are deleted from the list.

Culturally sensitive social work practice is another area often studied using the case study approach. Research may look at interventions that have been studied with the dominant cultural groups but have not specifically focused on certain minority groups. Other studies look specifically at issues that are relevant to a particular ethnic or cultural group and analyze the effects of interventions taking these cultural phenomena into consideration. An example of this is a case study by Trinidad (2009) that studied the effects of colonization on Hawaiian youth, including persistent structural discrimination and loss of land and indigenous ways of knowing. This case study of a community-based youth program analyzed how these issues influence the risk,

Research-informed Practice or Practice-informed Research

Behavior: Apply critical thinking to engage in analysis of quantitative and qualitative research methods and research findings.

Critical Thinking Question: Once a substantial amount of research has been conducted on a subject area, why are case studies rendered less appropriate for further research?

treatment, and prevention of youth violence, suicide, substance abuse, and juvenile delinquency. Semi-structured interviews were conducted and then analyzed using content analysis. The researchers used critical indigenous qualitative research to build a model for violence prevention that provides opportunities for active participation by the Native Hawaiian young adults.

Strengths and Limitations

Case studies enable researchers to achieve insights (such as how people feel about and experience certain phenomena) that cannot be obtained using more quantitative methods. They are also among the most interesting and gratifying types of research that can be conducted. When conducting a case study, we can experience a feeling of being on the very cutting edge of knowledge building about a problem or question.

A major limitation of the case study is its inability to generate knowledge that could be described as definitive. Any conclusions should be carefully qualified. Because the number of participants is small and because they cannot be considered representative, few real conclusions emerge from case histories. Often, the most that can be said about data collected is something like "These are some of the problems that were found," "These are some of the ways that some people experience them," or "This is what some people think can be done about them." A case study does not allow the researcher to generalize beyond the research participants. Thus, the external validity of any findings is low or even nonexistent. Findings are often used as the starting point for other types of research.

Grounded Theory

Grounded theory is one of the best known and one of the purest types of qualitative research. It falls in the exploratory-descriptive area. It is more likely to be cross-sectional than longitudinal in the purest sense; however, data collection can occur over an extended period of time and entails the use of multiple interviews with the same research participants. It relies heavily on skillful interviewing and content data analysis. Grounded theory research seeks to learn what meanings people give to certain events in their lives. Like most qualitative research, it seeks to generate hypotheses, not test them, and attempts to <u>build</u> theory from data, in contrast to quantitative research, which often tests theories using data.

Researchers conducting grounded theory research constantly monitor and reshape their developing theories. The method involves a recurring process of proposing (on the basis of analysis of completed interview data) and checking and verifying what has been proposed (with subsequent interviews). In grounded theory research, sample selection, data collection, and data analysis occur simultaneously rather than in a pre-established sequence. Analysis of data gathered early in the study guides and shapes subsequent sample selection and the focus of future data collection. Researchers use emerging theoretical categories to influence both the ways in which subsequent data collection will be accomplished and from whom. For example, in early interviews, we might begin by asking general research questions on the basis of whatever clues the literature may provide as to what those questions might find. If some questions turn out to be irrelevant or nonproductive, they are dropped in subsequent interviews. Other, new questions, suggested by what they learned in earlier interviews, may be added. Similarly, if certain types of participants seem to be providing more enlightenment for the emerging theories than others, subsequent interviews may target only those people who show the greatest potential to verify (or refute) their theories.

Data Analysis

Despite its somewhat unconventional approaches to data collection and case sampling, grounded theory is definitely not a haphazard or unscientific method of conducting research. It employs a systematic sequence of steps. For example, after the first batch of data is collected (often using DVD recordings of interviews), the process of coding, analyzing, conceptualizing, and categorizing the data is begun. In the early stages of analysis, a process called open coding entails broadly conceptualizing what the data seem to mean and beginning to assign responses to different categories. It requires a careful dissection of interviews, sometimes word by word. Questions such as "What is this?" or "What does this seem to mean?" are common at this stage of the data analysis. Eventually, as proposed relationships between categories gain support as more data are collected, the researcher produces what is referred to as a story line, a brief narrative description of what was observed. This is analyzed and distilled further to form what is called a core category. Finally, a theory or hypothesis emerges as a product of the research.

We looked at a study by Taylor (1998) in our earlier discussion of dual-role relationships in Chapter 2. In her research on parents who experienced the death of an adult child to AIDS, Taylor developed the theory statement, "Parents of persons with AIDS employ a combination of spiritual strengths and self-talk, along with a network of social supports and confidants, to arrive at a level of acceptance and confidence" (p. 237). Note that several terms in the statement (*spiritual strengths, self-talk, social supports, confidants, acceptance,* and *confidence*) were codes that Taylor developed through the process of analyzing the interviews and conceptualizing what was heard and observed.

Grounded theory is based on the premise that the meanings that people give to events in their lives are important in understanding their responses to the events and the amount of their resilience afterward. It is based primarily on theories of symbolic interaction, which hold that people construct their own meanings for events in part on the basis of their interactions with others. Grounded theory research thus seems especially well suited to acquiring the kinds of knowledge needed by social workers. Conducting it also requires many of the very attributes (interviewing skills, ability to form relationships, and so forth) that social workers possess.

Content analysis is often used in conjunction with grounded theory as a way of analyzing all types of data, including interviews, journals, and meeting minutes. One study (Takahashi et al., 2009) used the grounded theory approach along with content analysis to examine the effects of Internet-based social support groups on people with depression. Ayon (2009) used grounded theory methods to complete a content analysis of the paths to mandated child welfare services experienced by Mexican families who had recently immigrated to the United States.

Ethnographic Research

Ethnographic research is primarily descriptive research and is usually cross-sectional, although it can be longitudinal. Ethnographic research uses a combination of quantitative and qualitative research methods to answer research questions about individuals within their social context. It entails observations and measurement of behaviors (quantitative), but it also seeks to understand the beliefs, attitudes, values, social roles, social structures, and norms of behavior in social environments that are different from that of the researcher (qualitative). It often relies on various forms of systematic observation (see Chapter 11) to accomplish these goals.

Emic and Etic Perspectives

Two concepts embedded in ethnographic research methods are *emic* and *etic* perspectives, related to our earlier discussion of the observer-participant roles. The emic perspective is that of the insider who is indigenous to the group being studied. This perspective is an experiential one based on an individual having been socialized to daily living in the culture and participating fully in all its psychosocial aspects. The etic perspective is that of the outsider—the stance traditionally assumed by researchers who study a culture that is not their own. An assumption of ethnographic research is that each perspective has advantages and disadvantages. For example, although the emic perspective permits an intricate understanding of even the most subtle cultural nuances, its requirement of familiarity with the cultural context may fail to raise critical questions about why things are the way they are or what maintains the status quo. On the other hand, although the etic perspective may miss important cultural nuances, it allows researchers to raise questions of context and purpose that would never occur to an insider. Ethnographic research attempts to blend these two perspectives by allowing the outside investigator to function as an insider through participant observation and other methods that will enhance the understanding of the cultural context. As in other types of research that rely on participant observation, the extent to which the very presence of the outsider changes the natural order of the cultural dynamics of insiders (reactivity) is a potential source of distortion of data thus collected.

> The emic perspective is that of the insider who is indigenous to the group being studied. The etic perspective is that of the outsider—the stance traditionally assumed by researchers who study a culture that is not their own.

Data Collection

Although participant observation is the data collection methodology most often associated with ethnographic research, there are now other methodological approaches that can help investigators understand different cultures. These include eco-mapping, geographic information system mapping, formal and informal interviews, life histories, kinship charts, and analysis of religious practices, myths, music, and other forms of folklore.

Because of negative historical and political encounters between ethnic communities and mainstream governmental or social welfare institutions, gaining access to study samples in ethnic communities may be problematic. Resistance is often encountered because of (1) mistrust of the researcher's motives for conducting the research, and (2) fear of how the data may be used. In addition, in the past ethnic communities have been used as study sites, with little or no feedback provided to them about what was learned through the research. Even when feedback has been given, it sometimes has not been in a form that is helpful to the community for understanding and/or addressing its problems. Providing information in a manner that is useful to the community may be empowering for them and contribute to social justice which is a goal of the social work profession.

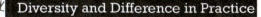

Diversity and Difference in Practice

Behavior: Present themselves as learners and engage clients and constituencies as experts of their own experiences.

Critical Thinking Question: In what ways would living with the research participants potentially change the data collected by the researcher?

Use of Key Informants

Key informants are often very helpful in conducting ethnographic research. A key informant is usually a member of, and frequently a leader (formal or informal) in, a community or group. Sometimes it can even be an "outsider" who is especially knowledgeable about a group and can provide insights that we lack. For example, it might be someone who has previously conducted research there and who has learned from his or her experiences. We can seek the assistance of a key informant through unstructured personal interviews or open-ended questions to them through mailed or electronic communication. These methods enable us to gain the advice and support of people who can offer a needed perspective on how to gain the trust of community members and how to conduct the research in a culturally sensitive way in a setting or context that is unfamiliar to us.

Key informants can be helpful in other ways too. They can provide guidance on where to find needed information and resources on topics of study interest, and even how to interpret study findings. Key informant surveys are also a way of forging alliances with community leaders and influential citizens who can endorse the research endeavor, thus helping to reduce suspicion about why it is being conducted. Who, specifically, qualifies as a potential key informant? The answer to this question is sometimes especially hard to determine in ethnic communities. Leaders designated by funding sources or university advisory boards may not be regarded as leaders by the members of their ethnic group; neither may certain appointed or elected officials. Butler (1992) points out, for example, that whereas funding sources may rely on academic credentials, work experience, or political connections to select leaders, members of some African-American communities are more likely to locate leadership in individuals who embody the community values of spirituality, wisdom, strength of character, and style. This suggests that key informants should be selected on the basis of a wide variety of criteria based on what personal characteristics are most valued and respected within the ethnic community involved in the research.

Examples

Ethnographic methods were first developed in the field of anthropology to guide participant observation and the qualitative field research of Western investigators studying behavior in primitive societies. However, ethnographic methods are now used to understand groups within modern dominant cultures. Those groups may exist based on shared race, culture, class, religion, or some other characteristic that in some way differentiates the subgroup from the mainstream culture.

One example of ethnographic research is a study by Haight (2002), which focuses on the spiritual socialization of African-American children through the African-American Baptist church and Sunday school. Many researchers have discussed the sociocultural significance of the church in the history of the African-American community. Haight looked at adult-child interactions, storytelling, and elderly Sunday school teachers focusing on the role of religion in the development of resilience among African-American children and families. Smith (2009) completed an ethnographic study of Afghan refugees in California to determine how to contact gatekeepers and other members within the community to help preserve autonomy, ensure confidentiality, build trust, and improve the accuracy of the results.

Ethical and Professional Practice

Behavior: Make ethical decision by applying the standards of the NASW Code of Ethics, relevant laws and regulations, models for ethical decision-making, ethical conduct of research, and additional codes of ethics as appropriate to context.

Critical Thinking Question: What possible ethical issues might a researcher face in conducting an ethnographic study of a group of Mexican immigrants?

It is to the researcher's advantage to understand the specific historical and cultural traits of the target community to (1) anticipate the degree and nature of resistance to participation and (2) seek advice from knowledgeable individuals on overcoming resistance to participation.

Some ethnic communities have set up stringent review and approval procedures before granting permission to conduct research. Notable among these are some of the Native-American tribal groups. Any researcher wishing to conduct studies that are on tribal lands or involve people who are members of their tribal group must be prepared to comply with their particular approval process. Typically, researchers must present a proposal before a tribal, community, or village governing body that exercises some degree of control over the research process. Beauvais and Trimble (1992) found the following guidelines in place in one Native-American tribe: (1) assignment of a tribal or village member to monitor study implementation; (2) community's right to review and edit guidelines concerning respondent selection procedures; (3) community's right to review and edit questionnaires, interview schedules, and field notes, and so on; (4) community's right to review and edit research reports and restrict or prevent the circulation and distribution of findings; and (5) ownership of the raw data and findings granted to the tribe or village. There are a few tribes that forbid any outside research within their boundaries; as sovereign states, they can legally do so.

It is to the researcher's advantage to understand the specific historical and cultural traits of the target community to (1) anticipate the degree and nature of resistance to participation and (2) seek advice from knowledgeable individuals on overcoming resistance to participation. For example, Kim, McLeod, and Shantzis (1992) presented some practical issues that should be considered when developing and evaluating drug and alcohol abuse prevention programs for the Asian-American and Pacific Island-American communities, such as:

- Conduct data collection in private settings.
- Provide refreshments (because of the importance of food and communal meals in social gatherings).
- Use personal contacts, such as telephone calls or word-of-mouth invitations, to invite participation in the study, rather than sending formal letters for appointments.
- Compensate respondents for their time (because research and evaluation are less important to many Asian-Americans than work in exchange for compensation).
- Provide transportation and child care (because many Asian-American families are accustomed to having children present at semiformal gatherings).

Other research has looked at utilizing the Internet in gathering data for ethnographic research. Garcia, Standlee, Bechkoff, and Cui (2009) look at the strengths and weaknesses of technologically mediated communications. While such communications prevent the researcher from directly observing the participant, they enlarge the possible pool of participants and can allow the participant to remain anonymous. The authors offer suggestions on how to conduct participant observations and interviews, how to obtain access to settings and subjects, and how to deal with specific ethical issues related to Internet usage. For a more thorough discussion of the use of ethnographic research methods, see Lowery (2010).

Cross-Cultural Research

Cross-cultural research is related to ethnographic research, and is primarily descriptive research. It is interested in looking at people within the context of their ethnic community, and it employs both quantitative and qualitative methods. However, cross-cultural research has its own unique focus—it seeks to describe cultural similarities (universalities that exist across cultures) and differences between and among cultures. It is being used more frequently than in past years because of a number of factors, including the opening of previously sealed international borders, large migration streams, globalization of the economic market, international tourism, increased cross-cultural communication, and technological innovations that make communication and scholarship in other countries possible (Van de Vijver & Leung, 1997). In cross-cultural research, investigators face some unique methodological challenges usually related to definitions of theoretical constructs and their valid measurement in different cultural contexts. Other problems relate to obtaining a representative sample and accuracy of translation of data collection instruments into foreign languages.

Cross–cultural research is most frequently conducted by sociologists or anthropologists. But social workers wishing to conduct research and/or to use its findings in their practice across multiple cultures or countries will be especially interested in cross-cultural studies of human behavior, family systems, and other social organizations, as well as epidemiological studies of health and mental health disorders and their treatment in various cultural contexts. Cross-cultural research may also be conducted with ethnic and racial groups within the North American culture.

Examples

One cross-cultural study (Dwairy et al., 2010) analyzed the differences between adolescents in nine countries. The researchers looked at psychological disorders and how they differ across cultures on the basis of the presence of different parenting factors, such as control, consistency, and rejection. Leenaars et al. (2010) conducted a thematic analysis of sixty suicide notes drawn from Turkey and the United States to identify common cultural themes as well as specific differences. They found more common factors than differences, although they did find that suicide notes written by Turkish subjects more often indicated that there were reasons for the suicide that were not included in the suicide note. The authors concluded that there is much to be learned through cross-cultural research in the field of suicidology.

Marin and Marin (1991) offer several suggestions for researchers who plan to undertake cross-cultural research. These suggestions are designed to reduce the risk of cultural encapsulation (i.e., depending entirely on one's own cultural frame of reference to formulate assumptions and define research constructs) and increase cultural relativity (i.e., the ability to understand behaviors, attitudes, and values within the context of the culture in which it occurs). Although these suggestions were offered many years ago, these strategies are still very relevant today:

- Cultural immersion in the group to be studied.
- The obtaining of information directly from cultural minorities about values and normative behavior rooted in the culture (i.e., what is normal and what is pathological for that specific culture).

- Collaboration with key informants from the culture to be studied on all aspects of the study design prior to initiating the study.

Feminist Research

Feminist research is distinguished primarily by two things—its focus and its purpose. It is research that seeks to build knowledge about women, specifically, about their unique problems or issues and the social institutions that affect them. When the label feminist research is used to describe a research study, it conveys little about what research methods were used. That is because feminist research employs all available methods, often in combination. It can be predominantly quantitative or qualitative, exploratory, descriptive, or (less frequently) explanatory, and may employ cross-sectional, longitudinal, or pretest-posttest designs.

Goals and Assumptions

In her early work in feminist research, Shulamit Reinharz (1992) pointed out that feminist research relates to "women's ways of knowing," a concept that women acquire knowledge differently than men. Feminist research is designed to hear the voices and other communications that more traditional, male-oriented approaches to knowledge building may miss. That would seem to suggest that (1) it is only qualitative research and (2) it can be conducted only by women. Both of these assumptions would be incorrect. However, it is conducted by people (men and women) who generally identify themselves as feminists and are concerned with the status and well-being of women.

Feminist research is often a form of action research: research designed to bring about change in women's lives by confronting sexism and attempting to alter those social institutions that may promote or perpetuate it. It results in consciousness raising and awareness of women's issues. The fact that feminist researchers study problems such as rape, sexual harassment, sexism, and salary inequity stimulates reflection and discussion about these issues by others.

Feminist research rests on the assumption that gender is critical to understanding women and culture. It has produced a wealth of data about women. For example, knowledge about domestic violence, date rape, marital rape, women's health issues, and women's work at home and in the community has been developed through feminist research. Knowledge derived from feminist research is used to validate women's lives and experiences and is useful for understanding women's issues, problems, and strengths. It has also been used to suggest additional research relevant to women that is needed to influence the development of social policy that directly affects women.

A Response to Traditional Research Methods

Knowledge developed through feminist research is often contextual and relative. This is justified by feminist scholars based on the assertion that traditional approaches to scientific research often assume objectivity about the world that is irrelevant to women's lives. More traditional methods of inquiry are believed to ignore and distort women's realities. For example, many widely accepted measurement procedures such as scales or tests were developed by and standardized using men only, thus making their value in understanding women's characteristics or experiences questionable. In addition, many life experiences that are important to the lives of women, such as sexual harassment in the workplace and post-partum depression, were historically neglected by researchers using traditional research methods. Feminist research uses perspectives of culture to select research problems and research methods for interpreting data. Feminist researchers argue that their methods of conducting research allow them to critique knowledge that has been developed by others while using more traditional models of inquiry.

Feminist researchers have described the more traditional methods of inquiry (especially experimental designs) as being antithetical to the purposes of feminist research. For example, experimental research generally is conducted "in the laboratory" under tightly controlled research conditions. Feminists have argued that these types of designs have tended to exploit and objectify women through a sexist bias in the ways that questions are asked and answered and the way that data are interpreted. They assert that the artificiality of the research laboratory is not conducive to a true understanding of people and their relationships. Feminist research, with its emphasis on more egalitarian approaches to interacting with research participants, is believed to be less exploitive than traditional methods in its approach to data collection. The relationship between the researcher and the person being studied is more one of equality. In feminist research, research participants often are referred to as *research partners* rather than research participants.

Human Rights and Justice

Behavior: Apply their understanding of social, economic, and environmental justice to advocate for human rights at the individual and system levels.

Critical Thinking Question: Why do you think research has historically concentrated on men in our society?

Design Characteristics

Methodologically, feminist research has been described using such terms as open, contextual, relative, interpretive, experiential, empowering, and social change–oriented. These descriptors suggest the wide range of research designs used by and for feminist scholarship. Feminist research relies heavily on a variety of qualitative (and, less frequently, quantitative) techniques. Feminist research designs are often hybrids, combining features of two or more approaches to knowledge building. For example, quantitative data may be collected and analyzed, but then participants may be asked if they would like to meet with a member of the research team to discuss their responses more fully in order to more clearly communicate the meaning of their answers to the researchers.

Like some of the other forms of research described in this chapter, feminist methods are characterized by relatively open relationships between researchers and research participants. Researchers may get involved with the lives of participants by establishing relationships with them that go beyond simple data collection. They may serve as resources to participants by providing information about community resources or may assist them in bringing about social change. The relationship between researchers and participants is viewed as critical to the development of knowledge about women. Questions asked often emanate from researchers' own concerns and experiences, rather than out of some previously developed interview schedule or agenda. The knowledge acquired through this kind of interpersonal interaction leads to an interpretive approach to data analysis that makes no claims of total objectivity.

Feminist research usually does not emphasize the testing of pre-specified hypotheses. It focuses instead on the development of a wide range of information and understanding. It has been described as emergent; it is not highly controlled. It often seeks to gather a wide array of descriptive, contextual information to provide data that are as complete as possible for analysis.

A predominantly qualitative approach to data collection and analysis—*naturalistic inquiry* (a form of unstructured systematic observation)—attempts to document and understand women's behavior as it is influenced by their social contexts. Observations may be made in a variety of field settings, such as women's health organizations, women's work and social groups, and other groups and communities to which women belong. The data in naturalistic inquiries, as in most qualitative research, are typically rich in detail. In naturalistic inquiry, the researcher allows the patterns and themes contained in the data observed to emerge naturally.

There are many excellent examples of naturalistic inquiries in the literature. Many of these studies have been conducted by feminist sociologists and anthropologists. One study (Gagne, 1992) sought to better understand wife abuse in a rural community. On the basis of the findings from her naturalistic inquiry of violence and social control, the researcher conceptualized three categories of control. She then used them to assert that domestic violence is dependent on cultural and social structures that condone men's domination of women and that, without them, violence would be less effective as a means of social control.

Data Collection and Analysis

Virtually every research method that we have described so far has been used in feminist research. On the basis of our description, it should come as no surprise to you that some of the qualitative methods described earlier in this chapter (e.g., grounded theory, content analysis) are frequently used. Although feminist research has often used quantitative methods, since this chapter focuses on qualitative research methods, we will focus here on feminist research that has utilized mainly qualitative methods.

Semi-structured, open-ended questionnaires (administered by the researcher) are useful when the purpose of a study is to have participants respond to certain questions in their own words. Participants often become involved both in the interpretation of the meanings of their responses and in the refinement of data collection methods to be used in future research. Typically, this method of data collection entails the use of multiple sessions with participants. Because it is often impossible to anticipate the type of information that will be shared, the interviews are often a process of discovery for both the participants and the feminist researcher.

Examples

Studies have looked at various forms of violence against women based on the changing societal definitions of what connotes acceptable and non-acceptable levels of violence. One qualitative study (Lipman, 2002) used semi-structured clinical interviews to explore women's relational and sexual functioning after experiencing a date rape. Some of the major themes she found were distrust in men, feelings of powerlessness, and lack of desire and pleasure in the sex act. She also found the effects were more pronounced among women who were virgins at the time of the rape than among women who had previous sexual experiences.

Harmon (2010) completed interviews with thirty single white mothers who had children of mixed race, and found that these mothers experienced significant levels of racism and prejudice aimed at themselves and their children. Another qualitative study (Reid, 2009) explored the social support network of single African-American mothers living in a public housing community in a small town. The researcher found that most of these single mothers identified family members as their primary source of support. In addition, while communication with neighbors in the public housing community was often limited, most of the mothers had exchanged vital resources, such as food or transportation, with at least one other single mother living in the same housing project.

Because eating disorders have historically affected more women than men, feminist research has focused some attention on this area. Malson and Burns (2009) have analyzed feminist approaches to eating disorders and the shifts in the way cultures define gender, body weight, body management, and food. The researchers contend that eating disorders should not be viewed as static individual mental illness, but should instead be viewed as conditions that constantly change in response to cultural changes experienced by the individual.

Brown, Weber, and Ali (2008) use a feminist narrative approach to analyze cultural influences that not only shape the presence of eating disorders but can also be used to guide the treatment of eating disorders. They argue that a combination of feminist and narrative treatment approaches can be more effective in working with women with eating disorders than more traditional approaches. As we noted earlier, it is the specialized purpose and focus of feminist research that gives it its identity. Feminist research is designed specifically to develop needed knowledge about women and the social institutions that impact them.

Participatory Action Research

Participatory action research offers research participants the chance to conduct research on their own behalf. The focus of participatory action research is on some action or change based on the outcome or information generated by the research. It is used primarily to give a voice to marginalized groups of people. The researcher serves as a resource to the participants in the study, while the participants not only define the problem(s) to be studied but are also responsible for the research design needed to study the problem. It is argued that research has too often been in the hands of the majority groups rather than in the hands of those in the groups who often benefit most from increasing knowledge in the problem area. By placing the information in the hands of those who most need it, research participants are empowered to find the answers and help themselves and others.

Examples

One study using participatory action research methods (Happell et al., 2009) explored and evaluated mental health practices in the pediatric unit of a rural general hospital. Nursing staff were given the opportunity to actively participate in the design, direction, and outcomes of the research study. Focus groups with the nurses revealed that the nurses felt they were inadequately trained to provide effective mental health services to children. The participants (nurses) then requested further training by mental health specialists as well as the development of new policies and clinical guidelines to facilitate their care of mental health patients.

In another participatory action research study (Van der Velde, Williamson, & Ogilvie, 2009), focus groups with immigrants and refugees were conducted to identify practical strategies to encourage engagement and participation in immigrant and refugee communities. As in most of the methods described in this chapter, it is generally categorized as a qualitative research method, but the design of a participatory action research study can be predominantly qualitative, predominantly quantitative, or a mixture of both types of methods. For further information on completing participatory action research, see Blum, Heinonen, and White (2010).

EVALUATION CRITERIA FOR QUALITATIVE RESEARCH

Obviously, the research methods and epistemological frameworks used in qualitative research are diverse. Because of this diversity, it has been challenging to create a set of evaluation criteria for qualitative research. A group of social workers (Shek, Tang, & Han, 2005) evaluated research studies using qualitative methods that were published in the social work literature between 1990 and 2003, and found that the quality of many qualitative research studies was not high. They concluded that social workers need additional training in qualitative evaluation and that social workers conducting qualitative research should be sensitive to issues of quality. Another outcome of this study was a set of criteria for evaluating qualitative research studies. Shek et al. created a comprehensive list of criteria that has commonly been adopted in the field of qualitative research to cover the broad and diverse types of methods used. These criteria include the following:

1. Explicit statement of the philosophical base of the study (this includes a clear statement as to why specific approaches are chosen, such as grounded theory, ethnography, etc.)

2. Justifications for the number and nature of the participants of the study

3. Detailed description of the data collection procedures

4. Discussion of the biases and preoccupations of the researchers (this is particularly important since it is especially difficult to eliminate biases in qualitative research)

5. Description of the steps taken to guard against biases or arguments that should or could not be eliminated

6. Inclusion of measures of reliability, such as interrater reliability (the stability of interpretations across different researchers) and intrarater reliability (the stability of interpretations of the same researcher at different times)

7. Inclusion of measures of triangulation in terms of researchers and data types

8. Inclusion of peer-checking and member-checking procedures

9. Consciousness of the importance and development of audit trails

10. Consideration of alternative explanations for the observed findings

11. Inclusion of explanations for negative evidence

12. Clear statement of the limitations of the study (p. 184)

Since there is such a wide range of goals and procedures involved with the various qualitative methods, one should not expect every qualitative research study to meet all of these criteria. Criteria may have to be selected on the basis of the theory orientation of the researchers and the purposes of the study. However, when using qualitative methods we should keep these criteria in mind to ensure the highest possible quality of our study.

Shek et al. (2005) also suggested four possible reasons why the quality of the qualitative research they examined may have been lower than expected: (1) Some methods, such as peer checking and member checks, that could enhance the quality of a qualitative study, can be extremely costly in terms of time and money; (2) Journals rarely provide guidelines or standards to report qualitative research findings; (3) Space constraints in academic journals may force qualitative researchers to report their findings in a truncated and inadequate manner; and (4) Inadequate training in qualitative research methods among social workers may lower the quality of subsequent qualitative research (p. 191).

SUMMARY

In this chapter:

- We point out the key characteristics of qualitative research.
- We identify data collection and analysis techniques often used by qualitative researchers.
- We describe six types of research that rely most often on qualitative approaches to knowledge building: case studies, grounded theory, ethnographic research, cross-cultural research, feminist research, and participatory action research.
- We discussed evaluation criteria that can be used by researchers and the readers of research reports to evaluate the quality of qualitative research studies.

MyEducationLab® for Research

Start with the Topic 5 Assignments: Selecting a Sample and the Topic 5 Study Plan and then try the Topic 19 Assignments: Qualitative Data Collection and Topic 19 Study Plan.

For specific qualitative designs, try:
Topic 12 Assignments: Narrative Research and the Topic 12 Study Plan.
Topic 13 Assignments: Ethnographic Research and the Topic 13 Study Plan.
Topic 14 Assignments: Case-Study Research and Topic 14 Study Plan.

Chapter 6 Chapter Review Quiz.

Evaluating Programs

Evidence-based practice is possible today because of the work of researchers. While basic research has provided the knowledge of human behavior that has made it possible for us to understand human problems and their origins, it has been the findings of applied research that have allowed us to make practice decisions and offer interventions that we have reason to believe will be effective. The bulk of this applied research has taken one of four forms in recent years:

1. **Systematic review of research reports.** It focuses on the quality of the research design that produced its research findings.

2. **Meta-analysis.** It has informed us about which method of intervention has proven effective (or ineffective) with certain types of problems. It has been used to evaluate theories of intervention.

3. **Program evaluation** (the primary topic of this chapter). It has evaluated specific social programs at various stages of their development.

4. **Single system research** (the primary topic of Chapter 8). The services of individual social work practitioners have been evaluated in systematic ways to provide feedback to them about their effectiveness in working with some problem of a specific client or client system.

SYSTEMATIC REVIEWS

In reviewing reports of research published in journals or other venues, we are encouraged as responsible practitioners to seek out and pay greater attention to the findings of "higher quality" or "stronger" studies, rather than "lower quality" or "weaker" studies. Why? Stronger, well-designed research studies are assumed to be more capable of producing credible findings and recommendations than weaker ones. There are a number of simple guidelines on how to evaluate the design quality of research as described in our literature. (Pignotti & Thyer, 2009; Thyer, 1989, 1991). Most social workers also get some guidance on this topic in their research methods course-work. A newer approach that provides a more comprehensive look at a research study's design and the findings that it produced is the systematic review. Littell and Corcoran (2010) offer the following definition:

> Systematic reviews are carefully organized, comprehensive, and transparent studies of previous research on a particular topic. They follow written protocols (detailed plans) that specify their central objectives, concepts, and methods in advance. Systematic review methods include procedures for identifying, critically appraising, synthesizing, and presenting results of previous studies (p. 313).

The authors further point out that rigorous reviews always include precautions to minimize error and bias at every step in the process. In addition, each step in the process is documented so the readers can follow and evaluate the research methods being used in a systematic review.

There are two international and interdisciplinary organizations dedicated to commissioning, approving, and publishing systematic reviews, and these are known as the Cochrane Collaboration and the Campbell Collaboration. The former focuses on the preparation of systematic reviews in the general field of health care and the latter in the areas of social welfare, criminal justice, and education. Their end products are open-access and Web-based systematic reviews, which can be found in the Cochrane (www.cochrane.org) and Campbell (www.campbellcollaboration.org) libraries. In addition, systematic reviews are sometimes published as independent journal articles by governmental organizations or private groups and are not a formal part of either of these collaborations. However, such stand-alone systematic reviews are not usually held to the exemplary research standards maintained by either the Cochrane or Campbell groups. Standards and guidelines for systematic reviews have been developed by both the Cochrane and Campbell collaborations.

Following are examples of completed systematic reviews that can be found on the Cochrane Collaboration website that summarize the effectiveness of various psychosocial interventions:

- Advocacy interventions to reduce or eliminate violence and promote the physical and psychosocial well-being of women who experience intimate partner violence
- Culture-specific programs for children and adults from minority groups who have asthma
- Culturally appropriate health education for type 2 diabetes mellitus in ethnic minority groups
- Behavioral interventions for decreasing HIV infection in racial and ethnic minorities in high-income economies
- Day care for preschool children
- Indigenous health care worker involvement for indigenous adults and children with asthma
- Morita therapy for schizophrenia

The federal Substance Abuse and Mental Health Services Administration maintains a constantly updated searchable website called the National Registry of Evidence-Based

Programs and Practices (www.nrepp.samhsa.gov). This site contains descriptive information about a wide array of interventions and their outcomes, along with an appraisal of the quality of research, the intervention's readiness for use in community settings, and sources of contact information for social work researchers to learn more about providing the intervention. Of particular importance is an indication of the study populations with which the intervention has been used. This site can be very helpful during the initial planning phases of a research study, when we are searching for other research that looked at similar problems, interventions, and/or populations (Thyer & Myers, 2010).

Littell and Corcoran (2010) emphasize the importance of using a systematic approach when reviewing reports of research. Traditional reviews, sometimes referred to as *haphazard reviews*, often use convenience samples of published reports of research studies. However, a systematic review formulates the eligibility criteria that specify which studies will be included and excluded from the review and describes them in its report. The Cochrane Collaboration offers a PICO framework for delineating these criteria. PICO stands for *participants* (or *populations* or *patients*), *intervention, comparison or control group*, and *outcomes*. These are the four eligibility criteria that should be defined in detail. See Littell and Corcoran (2010) for a detailed discussion of the steps involved in conducting a systematic review.

META-ANALYSIS

Meta-analyses can be particularly helpful when completing a review of the literature on a certain topic, as they examine the reports from various research studies that focused on the same questions or tested the same hypotheses.

Another type of research that also uses the literature as its focus is the meta-analysis. Corcoran and Littell (2010) define *meta-analysis* as "a set of statistical methods for combining quantitative results from multiple studies to produce an overall summary of empirical knowledge on a given topic" (p. 299). Meta-analyses can be particularly helpful when completing a review of the literature on a certain topic, as they examine the reports from various research studies that focused on the same questions or tested the same hypotheses. These reports may be found in professional journals, research monographs, program evaluation documents, theses, dissertations, or any document in which research designs and findings are described in sufficient detail to be compared and analyzed critically.

Most meta-analysis is cross-sectional and is regarded as explanatory research. Thus, designs generally include hypothesis specification and testing and statistical analysis of data – characteristics of research studies that are more quantitative than qualitative. Designs can be highly rigorous and may contain various methods to control for problems of design bias and confounding variables, including both those that are unique to this type of research and some that are common to other forms of secondary analysis.

Meta-analysis has made major contributions to evidence-based practice. A common use of meta-analysis is to try to ascertain if a method or model of intervention is effective for addressing a problem or condition. For example, suppose you are completing a literature review prior to evaluating the effectiveness of a specific intervention used by school social workers. Early in your review, you could describe the meta-analysis by Franklin, Kim, and Tripodi (2009), in which they analyzed the overall effectiveness of school social work interventions. Or suppose you are conducting a literature review for a study in which you are analyzing the effectiveness of a specific treatment for children diagnosed with conduct disorder. You might want to describe Litschge, Vaughn, and McCrea's (2010) meta-analysis, in which they identified and summarized treatment effects for children and adolescents with conduct disorders on the basis of 2,000 studies! It would provide you with not only an excellent summary of research findings related to your area of interest but also the citations for those relevant research studies that were included in its meta-analysis, should you wish to learn more about any of them.

Because findings of meta-analyses are based on the reports of studies conducted by many researchers in different settings, they are often based (collectively) on data obtained from very large numbers of research participants. This has certain advantages. The large number of people on which the findings are based should make the likelihood of sampling error quite low. Also, while a particular design bias may have been present in one or two of the studies, it is unlikely to have been present in all of them. So, if all or most of the different designs included produced similar findings, this would suggest that the findings are likely to be valid. Thus, the findings of meta-analysis studies have the potential to possess a high level of both internal and external validity.

There are also several problems associated with the use of meta-analysis. Like all forms of secondary data analysis, meta-analysis studies are limited by the scope of the research findings and the research design that produced them. The report of one study may be comprehensive; the report of another may be sketchy. Or, one report may suggest that a strong research design was used, while another may suggest the use of a weaker one. This latter problem can be partially identified through the use of systematic review (explained above), but it does not answer the question, "Should the study with the weaker design be totally eliminated from the meta-analysis, or should it still be retained but somehow discounted (perhaps statistically) in the data analysis?"

A lack of comparability can cause problems in drawing conclusions about the use of the reports of different studies in other ways too. Unless one is a replication of the other, it is rare that two or more research studies that examined the same research questions used exactly the same research methods. Because of this, the researcher inevitably ends up asking, "How comparable must research methods be for me to include the report of a research study in a meta-analysis?"

Another potential problem relates to the selection processes that sometimes influence what gets into print—publication bias. As we have suggested elsewhere, professional journals may be more likely to publish articles that support the study's research hypotheses than studies where the variables of interest were found to be unrelated (null findings). If this is true, when professional journals represent a high percentage of the research reports included in a meta-analysis, it is possible to conclude from it that an intervention is more effective than it really is. However, certain statistical corrections and design features (beyond the scope of this book) have been developed to attempt to address the problem of publication bias in meta-analysis.

Despite its shortcomings, meta-analysis is growing in popularity among social work researchers. It is becoming more and more feasible as we accumulate reports of research that are either replications of earlier research or are reports of research that are similar enough that they lend themselves to this type of study.

Assessment

Behavior: Select appropriate intervention strategies based on the assessment, research knowledge, and values and preferences of clients and constituencies.

Critical Thinking Question: How can a meta-analysis assist the social work practitioner in the selection of the most effective intervention as well as a useful measurement instrument for use with a client?

WHAT IS PROGRAM EVALUATION?

Some of the examples that we used in the previous chapters referred to real and hypo-thetical program evaluations. Program evaluations can utilize any of the research meth-ods and designs already discussed, and have provided both clear examples of many of the methodological issues that were discussed and good illustrations of how research can inform practice and help us to make better decisions. However, program evaluation is such an important part of social work research activities today and such a major contrib-utor to evidence-based practice that we also believe it merits most of this chapter being devoted exclusively to it.

Program evaluation is an important enterprise. It constitutes the major activity of many research institutes both on college and university campuses and in the private, for-profit and not-for-profit sectors. There are many individuals who specialize in it, either as a pro-bono service to their profession or as a major source of their personal income. There are many books and articles that focus on program evaluation (see for example, Nugent, Sieppert, & Hudson, 2001; Rossi, Lipsey, & Freeman, 2003; Royse, Thyer, & Padgett, 2009; Thyer & Myers, 2007; Unrau, Gabor, & Grinnell, 2015; Weinbach, 2005). They go into great detail about the specific methods for conducting it. In this text, we will focus on developing a good general understanding of what program evaluation is, what different focuses it can assume, and how it relates to our discussion of social work research in earlier and later chapters.

Program evaluation encompasses a wide range of activities and attempts to answer many different questions about programs. In the broadest sense, program evaluation can be thought of as "the application of both quantitative and qualitative research methods to evaluate the merit, worth or value of a program" (Weinbach, 2005, p. 30). The focus of a program evaluation may be on an old, well-established program, a relatively new one, or one that is just being considered.

Programs are subunits of organizations, constructed in a unique way to address some social problem. They are more or less self-contained and autonomous. What they hope to accomplish should be consistent with the organization's mission and its vision state-ment. However, programs generally have their own goals, objectives, policies, rules, pro-cedures, strategies, services, staff, budget, space, and so forth, which may differ from other programs in the organization.

For social workers, the pressure to evaluate the effectiveness of our programs is increasing. Many of these pressures come from a program's stakeholders. A *stakeholder* is anyone who has a stake (an investment) in a program and its success. The most obvi-ous stakeholders might be donors—both voluntary donors and those who "donate" through their taxes or health insurance premiums. Other donors might be funding organizations such as The United Way or private foundations that provide financial support to programs. However, there are still other stakeholders. They might include board members who are responsible for an organization's operation, government reg-ulatory organizations, and the staff members who invest their time and talents to work in a program. Of course, we cannot forget clients—they have a very big investment in a program that they enter with the expectation that it will be of help with some prob-lem that they have.

Use of Logic Models

A program's logic model displays what the program is all about, what it hopes to accomplish, how it hopes to accomplish it, and how it will determine if it has been accomplished. It is both a description of a program and a management tool, since it suggests what a manager needs to do to keep the program on-focus. It describes a program in concise form and, if well-articulated, can result in a well-integrated, efficient program. A good one can also make the work of a program evaluator much easier. There is no single template for a logic model, but logic models generally consist of a description of the program's following components:

1. *Inputs* are all of the resources that are available to the program, both monetary and nonmonetary. Common inputs would be reflected in the program budget but would also include other resources that the program has, such as the services of volunteers or donations in kind.

2. *Activities* are how the program's inputs are used. Services to clients are generally a very important activity, but so are other actions that support services or make them possible, such as the work of program managers. For example, fundraising, marketing of the program, or development of referral sources would be important activities within a program.

3. *Outputs* are what the program produced; generally, what it accomplished in quantifiable terms. Examples of outputs might be number and demographic characteristics of clients served, number of workshops offered, or number of new cases opened.

4. *Outcomes* are the degree to which the program accomplished what it intended to accomplish, generally the elimination or reduction of the problem that the program sought to address. They are the degree to which clients or client systems benefited from the program—how much of a difference it made. Outcomes are often described as short term, intermediate term, and long term. A *short-term outcome* might be how clients who complete the program are different from how they were when they entered it. *Intermediate-term outcomes* often relate to objectives of continued client growth and progress following their completion of a program, such as the continued career advancement of clients who complete a job training program. *Long-term outcomes* (sometimes called *impacts*) often reflect a wide range of changes that may result from the program, such as reduction of the problem within a community, effect on the need for other programs, or the long-term impact on clients who completed it. Evaluating the degree of achievement of intermediate-term and long-term outcomes often requires follow-up of former clients and/or a longitudinal component in a program evaluation design. Of course, like short term outcomes for clients, not all longer term outcomes are always positive. Sometimes, unintended negative outcomes also occur, such as increased community antagonism toward the organization or the creation of a new problem that emerges in response to reduction in the original one.

5. *Indicators* are the methods used to evaluate the degree to which outcomes have been achieved. They are how program success is measured.

Box 7.1   Contents of a Typical Logic Model

Inputs	Activities	Outputs	Outcomes		
			Short-term	Intermediate	Long-term
Resources (human and material) allocated to the program	What takes place within the program; how inputs are used to attempt to produce outcomes	Products of a program's activities; what the program produced	How the problem was reduced by the program; how its clients benefitted	Continued effects of the program over time	Ultimate effects of the program on its clients and others

Box 7.1 reflects the contents of a relatively simple logic model. Note how its various components fit together. A program manager would articulate the logic model for a program by describing the various forms that each component would take. Indicators would be attached to each outcome objective. If a more complex logic model is used, it may also contain content on other factors that describe the program and the likelihood of its success. Two common ones are constraints and mandates. *Constraints* are limitations that affect the program. For example, there may be certain conditions imposed on it by the organization in which it is housed, the political climate in its community, by legal restrictions such as confidentiality requirements, or ethical limitations that will not allow it to function as it might in a less-restricted world. A *mandate* restricts the program in a related but somewhat different way. It is a requirement (often a legal one or one required for licensure or accreditation) that something must be in place or must happen in a certain way. For example, a program may be mandated to offer certain services or to offer them in some prescribed way that is designed to assure equal access to them among various groups.

A good logic model can help a program to stay "on track" and thus increase its likelihood of success. It can also help an evaluator to understand what a program hopes to accomplish and how it is designed to function. However, even the best logic model cannot guarantee success and should not be used as the primary indicator of a program's merit, worth, or value. Unless we are careful, we can slip into the trap of being overly impressed by a complete, well written logic model or thinking less of a program because it lacks one. It should be remembered that some programs (by the nature of what they do and how they go about accomplishing it) have an easy time "fitting into" a logic model. Others, for some of the same reasons, are more likely to struggle with it. In either case, it might be unfair if we were to reward or penalize the program based too much on the quality of its logic model.

Intervention

Behavior: Apply knowledge of human behavior and the social environment, person-in-environment, and other multidisciplinary theoretical frameworks in interventions with clients and constituencies.

Critical Thinking Question: Using the logic model, list some possible inputs, activities, and outcomes of a program that works with at-risk teenagers at the local high school to encourage them to graduate from high school.

Why We Conduct Program Evaluations

Program evaluation seeks to improve the quality of social programs. The programs may be involved in social action, prevention, treatment, or any other form of intervention that improves human conditions. The primary task of program evaluation is to test the theoretical models that underlie a social program. Most programs "sound good"—they seem like they ought to get underway easily and accomplish their objectives. But a program that sounds good "in theory" may not work or be what is actually needed in the real world.

As we have already mentioned, program evaluation occurs at all stages of program development. It occurs when programs are in the planning or formulation stage. Then the goal of the research is to describe accurately the need for a program and, if it is found to be needed, to tailor the program to meet that need. Once programs are underway, other forms of program evaluation look at how well a program has been implemented. Still other forms of program evaluation look at accountability issues such as, did the program achieve its objectives? The results of these evaluations are used for making a wide range of decisions about whether a program should be offered, continued, modified, or terminated.

Although program evaluations can and are planned to be undertaken at any time in the life cycle of a program, certain events sometimes precipitate them. For example, a politically prominent critic of the program may have questioned the need for the program, professionals or clients may have expressed doubt about its effectiveness, or a funding organization may have determined that extended funding will not be offered until it has demonstrated its ongoing accountability.

Historical Background

Program evaluation as it is currently employed is a relatively new form of research, first receiving widespread attention during the Great Depression and during and after World War II. The need for it became especially great in the 1970s and 1980s, when conservative government leaders carried through on election promises to take a careful (some would say hypercritical) look at social programs that were accused of having failed to solve problems like poverty, unemployment, delinquency, and substance abuse. Other constituencies also began to voice demands for accountability at about the same time. Members of the general public wanted to know how their taxes were being spent, and they sought documentation of the success of social programs that they were supporting. The consumer movement that surfaced in the 1960s and 1970s also produced another group of people—clients—who wanted proof that programs were accomplishing their objectives. Helping professionals themselves began to recognize the importance of evaluating the success of programs. Faced with threatened and real funding cutbacks, they sought methods to help them to use limited resources in the most economical and productive ways. In the late twentieth century, rising costs of health care and other publically subsidized services and the threats of privatization of what have historically been social work programs only increased the emphasis on program efficiency. It was not enough to demonstrate that a program accomplished some good things. We also had to be able to show that it did this at the least amount of cost or, frequently, more cheaply than some other program.

Of course, program evaluation of some form has always been around. However, in the past, methods for evaluating existing programs were often narrowly focused, limited to some aspect of a program that one or more stakeholders deemed especially important to program success. For example:

- Budget reviews determined if a program stayed within budget and whether expenditures in any area were excessive or extravagant.

- Social accounting examined program records to look for problems such as missing or incomplete client records, ambiguous categories of services, and the overall accuracy of record-keeping and recording.
- Audits were conducted by outside auditors to search for financial irregularities such as double billing of third parties for services or misuse of funds for the personal benefit of staff members.
- Administrative audits examined the degree to which a program was well managed. They determined whether managers performed the tasks of planning, staffing, organizing, controlling, and leading well. For example, they might look to see if employees received timely performance evaluations or whether there was an up-to-date manual outlining a program's rules, policies, and procedures.
- Time and motion studies examined how staff used their time. They sought to identify nonproductive activities or other areas of inefficiency such as inconvenient placement of office equipment that might reduce productivity or otherwise interfere with a program's functioning.
- Functional evaluations attempted to learn whether the program was run "properly," often operationalized as the degree to which clients were treated professionally.
- Structural evaluations focused on such factors as the academic credentials and diversity of staff, the aesthetics and healthiness of facilities, and the presence of state-of-the art technology. An accreditation review is often a form of structural evaluation.
- Cost-benefit analysis was used to compute a cost-benefit ratio when both costs and benefits could be measured in monetary terms. It was designed to determine the degree to which a program was able to produce a net overall saving for its stakeholders through its presence.
- Cost-effectiveness analysis was used to compute the cost of an individual program "success" by dividing the number of successes by the overall cost of the program. Then these costs could be compared with the cost effectiveness of other programs that might be attempting to accomplish the same objectives.

These methods of evaluating some component of a program are still around. Each has its merit. However, when they are used in today's program evaluations they are generally just one piece of the evaluation design. They contribute to an assessment of the overall value, worth, or merit of a program, but they are certainly not a sufficient indicator of it in themselves. Today's program evaluations are more comprehensive in scope, often using sophisticated research designs that combine quantitative and qualitative research methods for answering key questions.

At the time when demand for more comprehensive program evaluations first began to occur, social workers were fearful that it would result in the loss of many valuable programs. Although some worthwhile programs undoubtedly were lost, the fears proved to be mostly unfounded. By now we have become quite comfortable with program evaluations as a part of responsible practice. We recognize both their necessity and their value. We understand that many programs within human service organizations receive funding through grants and contracts with government organizations and private charitable organizations, and we acknowledge that these organizations, as stakeholders, have a right to know if the money that they provide is being used responsibly and productively. We are no longer surprised that almost all applications for funding contain a provision for how the program will be evaluated, often by an outside evaluator or evaluation team. We expect a rigorous evaluation of the way that monies are spent and some evaluation of our program's degree of success. And, if a program is not effective, we would like to know it anyway, so that we can revise it or phase it out and spend our time and resources on some other program with greater success potential.

TYPES OF PROGRAM EVALUATIONS

Programs can be described in general terms as either time limited or permanent. Time-limited programs are often grant funded and have a specified duration, for example, three or five years. They may or may not be funded for one or more additional "cycles," often depending on the results of program evaluations. Permanent programs may be mandated by law or may have begun as time-limited programs but are now a relatively permanent component of an agency or organization. Unless there is evidence to the contrary, they are assumed to be needed and will continue indefinitely. However, if their value or effectiveness continues to be questioned, they may be placed in time-limited status. For example, a program may appear to be becoming obsolete, based on changing societal values or a significant decline in the incidence of some problem. Then it may be given three years to demonstrate its merit, worth, or value. If this doesn't happen, it will be terminated.

There are three general categories of program evaluation. In time-limited programs they correspond roughly to the stage of development of the program. In permanent programs the parallel is less direct. The three categories are: (1) needs assessments, (2) formative evaluations, and (3) outcome (sometimes called summative) evaluations.

Needs Assessments

In the broadest sense, the purpose of a needs assessment for a considered or proposed program is to describe the need for such a program and, if it is found to be needed, to propose a program to best respond to that need. Typically, a needs assessment also defines the problem of concern, (actual conditions and how they differ from what is desirable), identifies unmet needs, and describes obstacles that might prevent a program from being effective in meeting them.

What type of questions does a researcher try to answer in determining if there is a need for a program? The most basic one is: Does the problem that we believe to exist really exist? Answering it often entails a documentation of the existence of the problem, who it affects, its magnitude, the forms that it takes, and the human and financial costs that result from it.

Almost always, the need for a program can be documented. After all, a program is often considered because we have already observed a need such as the absence of services that our clients require. However, just because the need for a program has been verified, that does not mean that we will offer the program as initially envisioned or even that we will offer it at all. That is why a needs assessment must address many other questions. Here are just some of them:

- What appear to be the causes of the problem in this community?
- How severe or widespread is it? Who appears to suffer most from it?
- Are we the best organization to address the problem?
- How adequate are existing programs for addressing it?
- What additional services appear to be needed?
- Do other organizations or programs have plans for offering them?
- Are there existing program models that could be successfully implemented here?
- What would be reasonable objectives for a program that would address the problem?
- What would be the budgetary and staffing requirements of such a program?
- Is there potential for outside funding for such a program? Where? What is the likelihood of acquiring it?
- Would the program have the potential to be self-supporting at some point?
- What organizations and individuals would welcome the proposed program? Who might oppose it?
- How might the program's existence affect other programs both inside and outside the organization?
- If offered, what potential clients should it target?
- How likely are targeted clients to use the program?
- What are potential referral sources for the program?
- How should the program be marketed in order to make it attractive to potential clients?
- What logistical obstacles to client participation exist? How could they be overcome?
- What would be a realistic timeframe for implementing the program?
- What tasks would have to be completed before the program would be operational?
- How, when, and by whom should the program be evaluated?

Accurate answers to these and other related questions are absolutely essential if the findings of a needs assessment are to have value. A needs assessment can be a valuable planning tool, or if it contains major design flaws, it can be a real liability to the achievement of the objectives of a program. A poor needs assessment is worse than none at all. It can mislead an administrator into making decisions based on an inaccurate reading of the true origin and nature of a problem and/or the requirements of a program to address it. Poor decisions will occur. Valuable resources will be misdirected and wasted.

One way to increase the likelihood of accurate answers to the questions in any program evaluation is to obtain several different perspectives, a process that researchers sometimes describe as *convergent analysis*. It means, essentially, collecting the same data from three (or more) sources, each having different perspectives on an issue. It can usually be assumed that no one group,

Research-Informed Practice or Practice-Informed Research

Behavior: Use and translate research evidence to inform and improve practice, policy, and service delivery.

Critical Thinking Question: What are five things that may be wasted if we fail to conduct a needs assessment before developing and implementing a social program?

influenced by its own concerns, priorities, experiences, and vested interests, can provide a totally accurate assessment of any situation. In convergent analysis, the different sources help to verify or to refute each other. Although any one source may be misleading, when data from all sources are examined together the truth will emerge.

How might convergent analysis, sometimes referred to as *triangulation*, work in a needs assessment? Suppose that a needs assessment is being conducted in preparation for the development of an HIV prevention program within a community judged to be at risk for high incidence of the disease. Politicians, medical professionals, public educators, clergy, elders, and potential recipients of services who might be surveyed or interviewed might all be knowledgeable about the problem and its solution to some extent, but also might provide very different answers to the same questions. Collectively, these people might be described as key informants. Still other answers might be suggested through an analysis of secondary data such as organization records, community demographics, and other sources of both qualitative and quantitative data previously collected for a variety of specialized uses.

Somewhere within all of the (often conflicting) data collected, there will be found the knowledge needed to create and implement a successful program. The researcher or research team conducting the needs assessment has the difficult job of finding it and conveying it accurately in a research report.

When data are comprehensive enough to construct one, an effective way to synthesize all data collected in a needs assessment is to create and present a clearly articulated logic model in the report. It describes the "ideal program," or at least the minimum required one, based on all that was learned. This allows administrators and others responsible for implementing the program to compare their personnel and financial resources with the model's requirements to assess the feasibility of such a program. They may conclude that the program is feasible, or they may conclude that, while such a program would be desirable, the organization lacks the capacity to offer the program at the current time. If it is the latter, they may still decide that even a scaled-down program would still be "better than nothing," or they may decide to wait until they have the resources to "do it right."

Although needs assessments are most often associated with programs that are in the planning stage, they are also conducted in more permanent programs. They can be used (1) to answer the basic question: Is this program still needed? *or* (2) to determine what changes in the program are necessary for it to retain its relevance. Conditions that create a need for a program change over time. A program that was once needed and made a valuable contribution to a community may now have its usefulness questioned, thus suggesting the appropriateness of a needs assessment.

What clues may suggest that a needs assessment of an existing program should be designed and implemented? Certain client groups may have stopped participating in the program, or the nature of the community (its economic well-being, age or ethnic mix, and so forth) may have changed. Perhaps other organizations may have begun similar programs that now compete with the program, or technological changes may have occurred that now make the way that it operates appear old fashioned or even obsolete. These and other changing conditions may suggest that it is time to conduct research that can be used either to justify continuing a program, to modify it, or to phase it out completely in a way that is least destructive to its clients and staff members. Data from a needs assessment can also be used to convince others of the continued need for a program, or to budget for either an expanded or scaled-down program. They can also help in marketing a program if it is concluded that it is still needed, and for planning for future changes designed to keep the program viable and relevant.

Formative Evaluations

Once a program is underway, program evaluation involves securing data about the degree to which the program is operational as planned and, if it is, what changes might be desirable for increasing the likelihood of it achieving its objectives. This form of program evaluation is referred to as a formative evaluation. In formative evaluations, we would try to determine if the program has been implemented on schedule and is doing what it was intended to do. We would seek to generate suggestions for overcoming any obstacles to program implementation that have been encountered and to recommend ways to improve the program based on how it is doing to date. Evaluating program implementation generally yields three kinds of data: (1) documentation that the program is really in operation as planned; (2) data designed to help program planners know how well program activities are being managed; and (3) data about program design defects or undesirable unintended consequences of the program. Emphasis is upon the support system that exists for services and on the services themselves as perceived by clients and staff members.

In many formative evaluations, the researcher's role is very close to that of consultant. Feedback to the sponsor of funded research is likely to be regular and ongoing. Interim reports may be provided, in addition to a final written report of the evaluation. As problems are identified, changes to the program are made and their success is then evaluated.

Formative evaluations often require the researcher to collect new data from a variety of sources. They might include many of the same sources that are used in conducting needs assessments, such as telephone surveys, mailed questionnaires, focus groups, interviews with key informants, structured and unstructured firsthand observation, and other methods that we have described elsewhere. However, secondary data analysis is often part of a formative evaluation, too. For example, daily attendance sheets might provide the evaluator with data about how well a program is recruiting and retaining clients, or personnel data might suggest whether staff turnover has become a problem.

A formative evaluation is designed to provide feedback (more accurately, "feedforward") to program administrators. When we conduct a formative evaluation we hope to identify the strengths and weaknesses of a program in its early stages and to recommend needed changes while the program is still in its earlier stages of development. In a formative evaluation, we would probably ask many of the same questions that a conscientious program manager asks on a regular basis. This function of managers is called *program monitoring*; the ongoing tracking of a program to be ensured that it is functioning as planned. However, as the evaluator in a formative evaluation we can offer an outsider's perspective. We have no vested interest in the program's success and thus we are more likely to provide constructive criticisms of the program (even its management) than is the manager of a program who is immersed in its day-to-day operation and has a vested interest in its success.

When we conduct a formative evaluation we hope to identify strengths and weaknesses of a program in its early stages and to recommend needed changes while the program is still in its earlier stages of development.

When another form of program evaluation is conducted later in the life cycle of a program, sometimes even when the program is nearing completion, a different term, *process evaluation*, is more appropriate. Unfortunately the term process evaluation is sometimes used interchangeably with the term formative evaluation. However, they not only usually occur at different points in a program's life cycle, they have different purposes as well. Like a formative evaluation, a process evaluation relies on a mixture of qualitative and quantitative data to gain insight into the functioning of a program. However, it is much like a systems analysis, looking to identify flaws in the functioning of the program as an integrated social system. Whereas a formative evaluation might try to learn what is working and what is not working to generate suggestions for improving it, a process evaluation would be more of a post mortem. It would try to learn why an objective will apparently not be achieved or why one component of a program has been successful whereas another was not, so that desirable changes can be made if the program is ever offered again or other programs can learn from the current program's mistakes.

Outcome Evaluations

Outcome evaluations (sometimes called *summative evaluations*) remain the best known form of evaluative research. We will briefly mention two recent examples of outcome evaluations, but they are numerous. One such study (Greaves & Salloun, 2015) was conducted on an outpatient program at an urban community mental health facility. Twenty-eight males, ages 11-17, who were identified as having sexual behavior problems participated in the program. Some findings were positive. Significant improvements occurred among the youths in their psychosocial functioning, in parenting stress, and in parent-child relationships. However, there was no significant change in sexual interests, attitudes, and behaviors.

In a second outcome evaluation (Kemp, Signal, Botros, Taylor, & Prentice, 2014), one designed to evaluate the effectiveness of a program in Australia that used equine facilitated therapy with children and adolescents who had been sexually abused, the psychological distress level of all 30 participants was measured at three different times. While no significant improvement occurred between Time 1 (intake into the program) and Time 2 (after 6 weeks), significant improvement occurred between Time 2 and Time 3 (after 9-10 weeks). The researchers concluded that the program had been successful overall.

Because the findings of outcome evaluations have the potential to threaten the existence of programs and the careers of people who work in them, they are sometimes also the most feared form of program evaluation. However, there are many benefits to outcome evaluations. They are beneficial to future clients by increasing the likelihood that they will receive services that work and will not receive services that are ineffective. The findings of outcome evaluations are also more likely to have utility for people not directly related to the program than the other types of program evaluation that we have discussed thus far. Why? When the results of an outcome evaluation are disseminated to others not involved in the program but working in the same area of practice, they are likely to learn something that is potentially useful to them in their work. If the outcome evaluation identified some component of a program that was unsuccessful, they may decide to not replicate it in their own proposed program. Or, if one of its components

Because the findings of outcome evaluations have the potential to threaten the existence of programs and the careers of people who work in them, they are sometimes also the most feared form of program evaluation.

was found to be highly successful, they may then wish to try the same type of intervention or adapt it to meet the needs of their own client population.

Even if a program is found to be unsuccessful overall in achieving its objectives, other professionals can still learn from its failings in important ways. For example, they might learn that the program was not well conceptualized in the first place. Or the program, though theoretically sound, might have failed to successfully address the problem for a variety of logistical reasons or because cultural issues were inadequately addressed. Another possibility is that the program was unsuccessful because the real problem was not what it was initially perceived to be. When this occurs, our understanding of the problem itself can be enhanced. Learning about why a program was unsuccessful can be very useful to other professionals seeking to address the same problem—it can keep them from making some of the same mistakes.

In the past, the success of programs was often evaluated based primarily on their outputs. For example, the conclusion that "This program offered services to 140 hospice patients and their families during the past year, an increase of more than 22 percent over the previous year" was adequate evidence that a program had been successful. However, accountability pressures now require documentation of how many people were served, and similar outputs are no longer adequate evidence of a program's success. Now a major emphasis is on outcomes, that is, the degree to which a program has been successful in achieving its objectives, but also at a reasonable cost. Thus, this kind of evaluation often involves a dual-focused emphasis on program effectiveness (achievement of objectives) and program efficiency (the relationship of outcome to expenditure of efforts and resources), often using yardsticks of cost-benefit analysis or cost-effectiveness. Comparisons between two related programs are often helpful in this regard. They might reveal that one program may be achieving its objectives, but at an extremely high cost per success, whereas another program may be achieving the same objectives, but at a much lower cost. Thus, both are effective, but they get very different marks in efficiency. We will use an extreme example to show how this could occur and how it is often difficult to determine which one is the better program.

Suppose that program A and program B are both job training programs. Program A carefully selected three clients and offered each client room, board, full tuition, and expenses to attend a junior college for two years, as well as free weekly counseling. At the end of two years, all three clients have found jobs (a success rate of 100 percent). The total cost of program A was $150,000, or $50,000 per success.

The total cost of program B was only $45,000, much lower than program A's. It was able to keep down costs by designing and offering its own intensive job training course. But program B also had a much lower success rate; only three of twelve (25 percent) of its graduates found good jobs. However, program B could claim that it had been successful in placing three clients (the same number as program A) and at a cost of only $15,000 per success!

It could be argued that program B was more efficient than program A, because the cost of each success in program B was less than one-third the cost of each success in program A. It could also be argued that program A was more effective because of its higher success rate. Or it could be argued that it was equally as effective as program B (but less efficient), because both programs successfully helped three clients to find good jobs. So, which was the more successful program? It is hard to say. We would probably be concerned about the per capita cost of helping people find employment under program A. But we also could not help being concerned about the low success rate of program B. What about the human costs related to those nine clients who completed the program, hopeful of getting good jobs, who were not successful in finding good employment?

Still other factors might further complicate a comparison of the two programs. Perhaps program B offered its clients more career choices. However, program A's clients were hired for better paying jobs or higher level jobs. The interaction between success (and failure) and their costs is never a simple one. Weighing the relative merits of effectiveness and efficiency objectively is one of the most difficult tasks that we face in an outcome evaluation. Studying program outcomes typically requires us to assess client gains and losses, the side effects and unintended consequences of the program, and the costs (including economic, social, and psychological) of operating it. As we have found with other forms of research, good outcome evaluation studies must rely heavily on the knowledge, skills, and professional values that we possess as social workers.

In time-limited programs, outcome evaluations are conducted at or near the completion of the program's funding cycle. They focus on the achievement of short-term outcomes, but the program design may also include additional follow-up in order to learn whether longer term objectives were achieved. In permanent programs or programs that are intended to be permanent, an outcome evaluation is generally conducted for the first time at the point where it would be fair to expect that the program should have demonstrated success. Then subsequent outcome evaluations may occur at periodic intervals, perhaps every five years, to determine if the program is continuing to be successful and remains valuable.

ISSUES INVOLVED IN CONDUCTING PROGRAM EVALUATIONS

Determining the Appropriate Design

There are many different ideas about what constitutes a fair yet rigorous evaluation design for a social program. It is probably safe to say that a design developed for any one program is ill- suited for another. That is why no two are alike. In order to design an appropriate evaluation, we must first identify the stage of program development of the program. Is it in the planning stages, laying the groundwork for future services? Is it offering some services but still seeking to expand through outreach and publicity? Or are most activities devoted to services that are in place, well known, and relatively stable? The stage of development of a program is determined by such factors as the activities of staff and how they spend most of their time, funding priorities within the program, and the kind of data (records) collected and used by it. It is often not synonymous with how long the program has been in existence. A program could be decades old but still actively seeking community sanction and client acceptance. Conversely, a program that is only a year or two old may devote most of its energies to the delivery of needed and community-legitimized services.

The pressure for accountability of social programs in recent years has produced a wide variety of different evaluation designs and strategies. Many have been borrowed from basic research designs such as those in Chapter 5 and modified to a greater or lesser degree to adapt them to social programs. Some have come into fashion quickly and fallen out of fashion about as quickly. We will not attempt to examine individual evaluation models (presented in many books and government documents, and a topic for advanced study). However, we will offer some general principles relating to the design of evaluation studies in each of the three categories that we have discussed.

As we noted, all program evaluations now typically combine elements of both quantitative and qualitative research methods. In needs assessments, the methods employed are generally a combination of exploratory and descriptive research. For example, the open-ended question—Do you think there is a need for an HIV infection prevention program in our community?—might be asked of people representing a wide variety of backgrounds and perspectives in either one-on-one interviews or in a focus group. Or the same question (along with others) could be part of a mailed survey sent to community leaders. Much of the data required in needs assessments can also be found through secondary analysis of social indicators such as public health data, census data, and other sources of data collected for some other purpose.

Formative (or process) evaluations tend to be primarily descriptive. For example, the evaluator may wish to gather a wide array of descriptive data (including personal observations) to evaluate how well a program seems to have gotten off the ground and to make recommendations for needed changes. Descriptive designs may also be used to answer other questions about program implementation, for example: Are the clients who were targeted for services actually those being served? Confidential, in-depth interviews with clients and staff may be conducted and the content of interviews examined using content analysis.

Outcome evaluations strive to be explanatory. Thus, when possible, they often employ the same basic explanatory designs that we described in Chapter 5 (experimental and quasi-experimental) to attempt to learn not only whether or not a program achieved its objectives but also whether or not the program can "take credit" for any changes that occurred. They test the null hypotheses about program effectiveness by using inferential statistical analyses to learn the probability that the relationship between the program and some indicator or indicators of success was a real one, and not just a function of sampling or random error. By using designs that rely on random assignment of clients to programs (and to control groups), it is also possible to conclude that it was the program, and not something else, that produced any successes (the issue of internal validity). Of course, for ethical and logistical reasons, it is not always possible to use explanatory designs. Then, designs that are more descriptive are used. They contain a mixture of qualitative and quantitative methods.

Researchers conducting outcome evaluations attempt to rely on measurement that is as quantitative as possible. However, even when explanatory designs can be used and quantitative measurements of the achievement of program objectives are available, qualitative methods are still likely to be used to gather some data. Sometimes they are used to attempt to confirm impressions obtained using more quantitative measures. For example, confidential follow-up interviews might be used to try to better understand the high number of responses in a survey of staff members that seem to suggest that efforts to recruit staff for the program did not seem to produce sufficient cultural diversity. Qualitative research methods may also be used to assess other indicators of the merit of a program. For example, interviews might be conducted with key informants to attempt to learn the reputation of the program in the community or how well its staff members are perceived as collaborating with staff members from other programs that address the same problem. Interviews with the program manager or grant writer might be used to learn how much progress is being made in moving toward financial independence. Or, a focus group of staff members might help in evaluating the quality of materials developed by program staff (for example, training manuals or computer software) to attempt to learn if they represent a valuable contribution to program functioning.

If experimental or quasi-experimental designs are ethically feasible and if program outcomes have been well stated and quantified (for example, "Following completion of the program, clients who completed the program will have a lower rate of re-hospitalization than those who did not participate in the program"), the determination of whether or not the program achieved its objective is a relatively simple, statistical one. However, if the objectives of the program were never well-articulated or the program was never implemented as articulated in its logic model, then any conclusions relating to the value, worth, or merit of such a program become much more difficult. When this happens, someone (often another evaluator) may first have to examine the program's activities and, based on them, use an inductive process to identify and specify the program's mission, goals, and objectives. This is known as *evaluability assessment*. It makes outcome evaluation more possible.

When conducting an outcome evaluation, we must have a clear understanding of the anticipated outcomes of a program and be very careful in the selection (if we have that option) and use of appropriate outcome measures (indicators). If judgments are to be made on the basis of its outcomes, then rigorous but fair outcome measures are needed. Often they are already specified in a grant proposal or contract with a funding agency. If not, they may be available in the form of standardized indexes or scales. But it may be that, in the interest of fairness, original evaluation instruments will need to be developed for the evaluation. If this is necessary, then we must use instrument development procedures that will ensure that measurement will be valid (see Chapter 12).

One notable trend has been evident in recent years. Increasingly, evaluations of existing programs are being required by outside funding sources to include input from consumers of services (clients). This trend has generally met with little resistance from social workers since, when asked (or perhaps because they are asked), clients generally report a high level of satisfaction with programs and services. Besides, it just seems right that we should ask our clients about their impressions of our programs. However, the validity of any findings from client satisfaction surveys are highly suspect for several reasons, the most obvious being that client satisfaction is not a valid indicator of program effectiveness. Clients can be satisfied or dissatisfied with a program for any number of reasons that do not relate to the quality of the program. They may be highly satisfied with a program because, for example, it allows them to take time off from work, provides necessary respite in the form of child care, or they simply like program staff and most of the other clients. In some fields of practice (for example, protective services or the juvenile justice system) where clients are "involuntary," some social workers have argued especially vehemently that consumer satisfaction (which understandably is usually low) is an unfair yardstick for measuring program success.

Most outcome evaluation designs focus on short-range success (outcome). However, there has been concern that they do not adequately address two issues: (1) the program's success may not hold up over time and (2) they give inadequate attention to the impact of the program on other programs and services of the program's organization or of other organizations—the unintended consequences of the program. In response to these concerns, some evaluation models have attempted to address them. They determine whether programs have resulted in permanent desirable changes. For example, they might ask whether street crime rates and unemployment rates stayed low or declined even more following the completion of athletic and recreational programs for youth.

Program evaluations that look at the long-term impacts of a program also look beyond a program itself to examine how the program's presence may have affected other programs or phenomena. They are a recognition (consistent with systems theory) that almost any change or innovation within a system is likely to produce both anticipated and unanticipated changes within other system components. For example, if this type of evaluation were used to evaluate a hospital's new bereavement program for caregivers of terminally ill patients who have recently died, many questions that would go beyond whether the program itself was effective would be asked. They might include, for example,

- How has the program changed the daily activities of social workers in the hospital's existing hospice program?
- How has the morale of the hospice social workers been affected?
- How has the new program's presence changed the informal power structure of the social work department?
- How has reallocation of funding affected the work of other staff?
- Are former caregivers more likely to serve as volunteers (after the required waiting period) than they were prior to the existence of the program?

Evaluating program impact requires the evaluator to extrapolate from the data collected in program outcome studies and to creatively use current social indicators. A problem with studies that include an assessment of a program's impact is the presence of a multitude of other variables that may have produced apparent impacts, especially because these studies generally employ a longer time framework for conducting an evaluation. So many different events and circumstances can intervene that it becomes very difficult to attribute any apparent impact directly to the effects of a program. In our previous example, it would be very hard to attribute changes within the hospice social work program directly to the presence of the new bereavement program rather than to other events or phenomena. For example, staff turnover, the lack of pay raises in more than three years, or staff burnout might have been the real reasons for any changes. Perhaps no changes were produced by the program at all. Or they might have been even more dramatic if the bereavement program had not been implemented!

The difficulty of isolating the longer term impact of a program and of determining how other (confounding) variables may relate to any apparent program impact is certainly not unique to social work program evaluations. For example, impact studies in the 1980s were used to examine the relationship between lower speed limits and rate of traffic fatalities. But how can people say (as many do) that fewer fatal accidents in the 1970s and the early 1980s were the result of federally imposed 55-mile-per-hour speed limits or that an increase in fatalities in the late 1990s occurred because speed limits were relaxed? One would need to control for many other possibly intervening variables, such as gasoline prices, number of miles driven, the work of Mothers Against Drunk Drivers (MADD), inconsistent punishments for driving while under the influence of alcohol or drugs, changes in automobile safety equipment, changes in size and design of automobiles, the advent of cellular phones, and literally hundreds of other variables that may contribute to traffic fatality rates. Similarly, it would be very difficult to learn whether a program to reduce teen smoking has been successful in achieving its objectives when, during its operation, smoking was made illegal in restaurants and other public places, the sales tax on cigarettes was increased, the dangers of second-hand smoke were widely publicized, and public hostility toward smokers was on the increase.

Ultimately, since an outcome evaluation is designed to learn whether a program reduced or alleviated a problem (a cause–effect relationship between two variables was demonstrated), the value of an outcome evaluation design and the findings that it produced come down to questions of *validity*, a term that is used with different modifiers in research. They have a specific meaning in outcome evaluations:

1. **Construct validity.** Was the intended program implemented as planned, and were intended outcomes measured using appropriate indicators?

2. **Conclusion validity.** Do the evaluator's conclusions about the program appear to be sufficiently justified?

3. **Internal validity.** Were desirable changes in the problem *caused by* the program?

4. **External validity.** To what extent would other programs benefit from the findings of the evaluation?

Who Conducts Program Evaluations?

In a general sense every social work professional is involved in program evaluation to a greater or lesser extent. It is a requirement for social workers in the twenty-first century, one that is consistent with the goal of evidence-based practice. At the very least, as employees of social programs or as professionals familiar with them, we are a potential data source for program evaluations. We possess a valuable perspective on them. At some point we will be called upon to share that perspective as research participants. Or, we may more actively assist others conducting program evaluations, perhaps by providing help in conducting research interviews or assisting in data tabulation and analysis. Or, if we have a little more expertise and a special interest in evaluation research, we may participate in both the design and implementation of program evaluations.

College and university faculty members may design and conduct program evaluations from time to time as part of their research agenda or as a service to their community or profession. Still other individuals who we might describe as social work program evaluation specialists spend most or all of their professional time designing and conducting program evaluations. Some are employees of large human service organizations. One of their major responsibilities is to conduct evaluations of its programs. Other evaluation specialists are employed within institutes or centers associated with universities or in the private, for-profit sector. Their program evaluation services can be purchased through contract.

In a general sense every social work professional is involved in program evaluation to a greater or lesser extent. It is a requirement for social workers in the twenty-first century, one that is consistent with the goal of evidence-based practice.

From the perspective of the program, the issue of who is the best person to design and conduct a program evaluation often centers around one question: Is it better for the evaluator to be in house or external to the organization and its programs? In making this determination, three factors may be considered: (1) requirements, (2) convention, and (3) advantages and disadvantages.

As we noted earlier, if major funding for the program was provided by some foundation or similar organization that awarded a grant to support all or part of the program, it may be stipulated in the agreement signed by all parties involved that an outside evaluator must be used. The evaluator may be an employee of the funding organization or an outside evaluation expert with whom they regularly contract. Or, a list of approved evaluators may be provided to the program manager. Then he or she may select an individual to hire with funds designated for evaluation within the grant's budget. An external evaluator is most likely to be required for an outcome evaluation, but sometimes it is a requirement for a formative evaluation as well. Less frequently, it is a requirement for a needs assessment unless one is mandated as part of a grant application when money was sought to conduct it.

Even if there is no requirement for an outside evaluator, convention suggests when an in-house evaluator or an external one is more appropriate. Needs assessments are generally conducted by agency employees, often as a cost-saving measure. However, if funds are available, they may be contracted out in order to get what is likely to be a more objective assessment. Formative evaluations may be conducted in-house, but they are more often conducted by external evaluators with no personal or professional investment in the program. When this is the case, the evaluator still receives considerable assistance from program staff, especially managers and/or quality control personnel, who should already have been collecting data and interpreting it as part of their own program monitoring. While outcome evaluations are sometimes conducted in-house, they still may be designed and conducted by outside evaluators. Since so much (jobs, funding, and so forth) is at stake in an outcome evaluation, employees of the program cannot be expected to be totally objective. If an outcome evaluation is conducted in-house (as sometimes occurs when the program receives no outside funding), the credibility of the research findings can be easily questioned.

Assuming there is a choice in the matter, another issue to be considered is the relative advantages and disadvantages of using in-house evaluators or external ones. One advantage to using in-house evaluators is that they are already familiar with the organization's functions, policies, programs, people, and politics. There is little need to acquaint in-house evaluators with any of these aspects of an organization; they can hit the ground running. Because they are in-house, they should also have sensitivity to the client populations served and an understanding of the organization's mission and a program's relation to it. This knowledge should help them in selecting or developing appropriate and sensitive methods of measuring key variables. Assuming that in-house evaluators also have expertise in data analysis and interpretation or have access to consultation for these purposes, the evaluation study can proceed smoothly and at minimal cost to the organization. Because they are already on the payroll of an organization, no additional expenses are incurred. However, there is still a cost. In-house evaluators need release time from their usual duties. Other staff may need to be hired to cover for them while they conduct their program evaluations.

Of course, there also are disadvantages to using an in-house evaluator. One relates to a given evaluator's experience and expertise in program evaluation. Many individuals claim to be knowledgeable in the areas of research and statistics, and some are. But program evaluation has important differences from most other forms of research, and few persons who are employed within organizations perform program evaluations on a regular basis. Unless the person is competent to perform all necessary research tasks, the quality of the evaluation may suffer. Of course, outside consultants may be hired to help perform specialized tasks; this may be necessary to successfully implement an evaluation that uses an in-house evaluator.

A second disadvantage, one that was suggested earlier, involves the extent to which in-house evaluators can be objective about the findings of a program evaluation in the organization where they are employed. Evaluation involves making judgments about programs; these judgments should be based on the data collected and on nothing else. In-house evaluators may have difficulty being objective (an understandable difficulty if the evaluator has had even minimal involvement with the program or has acquaintances or friends who have). Or, as an employee of the organization, the evaluator might feel pressured to present findings in a way consistent with the wishes of administrators—an ethical dilemma that a nonemployee would be less likely to face. If, for whatever reason, the evaluator's objectivity is compromised, the quality and credibility of the research findings can be severely damaged.

A third disadvantage involves the way that other staff may perceive the in-house evaluator. Suddenly the evaluator may appear to have been elevated in status (perhaps with justification). He or she may have the power to influence the functions and even the job status of coworkers. This may result in staff resentment and resistance (more than if an outside evaluator were to be used), and it may prompt staff to be uncooperative or even to sabotage the evaluator's work. After completing the evaluation, the in-house evaluator may find relationships with coworkers to be negatively affected or even irreparably damaged. This can be costly to the organization as well as to the individuals involved.

Expertise and objectivity are two major advantages to using outside evaluators. Unfortunately, there are also distinct disadvantages to using them. Hiring an outside evaluator often requires an organization to find the money to pay someone to design and conduct a program evaluation. Given the austere budgets that often characterize human service organizations, the cost of hiring outside evaluators may be prohibitive. Outside evaluators are generally paid well for their time and expertise, and they may require more time to conduct an evaluation than would an in-house evaluator. Before they can even begin to design and implement an evaluation, an external evaluator first needs to learn about the organization and its programs. If this is not done, an evaluation design that is inappropriate and unfair may result. The amount of time needed to educate an outside evaluator varies with the complexity of the organization and its programs. But it is always necessary for an outside evaluator to spend time trying to understand what a program is trying to accomplish (its goals and objectives), the ways in which it goes about trying to accomplish them, and the stage of development of the program.

Another potential disadvantage concerns the extent to which external evaluators (particularly those who are not social workers working in a related practice setting) are likely to be insensitive to certain realities within which a program must operate. They may have difficulty understanding the many sources of resistance that confront clients seeking to change some aspect of their lives or the hostile task environment that exists for many unpopular programs that social workers offer. For example, they may not understand that programs designed to protect children from abuse or to prevent the spread of sexually transmitted diseases are often resented by community members who may create obstacles to their success. An outside evaluator may also have difficulty developing appropriate evaluation instruments and standards to assess the success level of such programs. Can an outside evaluator understand that a 30 percent success rate for a program to train people who are chronically unemployed may constitute an acceptable level of success? Or that historically, treatment programs for people who are repeated sex offenders have had a very low rate of success? Of course, if the program has clearly articulated realistic objectives from the outset and if the program is evaluated based on them, this problem can be greatly reduced.

The advantages of external and in-house evaluators can be maximized while minimizing the disadvantages of both. *Empowerment evaluation* is an approach to program evaluation that combines the use of in-house and external evaluators in a unique way. It has the expressed purpose of helping program staff evaluate themselves and their programs in order to improve practice and foster self-determination. Like other forms of program evaluation, it employs both qualitative and quantitative methodologies. Program staff members conduct their own evaluations using a form of self-evaluation and reflection; it is very process oriented. An outside evaluator acts as a coach or facilitator depending on the capabilities of program participants and staff.

Empowerment evaluation is consistent with social work professional values. It is being used in a variety of human service organizations in many different countries, particularly with those that serve more powerless and historically disenfranchised populations. Through this type of evaluation, people develop skills to become independent problem solvers and decision makers. Because all of the program staff (and, to a lesser degree, clients) are involved with the evaluation from its inception and form a team with the external evaluator, some of the power dynamics and areas of distrust typically associated with external evaluations are minimized.

The assessment of a program's value is not the end point of empowerment evaluation, but part of an ongoing process of service and quality improvement. The goal is to have program staff internalize and institutionalize self-evaluation practices. It allows them to practice ongoing program evaluation and improvement in the face of population shifts, changing knowledge about practice, and evolving external political forces that affect the social welfare environment. Fetterman, Kaftarian, and Wandersman (1996) identify several facets of empowerment evaluation: training, facilitation, advocacy, illumination, and liberation.

1. **Training.** Skilled evaluators teach program staff how to conduct their own evaluations with a focus on mastery and internalization of evaluation principles and practices as an integral part of program planning.

2. **Facilitation.** Skilled evaluators serve as coaches to help program staff conduct their own self-evaluations. Tasks include goal setting, specifying of performance indicators, establishing baselines, developing rating scales, and monitoring goal attainment.

3. **Advocacy.** Program staff members are helped to use the findings of the evaluation to gain more leverage over resources and to participate in the political process. Advocate evaluators use findings to try to change public opinion and influence the policy decision-making process.

4. **Illumination.** Program staff members are helped to gain new insights and understanding about program dynamics and roles of various stakeholders.

5. **Liberation.** Liberation is the ultimate outcome of empowerment evaluation. It is a process through which program staff members are freed from preexisting roles and constraints as they learn more about what works and what does not work. They are helped to discover new opportunities, to use existing resources in innovative ways, and to redefine the roles they play in continuous program improvement.

Participating in Program Evaluations

When we and other professional staff are asked to be involved in the implementation phase of a program evaluation, we may be involved in data-gathering activities, such as submitting work documents to the evaluation team, completing questionnaires or interviews, or asking our clients to provide evaluative data. We may experience concern and skepticism when asked to supply data that will be used for evaluating a program. We may be fearful both for the future of the program and for our own job security.

One possible recommendation of an outcome evaluation is that a planned or existing program should be terminated or significantly modified. Even if the decisions that are to be made about a program and its future aren't of the "continue" versus "terminate" type, we are aware that the process of evaluating always entails making a judgment (either directly or implicitly) about the value of a given program. We also know that good outcome measures are sometimes difficult to develop and that the real, lasting achievements of a program and its overall merit, worth, or value may not be evident for many years. Thus, we fear that what they perceive to be a valuable program may show up in a bad light or even prematurely terminated.

There may also be concern that our individual work performance will be assessed by the evaluator using data provided and then shared with administrators or supervisors. The study design may, in fact, require that individual workers submit time sheets, activity logs, and other process documents and even reports of single system research (Chapter 8). However, the goal of program evaluation studies is typically not to evaluate individual work performance (although they almost always reflect on the performance of a program's managers). Individual employee performance evaluations are generally conducted at regularly scheduled intervals (often, annually) by a supervisor and are separate and unrelated to program evaluation studies. An evaluator is likely to receive better cooperation from staff members if they are reminded of this.

A program evaluation should also be viewed as part of a greater political process for two major, related reasons. The first has to do with the purpose of the study, and the second concerns the use and potential misuse of evaluation data. As we have noted, program evaluation studies are sometimes conducted at the request or mandate of organizations that have provided funding for a program. They are conducted to address accountability concerns or to assist in answering some question, for example: Should the program be funded for another year or cycle?

In addition, program evaluations can legitimately be requested by boards of directors and funding organizations at any time. Unfortunately, such a request may not always be based on a desire for constructive feedback or other evaluation data designed to improve the program being evaluated; there may be another hidden agenda. Sometimes evaluations are requested because boards of directors simply wish to secure damaging evidence about an unpopular program or its administrator. For example, an evaluator may be hired because the board is seeking documentation to justify the firing of a program's director. Or, if a program provides desirable employment for friends or relatives, the board may be seeking justification to continue or expand it, despite the fact that it is believed to be ineffective. As we suggested earlier, an external evaluator is likely to have more credibility and is assumed to be more objective than an employee of the organization where a program is based. However, even an external evaluator is vulnerable to being "used" unless (1) they are politically astute, and (2) they adhere to ethical standards and insist on reporting their findings in a way that presents a complete and accurate picture of a program.

Hidden agendas are a fact of life in many program evaluations and are often the impetus for them. When an evaluator from outside (or even within) an organization is asked to conduct a program evaluation, he or she needs to remember that there may be motives for conducting it besides a desire to improve the program. Skilled evaluators attempt to determine if they exist before agreeing to conduct program evaluations. They ask questions about the purpose of proposed evaluations and explore what possible uses may be made of the data. If it appears after some inquiry that something other than an honest evaluation is being sought, and that the evaluation will simply be used to support a decision that has already been made an ethical evaluator may refuse to participate in it. However, if the decision is not irreversible and assurances are made that the findings of the evaluation will be considered with an "open mind," the evaluator may agree to conduct it.

Other Ethical Issues

There are ethical issues in any type of research. We discussed some of the more general ones in Chapter 2. They apply to program evaluations as well as to research that is designed to build general knowledge for our profession. For example, confidentiality, anonymity, and informed consent issues must be addressed, because people who provide data for program evaluations are often vulnerable to retaliation if they are critical of a program and the source of their comments is revealed to administrators. When conducting program evaluations, however, there are also some very specific ethical dilemmas that must be confronted. Because the evaluator usually has a considerable amount of latitude in making certain critical decisions about how the research will be conducted, it is quite easy for unethical evaluators to influence the results of an evaluation.

Suppose that you have been asked to conduct an outcome evaluation of a program that was established to provide assistance to couples and individuals seeking to adopt children from Asian or North African countries. The program is a new one to the agency, which had not previously offered international adoption services. If you were unethical, could you "stack" the evaluation so that the program would look highly successful and so that your friend who works in the program can remain employed? Yes. Or, conversely, could you design the research to make the program appear ineffective? Yes.

We would need to make a number of important design decisions, sometimes with the "help" of powerful people like administrators, but often unilaterally. Most likely, the program has several objectives, some of which have been achieved and some of which have not been achieved. By choosing to focus on those where we know the program has been successful (for example, in expediting paperwork) and either not addressing or deemphasizing those where it has not been successful, it is possible to make a program look better than it really is. Conversely, a focus on the program's shortcomings (for example, its failure to attract single parents) could make it appear worse than it really is.

Similarly, the decision of who will provide data (sampling bias issues) can distort results. Interviewing parents of newly adopted children (as opposed to those who dropped out before the adoption process was completed) can make the program look good. Interviewing staff from agencies that compete with the program for clients can make it look bad. Or, knowing what we do about different methods of data collection (for example, that in-person interviews have very high completion rates but mailed questionnaires have lower, often biased completion rates), it would be possible to get whatever results are sought. Statistical analysis and interpretation of findings would also provide opportunities to deliberately misrepresent the results of the evaluation.

> **Ethical and Professional Behavior**
>
> **Behavior: Make ethical decisions by applying the standards of the NASW Code of Ethics, relevant laws and regulations, models for ethical decision-making, ethical conduct of research, and additional codes of ethics as appropriate to context.**
>
> **Critical Thinking Question:** Describe an example of how an unethical evaluator could purposefully bias the outcome evaluation of a social program.

In contrast, as an ethical researcher, we would strive to produce an evaluation that is feasible given budgetary constraints and given the need to not disrupt client services, but also one that is fair and accurate. Fairness would entail getting a wide array of perspectives on the program and reporting them in a way that no group feels that their input was ignored. Accuracy would relate to the reliability and validity of the data, as well as to the correct use and interpretation of statistical analyses.

SUMMARY

In this chapter and the next one we focus on the direct contributions of research to evidence-based practice. In Chapter 7, we focused on

- How research methods are utilized to assess the merit, worth, or value of social programs.
- An overview of systemic reviews and meta-analysis and how they are sometimes used for evaluating reports of research in our professional literature that describe the effectiveness of services and programs.
- How both qualitative and quantitative research methods are used to evaluate both proposed and existing programs. Program evaluation is, in part, a response to demands for accountability by the stakeholders of programs. We emphasized that program evaluation should be perceived as a critical component in an ongoing process of planning for, fine-tuning, and passing judgment on programs.

- The three major types of evaluation studies: needs assessments, formative evaluations, and outcome or summative evaluations. These evaluation studies differ in purpose and the research questions that they attempt to answer. All program evaluations employ unique research designs, a variety of data sources, and data-gathering techniques.
- The complex decision to use either an in-house or an outside evaluator to conduct program evaluations, when the option is available. Both alternatives have advantages and disadvantages. An alternative that uses both in-house and outside evaluators—empowerment evaluation—is a compromise that often that may combine the best features of both.
- How program evaluations are action-oriented and decision-oriented research; decisions about programs and their continuation are likely to be made as a result of them. This fact and others were discussed in the context of political and ethical factors that can affect our desire and capacity to participate in, design, and conduct program evaluations.

MyEducationLab® for Research
Chapter 7 Chapter Review Quiz.

8

Evaluating Individual Practice Effectiveness

In the previous chapter, we saw how many of the research concepts and methods that we discussed in earlier chapters are also useful for evaluating social programs. However, social work practitioners also need to know how well they are doing in their individual practice interventions; that is, in the services they offer to clients and client groups. We require regular feedback if we are to be evidence-based practitioners. In this chapter, we will look at how research methods can be used to provide it.

As we have suggested repeatedly throughout this book, there are many potential sources of research data. The data that social workers need to assess their effectiveness can also come from a variety of sources. We will mention a few of them briefly and then shift our focus to what we believe to be an especially good way to evaluate individual practice effectiveness—single-system evaluations.

SUPERVISOR FEEDBACK

A potential source of data for feedback on one's practice effectiveness is the social worker's supervisor. In supervisory conferences, social workers are encouraged to objectively evaluate their progress in working with individual clients or larger client systems. Along with the supervisor (often a very experienced, accomplished practitioner), achievements are identified and applauded, and shortcomings are analyzed. The supervisor may suggest better ways to accomplish the goals of intervention. At least, that is the way it is supposed to work. Unfortunately, supervisory conferences may have another agenda that gets in the way of useful feedback. One problem is that supervisors are also asked to perform annual performance evaluations of their subordinates, often with little knowledge of their work other than what they learn during supervisory conferences. Thus, while trying to be helpful, they are also evaluating. Not surprisingly, supervisees are not always totally candid when discussing their interventions. They sometimes are unwilling to jeopardize salary increases or promotions by describing those situations in which they appear to be less than effective. Thus, they are deprived of much of the feedback that might have helped them to become more effective practitioners.

LEARNING OUTCOMES

- Examine supervisor feedback as a method of evaluating individual practice effectiveness.
- Consider the strengths and weaknesses of using consumer feedback to evaluate individual practice effectiveness.
- Analyze goal attainment scaling as a potential method for evaluating individual practice effectiveness.
- Compare and contrast group research designs and single-system evaluation designs.
- Distinguish between various single-system evaluation designs and identify the strengths and weaknesses of each.

CHAPTER OUTLINE

In recent years, trends within our profession have made supervision an even less likely source of useful feedback. Cost-cutting measures in many settings, such as hospitals and psychiatric facilities, have eliminated many supervisory positions. If a social worker has a supervisor at all, it is likely to be someone who is seen only rarely, is unfamiliar with their work, and may belong to another professional discipline. In other settings, alternative models of supervision (for example, group supervision, peer supervision, or even supervision via electronic communication) have replaced the former supervisor–supervisee relationship.

Even annual performance evaluations that supervisors or others conduct have limited value as indicators of practice effectiveness. If data collection instruments are used at all, they have rarely undergone validation using scientific methods. Often, written evaluations consist of subjective judgments based on occasional firsthand observations, data provided by the individual being evaluated, and impressions shared gratuitously by other staff members.

CONSUMER FEEDBACK

If feedback from supervisors is of little value, why not get it directly from those consumers who are supposed to benefit from our interventions? Aren't they in the best position to tell us if we are helping or making a difference in their lives? Yes, but unfortunately, our clients often fail to provide honest answers.

Suppose, for example, that a social worker decided to draw a random sample of past and/or current clients and to construct and mail out a brief questionnaire asking them to evaluate the services received. Would this provide an accurate assessment of the social worker's effectiveness? Probably not. First, those clients most likely to return the data collection instrument would be those most satisfied with services and, perhaps, a smaller number who were least satisfied with them—an uneven, biased response rate. Others who might really be less than totally satisfied might still report that they were satisfied, simply because they were impressed that the social worker cared enough to ask. For a variety of reasons, the presence of a past or present helping relationship with individual clients and client groups tends to influence the results of a client satisfaction survey. We alluded to this problem in the previous chapter when we referred to client satisfaction surveys as a component of program evaluations. We also noted that satisfaction is not synonymous with successful intervention. Thus, if social workers use client satisfaction as an indicator of their effectiveness in their individual practice, they may learn a considerable amount about how satisfied their clients are, but little about how effective their interventions are. A client might be satisfied with the intervention because it was convenient or inexpensive, because the social worker seemed to really "care," or for any number of other reasons, even though no progress in addressing their problem was made. Conversely, dissatisfaction may have occurred because the services were court ordered and not sought or the social worker offered some needed but unpleasant form of intervention (for example, confrontation) that ultimately proved effective. Even if clients are surveyed in such a way that questions focus on client progress rather than on satisfaction, it is almost impossible for satisfaction to not influence the results. (This phenomenon often occurs when students are asked to evaluate the teaching effectiveness of their instructors.)

Despite these problems, client surveys can sometimes provide useful feedback of individual practice effectiveness. They are most likely to yield useful data when carefully developed data collection instruments are used that contain some open-ended questions (for example: What help did you want or were you expecting to receive?), along with fixed-alternative items or scales that measure the client's progress in reducing their problem.

GOAL ATTAINMENT SCALING

Another method of evaluating the success of an individual social worker's intervention methods, goal attainment scaling (GAS), frequently relies on consumers (clients) to provide data. However, the data reported are the behaviors of clients or client systems rather than their satisfaction with services. Thus, it is believed to be less vulnerable to bias.

GAS has a relatively long history of use by social workers; it was first used back in the 1960s among therapists working with psychiatric patients. Since then, it has been used in a wide variety of settings where social workers are employed. When using it, a social worker identifies (along with the client or client system) a small number (usually, three to five) of specific behavioral problems. They should be problems of importance to the client and ones for which it is reasonable to expect that social work intervention might produce some positive changes. Although GAS is used most frequently to evaluate the success of interventions with individual clients, it is also applicable when working with problems within groups, families, institutions, or communities, as long as the problem and its incidence can be easily quantified. For example, if we are employed in a community agency we might use it to assess our effectiveness in increasing the percentage of the local population who register to vote in an upcoming election.

Once having identified and specified a small number of problems and the goals of intervention associated with them, a range of five levels of goal attainment are specified and listed in rank order. They are assigned a number between −2 and +2. Zero is assigned to what will be the expected outcome if intervention is successful. Plus scores are assigned to goal attainment that is greater than expected and minus scores to goal attainment levels that are less than expected. To return to our previous example—attempting to increase voter registration prior to a presidential election in a community where current registration is only 20 percent—we might use the following scale:

Most unfavorable outcome (−2)	20% or less
Less than expected outcome (−1)	21–25%
Expected outcome (0)	26–30%
More than expected outcome (+1)	31–35%
Most favorable outcome (+2)	over 35%

The decision as to which percentage of registration would represent the expected outcome (0) and which percentage would be appropriate for the other four levels would be based on a combination of an assessment of what we believe to be realistic, given the time available for the intervention, and what past experience has taught us about the likely impact of the intervention. It would also require a good understanding of the community and the reasons for low voter turnout in the past.

The results of goal attainment in addressing different problems in the same client system (perhaps, in our example, participation at community meetings or attendance at PTA meetings) could then be combined mathematically to suggest, overall, how effective we have been in working with that system. The different problems could also be weighted to reflect their relative importance. Methods are even available to convert the results to a scale with scores ranging between 1 and 100.

GAS is designed for use with well-motivated clients who will work to set realistic goals and honestly report their behaviors, as well as with larger client systems where valid measurement of behaviors is possible. It is also designed for social workers who want honest feedback about their effectiveness, not social workers who just want to appear successful. If, either unintentionally or deliberately, the different levels of success are scaled too high or too low or if the measurement of success is inappropriate for some other reason, the results of GAS will be of little value as feedback. For example, if both a social worker and an adolescent with a problem of severe shyness in social situations set an expected goal of two Internet chat-room conversations per week ($+2 = 4$ chats; $0 = 2$ chats; $-2 =$ no chats), a 0 level or even a $+2$ level might be accomplished. It would make the social worker appear successful, but would this really represent successful intervention for the client's shyness? Probably not, because the goal levels were set so low that they could easily be achieved. In addition, the goal itself may have been inappropriate, because there is little reason to believe that increased Internet conversations might help the underlying problem of shyness in actual social situations.

SINGLE-SYSTEM EVALUATIONS

Next, we will look at a useful method of evaluating individual social worker effectiveness called single-system research. In Chapter 5, we looked at group research designs that are used when groups of people or client systems (e.g., families, neighborhoods) participate in the research process. In the most rigorous designs (experimental), the participants are randomly assigned to either a control group or an experimental group and data from both groups are compared. In less rigorous designs (pre-experimental and quasi-experimental), either no comparison group is available or the groups cannot be randomly assigned for ethical or logistical reasons. We briefly described one of these, the time series design, which uses repeated measures before and after the introduction of the independent variable in the absence of a control group. It is a variation of this design that is the basis for single-system research.

In a time series design, repeated measures of the dependent variable make it possible to compare measurements of it before the independent variable is introduced with measurements of it after the independent variable is introduced. Thus, it provides at least a tentative assessment of the impact of the independent variable on the dependent variable.

In single-system research (also commonly referred to as single-subject designs, single-case designs, and $n = 1$ research), we also use repeated measures and the analysis of any trends in measurements of the dependent variable (the problem of a client or client system) both before and after the introduction of the independent variable (an intervention). However, unlike the basic time series design in which measurements are taken of the dependent variable before and after the independent variable is introduced, single-system designs involve taking measurements of the client or client system's problem before the intervention is introduced, throughout the time period while the intervention is being employed, and often after it is completed or withdrawn. The more stable the trends (e.g., rising, falling, or stable) are in the measurements of the problem before, during, and after the intervention, and the more pronounced any changes are, the stronger the argument for inferring that our intervention may have produced those changes.

Differences between Group Designs and Single-System Evaluation Designs

There are several differences between single-system designs and group research designs. The main difference, of course, is that group designs require that a group (sample or population) of research participants be involved in the study. Single-system designs use a single client or client system, whether that be an individual, family, school, community, or whatever system level is the focus of our intervention. Another important difference is that while group design research is often conducted by research specialists who may do little else but conduct research studies, single-system evaluations are generally conducted by practitioners for their own use (feedback about their practice effectiveness).

Single-system evaluation research is similar to group research in that, just as there are a variety of group research designs, there are different types of single-system designs, some more rigorous than others. Generally speaking, the more times the dependent variable is measured and the more times the independent variable is introduced and withdrawn (or, less frequently, manipulated), the stronger the single-system design. This principle is based on the concept of unlikely coincidences. That is, if we can see clear trends in the measurements of the problem, and these trends change one or more times coinciding with when the intervention is introduced and withdrawn, it becomes increasingly unlikely that the changes are a coincidence (or are caused by something other than the intervention).

Terminology

Much of the terminology used in single-system evaluation research is common to all forms of research. However, in single-system designs, many other terms have different, specific meanings. Still other research terms are not often used, but they are implicit in the designs of single-system studies. This can be confusing, so we have grouped some of the more important research terms in Box 8.1 along with how they are understood to exist in single-system evaluation research. The reader may wish to refer back to them in the discussion that follows.

When Are Single-System Evaluations Appropriate?

Single-system evaluations are best suited to those situations in which (1) a primary treatment goal is change in a client behavior, attitude, perception, or other characteristic and (2) whatever we are seeking to change (the target problem) can be accurately measured. In order to conduct a single-system evaluation, we must be able to specify exactly what change in the problem is sought and how it will be measured, as well as the intervention that will be used to attempt to change it. If progress toward attainment of a goal cannot be measured, or if the intervention method cannot be clearly specified, a single-system

Box 8.1   Research Terms and Their Equivalents in Single-System Evaluation

Baseline Phase (A phase) – The measurements taken during the absence of the intervention. This can be before the intervention is introduced the first time (*true baseline*) or it can be during later phases after the intervention is withdrawn.

Treatment Phase (B phase, C phase, etc.)—The time period(s) during which the intervention is being offered and measurements are taken.

Design—The number and sequence of alternating A (baseline) and B (treatment) phases.

Exploratory design—A design with no A phase (baseline), e.g., BC or BCD.
Descriptive design—A design with a true baseline and one or more interventions, e.g., AB or ABC.
Explanatory design—A design that uses repetition or withdrawal of the intervention to observe whether a pattern among the measurements of the dependent variable occurs, e.g., BCBC, ABA.

Independent variable—The intervention or its absence (or, less frequently, the magnitude of the intervention). It is almost always a nominal-level variable, a categorical variable with two or more distinct values (see Chapter 10 for a detailed discussion of the levels of measurement).

Dependent variable—The severity of the client or client system's problem or its incidence as measured through all phases of the evaluation. It can be any level of measurement.

Case—A single measurement of the dependent variable in either an A phase or a B phase.

Sample—The total number of measurements of the dependent variable in an A phase or B phase.

Control group—The measurements of the dependent variable during an A phase.

Experimental group—The measurements of dependent variable during the B phase.

Sampling error—The normal fluctuation of the dependent variable; an alternative reason (other than the presence or absence of the intervention) why measurements in an A phase may differ from those in a subsequent B phase.

Sampling bias—The tendency of a sample of measurements of the dependent variable (especially in a true baseline) to be atypical for the client or client system.

Target problem—The problem of the client or client system that the intervention is designed to influence.

evaluation is not appropriate. See Box 8.2 for some of the practice situations in which a single-system evaluation may not be appropriate.

The last item in Box 8.2 makes the point that the target problem in single-system evaluation research can only be something that we can directly influence, not something we are helping others to try to influence. For example, a school social worker should not use single-system research to evaluate her success in consulting with a teacher about how to handle a child's disruptive behaviors in the classroom by using the number of his disruptions as the target problem. The social worker would not be directly affecting the target problem through her intervention; the teacher would be. So, any success in changing the child's behaviors might be a function of how well the teacher applied the methods the social worker suggested, not how good the suggestions were or how well the social worker communicated them.

The target problem must also be something that can be measured repeatedly over some period of time. Thus, research that entails only a few or just two measurements (e.g., a pretest-posttest design) is not a single-system evaluation.

As we have already noted, under the right conditions we can use single-system evaluation to evaluate our own practice with any client system—individuals, couples, families, schools, hospitals, neighborhoods, or communities. This is why we have chosen to use the term *single-system* rather than one of the other terms, such as *single-subject*, as it

---

Box 8.2   Some Situations Where Single-System Evaluation Is <u>Not</u> Appropriate

- When the target problem or problems cannot be easily and accurately measured
- When multiple measurements of target problems over time are not logistically possible, as is often the case with short-term or crisis interventions
- When the intervention is complex or otherwise cannot be clearly specified

- When the intervention is "one shot," as in making a referral or conducting discharge planning
- When the intervention is "indirect," as in working with teachers around how to better manage classroom behaviors or in working with community members to help them reduce gang violence

---

emphasizes the fact that our effectiveness with any level of system, micro (individual), mezzo (small group, including family, work group, social group, etc.), or macro (larger group, including communities, organizations, etc.), can be evaluated using this method.

Single-system evaluations can be used in situations where selecting a larger group of participants is either impossible or unethical. Mattaini (2010) argues that, in many cases, a single-system evaluation is the most appropriate form of research and evaluation for social workers:

> Single-system research is, in many ways, an ideal methodology for social work research. Social worker practitioners commonly work with one system at a time, under often unique contextual conditions, and single-system methods have the potential to make such work much more powerful. Every client's world and behavioral history are different, and . . . standardized treatments are unlikely to be widely applicable without individualization (p. 268).

Over the past few decades, researchers and theoreticians have greatly expanded the number of practice situations where single-system evaluation can be used. Progress has come from at least three sources:

1. Social work researchers and practitioners have created and refined scales for the measurement of such hard-to-measure variables as marital adjustment and family relations. Corcoran and Fischer (2013a, 2013b) have compiled a two-volume book of hundreds of scales that can be used in single-system evaluation research. Many of these scales have been shown to possess both reliability (consistency in measurement) and validity (they measure what is intended to be measured) when used repeatedly with the same clients or client systems.

2. Scholars have designed highly sophisticated single-system evaluation designs. There is a design that is suitable for nearly every practice situation (Weinbach, 2005).

3. Still other scholars have developed computer software to make the recording and analysis of data nearly effortless for the practitioner (Bloom, Fischer, & Orme, 1999).

Elements of Single-System Evaluation Designs

There is a general sequence of steps that are followed in conducting a single-system evaluation. These steps are presented in Box 8.3. Notice that seven of the eleven steps are conducted before the data are collected. As we have emphasized in earlier chapters,

Box 8.3   The Usual Steps for Conducting Single-System Evaluations

1. Describe the client's problem (or at least its symptoms).
2. Specify the target problem—the behavior, attitude, and so on (the dependent variable)—and how you propose to measure it.
3. Identify the pattern of the target problem believed to exist (stable, rising, falling, and so forth).
4. Identify professional literature that describes the problem or something similar and suggests the interventions that may be effective.
5. Briefly specify the precise treatment or intervention to be used and how it will relate to other ongoing services to the client.
6. Select from among the various single-system designs the one that you will use. Justify why it is best, given such factors as time, ethical constraints, need to control for other variables, treatment goals, and so forth.

7. Determine which pattern of the target problem would indicate that your intervention may be related to a desired effect, that is, the treatment goal. Also determine which pattern(s) would suggest the possibility that your intervention may have promoted unhealthy dependency or some other unintended consequence.
8. Conduct the research, carefully graphing measurements of the target problem over time.
9. Analyze the results of the research relative to step 7.
10. If the intervention appears to have been associated with success, consider replicating the research with other similar clients or client groups who might also benefit from it.
11. Disseminate the results of the research to colleagues who might benefit from knowing them.

A slightly different version of this box appeared in Compton, B., Galaway, B., & Cournoyer, B. (2005) and Weinbach, R. (2005).

careful planning is critical to research success. With single-system evaluation, steps 2 and 4 take on special importance if researchers are to learn about their practice effectiveness. They need to specify exactly what their intervention is (the independent variable) and what it is that they hope it is influencing (the dependent variable). Otherwise, findings would be of little practical value.

Before we look at the various single-system evaluation designs, let us examine in more detail six of the major elements of a single-system evaluation: (1) Defining the outcome or dependent variable; (2) Measuring the outcome or dependent variable; (3) Defining the independent variable or intervention; (4) Conducting the baseline phase(s); (5) Conducting the intervention phase(s); (6) Graphing and analyzing the outcome data.

Assessment

Behavior: Develop mutually agreed-on intervention goals and objectives based on the critical assessment of strengths, needs, and challenges within clients and constituencies.

Critical Thinking Question: How could you translate the goal "reduce the number of times the student with ADHD disrupts the class" to a more positive goal?

Defining the Outcome or Dependent Variable

Defining the outcome or dependent variable as well as how it will be measured is key to single-system evaluation because it relates directly to the client's problem. The dependent variable is generally the main target (although it doesn't have to be) that the intervention is attempting to change. Whenever possible, it is preferable to define the goal of intervention (the dependent variable) in a positive way. This is consistent with practice values that stress building on client strengths (the *strengths perspective*). For example, it would be preferable to define a goal as "increasing the number of reinforcing comments made by Ms. X to her son" rather than "decreasing the number of critical comments made by Ms. X to her son."

If the subject of the evaluation is an individual client, couple, or family, the dependent variable might be, for example, a client's score on an assertiveness scale, the number of parenting responsibilities shared by a couple, the number of meals per week in which all family members are present, or any of the myriad of possible targets of our intervention. If the client system is a school, the dependent variable might be, for example, the percent of students participating in a community service project in the school or the percent of students present and on-time each day. If the client system is a community, the dependent variable might be, for example, the number of people participating in neighborhood watch groups or the number of children involved in a community center after-school program. There is no limit to the dependent variables that can be defined for single-system evaluations.

It should be noted that, in single-system evaluations, the dependent variable defined need not be the central problem or the major focus of the social worker's treatment plan. It can be just one symptom of the problem (it often is) or even something that may be only tangentially related to the central problem but is negatively contributing to the client's or client system's functioning in some way. For example, we might use an intervention to attempt to increase how frequently our client, a woman with a diagnosis of schizophrenia, does not verbally respond to voices that she is hearing. If we are successful, the change in her behavior would have no impact on the underlying problem (her psychiatric diagnosis), but it might help her to function better in social situations.

If a symptom of a problem is the target problem, we need to be careful not to define it either too broadly or too narrowly. If we define it too broadly (for example, "antisocial behavior" by a male in-patient psychiatric patient) it will be difficult to know if and when the problem occurred. If the patient verbally abuses another patient, should that "count"? What if he refuses to come out of his room for a meal? What if he fails to speak for an entire day, is that just one incident, or should it "count" for more? However, if we define the target problem too narrowly that can result in another problem, *symptom substitution*. Suppose, using the same example, we define the target problem as "striking another patient." When an intervention is offered over a period of time (perhaps by offering daily opportunities for the patient to vent his anger), the behavior may show an obvious decline, suggesting that the intervention was successful. But, in fact, while the patient is no longer attempting to strike other patients, he has now begun to frequently strike nurses and other staff members, and even you! He has simply substituted one symptom of his problem for another. A possible definition of the target problem that is neither too broad nor too narrow might be "physically striking others."

Measuring the Outcome or Dependent Variable

Once the outcome or dependent variable has been identified and clearly defined, we then determine how it is to be measured. When using single-system designs, regular measurements of the target problem are made over the entire course of the study. Ideally, this involves using more than one observer or method in order to increase the likelihood that the measurements are both reliable and valid. Measurements are recorded as they are made, usually using standard graph paper or a computer software

---

Engage in Practice-Informed Research and Research-Informed Practice

Behavior: Apply critical thinking to engage in analysis of quantitative and qualitative research methods and research findings.

Critical Thinking Question: How could depression be measured using frequency, duration, interval, magnitude, and presence or absence?

package designed to produce the line graphs that are characteristic of a single-system evaluation.

As we have already noted, a variety of types of measurements can be used in a single-system evaluation, including standardized questionnaires or instruments and direct observation of behavior. When measuring behavior, some common methods used include:

1. **Frequency.** For example, we might measure the number of times that an inpatient psychiatric patient attends recreational therapy each week.

2. **Duration.** For example, we might measure the length of time that family members spend eating their evening meal together over a two-month period.

3. **Interval.** For example, we might measure the length of time between incidents of racial conflict within a community over a period of five years.

4. **Magnitude.** For example, we might measure the intensity of a client's clinical depression each week as measured by a depression inventory.

5. **Presence or absence.** For example, we might record whether or not a high school student attends school on-time each weekday.

The availability of valid measurement instruments may be an important consideration, especially if the target problem is one that is not easily measured. For example, we may find a standardized measurement instrument to measure the overall positive and/or negative intensity of a parent-child relationship, but it may be much more difficult to develop a log that will enable the parent and child to accurately (reliably and validly) document the number and duration of individual positive and negative interchanges throughout the day. In another example, the frequency of drug use may be difficult to measure with precision, but its presence or absence each day or the interval between occurrences may be easier to measure as well as more relevant to the intervention goals.

The goal of intervention is an especially important consideration in determining how the dependent variable will be measured. For example, suppose two parents have frequent, but superficial and brief, discussions with each other regarding their child-rearing practices. If the treatment goal is to increase the depth of their discussions, then measuring the duration of the discussions may be more consistent with the treatment goal than counting the number of times the parents discuss child-rearing practices. We operationally define our outcome variable based on what we see as the goal of the intervention, as well as on the best available tool for measuring progress toward achieving it.

A measurement issue that occurs in single-system evaluation (and also in some other time-series group designs) is the need for measurement to be repeated many times throughout the study. This may eliminate measurement instruments or methods that would be too tedious or difficult to measure over and over (e.g., a questionnaire with 200 items). Even if the instrument used to measure the target problem is a short and simple one, the process of repeating it over and over can itself influence the measurements of the dependent variable. Something other than the intervention (for example, boredom, carelessness or a desire among people to be consistent in what they report) may influence any apparent changes (or lack of them) in the target problem.

Measurement of a variable should be sensitive enough that it will record meaningful changes, yet not so sensitive that it will record changes that are meaningless in relation to the goals of the intervention. It should also be as unobtrusive as possible, so that it does not interfere with the intervention itself. Measurement must also be acceptable to the client or client system. This is in part an ethical issue. Because a power differential exists and because they may fear displeasing us, clients might agree to provide data that they would prefer not to provide or to permit measurement in a way that they might otherwise resist. Thus, it is our responsibility to ensure that both the measurement itself and its method of collection are acceptable to the client or client system.

Defining the Independent Variable or Intervention

Once the target problem has been identified and the method for measuring it has been selected, the next step in single-system research is to specify the intervention that will be used. As in all quantitative research (and in evidence-based practice), this step should be undertaken after a review of the literature to determine the most effective treatment or intervention available to address the target problem. Once it has been identified, it should be operationally defined so it can be clearly described in a written report or case notes. This would enable us or some other practitioner to replicate the study at a later time using the same intervention or a variation of it.

The basic assumption underlying single-system designs is that, if an intervention makes a difference, a client or client system will show a response to it (change). With most designs, practitioners expect (hope?) that the target problem will change when the intervention is introduced. The stronger the pattern of agreement between the presence or absence of the intervention and corresponding changes in its target, the greater the evidence that the intervention makes a difference. For example, if one pattern is evident during the presence of the intervention and another pattern can be seen both before the intervention is introduced and after it is removed, the evidence that the intervention makes a difference is especially strong. Such consistent patterns would constitute an unlikely coincidence, and would suggest that the presence of the intervention and changes in the target problem are related. Of course, we would hope to demonstrate that the intervention is accompanied by a desirable change in the target, one that is consistent with intervention goals. But the observation that the presence of the intervention is accompanied by undesirable change in the target problem or even that it makes no difference would still be valuable feedback to the practitioner. Either would suggest that the intervention was not successful, at least not with that particular client or client system.

Conducting the Baseline Phase

Baseline data are the measurements taken before the intervention is introduced and at any time that the intervention is withdrawn. The time period during which the baseline data are collected is the baseline phase, referred to symbolically as the A phase. As we will see later in the chapter, not all single-system evaluations include a baseline phase, but most do. While the intervention being evaluated is withheld during the baseline or A phase, the client or client system may receive no intervention or may receive other forms of assistance, such as the usual treatment.

If an A phase occurs before the intervention is first introduced, it is known as a true baseline or sometimes just a baseline. It is used to represent the usual pattern of

*An A phase serves the
same general function
as a control group
does in an experimen-
tal research design,
providing a source of
comparison by indicat-
ing what occurs with
the target problem
when the intervention
either (1) has not yet
been introduced or
(2) is withdrawn.*

the behavior or other target of the intervention, the starting point for the intervention. Depending on the design being used, there may be additional A phases later in the process. In these instances, the intervention is withdrawn to see how the target problem is affected. However, once the intervention has been introduced, any subsequent A phase is no longer considered a true baseline, because the intervention may continue to influence the dependent variable even after it is withdrawn. An A phase serves the same general function as a control group does in an experimental research design, providing a source of comparison by indicating what occurs with the target problem when the intervention either (1) has not yet been introduced or (2) is withdrawn.

There is no consensus as to what constitutes an adequate baseline. The rule of thumb is that at least three measurements should be collected during the baseline phase, although many researchers argue for at least 5 to 10 baseline data points. Ideally, the baseline should contain a large enough number of measurements so the practitioner can identify the normal fluctuations of the dependent variable in the absence of the intervention. Thus, it can later be determined if there was a meaningful change in the pattern after the intervention was introduced. However, because of time constraints and logistical problems, this is not always possible. So, can just five or ten measurements of the problem constitute a baseline? Or, are more needed? The answer is, it depends. Theoretically, a good baseline can be established using relatively few measurements if they accurately reflect the usual pattern of the target of the intervention. The decision on the adequacy of baseline data often comes down to our subjective judgment, our answer to the question, "Have I captured the usual pattern of the target problem prior to offering my intervention?"

Fortunately, a baseline containing a large number of measurements can sometimes be created retroactively. If good records have been kept and are available (e.g., school attendance records), baseline data that have already been gathered can be used to create the baseline phase. This entails secondary data analysis, which can have serious limitations (see Chapter 11). Among other things, it is dependent on the ways in which the problem was conceptualized and operationalized by other people and how conscientiously it was measured. We would need to determine if the retroactive data are dependable enough to be used or if additional baseline data must be gathered. Generally speaking, recorded data, such as grades, attendance records, doctors' records of appointments, court records, and other similar data are considered reliable data that can be used to create a retroactive baseline phase.

While the required number of baseline data points cannot be easily specified, the goal is to collect enough baseline data that a trend becomes apparent. Once a clear trend has been established, it is more likely that any change in the trend that occurs after the intervention is introduced is due to the intervention itself. In other words, the internal validity of the design is improved if the researcher takes enough baseline measurements so that a clear trend has been established. During the baseline phase, there are several possible trends that researchers might observe in measurements of the target problem: increasing, decreasing, stable or unchanging, cyclical, or unstable. *Increasing* is when the values of the outcome measure are steadily increasing, while *decreasing* is when the values are steadily decreasing. *Stable* is when the values are staying essentially the same, or changing very little. *Cyclical* is when there is an up-and-down pattern that is happening regularly over a certain time period. An *unstable* trend is when there is no clearly

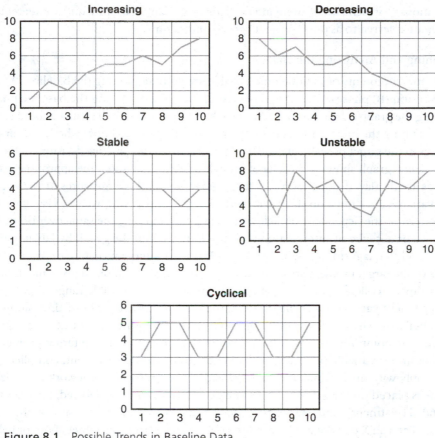

Figure 8.1   Possible Trends in Baseline Data

identified trend. If the data are unstable, it is usually preferable to keep collecting further baseline measurements until a trend is achieved. Otherwise, the baseline data offer us little in the way of comparison once the intervention is introduced (see Figure 8.1 for diagrams of these trends). However, in those relatively rare situations when we plan to use an intervention to stabilize an unstable target problem (for example, sporadic attendance at support group meetings) we might use the unstable measurements of the target problem as a baseline phase in our evaluation of our intervention's effectiveness.

Conducting the Intervention Phase

In those designs where baseline data are gathered first (there is a true baseline), a second phase, the intervention phase, follows. An intervention phase is a time period during which the intervention is present and the dependent variable continues to be measured. It is represented symbolically as a B phase. Thus the absence (during an A phase) or the presence (during a B phase) of the intervention are the two possible variations (value categories) of the independent variable.

As we shall see later in this chapter, different single-system designs can also be used to compare the relative effectiveness of different interventions, to attempt to learn which sequence of interventions worked best, and even to examine whether a given intervention seems to work more effectively with one target problem than with another. In

Generally speaking, recorded data, such as grades, attendance records, doctors' records of appointments, court records, and other similar data are considered reliable data that can be used to create a retroactive baseline phase.

evaluations in which two or more interventions are examined, subsequent intervention phases are referred to as the C phase, D phase, and so on.

Graphing and Analyzing the Data.

As the measurements of the outcome variable are gathered during the baseline (A) and intervention (B) phases, they are graphed on a line graph. During the baseline phase, studying the graph enables us to determine when a clear trend in the data has been established. During the intervention phase, the graph enables us to know whether desirable changes in the target problem are occurring, and thus guides practice decision-making.

In a line graph showing the data of a single-system evaluation, the appropriate time periods are displayed along the *x* axis (horizontal axis) and the measures of the dependent variable are shown on the *y* axis (vertical axis). In this way, we can visually see if the pattern of the dependent variable is changing or remaining the same over time. The presence or absence of intervention is clearly indicated on the graph by labeling time intervals either as A (for a baseline phase) or B (for an intervention phase). If measurements of the target problem are numeric (e.g., score on a standardized instrument, number of times a college student is on-time for class, etc.), the possible range of values of the dependent variable are displayed along the vertical axis and units of time along the horizontal axis. Thus, each dot on the graph reflects a measurement of the target problem and the point in time when the measurement took place. If the target problem is a dichotomous variable (e.g., attended/did not attend group treatment, complied/did not comply with medication, or completed/did not complete all homework), a horizontal line is placed on the graph with one value category above it (labeled, for example, "attended treatment") and one below it (labeled "did not attend treatment") on the vertical axis. Then an X or a dot is placed at the same distance from and either above or below the line each time that the target problem is measured to reflect its measurement.

The most common form of data analysis used in single-system evaluation is visual analysis. In other words, the data are graphed on a line graph, and we look carefully for trends in the data and changes in these trends in relation to when interventions were present or absent. Many social workers using single-system designs believe that only those effects that can be easily seen on a line graph should be considered meaningful. If there is no improvement, or if there may be improvement but it is not obvious, the null hypothesis (that there is no relationship between the independent and dependent variables) cannot be rejected. In other words, any change in the target problem is so small that it is likely to be due to the normal fluctuation of the target problem, rather than to the intervention.

The measurements of the target problem during the intervention phase are interpreted by comparing them with the trends in the measurements observed during the baseline phase. For example, consider a client whose score on a clinical depression inventory during a baseline phase is steadily increasing (indicating increased depressive symptoms). If the increase stops after the intervention is introduced, we could argue that the intervention may be helping in that the problem at least stopped getting worse. What if the target problem was getting slowly better during the baseline phase, and then continued to get slowly better after the intervention was introduced? On first glance, it might seem the intervention could be helping. However, since the client was already improving before the intervention was introduced, the intervention may actually be having little or no effect on the dependent variable (see Figure 8.2 for examples of these and other data trends).

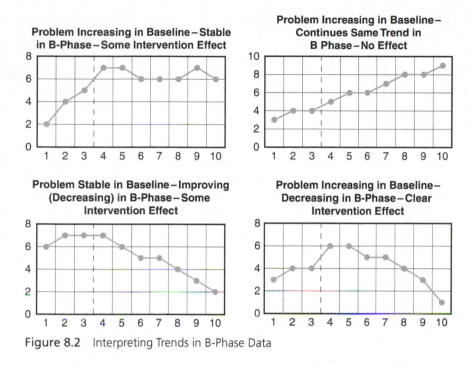

Figure 8.2 Interpreting Trends in B-Phase Data

In single-system evaluations where there is a baseline A phase followed by an intervention B phase, statistical analyses are sometimes used to determine the mathematical probability that differences in the measurements of the dependent variable between the A and B phases represent nothing more than normal fluctuation. There are several easily computed tests that can tell us if the difference between the measurements in the A phase and the subsequent B phase is statistically significant, that is, it is large enough that the probability of its representing just normal fluctuation over time is quite small. While these methods are beyond the scope of this chapter, you can find a thorough discussion in Mattaini (2010). These methods are based on the following assumptions:

- The A (baseline) phase is an accurate representation of the dependent variable and its variability (measurements constitute a representative sample).
- The same pattern of variability of the dependent variable would continue following the A phase if the intervention were not introduced.
- Any difference between the pattern of the dependent variable in the A and subsequent B phases may be attributable to the presence of the intervention during the B phase.

Single-System Evaluation Designs

Just like the research designs that we discussed in the previous chapter, different single-system designs have been created to answer different questions. Some are exploratory. They lack a baseline (A) phase and seek simply to answer the question, "Do changes occur in the target problem during the time an intervention is present?" Other designs are descriptive. They contain a baseline (A) phase and an intervention (B) phase and are used to answer the question, "Did change occur in the target problem and how much did it change when an intervention is introduced?" Still others are described as explanatory. They contain a series of alternating A and B phases and attempt to answer the question, "Did the intervention actually cause changes in the target problem?" Explanatory designs tend to be the most complex because they must attempt to control for threats to internal validity. We will look at examples of all three types, paying special attention to their specialized uses.

B Design

The most basic single-system exploratory design is the B design. It consists of the introduction and continuation of an intervention while measurements of the target problem or dependent variable are carried out and recorded. It is exactly what most responsible practitioners already do to some degree. However, for the monitoring to be considered single-system evaluation, the practitioner would have to (1) operationally define the target problem and the intervention; (2) measure the target problem repeatedly throughout the intervention; and (3) graph and interpret the data.

Other exploratory single-system designs include the BC or BCD designs. In the BC design, the first intervention (B phase) is withdrawn and a second, different intervention is introduced during a C phase. The target problem continues to be measured throughout the completion of the second intervention to learn what changes occur. In a BCD design, a D phase is added after the second intervention (C phase) is withdrawn. The target problem continues to be measured. These designs allow the practitioner to explore the possible effects of a series of one or more interventions on a target problem.

AB Design

An AB design is considered *descriptive*. It consists of two phases: (1) a baseline (A) phase, during which the target problem is measured and graphed and the intervention being evaluated is not offered, and (2) an intervention (B) phase, during which the intervention is present and the target problem continues to be measured (see Figure 8.3 for an example).

When using an AB design, the intervention being evaluated is not offered until a true baseline phase of measurement takes place or is constructed from available data. Thus, we might have an ethical objection to using an AB design with a client or client system that is in imminent danger because the target problem is life threatening or otherwise destructive. For example, we would not use an AB design to see if a promising intervention is effective in reducing the number of times that a client at high risk for contracting an HIV infection engages in unsafe sexual practices. We could not ethically justify waiting to offer the intervention just because we preferred to use an AB design. However, if we already have or can acquire valid measurements of the client's usual sexual practices prior to seeking assistance, we might be able to use these measurements to create a retroactive baseline.

AB is often the design of choice when permanent learning or nonreversible behavior or attitudes are a likely consequence (and a goal) of the intervention. As we will discuss later, some single-system designs (withdrawal designs) withdraw the intervention

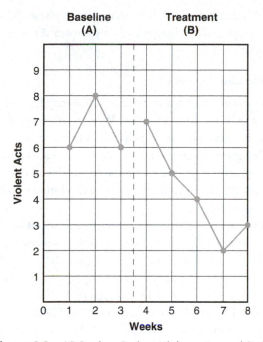

Figure 8.3   AB Design: Patient Violence toward Staff

and return to a second baseline phase. If the target problem reverts to the level of the initial baseline, we might conclude that the intervention caused the change in the target problem. If, however, the behaviors, once learned, are not likely to spontaneously return to their original levels if the intervention is withdrawn, withdrawal designs are not appropriate. In these cases, an AB is more appropriate. For example, we might select a specific intervention to increase the frequency of assertive behaviors of a client. The intervention may be accompanied by an increase in these behaviors, as reflected in the B phase of the design, suggesting that our intervention was effective. However, the literature and experience tell us that, once people become more assertive, they are likely to continue assertive behaviors when appropriate because assertiveness is self-reinforcing. It promotes desirable responses from others. So, a second A phase could be misleading about our intervention's effectiveness. If additional data were collected after the intervention concluded (after the B phase), they should be used primarily to learn if the increase in assertiveness stabilizes or even continues to increase over time after the intervention was withdrawn.

When using descriptive designs such as AB (or ABC or ABCD), we do not control for other variables (besides the intervention) that might produce change in the target problem. In the evaluation portrayed in Figure 8.3, for example, the decrease in attacks on staff during the B phase may have been the effect of the intervention, but may also have been the result of changes in the patient's diet or medication, help offered by other staff, visits from the patient's relatives, pressure from other patients, the passage of time, and any of hundreds of other factors working alone or in concert. Perhaps the A phase (baseline) was an atypical time for the patient and the B phase is simply more typical of the patient's behavior. Or perhaps the difference between the A and B phases just represents normal fluctuation for the client, and the B phase did not really reflect change at all. Descriptive single-system designs can only answer the question, "Did change occur and how much did it occur?

Successive Intervention Designs

Sometimes, we know of several interventions that may be effective, but none of them is clearly indicated to be the most effective. We seek some general guidance as to which may be best or, to be more precise, which intervention or series of interventions seems to work best with a given client or client system. Successive intervention single-system designs can examine several interventions, each introduced one at a time. These designs are used to examine the relationship between several interventions and a single dependent variable (a target problem).

Figure 8.4 illustrates the efforts of a public health social worker to evaluate the relative effectiveness of several interventions with a client in a smoking-cessation program. This evaluation started with a baseline phase (A), during which the number of cigarettes smoked by the client was recorded and graphed for ten days. Next, three interventions were introduced consecutively (B, C, and D), during which time the dependent variable (cigarettes smoked) continued to be recorded. This constitutes an ABCD single-system design. If there had been four interventions used, the design would have been ABCDE, and so forth.

When using a successive intervention design, the potential for treatment carryover from one phase into subsequent ones can make it difficult to determine just which

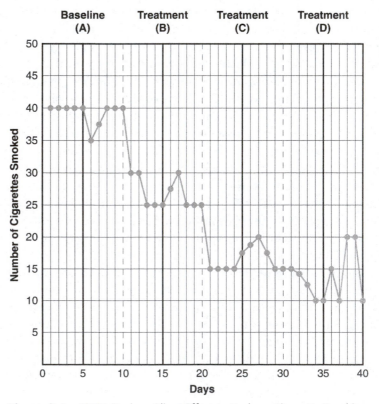

Figure 8.4   ABCD Design: Client Effort to Reduce Cigarette Smoking

intervention produced the most change in the dependent variable (target problem). For example, the continuation of a desired behavior at approximately the same level following the shift from one intervention to another, as in the D phase in Figure 8.4, may mean that interventions C and D are equally effective. It may also mean that the effects of intervention C continued on through the D phase. If so, it may be this carryover effect and not intervention D that produced the level of the desired behavior in the D phase. But how can we know this is what happened? The possibility of treatment carryover can severely limit any conclusions about the relative effectiveness of different interventions when successive designs are used. To avoid effects of treatment carryover, the social worker may want to add a brief baseline phase between each intervention to have a clearer idea of the effectiveness of each individual intervention. While the previous intervention may continue to affect the data during the baseline phase, there may also be some change when one or more of the interventions is withdrawn making it easier to analyze the effects of various interventions.

Look back at the example (see Figure 8.4) in which the baseline phase was followed by three successive interventions (ABCD design). If the withdrawal method had been added to this study, we would have had another design (ABACAD). Such a design would give us a clearer indication of the relative effectiveness of the three interventions. Its downside (besides treatment carryover) would be that the cumulative effect of treatments B, C, and D may have been more difficult to determine because of the presence of baseline phases between each treatment. If we prefer to keep the effects of the different interventions as separate as possible, the ABACAD design may be preferable. However, if we are more interested in looking at the cumulative effects of the interventions, the simpler ABCD design may be more helpful.

Another method for gaining useful information about the relative effectiveness of different interventions for addressing a target problem is by changing the order of the interventions in subsequent studies. If the smoking-cessation intervention in the earlier example was unsuccessful, the practitioner could use the same participant again (or another one with a similar problem), but this time, the practitioner could begin with an A phase and then introduce interventions C, B, and D, in that sequence. Another study might order the interventions D, C, and B, and so forth. Eventually, the best sequence of treatments might be identified, especially if the study were to be replicated many times with similar participants. In situations where problem recidivism is common (e.g., family violence, substance abuse, truancy, bullying), the repeated use of the ABCD design with the same client using different sequencing of interventions can be quite enlightening.

Ethical concerns related to use of ABCD designs are not as great as with some other designs. One issue sometimes voiced relates to withdrawing an apparently successful intervention to substitute one that may not be found to work as well. But this is not as problematic as it might seem at first, because most often the withdrawal of an apparently successful intervention is soon or immediately followed by another promising intervention. A greater ethical issue occurs when a successful intervention is withdrawn completely and is followed by a second baseline phase, such as in an ABACAD design.

Research-Informed Practice and Practice-Informed Research

Behavior: Use and translate research evidence to inform and improve practice, policy, and service delivery.

Critical Thinking Question: Describe why the ABACAD design can help the social worker see the individual effects of the interventions better than the ABCD design.

Withdrawal Designs

Single-system withdrawal designs include any design that introduces a single intervention (B phase) and then subsequently withdraws it and returns to a baseline phase (A phase). In some cases, such as the ABA or ABAB designs, there is a true baseline phase at the beginning of the evaluation.

An ABA design consists of an initial baseline phase (A), followed by the intervention phase (B), followed by a third phase in which the intervention is withdrawn to create a second baseline phase (A) of observation and measurement. This explanatory design attempts to address potential threats to internal validity. If the target problem shows improvement during the intervention phase and seems to get worse again during the second baseline phase, evidence exists that the intervention (and not something else) may have caused the problem to diminish. Of course, this type of design is only useful when the effects of the intervention are not expected to carry over once the intervention is withdrawn. For example, if some aspect of cognitive-behavioral therapy is used to attempt to reduce a symptom of a client with a diagnosis of bi-polar disorder, it would not make sense to use a withdrawal design, because, once the treatment is completed and withdrawn, it is hoped that the treatment's effect will continue. In this case, subsequent measurements will offer follow-up measures to see if the treatment's effect is long lasting.

In situations when we would expect the effects of our intervention to stop once the intervention is withdrawn, the withdrawal designs are a very effective way to suggest a causal relationship between the presence of the intervention and change in the target problem. Suppose, for example, we offer children in a residential foster care facility tokens for completing their chores each week. These tokens can be traded for television, computer, and video game time. If the token system is used for six weeks and seems to be working successfully, we could withdraw the system for three weeks and return to baseline measurements to see how well the children complete their chores without the tokens. Because we would expect the effects of the intervention to significantly reduce after the intervention is withdrawn, the ABA design might be appropriate (see Figure 8.5) in this scenario. If the second baseline data shows a reduction in chores done, the next step might be to reintroduce the intervention and leave it in place indefinitely (making it an ABAB design).

Although an ABA design can tell us what happens to the target behavior after the intervention is withdrawn (which an AB design cannot do), there are possible ethical issues that must be considered. Many social workers question whether it is ethical to withdraw an intervention believed to be effective. But two things should be kept in mind. First, with only an AB design in place, if improvement in the target problem occurs during the B phase we cannot claim that the intervention produced any or all of it. Many other factors could be affecting the measurements of the target problem. By withdrawing the intervention, we can be more confident that the intervention really was effective. Second, we would simply not use a withdrawal design in situations in which discontinuing the treatment could be dangerous to the client. For example, in the situation above, we were trying to encourage children in a group foster care home to complete their chores. By withdrawing the intervention, it became clearer that the tokens being offered were increasing the completion of the chores. But withdrawing the tokens for a period of weeks did not present any danger to the children. It is up to us to decide when it is appropriate and ethical to use a withdrawal design. Because the ethical issue for many social workers is ending the research in an A phase, the next design that we will discuss, the ABAB design, is sometimes preferred.

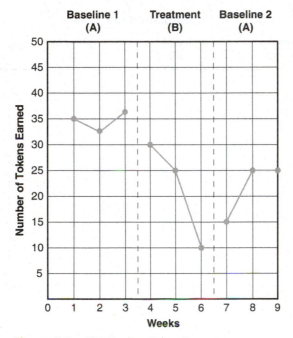

Figure 8.5 ABA Design: Token Economy

The ABAB design ends with an intervention phase. The addition of one or more alternating A and B phases helps to provide additional evidence for a possible cause-effect relationship between the intervention and the target problem. When using an AB design, there is only one point in time that the intervention is introduced. Many other events could have taken place in the client's life to affect the dependent variable at that point in time. In the ABAB design, there are now three points in time that the independent variable is manipulated: when the intervention is introduced, withdrawn, and then introduced again. If the measures of the dependent variable change at each of these three points in time and in a consistent pattern, we could argue that the intervention is indeed affecting the dependent variable. In other words, it becomes less and less likely that other factors could have coincidentally affected the dependent variable at all three of these points in time.

Let's continue our hypothetical example of the token economy being used to encourage children to complete their chores. Figure 8.6 shows the graph of an ABAB design, in which the dependent variable (percent of chores completed by all children in home) is shown on the y axis and time is shown on the x axis. The baseline data are gathered for four weeks and reflect a relatively stable trend in the data. The intervention starts and the target problem continues to be measured for the next four weeks. The number of completed chores increases. However, we need to provide better evidence to our supervisor in support of the intervention in order to justify continuing to use it. So, we decide to use a withdrawal design. We stop offering tokens to the children, and continue to measure the dependent variable for four more weeks. If it is clear that there is a significant drop in the percent of chores being completed, then we offer the intervention again for four weeks, continuing to measure and record chore completion. It increases again. Our supervisor would probably agree with our conclusion that the intervention was successful and allow it to continue indefinitely.

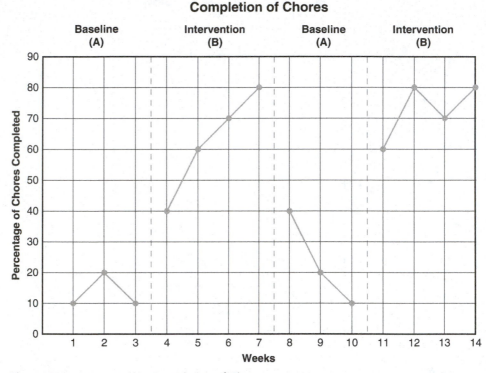

Figure 8.6 ABAB Design: Completion of Chores

The BAB design can be used in cases where a withdrawal design is desirable, but it is impractical to gather baseline measurements before the intervention is introduced. It is popular, because, like the ABAB design, it ends with an intervention (B) phase, a characteristic that appears to be consistent with social work practice values and ethics. This design is especially well suited to crisis situations where we believe that conducting a baseline measurement prior to offering the intervention would be unethical, but where it is believed that the intervention can safely be withdrawn after a short period of time.

Figure 8.7 illustrates a BAB single-system evaluation design. Suppose a teacher asks you, a school social worker, for help with a boy who has been observed hitting other children in the classroom. The teacher does not want to wait for the time required for baseline data collection. She is already convinced it is a serious problem, which is why she came to you. In your counseling with the boy, you immediately implement an intervention that entails a reward system—allowing him to play computer games a certain amount of time during your counseling contingent on the number of days the previous week that he did not hit or physically hurt another child in the classroom. After six weeks, the data show a marked improvement in the boy's behavior. However, you are aware that other factors in the boy's life may have caused the improvement (e.g., possible additional treatment outside of school; a new friend in the classroom; change in diet, sleep, or exercise). In addition, without baseline data before the intervention started, there is no way to know for sure how many incidents the boy was having before the intervention. To be more confident that the intervention is having a positive effect on his improved behavior, the reward program is withdrawn. Baseline data are gathered for six weeks. The number of incidents during this baseline phase increases significantly, giving you more confidence that your intervention is

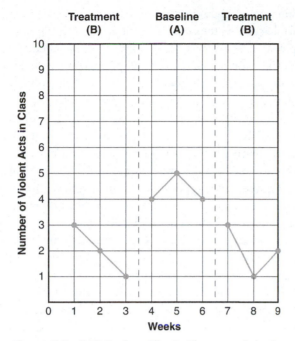

Figure 8.7   BAB Design: Client's Classroom Behavior

having a positive effect on the boy's behavior. The reward system is then put back into place and the behavior again improves. At this point, you would need to decide whether it is appropriate to leave the intervention in place indefinitely or, perhaps, to withdraw it while continuing to monitor the child's behavior.

In using a BAB design, ethical concerns often center around the timing of the decision to withdraw intervention, that is, to move from the first B phase into the A phase. Without extensive foreknowledge of the client and the target problem pattern, it may be difficult to know when it should be considered safe to withdraw the intervention. If in your professional judgment it would be detrimental to the client to withdraw the intervention at the time that the design calls for it to be withdrawn, the intervention would simply continue. When using any single-system research design, the best interests of the client or client group should always take priority.

Multiple-Baseline Design

In situations where it is not appropriate to withdraw an intervention, either because of possible detrimental effects on the client or client system or because the intervention effects are likely to continue anyway even after the intervention is withdrawn, the multiple-baseline design may be a good choice. It is also a design with relatively strong internal validity. In other words, it can help us to determine the likelihood that something other than the intervention caused the observed effects on the target problem. This design is most often used to examine the relative effectiveness of one (the same) method of intervention when it is used with two or more clients or client groups, two or more (usually related) target problems, or in two or more settings (e.g., school, home, child care setting).

It should be noted that the intervention is the same across all of the targets, whether you are looking at multiple target problems, clients, or settings. If multiple target

In situations where it is not appropriate to withdraw an intervention, either because of possible detrimental effects on the client or client system or because the intervention effects are likely to continue anyway even after the intervention is withdrawn, the multiple-baseline design may be a good choice.

problems are being studied, then the client and settings also stay the same across cases. Likewise, if multiple clients are used, the settings and target problems stay the same. Finally, if multiple settings are being examined, then the clients and target problems stay the same. In other words, in any one multiple-baseline evaluation, only one factor changes while the others remain constant.

When using a multiple-baseline design, an A phase precedes the introduction of the intervention for all of the clients, target problems, or settings. For the remainder of this discussion, we will use the term 'target' to refer to the clients, target problems, or settings being evaluated. During this phase, baseline measurements of the dependent variable or variables are taken. Then the intervention is introduced to attempt to influence one of the targets. Generally, it is applied first to the target that has reflected the clearest trend during the initial baseline (A) phase. As the intervention is offered to the first target, baseline measurements for the other targets continue, thus creating an extended A phase. After the intervention is used for some period of time with the first target, the intervention is introduced for the second client, target problem, or setting. During this time, the baseline measurements continue to be taken for the remaining targets. This continues until the intervention is introduced to all of the targets.

Let's look at some examples of this design. Figure 8.8 illustrates an application of a multiple-baseline design that looked at one client across three target problems. In this study, a fourth grade boy diagnosed with ADHD was having problems in his classroom, leaving his seat at inappropriate times, kicking the chair in front of him, and talking out of turn. It might be best to tackle them one at a time. We might observe the boy for thirty minutes each day right after lunch, a time when his teacher said the boy's behaviors were particularly troublesome. After we had observed and recorded the target behaviors for five days, we would start the intervention (legos and rewards for not exhibiting the behavior) with the boy's habit of talking out of turn. This was chosen first because the baseline data was extremely stable after the first five days of recording. After five days, this behavior had subsided dramatically, so we would begin the intervention with the boy's kicking the desk in front of him. Again, dramatic gains were observed, this time after ten days. Finally, the intervention would be used to try to control the child's tendency to get out of his seat. Again, the intervention seemed successful, after one week. So, as Figure 8.8 seems to suggest, it was apparently successful in reducing all three problem behaviors, and with little difference in success rate.

Figure 8.9 illustrates the data from a multiple-baseline design to evaluate the relative effectiveness of an intervention across client systems, specifically within three different communities. Suppose a community social worker conducts a crime reduction program in three high-crime neighborhoods in her city (her client systems in this example). Monthly crime statistics were gathered from city records for the six months preceding the start of the study, thus creating a retroactive baseline. The program was started in neighborhood A. Baseline data continued to be gathered for the other two neighborhoods. After three months, the program was started in neighborhood B, while baseline data continued to be gathered on the third neighborhood. Finally, three months later, the program was introduced to neighborhood C. As we can see from the data, the crime rates in each of the neighborhoods started to reduce soon after the intervention was started.

As in our previous example, the intervention appeared successful with all three client systems. However, this is not always what we find when using a multiple baseline

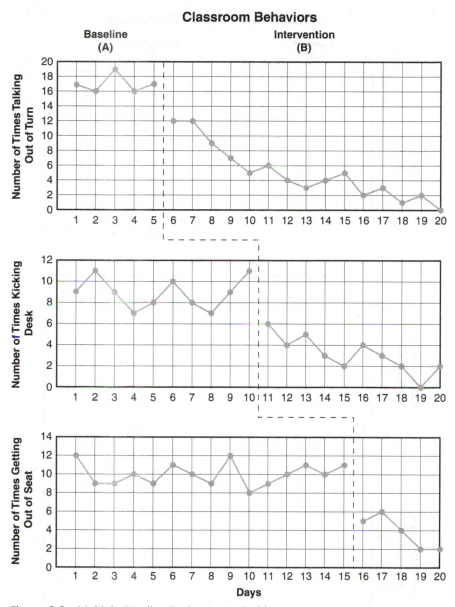

Figure 8.8 Multiple-Baseline Design across Problems

evaluation. Sometimes, there are significant differences among the outcomes observed with three clients or client systems, target problems, or settings. For example, if the intervention had been more successful with Community A than with the other two communities, we would see the greater decline on the chart during Community A's B phase. If the intervention had been successful with Communities A and B but not with C, the decline in crime rates would be considerably greater in Communities A and B than the decline during Community C's B phase.

This design offers a much stronger argument than a simple AB design would that the intervention actually caused the change. If, for example, the same program had been

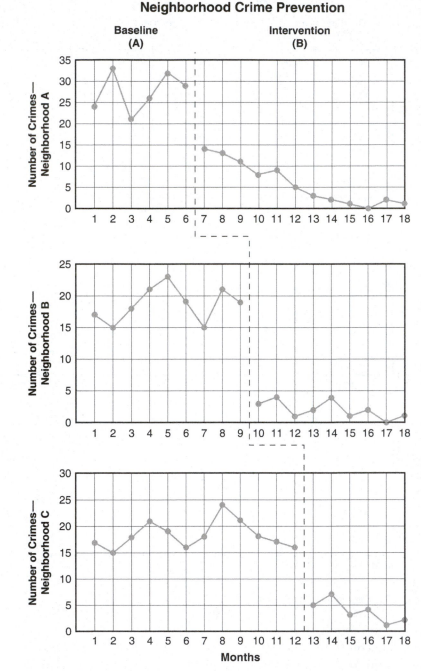

Figure 8.9   Multiple Baseline across Client Systems

started in all three neighborhoods at the same time, the social worker would not have known whether something else had happened at the same time that caused the reduction in crime (e.g., new stiffer penalties, seasonal change in weather, increased police presence). It would be much less likely that something else happened at all three times the program was initiated in the different neighborhoods to cause the reduction. This is the primary strength of the multiple-baseline design.

Another use of single-system evaluation is when we implement an intervention across multiple settings. For example, a social worker trying to help a young mother reduce the number of temper tantrums thrown by her 3-year-old son may use an intervention with the mother at the child's home, with the preschool teacher at the child's school, and with the grandmother at her home where the child stays on weekends. We may decide to use a multiple-baseline design to evaluate the client's progress in all three settings so we can be more confident that the intervention is actually causing the improvement in the child's behavior.

Strengths and Weaknesses of Single-System Evaluations

An objective assessment of the place of single-system evaluation research in social work must recognize both its strengths and weaknesses. On the positive side, single-system evaluations are inexpensive to implement. They cost little in time and other resources, something that generally cannot be said of many of the other forms of research we have described. Single-system evaluations are easily understood; a short workshop or staff development program is all that is needed to get staff members started in using them to evaluate their practice. They offer almost instantaneous feedback regarding a social worker's practice effectiveness. There is no need to wait months or years to acquire and analyze research findings—a phenomenon that is typical of most other forms of research. In single-system evaluations, data are collected and interpreted on an ongoing basis while practice intervention continues. Application of findings is thus easily and quickly accomplished.

Findings from single-system evaluations are typically not hard to understand; they are in a form that is amenable to immediate utilization. They can provide useful early feedback about new or experimental intervention methods. The interventions can be quickly evaluated and either discarded or, if they seem to be promising, evaluated more thoroughly using other types of research.

Single-system evaluations provide good feedback for evaluating the effectiveness of practice intervention methods, especially those that are primarily task-centered or problem-solving in nature. Sometimes, a series of studies using the same intervention, the same target problem, the same designs, and the same or similar participants can begin to suggest knowledge that transcends any one case. This method (replication) is the only way that single-system studies can make any claim to generalized knowledge building or to producing findings with external validity (being able to generalize any findings to the larger population). However, any such claim is a tenuous one at best, given what we know about the uniqueness of people and their situations.

There are also a number of inherent design weaknesses in single-system evaluation research. It often must depend on a client's own measurement and self-report of measurements of target problems or the reports of others such as friends or relatives (especially when used anywhere other than in institutional settings). The accuracy of this method of measurement can easily be questioned. Of course, this potential problem is no stranger to the social worker. Almost all intervention and evaluation must rely heavily on the belief that what others tell us is truthful and accurate.

Another problem related to single-system evaluation research is that it cannot be used productively unless work environments support its use. Even though this type of evaluation requires relatively little time and effort on the part of the practitioner, problems can occur unless administrators and supervisors are convinced of its value.

A supervisor who fails to share a commitment to it and who does not understand it may view it with suspicion and even perceive a supervisee to be wasting time conducting it. No one will want to conduct single-system evaluations if a supervisor demands to know why the social worker is "fooling around with those graphs when you should be seeing clients or keeping your records up to date."

Single-system evaluations are vulnerable to misuse. A supervisor may attempt to use the evaluation findings (including graphs) as evidence of the supervisee's competence (or lack of it). They may be used as input for annual performance evaluations or to justify personnel actions. This practice can be tempting for supervisors seeking "objective" criteria to validate their actions. But it is a gross misuse of single-system evaluation research. Evaluation data are not intended as a vehicle to assist the supervisor in evaluating the social work practitioner; it is intended as feedback for us, as researchers/practitioners. Use for any other purpose will quickly discourage us from conducting single system research. However, if our supervisor has understood and appreciated the purpose of single-system evaluations, we can discuss our findings safely and productively in case supervision conferences designed to help us become more effective practitioners.

Single-system evaluation research has also proven vulnerable to misuse in another way. Ironically, this misuse has occurred because of the increased popularity of and need for program evaluations (Chapter 7). As evaluators and program managers have sought ways to demonstrate the effectiveness of services, they have sometimes turned to reports of single-system studies (conducted by social workers for their own use) as evidence of successful or unsuccessful programs. They have increasingly been used as indicators of a program's achievement of its outcomes. Like their use to evaluate individual professional competence, this trend could easily tempt us to distort findings to look more favorable and thus to defeat the purpose of why we conducted single-system evaluations in the first place—to receive honest, objective feedback about our practice effectiveness.

Ethical Issues

We have already mentioned a number of ethical concerns that have been voiced regarding the use of single-system evaluation research. As we noted earlier, there are clearly times when we must decide between continuing the study as planned and what is best for the client or client system. Even the strongest advocates of single-system research would never suggest that the study and its potential findings should take precedence over the welfare of our clients. Practice values must prevail over our desire for knowledge-building. This same principle applies in all forms of research. Luckily, when single-system designs are used, the cost in time and resources of ending a study prematurely or changing its design for ethical reasons is rarely great. In many other types of research, such changes can be much more costly.

There are a few ethical issues that have yet to be resolved. They relate to what we discussed back in Chapter 2. Some people might claim that conducting evaluation research with one's clients comes dangerously close to a dual relationship and may therefore be unethical. Others might suggest that the only way to avoid this conflict is to have clients sign consent forms, thus ensuring that the principle of voluntary informed consent has not been violated. Still others might contend that single-system evaluation is just part of good practice; it is not research per se. Thus, a signed consent form is not necessary. They would see nothing unethical about using a method to systematically monitor and evaluate one's practice to ensure that the best possible interventions are offered. In fact, they would suggest, it would be irresponsible for a professional not to do so.

Different agencies and organizations have different rules and policies on the use of consent forms and the necessity of review of single-system proposals by institutional review boards (IRBs). Administrators in some settings (e.g., teaching hospitals) contend that a patient receiving services has already agreed to participate in research and that no additional requirements must be met. Other settings may require consent forms and reviews by IRBs for their legal protection. Even universities have different policies on the issues. The university where one of the authors of this book once worked requires professors of students conducting single-system evaluations to submit a summary of all proposed studies to an IRB for approval and that all participants must sign an informed voluntary consent form. At the university where one of the authors now teaches, there are no such requirements, because single-system evaluation is seen more as a part of social work practice than as research.

Because there is a lack of consensus on a number of ethical issues related to single-system evaluation research, we must be familiar with the rules and policies that are in force in the agency or other institution under whose auspices the research will be conducted. The rules or policies regarding single-system evaluation are generally not prohibitive and should not discourage us as social work professionals from using this method to evaluate our practice effectiveness.

SUMMARY

In this chapter,

- We examined various methods for evaluating our individual practice effectiveness, including supervision, consumer feedback, and goal attainment scaling.
- We focused on single-system evaluation, involving a careful monitoring of changes in certain behaviors, attitudes, perceptions, or other problems of clients or client systems. Single-system evaluations attempt to learn if these changes may be associated with the presence or absence of some specific intervention that we introduce with the client.
- Single-system design variations are employed to attempt to answer different questions, to attempt to control for the effect of other variables, and to be able to conduct evaluation in a way that is not in conflict with professional values and practice ethics.
- We discussed several of the designs that can be used, stressing their specialized usage and individual strengths and shortcomings. We demonstrated the importance (and the complexity) of interpreting the evaluation findings.
- Finally, we examined some of the ethical issues that are sometimes discussed in relation to single system research.

MyEducationLab® for Research

Try the Topic 11 Assignments: Single-Subject Experimental Research and the Topic 11 Study Plan.

Chapter 8 Chapter Review Quiz.

Sampling Issues and Options

In the previous chapters, there were numerous references to two important components of research design: sampling (sometimes referred to as *case sampling*) and measurement. Because of their importance (especially in quantitative research), we will examine them in greater detail in this chapter and the three that follow.

In social work research, a sample is often a group of people chosen to represent a larger group of people. For example, it might be a group of active clients with some problem who are chosen to represent all clients with that problem. Or it might be a group of staff members who are chosen to participate in a focus group to represent all staff members. Samples can also be inanimate, for example, a group of

- case records selected to estimate the extent of some problem, such as the error rate in service eligibility determination;
- social agencies selected from among all agencies that serve a certain client population;
- research reports that meet certain criteria and are evaluations of a particular method of intervention in a meta-analysis (see Chapter 7);
- records of human communication, such as the minutes of business meetings, recordings of oral histories, television programs, or Internet websites that are used for content analysis (see Chapter 6).

In exploratory studies in which the researcher hopes only to acquire a better understanding of a problem or other phenomenon, samples are often chosen more for their availability than anything else. There can be little pretense that what is learned from them can be generalized to cases not studied. This is also true in many studies that are primarily qualitative that seek to learn about the different ways people perceive or experience a problem or an event and the meanings they attribute to it. In many descriptive studies and in explanatory studies that attempt to test hypotheses about relationships between variables (studies that tend to rely more on quantitative research methods), sampling methods are used to increase the likelihood that findings from the sample can be generalized beyond the sample to the larger population. In short, every effort is made to produce findings that possess good external validity.

The reason for sampling is efficiency and practicality. By using one or more research samples, researchers hope to learn something at less cost using less time than would be involved if they had to study all of the people or objects that meet some criteria. Whether the research is designed to determine if there is support for hypotheses, describe a problem more accurately, or achieve any other purpose for which research is conducted, the composition of the research sample is important. Not just any sample will do. Researchers seek the sample or samples that will best accomplish their purpose.

TERMINOLOGY

When used in a discussion of sampling, some terms take on very specific meanings. Let us look at some of the most important ones.

Case

A case (sometimes called an *element* if it refers to an inanimate object) is the basic unit of analysis in a given research study. If the unit of analysis is a person (as is often the situation in social work research), the term is used to denote each person who is selected for study. Collectively, those people selected as research participants for the study constitute the sample. The term *case* may refer to many different units of analysis, for example, a family, a group, an organization, a community, or even a nation.

Universe, Theoretical Population, and Accessible Population

The word *universe* is sometimes used in discussions of sampling to refer to the entire collection of people (or elements) that share some defined characteristics. The universe is sometimes referred to as the *theoretical population*. Depending on the theoretical population being defined, the universe for a research study may never really be known. For example, suppose we try to define the universe of all incidents of child abuse in North America. We can never fully define this population, because (1) some incidents of child abuse are never reported; (2) there are always going to be cases that are currently being investigated; and (3) there are continually new cases being reported and others being closed. If we defined our population as all incidents of child abuse reported in the United States during a specific time period, we would come closer to being able to compile an accurate list. However, it would still be extremely difficult, because we would have to rely on records from hundreds of agencies across the country. And, the chance of our list of cases being completely accurate would be extremely low.

Another term, *accessible population* (we will use simply the term *population* after this initial discussion), has a somewhat narrower connotation. It refers to only those cases that theoretically might be selected as research participants—those that are potentially accessible to the researcher because of geography, time, methods of data collection, and budget limitations or other constraints. In the preceding example, we may be interested in the theoretical population of all incidents of child abuse in the country or in our state. However, it is obvious that we will never have access to those incidents that are not reported. Therefore, our accessible population will include only reported child abuse incidents.

Sampling Frame

When defining certain populations, we could create a perfect listing of all cases in our population. For example, if we wanted to survey all presidents of state universities in the country or all high school principals in our state, we could probably create a completely accurate listing as of some point in time. When defining other populations, such as all reported child abuse incidents, we would most likely never be able to compile a completely accurate listing. An actual list of potential cases from which our sample is drawn is called a *sampling frame*. We hope that a sampling frame constitutes at least a reasonable approximation of the population. But we all know that lists, no matter how meticulously they have been compiled, are often incomplete or contain some people or objects that should not be included. For example, if we are interested in studying some characteristic of social work students, the population may be defined as all current BSW and MSW students at XYZ University, and the sampling frame may be an actual list of social work students supplied by the dean's office. It would not include all students who registered after the day the list was compiled, and it may contain the names of some students who recently have withdrawn from social work courses but have not completed the necessary paperwork or notified the dean.

A population is what we would like to use for selecting cases, whereas a sampling frame is an available list that is the next best thing to a population. Frequently, a sampling frame is all that is available. Then one has no choice but to use a sampling frame, knowing full well that it is not a 100 percent accurate representation of the population. When we study a problem that carries a social stigma or is illegal, use of a sampling frame is almost always inevitable. In some cases, the sampling frame may not even be a close approximation of the population. For example, suppose we wish to interview victims of date rape during the past six months in our state to determine what percentage of victims seem to be suffering from post-traumatic stress disorder. No master list of date rape victims for the time period would be available. But a sampling frame containing the names of at least some victims might be compiled with the help of local law enforcement officials if they could be convinced that we would protect participants' confidentiality and conduct the research ethically. We might use this sampling frame, although it probably differs in some important ways from the population. For example, it would not contain the names of date rape victims who did not go to the police or refused to press charges against their attacker.

Sample

We have used the term *sample* many times in this book. What exactly does it mean? A sample is a subset of cases selected for study from among people or objects within a defined population. It is chosen to represent the population. If there are two or more subgroups of cases within a sample, they are referred to as *subsamples*.

Usually, we conclude that it is unfeasible or unnecessary to study the entire population or all potential cases. The population may be too large and/or too costly to study or we may conclude that it is possible to learn almost as much (and at far less cost) by studying only a portion of the population (or sampling frame), so we select a sample of cases from it.

Representativeness

In Chapter 5, we mentioned the importance of using a representative sample in quantitative research. The representativeness of a sample impacts both the internal and external validity of research findings. Although it is desirable in all research, representativeness is less critical in most qualitative studies, which often do not seek support for hypotheses (so internal validity is not an issue) or to generalize their research findings from the sample to its population (so external validity is less of an issue).

Representativeness is one of two criteria generally applied in evaluating the quality of a research sample. It refers to the degree to which a research sample is similar to the population from which it was drawn. Thus, representativeness should be regarded as a relative term. Ideally, we would like to study cases that are identical in all respects to the members of the population from which they were selected. Of course, the only way that this can happen is if we do not sample at all, but study the entire population instead. But if we did, the major benefit of sampling (conservation of research resources) would be lost. Fortunately, perfect representativeness in every respect within a sample is not really necessary—a sample can be sufficiently representative of a population if it resembles the population as a whole with respect to a limited number of relevant variables, most often, the dependent, independent, and any potentially confounding variables.

In Chapter 5, we mentioned three sampling methods that are used in longitudinal studies: trend study, cohort study, and panel study. Generally, sample representativeness is important in this type of research. Longitudinal studies entail costly and time-consuming study of participants who, it is hoped, will provide an accurate picture of changes that occur within the population. A special problem in panel studies (which study the same group of participants over time) is the likelihood that participants may drop out or otherwise become unavailable as the study progresses. Because of death, participant mobility, or other forms of attrition, referred to as *experimental mortality*, the number of participants who are available over the entire course of the study is often much reduced from the number of participants who had initially agreed to participate in the study. If the causes for dropout are not related to central research questions, the problem can be handled by anticipating sizable participant loss and beginning with enough extra participants to absorb it. However, some participants may drop out because of factors relevant to the central focus of the research. If this occurs, their presence can be missed and can affect the credibility of any research findings.

For example, suppose we wish to conduct a panel study to study the long term benefits of a job training program by regularly assessing the employment status of the people who completed the program. Because of attrition, they themselves would not be a representative sample of those people who simply participated in the program, since those who dropped out of the program and were unavailable to us may have differed from the people who completed the program in important ways. Perhaps they found work, experienced a health problem, determined that the program was not worthwhile, etc. But even in our panel study of only those people who completed the program, we would undoubtedly have some experimental mortality too, that is, we would lose contact with some people over time. And who might they be? They might be people who left the area to take a better job or become available for a job promotion. But they might also have become unavailable because they are now unemployed and homeless. In either case, we may have no way of knowing. However, their loss from our study population (experimental mortality) would be closely related to the purpose of our study and could distort any conclusions we might draw about the long-term success of the program.

Sample Size

Another criterion that is considered in assessing the quality of a research sample is the sample size. *Sample size* refers simply to the number of cases the sample contains, not to the percentage of the population or sampling frame that it contains. This is an important distinction and one often misunderstood. Although it seems logical that a sample that includes only a small percent of the population could not possibly be a good sample, this is not necessarily true. Political pollsters using large samples (1,800 to 2,200) have been generally successful in predicting the results of most close elections. Yet their samples consistently have included far less than 1 percent of registered voters. Why have they been so successful? A sample of 1,800 to 2,200 is large in the absolute sense. In addition, the cases within their samples were carefully selected using methods designed to increase the likelihood of the sample's representativeness.

In sampling, size and representativeness are interrelated. A sample's size affects its potential to be representative. For example, if we draw two samples from the same population, one larger than the other, and use the same method for drawing them, the larger sample is more likely to be representative of the population than the smaller one. However, the relationship between sample size and representativeness is not usually that simple and is not as direct as we might logically assume.

When is a sample considered to be large? When is it so small that it is almost surely not representative? Although these would seem like easy questions to answer, they are not. There is no general rule, no absolute definition of what is a large sample or a small one. A small sample is not one, for example, that is always less than 30, less than 100, and so forth; the same applies to what is a large sample. In short—it depends. However, there are several principles that address the issue of sample size and its relationship to representativeness. These principles assume that a sample is a random one (discussed later in this chapter) and relate to (1) the size of the population from which the sample is drawn and (2) the amount of variability within the population.

- If the number of people or elements in the population is small (e.g., less than 100), even a relatively small increase in sample size (drawing just a few more cases) is likely to make the sample more representative. Conversely, if the population size is large, adding a few more cases to the sample will most likely have little effect on its representativeness. A point of "diminishing returns" will have been reached.

- If the number of people or elements in the population is small, the sample may have to include a fairly large percentage of the population (referred to as *sampling ratio* or *sample to population ratio*), perhaps 25 or 30 percent, to be sufficiently representative. If the population is very large (in the hundreds of thousands or even millions, as in the example of political polls mentioned earlier), a very small sampling ratio, 1 percent or even less, should provide a sufficiently representative sample.
- If the population varies widely (it is heterogeneous) in relation to the variables being examined, a larger sample may be required to achieve sample representativeness than if the population is more similar in relation to the variables being examined (it is more homogeneous).

These principles can be helpful in deciding what sample size is most likely to produce the degree of representativeness required. However, they still do not produce a formula for determining the correct sample size. Another factor to be considered in evaluating whether a sample size is appropriate for a given research study is the statistical analysis that will be used to analyze the data. A sample can be considered too small if the sample or one or more of its subsamples is smaller than the size for which a statistical test was designed. Conversely, it is too large if it is larger than the size recommended for a given statistical test. If it is concluded that a sample is of an appropriate size for the statistical analysis being used and has been selected in such a way that it produces a high likelihood of representativeness, it is likely to be considered a good one, especially if we hope to produce findings that possess a high degree of external validity.

Assessment

Behavior: Collect and organize data, and apply critical thinking to interpret information from clients and constituencies.

Critical Thinking Question: Why would a population that varies widely in relation to the variables being examined require a larger sample size than a population that is more similar in relation to the variables of interest?

Sampling Error

There are two reasons why a sample may differ from its population: sampling error and sampling bias (see Box 9.1). The difference that occurs naturally when a sample is drawn from a population or sampling frame is referred to as *sampling error*. All samples, especially smaller ones, are likely to differ from the population from which they are drawn. Even two or more identically sized samples drawn from the same population are likely to differ in relation to measurements of any variables that we may wish to study. For example, two samples of twenty students drawn independently from a class of social work students would be expected to differ from each other in relation to their average grade point, years of work experience, number of siblings, etc. The concept of sampling error is critical to an understanding of how certain types of statistical tests work (see Chapter 13). Sampling error can make variables appear to be related when they really are not, or it can hide true relationships between or among variables.

The relationship between sample size and the amount of sampling error present in a sample can be easily demonstrated by thinking of a class of fifty social work students. Suppose the average age (referred to as the *mean* in statistical analysis) of the class is 30, with most students being between 27 and 33. The oldest is 39, and the youngest is 21. The ages of the students might form a bell shape, or normal distribution, if we were to create a graph of everyone's ages.

Box 9.1   Two Reasons Samples May Differ from the Population from Which They Were Drawn

1. **Sampling error.** The normal tendency of a sample to differ from its population.

2. **Sampling bias.** The intentional or unintentional systematic distortion of a sample.

If we were to draw a sample of five students from the class, we would not expect the average age of the sample of five to be exactly 30. It might be 28 or 32 or even 25 or 35. The difference between the mean of the sample and the mean of the class (population) would be the amount of sampling error in the sample. If we drew many repeated samples of five students from the class, most of the samples would not have a mean age of exactly 30. The average ages of the respective samples of five students would differ from the class mean (30) and from each other. Thus, most of the time, the mean age of any sample would be a poor estimate of the mean age of the class—the sample would not be very representative of the class for the variable "age."

Research-Informed Practice or Practice-Informed Research

Behavior: Apply critical thinking to engage in analysis of quantitative and qualitative research methods and research findings.

Critical Thinking Question: Why are larger samples more likely to be representative of the population than smaller samples?

It is important to remember that it is the number of cases in a sample and the amount of variability within its population (and not simply the percentage of the population that a sample represents) that are important in estimating the amount of sampling error within a sample.

Now suppose that we had drawn samples of fifteen students from the same population (class) of fifty. We would still expect the mean ages of most of the samples to not be exactly 30. However, we would expect more of the samples to be closer to 30 than when we drew samples of only five. Why? Because with samples of fifteen, there is likely to be less sampling error than with samples of only five. A sample of five might contain, for example, five of the oldest students in the class. Then the sampling error might be large. In sampling fifteen students from the class, our first five selections might be the same five older students. But as we select more cases for the sample, the likelihood of drawing younger-than-average students (to balance off the first five) would now be increased, because the average age of the remaining pool of students would now be less than 30. As samples get larger, they begin to look more and more like their population. So, if we had drawn samples of 49 students each, we could expect that the average age of the students in the samples would be very close to the class average of 30. Only if we selected the entire population of all 50 students could we eliminate sampling error. But this would defeat the purpose of sampling, which is to build knowledge in the most efficient way.

Since samples are likely to vary from their populations, we cannot assume that measurements of a sample's characteristics are the same as those of its population. But how much do they differ? An estimate of the similarity of a sample to its population can help us gauge to what degree a drawn sample is sufficiently representative of the population in relation to one or more variables. But how similar can we expect a given sample to be to its population?

There are methods and formulas to help us determine the minimum sample size that will produce an acceptably low sampling error (for more detailed discussions of these methods, see Cohen, 1988; Rosenthal, 2001; Weinbach & Grinnell, 2015). It is important to remember that it is the <u>number</u> of cases in a sample and the amount of variability within its population (and not simply the percentage of the population that a sample represents) that are important in estimating the amount of sampling error within a sample.

Sampling Bias

Even if a sample is relatively large and tables and/or statistical analysis seem to suggest that the amount of sampling error is estimated to be quite small, the sample may still not be adequately representative. It may contain too much *sampling bias*. Sampling bias refers to the systematic distortion of a sample. It can occur either intentionally or unintentionally. It is caused by such factors as the methods used to select a sample or when and where a sample was selected. A biased sample contains overrepresentation of some types of cases and underrepresentation of others (relative to the population from which it was drawn).

A biased sample can seriously limit the usefulness of our data and the credibility of our findings, especially in predominantly quantitative studies. If a sample does not adequately represent its population, nearly anything we find out about cases in the sample will be of limited value. We may know a great deal about a particular (biased) group of cases, but we will be unable to generalize this knowledge to the population from which the sample was drawn. Thus, the external validity of findings generated by a study of a badly biased sample (or of one containing too much sampling error, for that matter) would be low.

Some samples almost invariably contain sampling bias. For example, as we discussed earlier, client satisfaction surveys tend to contain a disproportionately high number of responses from clients who are most satisfied with services (and sometimes those who are most dissatisfied), because they are the people who are most likely to complete the survey. However, there are ways to decrease the likelihood that sampling bias will occur. By controlling the conditions under which a sample is selected using strategies discussed later in this chapter, we can increase the representativeness of research samples.

Statistic and Parameter

The terms *statistic* and *parameter* are closely related. Statistics describe the distribution of variables within samples. Parameters describe the distribution of variables within populations. In predominantly quantitative research studies, we often secure statistics from our sample data that we hope will provide a good estimate of the parameters of the same variables within the population that the sample is supposed to represent. For example, we may calculate the mean (average) age of people within the sample (a statistic) and hope to be able to use that statistic as an estimate of the mean age of the population (a parameter). In those less common situations in which we attempt to study the entire population, we would summarize the findings of the research study as parameters. For example, if we conducted a thorough analysis of all active case records in a human service organization and then summarized the demographic characteristics of those clients currently being served, we would refer to our summaries as parameters.

Random Selection

Random selection entails drawing the cases for a sample or subsample so that all cases have an equal probability of being selected. It is designed to preclude sampling bias and

	Was is it?	Desired Effect?	Purpose
Random Selection	The process of randomly selecting cases from the larger population	Equivalence of a sample and the population	Increase the external validity of research findings
Random Assignment	The process of randomly assigning cases in a sample to the various sub-groups in a study	Equivalence of the sub-groups in a study	Increase the internal validity of research findings

Box 9.2   Random Selection versus Random Assignment

produce a more representative sample. By enhancing sample representativeness, random selection can increase the external validity of research findings.

Random selection should not be confused with random assignment. These two terms can be confusing. Random selection is the process of randomly selecting cases from the population so that our sample is believed to be roughly equivalent to the larger population in relation to all variables of interest. *Random assignment* is the process of randomly assigning the cases to subgroups after they are selected for your sample. Why would we do this? When cases are randomly assigned to, for example, an experimental group and a control group, the two groups will theoretically be closely equivalent to one another on all variables of interest, and even any other variable that we may have failed to identify as relevant to our study! Random assignment is used to increase the internal validity of our research findings by controlling for common threats to internal validity. See Box 9.2 for an overview of this comparison.

Random Sample

A random sample is a sample that is drawn from the population using random selection. There are distinct advantages to random samples. They control for sampling bias, by making it impossible for the researcher to inadvertently distort the sample in some systematic way. Random samples cannot eliminate sampling error. However, when using random sampling we can, using probability theory, estimate the amount of sampling error within the sample and statistically determine the probability that certain relationships between variables within the sample may have been the work of sampling error (Weinbach & Grinnell, 2015).

Random samples are used in social work research when a representative sample is important. However, several factors explain why they are not used more frequently. To draw a random sample, we must have access to a list of all cases in a population or at least a sampling frame that is a good approximation of the population. Often such a sampling frame is not available, and even if it is available, the cost of acquiring a random sample from it may be prohibitive. Many organizations that maintain such lists cannot make them available to outside researchers for legal reasons (e.g., HIPPA laws that apply to medical records) or choose not to share them. Or, even if they are made available, it may simply be too expensive to collect data from cases in a random sample drawn from them when cases are geographically scattered and in-person interviews are the data collection method of choice.

There may also be ethical reasons why random samples are not used. For example, we could draw a random sample of current clients to receive some new form of intervention, but our knowledge of certain clients in the sample might suggest that they would more likely benefit from the traditional treatment or that they might likely be harmed by the new one. Ethically, such clients could not be included, and thus our sample would no longer be considered random.

Summary of Terms

We can now summarize how the preceding terms relate to each other in the context of research sampling:

- *Universe* or *theoretical population* refers to the entire collection of people (or elements) that share some defined characteristic(s) that a researcher wishes to study.
- A *population* is that portion of the theoretical population that is realistically accessible to the researcher.
- A *sampling frame* is an available list that approximates a population but is likely to differ from it in some ways.
- A *sample* is a group of *cases* drawn from a sampling frame that is actually studied. The purpose of selecting a sample is to efficiently study a group of cases that (to a greater or lesser degree) represents a larger number of cases within the population.
- Two criteria used to evaluate the quality of a sample are its *representativeness* (the degree to which it resembles the population) and its *size* (the number of cases it contains).
- Samples may not be representative of the population because of (1) *sampling error*, which is the natural tendency of a sample to differ from its population and/or (2) *sampling bias*, which is the systematic distortion of a sample because of a variety of factors.
- In analyzing data collected from a *sample*, the researcher may calculate sample *statistics* and conduct statistical analysis as a way of estimating population *parameters* or, in explanatory studies, to determine the likelihood that sampling error might have produced a relationship between variables within the sample.
- *Random selection* entails selecting cases for a sample to ensure that all cases have an equal probability of being selected. Samples that are randomly selected are called *random samples*.
- *Random assignment* is the process of randomly assigning randomly selected cases to subgroups (subsamples).

PROBABILITY SAMPLING

There are two general categories of sampling methods available to researchers: probability sampling and nonprobability sampling. *Probability sampling techniques* use random selection, and *nonprobability sampling techniques* do not use random selection. With probability sampling, it is possible to calculate the statistical probability that any case within a sampling frame or population will be selected as part of the research sample. When we use random sampling techniques to select our sample, we ensure that our sample is as close to the population as possible. This allows us to generalize our findings from our sample to the larger population (external validity). There are several probability sampling techniques that can be used to randomly select a sample.

Simple Random Sampling

Simple random sampling is the most well-known type of probability sampling. It entails randomly selecting a predetermined number of cases from the sampling frame or population. If we wanted to select a 25 percent sample (25 people) from a sampling frame of 100, we could write each person's name on an individual 3 by 5 file card and then randomly select 25 cards from a container. If the cards were identical except for the names on them and were mixed in the container in a way that each had an equal probability of being selected, a simple random sample would result.

For drawing larger samples, we could consult a table of mathematically generated random numbers to assist in the selection of cases. Tables of random numbers are available in many research textbooks (see, for example, Rubin & Babbie, 2007). To use a table of random numbers, we would first assign consecutive numbers to all cases in the sampling frame. Then we would enter the random number table at some random point (selecting any number off the table arbitrarily) and then move through the table in some systematic way (e.g., moving horizontally and selecting every fourth number) until the required number of random numbers has been selected. The cases that correspond to the random numbers selected from the table would then be selected to be included in the sample.

Another common method for selecting a simple random sample is to use computer software designed to generate numbers at random. Many statistical software packages now offer a random number function. All cases in the sampling frame or population are assigned consecutive numbers. We would then enter the size of the sampling frame and the number of cases that will constitute the sample. The software produces a list of random numbers, and we would then select the cases assigned those numbers to constitute our research sample.

Intervention

Behavior: Apply knowledge of human behavior and the social environment, person-in-environment, and other multidisciplinary theoretical frameworks in interventions with clients and constituencies.

Critical Thinking Question: Under what circumstances might simple random sampling be considered unethical?

Systematic Random Sampling

Systematic random sampling is popular because of its simplicity. No table of random numbers is needed, and no computer programs are required. It uses a three-step process. An example will help to explain how it works.

Suppose we wish to conduct a client satisfaction survey using a 25 percent sample of all 100 active clients in a human service organization. The case records for the active clients (the sampling frame) are stored in a locked file drawer or as an electronic file. The first 25 case records in the file could be selected, but they would not constitute a probability sample since the other 75 active cases would have zero probability of being selected. Such a sample might also be biased. For example, because files are stored alphabetically, the first 25 cases would include only those cases whose last names start with a letter early in the alphabet. That might produce a bias in terms of ethnicity, since surnames beginning with certain letters are more common in some parts of the world than in others. So, a systematic random sample would be preferable; it would control for this potential source of bias.

How would a systematic sample be drawn in this case? First, the necessary sampling interval (k) would have to be computed. The sampling interval is determined by dividing the number of cases in the sampling frame by the number of cases needed for the sample. To select a sample of 25 cases from a sampling frame of 100, we would calculate our sampling interval as follows:

$$k = \frac{\text{numbers of cases in sampling frame}}{\text{numbers of cases desired for sample}}$$

$$k = 100/25$$

$$k = 4$$

Therefore, the sampling interval (k) would be 4. Next, we would randomly select a number from 1 to k (4 in this case). Let us say that it is 3. This number would be the starting point—the third case in the file would be the first case selected. Then, we would select every fourth case after that; that is, the seventh case, the eleventh, the fifteenth, the nineteenth, and so forth. The initial, random selection of a starting point is an important step, and it cannot be ignored. It is necessary so that, when we began, every case in the file had an equal chance of being selected for the sample.

Stratified Random Sampling

Stratified random sampling is another probability sampling method, and can be used (1) to reduce the amount of sampling error when using a simple or systematic random sample or (2) to ensure that there are enough cases within different value or value label categories of a variable for comparison purposes. For either purpose, a two-stage sampling method is used.

The first stage of stratified sampling requires that we divide the population into homogeneous categories, or strata. That is, people or objects are separated into two or more strata (subgroups of the population or sampling frame) on the basis of the variables of interest. Thus, within strata, members are homogeneous with regard to this variable (e.g., all social workers in one stratum and all physicians in another stratum for the variable "profession" or all women in one stratum and all men in the other stratum for the variable "gender"). In the second stage, the desired number of cases is selected from each stratum by simple random sampling or systematic random sampling.

Stratified random sampling is another probability sampling method and can be used (1) to reduce the amount of sampling error when using a simple or systematic random sample or (2) to ensure that there are enough cases within different value or value label categories of a variable for comparison purposes.

Proportionate Stratified Random Sampling

There are two types of stratified random sampling: proportionate stratified random sampling and disproportionate stratified random sampling. In *proportionate stratified random sampling,* we would stratify cases on the basis of a variable that could distort the research findings if not proportionately represented in the research sample (i.e., one that is a potentially confounding variable). For example, if we are wishing to study the effectiveness of treatment intervention on a group of clients who have been diagnosed as clinically depressed we might have good reason to stratify the sample by gender. There might be concern that client gender may be a confounding variable that relates to treatment success. Thus, a method is needed to ensure that the sample does not consist of a disproportionate (relative to the sampling frame) number of either men or women.

Let us assume that the sampling frame from which the sample is drawn consists of 1,000 cases, of which 900 are women and 100 are men. A 5 percent sample (consisting of 50 cases) is to be drawn. To draw a proportionate stratified random sample, the cases would first be sorted into two strata consisting of (1) the 900 women and (2) the 100 men. Then 5 percent of the women (45 cases) would be selected from the group of women at random and 5 percent of the men (5 cases) from the group of men at random. The sample, like the sampling frame, would thus be 90 percent women—perfectly representative of the population with regard to gender. The sample thus produced might be biased in some other respects, but it is definitely not biased regarding gender. And, initially every case in the sampling frame had an equal likelihood of being selected (0.05, or 5 percent), so the sample is considered to be a random one.

But what if we wished to determine if the treatment intervention is more effective with men or with women? If a proportionate stratified random sample were used, it would require comparing the clinical depression level of one subsample of 45 women (probably an acceptable size) with the other subsample consisting of only 5 men. We might be uncomfortable with allowing only 5 men to represent all male clients. Could only 5 cases be representative of all male clients? Five is a very small subsample size; the likelihood of sampling error might be high, and certain potentially useful forms of statistical analysis that require larger samples would have to be eliminated.

Diversity and Difference in Practice

Behavior: Apply and communicate understanding of the importance of diversity and difference in shaping life experiences in practice at the micro, mezzo, and macro levels.

Critical Thinking Question: How would you use proportionate stratified random sampling to make sure your sample is representative of the population with regard to race?

Disproportionate Stratified Random Sampling

An alternative method of sampling that also relies on the use of strata (homogeneous subgroups) is *disproportionate stratified random sampling*. It can be used to produce subsamples of comparable size for comparison purposes by over-sampling from one group and under-sampling from another. For example, in the previous example we might randomly select a subsample of 25 women and another of 25 men from their respective strata. In the total sample (men and women), there would be a disproportionate number of men relative to the sampling frame. In the sample, 50 percent of the cases would be men, although in the sampling frame the percentage of men is only 10 percent. Male and female clients would clearly have a different probability of being selected for the research sample. But it is still possible to calculate the likelihood of their being selected for the research sample—thus, the sample would still be a probability sample (but not a random one). Each male client would have a 25 percent chance of being selected for the sample (25 out of 100), while each female client would have a less than 3 percent (25 out of 900) chance of being selected for the sample.

Cluster Sampling

Cluster sampling involves a multistage process. It is more likely to be used in large-scale surveys or studies that involve cases that are geographically distant from each other than in small, organization-based studies. There are some research situations where it is extremely useful for putting together a sample that is both representative and sufficiently large, while conserving the resources of the researcher.

In cluster sampling, we would identify clusters of cases. Next, we would randomly select a predetermined number of clusters. Then all cases (or sometimes a random sample of all cases) within each of the selected clusters is selected to constitute the research sample. The following example should help clarify how cluster sampling is accomplished. Suppose we wish to collect data to describe the characteristics of a random sample of women who have experienced domestic violence who are currently residing in domestic violence shelters within our state. For various reasons (e.g., the women's safety), there is unlikely to exist a readily available master list of these women. Thus, a simple random sampling method cannot be used. However, a list of all shelters within a particular state may exist. Each shelter can be thought of as a cluster of cases. First, a random sample of these shelters (clusters) is selected. Then the administrators of the shelters selected could be asked to provide a list of all persons currently in the shelter (using numbers instead of names to preserve the clients' confidentiality). The lists from the shelters could comprise the research sample, or if the number of cases thus obtained would be too large, the desired number of cases could be selected from the lists using either simple or systematic random sampling.

Sometimes, even if a master list of potential research participants can be compiled, cluster sampling may still be the sampling method of choice. A major advantage of cluster sampling is that it allows us to collect data in a timely and cost-efficient way, while not greatly increasing the likelihood of sampling bias. In our example, we would be able to collect data about a large number of people in relatively few locations (those shelters that were selected) using cluster sampling. Even if a simple random sample of all cases currently active in the shelters could have been drawn, a considerable amount of time and money would have been spent requesting assistance in acquiring data or even traveling around the state to collect data on just one or two cases in each of many shelters.

NONPROBABILITY SAMPLING

In a nonprobability sample, it is not possible to calculate the likelihood that a given person or element will be selected. It does not involve random selection, so some cases will have a greater likelihood of being selected than others. However, we cannot know how much greater. We also cannot estimate how much sampling error a sample contains. In many research studies in social work, a method that produces a probability sample (random selection) cannot be used. This happens most frequently when no population list or even sampling frame is available from which to draw the sample. In such situations, it would be impossible to use a probability sampling technique. This was the situation when one of the authors was involved in an exploratory study of women who delayed childbearing until after age 30. No sample drawn could possibly be a probability sample, because the population could not be identified or specified and no acceptable sampling frame was available.

Even when it is possible to draw a probability sample, it might not be the best sample to use to study a given problem or research question. A nonprobability sample may be preferable. In some types of research, sample representativeness is not as important as other sample characteristics. For example, in research studies where the emphasis is on exploring the nature and impact of a problem, it may make sense to study only individuals who are likely to have the best in-depth understanding of the problem, whether or not they represent a cross-section of the population experiencing it. In this type of study, we might deliberately exclude from the study those who might otherwise have been randomly selected as participants but who may contribute little or nothing new to an understanding of the problem.

There are four commonly used nonprobability sampling methods. All of these methods are suited to situations in which the researcher either (1) would prefer a representative sample but is unable to compile a population or sampling frame from which to randomly select the sample or (2) has decided that representativeness is less important to sample composition than one or more other characteristics.

Convenience Sampling

One type of nonprobability sampling method involves a very unscientific approach to sampling. Convenience sampling (sometimes called *accidental sampling*) entails selecting cases for study primarily because they happen to be readily accessible to the researcher. It is this type of sampling that is most likely to have been used when we hear on the evening news that a "random sample" of residents of our community was interviewed about their opinions regarding a news event. In fact, the sample was not at all random! Generally, the people interviewed were all in the same shopping mall or were sitting in the park near the television studio. They were selected mainly because of convenience. Clearly, some potential participants (those most readily available) had a greater likelihood of selection than others who were in some different place at the time that data were collected.

Like all sampling methods, convenience sampling <u>may</u> produce an acceptable level of representativeness but it is the method that is probably least likely to do so. The usefulness of convenience samples in social work research is limited. If we are just beginning to explore a new area of inquiry and it is hard to locate people with certain characteristics or obtain their permission to be research participants, it may be the only feasible alternative. But convenience samples present a major difficulty to us. How can we interpret the findings of our research? To whom do they apply? Under what conditions? Research designs that rely on convenience sampling have little or no claim to external validity. Findings are generally believed to be applicable only to those people or objects that were studied.

Purposive Sampling

Sometimes, cases are selected because researchers believe that the cases can provide them with access to a unique approach to a problem or situation, or a special perspective, insight, expertise, experience, characteristic, or condition that they wish to understand. For example, suppose we wish to know more about the variations in coping strategies used by people diagnosed with early-stage Alzheimer's disease. Although we might be able to produce a sampling frame of people who have recently been diagnosed with the disease and draw a random sample from it, the sample thus selected might not be what is needed for our research. For our research objective, a purposive sample might actually be preferable to a more representative one. It would be more likely to help us describe the wide variety of coping methods used.

How would we acquire a purposive sample of people recently diagnosed with Alzheimer's disease? From informal conversations with medical staff, we might learn of a number of people being treated at clinics and hospitals who use what staff members perceive as unique coping strategies. We might then select those twenty people with what seem like the most unique ways of coping and ask them to voluntarily take part in in-depth research interviews. Our sample would not be representative of the population or even of the available sampling frame. It would not contain the same distribution of coping strategies (percentage-wise) that exists within the population of people with Alzheimer's. For example, we might estimate that 40 percent of the population all use the same coping strategy, but we might select only one person for our sample of twenty (5 percent) who use that strategy. Because we would be seeking to learn about the diversity of coping strategies used by the population (heterogeneity), there might be little value in interviewing more than one person who uses any one coping strategy. That would be redundant.

There are other variations of purposive sampling that are used less frequently in social work research. One, *expert sampling*, selects cases on the basis of the criterion that they have a certain desired expertise. Thus, we might select and bring together a panel of researchers, all of whom have studied, for example, the problem of weight-based discrimination, or a group of primary care physicians who have set up their practices using a fee-based system (a system in which patients pay a fixed amount per year and are promised certain services at no additional charge). These "panels of experts" can then be surveyed, brought together in a focus group, or individually interviewed in an attempt to tap their experience and expertise.

Sometimes, we might prefer a group of people who are "typical" in some way. We would use a type of purposive sampling known as *mode instance sampling*. For example, in conducting a needs assessment to determine the level of perceived need for a proposed social program, we may want to assemble a sample of people who share certain characteristics, those individuals who might use the proposed program's services, to collect their opinions about how best to market the proposed program and what client needs it should address.

Still another form of purposive sampling is the opposite of mode instance sampling. It is *deviant case sampling*, and it seeks the most atypical cases for study. For example, in an exploratory qualitative study, we might wish to use a sample of investors who profited the most and/or lost the most money by lying on home loan applications to acquire real estate that they planned to resell ("flip"). They might then be interviewed in order to learn how they were ethically able to justify their illegal behavior.

Snowball Sampling

Snowball sampling does not select a sample at one point in time. When using snowball sampling, the sample is compiled as the research progresses. First, one or just a few people are identified as potential research participants. Then they are asked to provide the names of people they know or know about who, like themselves, have experienced a problem or who in other ways meet the necessary criteria for inclusion in the research study. The next potential participants are then contacted to determine whether they are eligible for inclusion in the sample, and, if so, whether they are willing to participate in the study. They may, in turn, be asked to provide the names of other potential participants. The process is repeated until enough participants are eligible and agree to take part in the study.

Snowball sampling could be used in the previously mentioned research study in which a sample of women who had given birth to their first child after age 30 were interviewed. An initial sample of women was identified by placing an ad in the paper (hardly a random selection procedure). Women who responded to the ad were interviewed by a member of the research team to ensure that they met the necessary criteria to be part of the research study, and an early draft of a research data collection instrument was completed. At the conclusion of the interview, they were asked if they knew other women who, like themselves, had borne their first child after age 30. These prospects were then followed up by the research team. The use of snowball sampling was appropriate because (1) the purpose of the study was to develop a research instrument for a subsequent study of delayed childbearing and (2) the researchers were not attempting to describe accurately the population of all women who delay childbearing.

Snowball sampling is often used if the problem or behavior is illegal or carries some social stigma, making it more difficult to locate potential research participants. Thus, it is frequently used in case studies, such as the ones described in Chapter 6. This sampling technique is also used in exploratory studies designed to learn more about either a new problem or one that has only recently been identified. For example, a sample of adolescents who are recent victims of *cyber-bullying* (harassment by peers using e-mail, Twitter, or other electronic communication) could be compiled by first identifying one victim and then asking him or her to provide the names of others who they know have had similar experiences. Of course, as this problem grows and more and more victims are identified, a sampling frame of victims will be able to be compiled. Other, perhaps better, methods of acquiring research samples (perhaps, simple random sampling) then can be used.

Quota Sampling

Another type of nonprobability sampling method, *quota sampling*, is used to obtain a sample that is (1) as representative as possible in relation to potentially confounding variables and (2) of a specified size (quota). The most common type of quota sampling, *proportional quota sampling*, begins with estimating the characteristics of the research population regarding selected variables. This description is built into a matrix, that is, a table displaying the percentage of people in the population believed to share each combination of characteristics. Then people are selected for study who have all of the characteristics described within each specific cell of the matrix. Sampling continues until there is a final sample of people selected that represents each of the cells. For example, in a survey being conducted at the mall, we may have decided upon a quota of interviewing 100 people, with individual characteristics proportional to the community's population characteristics of gender and race. Therefore, we would select individuals from the people walking by with specific values of gender and race until we have met the quota in each category. Quota sampling is generally used by political pollsters conducting exit polls. It has produced some accurate predictions but also some embarrassing wrong ones, such as in the United States 2016 presidential election. However, when the latter has occurred, it has usually been attributed to other factors such as people's unwillingness to admit for whom they had voted, not a flaw in the sampling method used.

Sometimes, it is logistically impossible (cost, time, geography) to use a large research sample. However, we still want to be sure that certain variables are adequately represented in the sample. If proportional quota sampling were used, characteristics of cases that occur relatively infrequently in the population might not be adequately represented. For example, a sample might contain only one person who is a Pacific Islander and has a disability. This one individual clearly cannot represent all people who have this combination of demographic characteristics—it would be better to have at least two or three cases. In such a situation, *nonproportional quota sampling*, a less common sampling method, might be preferred. It is considered the nonprobability equivalent of disproportionate stratified sampling. It entails determining the minimum number of cases required for each category or combination of characteristics (cell) and then sampling until that minimum is attained.

The use of nonproportional quota sampling, like many choices we make in research, is a trade-off. It is based on the assumption that sacrificing representativeness in the sample as a whole is preferable to the risk of having a category or combination of characteristics with a small number of cases and, thus, a high probability of sampling error within it. There is one major problem that frequently precludes the more frequent use of quota sampling of either type. If we do not have accurate estimates of the characteristics of the population of interest, we will be unable to develop an accurate quota matrix to determine how many cases we should select from each category. Quota sampling should be used only when (1) the researcher has confidence that the data needed to establish a quota matrix represent reasonably accurate estimates of the characteristics of the population and (2) an unbiased (ideally, random) method of selecting participants within each cell can be implemented after a matrix has been constructed.

SELECTING A GOOD SAMPLE

The sampling methods that we have just described might be regarded as options, or a menu of sampling alternatives. Sometimes, we simply select the one best suited to our needs and use it to draw a sample. However, sampling is often a little more complicated. We would then employ a *sampling plan*, a sequence of steps or stages that makes use of two or more of these methods. For example, in a study of the job satisfaction of social workers in large outpatient mental health clinics, we might first (using systematic random sampling) select the names of twenty clinics from a state-wide directory. The social workers in these clinics would then serve as a cluster sample. However, rather than selecting all of the social workers employed there to participate in our research study, we might draw a 20 percent simple random sample of workers to participate. After interviewing them, we might select ten social workers who are the most dissatisfied with their jobs (mode instance sampling) to participate in a focus group to discuss the reasons for their dissatisfaction. This multistage sampling plan would be designed to take advantage of the desirable features of each of the different sampling methods used.

When selecting the sampling method or methods to be used and determining the appropriate sample size, a number of important, interrelated issues must be addressed. Some of them relate to practical matters that are easily understood; others are a little more technical. The major issues that the researcher needs to consider are (1) available resources for securing the sample, (2) the overall design and purpose of the study, (3) the type of statistical analysis that will be used, and (4) the relative importance of sample representativeness.

Available Resources

If the study is being funded by a human service organization or some other organization that has been contracted to have it designed and implemented, the size of the sample to be used may have already been specified. If this is not the case, the researcher is free to use judgment in selecting an appropriate research sample size.

As we have noted, larger samples generally are more likely to be representative of the population than are smaller ones. When larger samples are chosen, the amount of sampling error should be reduced. But even in quantitative studies, where sample representativeness is usually critical to the credibility of the research findings, there is a point of diminishing returns. We can get to the point where an increase in sample size does not appreciably reduce the amount of sampling error that may be present. Besides, using large samples can be costly. As stated previously, the processes of compromise and trade-off are ongoing activities in conducting social work research. Resources spent collecting data from a large number of research participants leaves less time and resources for performing other essential tasks in the research process, for example, data analysis or report writing. If a smaller sample is used, some of the time and resources can be used to perform those other tasks, and the overall quality of the research study might actually be enhanced.

> *We can get to the point where an increase in sample size does not appreciably reduce the amount of sampling error that may be present.*

Overall Design and Purpose of the Study

Generally, we expect to see different size samples (and different sampling methods) with certain types of research. For example, qualitative research studies often use nonprobability sampling methods with smaller sample sizes than predominantly quantitative designs. Often, a representative sample is impossible to obtain because of the absence of an adequate sampling frame. And it may not be considered important anyway if the research is primarily exploratory. In contrast, large-scale descriptive studies such as mailed surveys that are primarily quantitative often use large samples (to reduce sampling error) and strive for representativeness by using random sampling methods, because the external validity of findings is considered important. If, for example, the purpose of a study is to describe accurately the characteristics of a client population, such as older people who have admitted to having been victims of financial abuse, and a good sampling frame is available, a randomly selected sample consisting of several hundred cases may be used to ensure the likelihood of a sufficiently representative sample. This increases the external validity of the study and allows us to generalize our findings to the larger population.

Other types of research use samples of various sizes, usually depending on financial resources available to support the research and the number of cases available for study. Research whose objective is primarily to develop measurement instruments to be used in subsequent research studies may use relatively small samples but may use many different samples representing different subpopulations and/or different times and settings for measurement. If a researcher wishes merely to pilot-test a research instrument (see Chapter 12) while anticipating that it will need to be revised, a small nonprobability sample is likely to be used.

It is sometimes helpful to consult reports of other similar research and note how many cases were used. This kind of information can be used as a general guide, but it should be remembered that errors in sample size selection are quite common. We would not want to repeat another researcher's mistakes. For a more in-depth discussion of sampling methods and issues, a text that is devoted solely to the topic of research sampling should be consulted (Levy & Lemeshow, 2008; Thompson, 2012).

Statistical Analyses to Be Used

In qualitative studies, statistical analysis is usually not an important consideration in designing a sampling plan. There are currently methods of analyzing qualitative data (primarily content analysis) that convert words to numbers that can then be analyzed statistically (see Chapter 13). However, since the sampling methods most frequently used (purposive, snowball, or convenience) rarely produce samples that can be considered representative, there is usually little value in conducting statistical analysis. Any conclusions regarding, for example, relationships between or among variables would be highly suspect.

In primarily quantitative studies, the size of a research sample and the type of sampling method used are important factors in the selection of the form of statistical analysis to be used. But sometimes it works the other way around. In some instances, the researcher knows in advance what analysis will have to be used, for example, when conducting grant-sponsored research that specifies which statistical tests are acceptable, or when replicating the research of others who used a specific form of statistical analysis. Then the size of the sample as well as the sampling method used (e.g., probability or nonprobability) is tailored to the requirements of the statistical analysis that must be used.

The relationship between types of statistical analysis and the most appropriate sample size is beyond the scope of this text. However, we should remember that sample size guidelines for various statistical analyses exist for a purpose. If a specific statistical test has been designed for a certain sample size, the sample size selected should be within the specified range, neither smaller nor larger. Samples that are either smaller or larger than recommended for a given statistical test can result in misleading conclusions regarding relationships between variables.

The Importance of Sample Representativeness

As noted earlier, quantitative studies place great importance on representative samples. There is a concentrated effort to avoid sampling bias and determine (statistically) the probability that sampling error may have produced a relationship between or among variables that are not related or masked a relationship that does exist. Thus, whenever possible, quantitative studies rely on probability samples and random sampling methods to increase the likelihood of representativeness within research samples.

Thus, whenever possible, quantitative studies rely on probability samples and random sampling methods to increase the likelihood of representativeness within research samples.

In predominantly qualitative studies, where representativeness is often impossible anyway, nonprobability sampling methods generally provide an adequate sample of cases. Both representativeness and size are less important than criteria such as the richness of data that a sample provides or the diversity of perceptions, meanings, experiences, and so forth contained within it.

SUMMARY

In this chapter,

- We focused on sample selection and its relationship to good research. Key terms relating to sampling were defined. Representativeness and size were identified as the two criteria most frequently used in evaluating the quality of a sample, at least in predominantly quantitative studies. Sampling methods are characterized as either probability or nonprobability, depending on whether it is possible to calculate the probability that an individual person or object will be selected to become a case within the research sample. Random samples are often regarded as superior to non-random ones because they are more likely to be representative of the population from which they are selected and they allow for the use of certain types of statistical analyses.
- Four types of probability sampling were described in this chapter: simple random sampling, systematic random sampling, cluster sampling, and proportionate and disproportionate stratified random sampling.
- For some research studies, probability samples may be neither feasible nor desirable. In some qualitative studies, for example, nonprobability sampling methods may yield samples that are exactly what is needed. Four common nonprobability sampling methods were described: convenience sampling, purposive sampling, snowball sampling, and quota sampling.
- Finally, we discussed four major issues that the researcher needs to consider when deciding which sampling method to use and how large a sample is needed. They are (1) available resources for securing the sample, (2) the overall design and purpose of the study, (3) the type of statistical analysis (if any) that will be used, and (4) the importance of sample representativeness to the research.

MyEducationLab® for Research

Try the Topic 5 Assignments: Selecting a Sample and the Topic 5 Study Plan.

Chapter 9 Chapter Review Quiz.

10

Measurement Concepts and Issues

Once we have determined how a sample of research participants will be selected, we generally focus on measurement issues. Specifically, we need to decide (1) what data will need to be collected and (2) what instruments or methods will be used to collect it.

In quantitative research, accurate measurement is of paramount importance. Whether the goal is to describe a problem or phenomenon (as in descriptive designs) or to attempt to learn if two or more variables are likely to be related in the population from which a research sample was drawn, research findings will be misleading if key variables are not measured accurately. For example, how could we know if a report of the incidence and severity of family violence in a community is accurate if it is unclear what exactly was meant by the term *family violence* or if the methods for measuring its severity appear to be highly subjective? Or, how can we trust a researcher's conclusion that clients' motivation and degree of success in counseling are positively correlated if motivation was determined solely on clients' own assessments or success in counseling was measured solely on the basis of the subjective impressions of their social workers?

Measurement is also important in qualitative studies. Researchers conducting qualitative studies acknowledge, however, that their measurements may be biased by their own presence or other factors and will necessarily have a certain degree of subjectivity; they expect that. But that does not absolve them of the responsibility to (1) measure even highly subjective variables, such as impressions, perceptions, or the meaning of certain events to participants, as accurately as possible and (2) measure more easily measured variables, such as their participants' demographic characteristics or behaviors, accurately. Thus, while Chapters 10–12 may seem to relate mostly to quantitative research, much of their content is equally applicable to predominantly qualitative research designs.

WHAT IS MEASUREMENT IN RESEARCH?

Most of us think we have a good understanding about measurement and how it works. After all, we have used it almost all of our lives; we measure the height of children, our weight, room dimensions and so on. But just to be sure we all agree on what it means, let's review it in the context of research. In research, *measurement* is the process of sorting and, when possible, quantifying information in a consistent, systematic fashion. It entails collecting data in relation to certain variables and assigning the appropriate value categories or values to individual cases. In the social work literature, there is disagreement as to how precisely one can measure certain variables. Some writers have taken the position that, with enough effort, virtually all variables can be accurately measured (Rubin & Babbie, 2014). They believe that most variables can be *quantified*, that is, a number can be assigned to describe accurately the exact amount of the variable present within a case. Other writers, especially those who espouse qualitative research methods, point out that because of the nature of many of the variables that are of interest to us as social workers they cannot be easily quantified using standardized measurement techniques. Our position is that, for most (if not all) variables, a measurement strategy can be developed that will yield useful data for researchers. However, we also acknowledge that many variables of interest do not readily lend themselves to quantification.

> *Our position is that, for most (if not all) variables, a measurement strategy can be developed that will yield useful data for researchers.*

PREPARATION FOR MEASUREMENT

Before any measurement can take place, two interrelated activities must take place. They are referred to as *conceptualization* and *operationalization*.

Conceptualization

Conceptualization entails two major processes, (1) selecting and specifying what we believe to be the most important or relevant variables to measure and (2) specifying as precisely as possible exactly what we mean by those variables. In performing these tasks, we would rely on both available knowledge (the literature) and our practice knowledge and experience. For example, the literature may have suggested that abuse (or nonabuse) of medication by people who have a terminal illness may be related to whether or not hospice care is provided. It may have suggested the hypothesis that terminally ill patients who receive hospice care will be less likely to abuse medication than terminally ill patients who do not receive hospice care. Two variables that clearly would need to be measured are (1) involvement (or noninvolvement) with hospice care, the independent variable, and (2) the presence or absence of medication abuse (the dependent or outcome variable). Specification of the independent variable (hospice involvement/noninvolvement) would be no problem. But we would need to specify exactly what we mean by *medication abuse* (the outcome or dependent variable). Would it be any use of medication—accidental or intentional—other than exactly as prescribed? Should it include taking less of a medicine than prescribed? What about the use of additional nonprescription medication? All of the preceding questions (and more) would need to be addressed before data collection begins, so that cases could be correctly and consistently assigned to value categories for the variable *medication abuse*. There are no right or wrong answers to these questions. We can answer them any way that seems logical or, perhaps, just answer them in the same way that a previous researcher addressed them in conceptualizing what he or she meant by the term "medication abuse." However we do it, the answers should be applied consistently with all research participants.

Sometimes, the answers are summarized at this point in what is referred to as a conceptual definition. A conceptual definition tells the reader of a research report exactly how the variable was defined in the current study. (Another researcher might apply still a different conceptual definition to the same variable in his or her research.) A conceptual definition says, in effect, "When I use a term in this research, this is what I mean by it." For example, we might construct the following conceptual definition:

> Medication abuse is the intentional misuse of a prescribed, controlled narcotic substance on at least three occasions by a person who is terminally ill.

Generally, conceptual definitions are then followed by operational definitions. Operational definitions of variables are presented (along with definitions of other terms that may need to be defined) at the end of a literature review or near the beginning of the methodology section of a research report. In our example, it would also be necessary to define operationally such terms as *terminally ill* and *hospice care*.

Operationalization

Operationalization is closely related to conceptualization and is the last step in preparation for measurement. It refers to specifying the actual measuring devices or methods that will be used to measure key variables. Thus, it further clarifies their meaning.

Generally, there are many ways that a variable can be measured. For example, measurement of the variable "medication abuse" might entail actual observations by nurses, social workers, caregivers, or aides. It might also include social workers' impressions based on mental alertness or other symptoms of medication abuse, self-reports of patients, or something as specific as a measurement of a certain chemical in the patient's bloodstream at regular intervals.

We noted that operational definitions of a term may vary from study to study. Similarly, different researchers may actually measure the same variable in different ways. Unless we are replicating the research of others (in which case the same method of measuring the variable should be used), that is fine. The only requirements for operationalization of a given variable are that it should be logical and justified (usually through the literature). Sometimes, researchers choose to include the method of measurement (operationalization) of a variable in their operational definition of the variable (Neuman, 1997). An example follows:

> Medication abuse is the intentional misuse of a prescribed, controlled narcotic substance on at least three occasions by a person who is terminally ill as reported by the patient's primary caregiver counting the number of pills missing from the medication dispenser.

Cultural Sensitivity in Operationalization

Certain theoretical concepts may have different meanings for research participants, depending on their ethnic and cultural backgrounds. When this is the case, every effort should be made to operationalize a variable in a way that is consistent with the culture of those individuals who are providing research data. For example, what if we need to measure the educational attainment of a group of research participants? Traditionally, "years

Diversity and Difference in Practice

Behavior: Apply and communicate the understanding of the importance of diversity and difference in shaping life experiences in practice at the micro, mezzo, and macro levels.

Critical Thinking Question: Identify another variable (similar to educational attainment) that might require the researcher be sensitive to cultural issues and/or definitions before creating the variable's operational definition.

of formal schooling completed as reported by the research participant" is the operational definition of educational attainment. This definition, however, may underestimate the actual educational experiences and degree of knowledge attainment in certain groups of people. For example, for some international populations, formal schooling may not be the only method of educating and preparing people for the workforce. Individuals may engage in mentorship programs, apprenticeship opportunities, or other less formal methods of educational preparation that do not occur in a traditional school setting. Thus, an accurate assessment of their educational attainment should include these less formal venues for education.

LEVELS OF MEASUREMENT

Levels (sometimes called *scales*) of measurement refer to the degree of precision with which a variable is to be measured. We must decide at what level each variable is to be measured, sometimes on the basis of the nature of the variable itself and more frequently on the method of measurement used (the way it was operationalized). Determining which of four possible levels of measurement are present in the measurement of each variable is a critical step for deciding which methods for any statistical analyses of data (see Chapter 13) would be appropriate. The four levels represent a hierarchy of measurement precision from lowest to highest as described below. See Box 10.1 for a summary and examples of the four levels of measurement.

Nominal Level

The nominal level represents the most basic form of measurement. It involves the use of a measurement scheme that simply sorts cases into exhaustive and mutually exclusive value categories of a variable. In a nominal-level measurement, a case must fall into one (exhaustive) and only one (mutually exclusive) category of a variable. The predictor variable in our previous example (involvement/non-involvement in hospice care) would be an example of a variable that would be considered nominal level. The different value categories of a variable reflect only a difference in kind, not a difference in the amount of the variable present within a given case. Even if a number is used as a label for a value category to make data entry into a computer database easier, the number has no quantitative significance. For example, in measuring the variable "gender identity," the researcher may assign the number 1 for individuals who identify as males and the number 2 for individuals who identify as females, or the other way around. In either case, the numbers do not reflect a quantitative difference—just a qualitative one. They are merely labels, substitutes for words.

In measuring many variables, nominal measurement is all that appears possible. Variables such as gender identity, whether one voted in the last election, whether one owns a car or not, is an undergraduate social work major, or one's religious affiliation are nominal by their very nature. A researcher might be interested in measuring the number of cars owned or degree of religiosity, but those are different variables, ones that have the potential for more precise levels of measurement.

Ordinal Level

Ordinal measurement meets all the criteria for nominal measurement. In addition, the value categories possess a logical rank-ordering. The term *ordinal level* is assigned to variables that have been measured using a range of categories, such as "always," "sometimes," "rarely," and "never" or "not improved," "slightly improved," "somewhat improved," and "greatly improved." Note that these categories can be rank ordered—anyone would arrange them in the same sequence to reflect the different quantities of some variable that each represents. But the value labels are not precise. For example, although we would all agree that "somewhat improved" reflects more improvement than "slightly improved," we cannot say exactly how much.

Ordinal measurement is used quite frequently in social work practice and research. For example, social workers may be interested in measuring the degree of cooperation displayed by families that have been court ordered to receive treatment. They might categorize degree of cooperation as (1) highly cooperative, (2) cooperative, or (3) uncooperative. Of course, it would be necessary to specify the criteria by which a rating (1, 2, or 3) would be assigned to a particular case. Note that the difference between successive points of measurement on the scale is not fixed. In other words, the difference between ratings of 2 and 3 on the scale is not assumed to be equal to the difference between ratings of 1 and 2. The numbers simply represent ranks.

Ordinal level variables in social work research include many sociodemographic variables such as age (when measured using the value categories "elderly," "middle-aged," "young adult," "adolescent," "preadolescent," and "child"), social class standing ("upper," "middle," and "lower"), and degree of educational attainment (when measured by the highest degree completed). Some measurement instruments, especially newly constructed ones, that measure psychosocial variables such as coping capacity or level of social functioning may generate only ordinal-level scores. For example, an instrument measuring level of social functioning may produce numeric scores. They can be placed in the value categories of "poor," "fair," "good," and "excellent," once the appropriate range of scores for each category has been determined. Then these labels can be assigned numbers again, for example "poor" might be assigned the number "1," "fair" the number "2," etc. These numbers could then be analyzed "as is," but any statistical analyses should be those designed for use with ordinal-level variables.

Interval Level

Interval-level measurements meet all of the criteria for ordinal-level measurement and additionally require that the exact differences between categories (values) of the variable are known and are equal to each other. Many standardized tests, especially those that have been refined over many years, are believed to produce interval-level measurements. For example, IQ tests, Scholastic Assessment Tests (SATs), or Graduate Record Exams (GREs) are believed to contain equal intervals. In theory at least, the difference between two equal intervals on an IQ test (say, between scores of 115 and 110 and between scores of 87 and 82) reflect equal quantities of the construct (intelligence) that the test is supposed to measure.

Interval-level measurement may use a zero as one of its values, but the zero represents a point on a range of measurement, not the total absence of the construct. For example, a scale measuring self-confidence may, for convenience, be scored on a range from 0 to 100. However, a person who scores a zero on this scale is not considered to be without any self-confidence. It might simply mean that the person answered every question on the scale in such a way as to suggest lower rather than higher self-confidence. Scores on an interval-level measurement may even be negative when using some measurement instruments. A simple example is a Fahrenheit thermometer. A temperature of 0 degrees Fahrenheit does not mean there is no heat present. It is only one point on a range of equidistant measurements that can be higher (e.g., 85 degrees) or lower (e.g., –220 degrees).

Ratio Level

Ratio-level measurement meets all of the criteria for interval measurement—values can be rank ordered with fixed, equal differences between them. However, a ratio-level measurement also meets another requirement—the presence of an *absolute zero*. The value zero is assigned to the point where there is no measurable quantity of the variable. Thus, no value can be less than zero (negative). For example, if the variable "income" were to be operationalized as "the actual gross earned annual income of clients as reported on their previous year's income tax return," the variable could be regarded as ratio level. A value of zero would mean no earned income. In addition, a person with an income of $60,000 could be said to have an income three times that of one with an income of $20,000. We could not make such statements about nominal-, ordinal-, or interval-level measurements.

In social work research, we might be interested in measuring how many children a client has, how many times a social worker has met with the client, or how many other organizations have offered services to the client. Each of these measurements could be regarded as ratio level since a value of zero would be a "true" or absolute zero, that is, it would reflect the total absence of the construct.

Box 10.1   Summary and Examples of Levels of Measurement

Level of Measurement	Brief Description	Examples
Nominal	Categorical measurement; order of categories is not important	Race, gender, marital status sexual orientation, ethnicity
Ordinal	Categorical measurement; order of categories is important and cannot be arbitrarily changed	Customer satisfaction (extremely satisfied, satisfied, dissatisfied, extremely dissatisfied)
Interval	Numeric measurement; either does not have a possible value of 0 or it is not an absolute 0	Beck Depression Inventory Temperature Fahrenheit IQ Score
Ratio	Numeric measurement; does have an absolute zero value, meaning a value of 0 indicates there is none of the variable being measured	Number of children Number of years of formal education Annual income

More on Levels of Measurement

The level of measurement of variables is often not a given in social work research. With many variables, the level of measurement is often dependent on how we ask a question or solicit data. For example, if we wanted to learn about research participants' life experiences with marriage using a self-administered questionnaire, we could ask, "Have you ever been married?" (yes or no). That would produce nominal-level measurement. If we ask married people the question, "How likely would you be to marry again?" (very likely, somewhat likely, not likely, very unlikely), answers would produce ordinal-level data. A standardized data collection instrument that measures marital satisfaction (with scores ranging from 25 to 100) included as part of the data collection instrument might produce interval-level data. Finally, the question "How many times have you been married?" would produce ratio-level data, where the value 0 (zero) would indicate no quantity of the variable.

In general, we seek to measure a variable as precisely as possible so that we can use the most powerful statistical analyses (tests) available, those that require higher levels of measurement. However, there are times when we might sacrifice precision for other priorities. Why would we ever do this? Sometimes, an estimate of a measurement is all that we require or can hope to receive, perhaps because participants might not remember the exact, correct answer. It might be better to obtain an accurate estimate than an incorrect precise answer. Or, we might need to measure variables that are considered quite "personal," for example, "income," "number of marriages," or "number of illegal substances that have been used." They probably could be measured with reasonable accuracy, and responses to questions would yield interval- or even ratio-level data. However, to ask about them very directly and require specific numbers might cause some potential research participants to not respond truthfully or even to refuse to provide an answer at all. Thus, it might be preferable to provide ranges of values for responses (which would result in only ordinal-level data) instead. The ranges would provide for a little more confidentiality for participants and thus might increase the percent who would provide needed data. So, we might choose to trade off measurement precision for a higher response rate—often a good trade-off.

Some variables that would seem to be inherently nominal level (gender identity, religious affiliation, living situation, and so forth) do not have to remain so. For example, the variable "living situation" might have three value categories (owning or buying a home; renting or staying with others; and homeless). It could be converted into two, ratio level variables. How? First, we might create a new variable that we could simply call "homelessness." A research participant who is homeless would be assigned the value 1, and a research participant who is renting or living with others would be assigned the value 0. So would a person who is a homeowner. A second variable would then be created. It might be labeled "home ownership," or something similar. A research participant who owns or is buying a home would be assigned the value 1; a person who is either renting or living with others or a person who is homeless would both be assigned the value 0. (There would be no need to create yet a third variable where people who are renting or staying with others would be assigned the value 1, since they would have already been included in the form of their two 0 values for the first two variables.) The two new variables thus created (called *dummy variables*) are really measurements of the original variable, but they are now considered ratio level, since the value 0 is assigned when a research participant has zero quantity of either of the two new variables. Why would we go to all this trouble? It is to attempt to improve statistical analyses of data. Researchers sometimes create dummy variables in order to include a variable in certain statistical analyses that could not be included in its original, nominal level form since the analyses require that some or all variables reflect the more precise level of measurement.

In measurement, the level of measurement of a variable is sometimes little more than a judgment call. Nominal-level variables can usually be easily distinguished from ordinal-level variables by our inability to rank order their value categories. However, distinguishing between ordinal- and interval-level measurements is especially difficult. Not surprisingly, even researchers sometimes disagree as to whether an item on a data collection instrument or a certain type of scale yields interval- or ordinal-level data. It often comes down to a judgment of whether or not the intervals reflected in the measurement are really equal in size. For example, does the difference between one client's score of 75 and another's score of 70 on an assertiveness scale (5 points) reflect the same difference in assertiveness as that between the second client's score of 70 and a score of 65 of a third client (also 5 points)? If the scale has undergone many years of rigorous development and refinement, we might argue that it now yields interval-level data. However, it could also be argued that assertiveness cannot be measured with that much precision or that the construct is dynamic, even within the same culture, and thus the measurements produced by the scale are just not that precise. If that is the case, only ordinal-level measurement should be claimed.

While deciding whether a measurement is at the ordinal level or interval level is an important decision, the distinction between interval- and ratio-level measurement is relatively unimportant, at least for purposes of most statistical analyses. In fact, in books on statistics, in describing the level of measurement requirements for using many statistical tests, the terms *nominal, ordinal,* and *interval/ratio* (or *scale*) are frequently used.

CRITERIA FOR GOOD MEASUREMENT

In Chapter 5, we discussed two criteria used in evaluating a research design, especially a quantitative one—external validity and internal validity. In Chapter 9, we presented two criteria for assessing the quality of a research sample—representativeness and sample size. There are also two criteria that are used to assess measurement quality (see Box 10.2). They are reliability and validity.

Box 10.2   Indications That the Measurement Procedure Is Good

1. **It is reliable.** We can demonstrate that it produces consistent results (e.g., 96, 96, 96, ...) when measuring the same object or individual in a variety of situations and under different conditions.
2. **It is valid.** We can demonstrate that it actually measures what we claim that it measures

(e.g., 96 = high level of aggression, not of assertiveness, anger, or some other construct).

Note: A measurement that is valid is both reliable and unbiased. Thus, a measurement that is valid is always reliable, but one that is reliable may not be valid.

Reliability

Reliability is closely related to the concept of consistency. It asks the question, "Does a measurement produce the same results under various conditions?" If the object or person being measured has not changed, a good measurement procedure or instrument should not produce different results under different conditions. For example, one indicator of reliability (test-retest reliability, discussed in the next section) is related to the extent to which a measurement produces the same results when it is conducted at one time as opposed to some other time. If there is no reason why a research participant's measurement score on a variable (such as attitude toward capital punishment or sexist beliefs) should have changed, measuring the participant a second time using the same method as the first time should yield the same or nearly identical results. If not, the method of measurement is not considered to be reliable.

> *If the object or person being measured has not changed, a good measurement procedure or instrument should not produce different results under different conditions.*

The degree to which a measurement is reliable is estimated and usually expressed in a *correlation coefficient*, a mathematical indicator of how much a measurement of a variable agrees (correlates) with a second measurement of the variable. A correlation coefficient reflects both the strength and the direction of the correlation between the two measurements. It consists of a number and a sign (– or +). Correlation coefficients range from –1.00 to +1.00. In using correlation coefficients as evidence of reliability, the researcher hopes to be able to produce correlation coefficients that are very high and positive (e.g., .85, .92).

High, positive correlation coefficients would result if, upon measuring people or objects twice (for example, on two different days, by two different researchers, using two different versions of the test, and so forth) using the same method of measuring the variable, the measurements for all or at least most people or objects are the same or nearly the same on both occasions. For example, if we claimed to be measuring assertiveness, a high, positive correlation coefficient would result if people tended to receive the same or nearly the same assertiveness score when measured on Monday and again on Friday. That would demonstrate the reliability of our method of measuring assertiveness.

Probably no method for measuring variables that are human attributes is universally reliable. A method is generally limited to certain groups or segments of the population. For example, some methods for measuring characteristics such as assertiveness or hostility may be considered reliable when used with men, but not with women. Others may be reliable within one socioeconomic class, ethnic group, or culture, but not within another, or with people above a certain age, but not younger than that age. This is because the indicators of an attribute, what we use to measure a variable, tend to be more or less socially appropriate (they vary) on the basis of gender, socioeconomic class, ethnicity, culture, age, and so forth. For researchers, the message is this: Be sure that the methods of measurement that you choose have been found to be reliable with *your* research participants.

> *For researchers, the message is this: Be sure that the methods of measurement that you choose have been found to be reliable with your research participants.*

There are several types of reliability that a measurement can possess. Some types are more important in some research studies; others are more important in others. The degree to which each one is present is demonstrated using a specific method. In any given research study, we are interested in the type of reliability that is most relevant to the purpose of the study and the way that the measurement instrument is to be used to achieve it.

Fortunately, in recent years, a great amount of time and energy has been devoted to developing better ways to measure variables that are of interest to social work researchers (see, for example, Hudson, 1988). Part of this process has involved *reliability testing*, determining the various types of reliability that a method of measurement of a variable possesses and the degree to which it possesses them. There are entire books published on measurement instruments (e.g., Corcoran & Fischer, 2013a, b) that include estimates of the amount of the different types of reliability that they possess (in the form of correlation coefficients) with regard to different subgroups of people and different settings. Often, it is possible to find exactly what we need—a measurement instrument that has been demonstrated to possess the type of reliability that we require for our measurement purposes. Even if none is quite appropriate, they can give us some beginning ideas for developing our own methods of measurement.

What are the different types of reliability that measurements of variables can contain? When is each of greatest interest? How do researchers and statisticians estimate the degree to which they are present? Let's examine each of the five types of reliability.

Test-Retest Reliability

An estimate of test-retest reliability requires testing the same participants twice, using the same measuring instrument to measure a variable both times, and then comparing the pair of measurements for each case. A correlation coefficient suggests the amount of agreement between the two sets of scores. The higher the positive correlation derived, the higher the test-retest reliability of the measurement instrument.

Test-retest reliability tells the researcher how consistently an instrument performs at different times. A time delay may occur between the first and second measurements of the variable, or they may be scheduled immediately after each other. If a delay between measurements is to be used, it can be as great as a week or even several months. Longer delays are most often used if (1) there is reason to believe that participants' measurements of the variable do not change naturally over time and (2) the researcher is concerned with avoiding the presence of a *testing effect*. A testing effect is the extent to which a participant's second measurement of the variable might be influenced by the experience of the first measurement if the two measurements occur too closely in time.

The degree to which test-retest reliability can be demonstrated is often an important criterion in assessing the quality of measurement in social work research and, ultimately, the quality of the research itself. For example, suppose the research entails the measurement of personality traits or certain behavior patterns, variables that should not change over a reasonably short period of time. Unless the method or instrument used to measure them can be demonstrated to possess test-retest reliability, any findings about the relationship between them, or between them and other variables such as success in treatment, length of treatment, and so forth, will have little credibility.

Parallel Forms Reliability

Sometimes, for various reasons, it is necessary to have two or more forms of a data collection instrument or test. While individual items on them will differ, the different forms should be comparable so that regardless of which form an individual completes, the results will be the same, that is, there should be a high degree of parallel forms reliability. An estimate of the parallel forms reliability (also called *alternate forms reliability* or *equivalent forms reliability*) of a measurement instrument is calculated by administering two or more forms of the same instrument to the same participants, with or without a delay between administrations. If the scores on the different forms of the same instrument are identical or nearly identical, parallel forms reliability has been demonstrated, also in the form of a high, positive correlation coefficient.

Parallel forms of a test have been developed for many standardized achievement and knowledge measures (e.g., SATs or GREs), as well as for tests designed to measure many attitudes or perceptions. The different forms are not identical; they contain different questions or items. If the tests possess a high degree of parallel forms reliability, no matter which form (variation) of the test a person completes, his or her score would be about the same. A person can also take one form of a test, and the persons sitting to his or her right and left could complete different forms of the same test. None of the three would have an advantage over the others since the different forms would all measure the same variable and would contain the same amount of difficulty.

When parallel forms of a measurement instrument are used, demonstration of parallel forms reliability is generally expected. For example, we might report that the different forms all produce distributions of scores that have the same or very similar means (averages) and a similar amount of variability.

While a demonstration of parallel forms reliability is important to people who develop and market standardized tests that require different forms of the same test, it is usually of less concern to social work researchers. However, it can be important in certain situations. Suppose we are conducting longitudinal research to learn when and under what conditions changes occur in clients in an intensive anger management treatment program. We might need to measure anger management skills of clients on a weekly basis. To use the same instrument for measuring the variable each week might be problematic. Clients would eventually learn the "best" or socially desirable answers from being asked the same questions every week and possibly discussing them with other clients or family members. However, if different forms of the instrument (perhaps containing different but similar scenarios) could be found or developed and it could be demonstrated that the forms are comparable (parallel forms reliability can be demonstrated statistically), some potential challenges to our findings could be avoided. For example, apparent improvement in clients' anger management skills could not be explained by either the fact that they took the same test repeatedly and learned how to respond to it or that they took different forms of the test that produced different results.

Split Half Reliability

An estimate of split half reliability entails dividing a single measurement instrument into two equal parts and correlating the total score on one half with the total score on the other half. The two halves may be derived by, for example, placing the even-numbered items in one group and the odd-numbered items in a second group. The reliability estimate derived from using the split half method is really an estimate of the internal consistency of the measure, that is, the degree to which half of the measurements within an instrument are correlated with the other half. Split half reliability estimates have been popular in the past, primarily because of the simplicity of their calculation. They are quickly and easily calculated by hand.

Professors who develop short answer tests designed to measure knowledge of a subject are often interested in an estimate of split half reliability. It can suggest the degree to which the test is consistent in its level of difficulty. If individual students' scores on one half of the test are about the same as their scores on the other half, split half reliability is high and the test is considered consistent in its level of difficulty throughout. However, if they vary considerably, split half reliability is low, and the items on the test vary in their level of difficulty.

Assessment

Behavior: Apply knowledge of human behavior and the social environment, person-in-environment, and other multi-disciplinary theoretical frameworks in the analysis of assessment data from clients and constituencies.

Critical Thinking Question: Can you think of a way to measure anger that would be more accurate than using a client self-report instrument?

In social work research, this indicator of reliability is most likely to be a concern if a variable being measured is the research participants' level of knowledge and the researcher wants the various items in the instrument to reflect equal difficulty. We might, for example, wish to measure social workers' knowledge of child abuse reporting laws by developing and administering a test to our research participants. It might consist of a series of forty true/false statements about current laws. The number of correct answers (out of forty) would be the participant's score. After administering the test, we could then determine its split half reliability by comparing the number of correct responses for even numbered statements for each social worker with his or her number of correct answers for odd numbered statements. If the estimate of split half reliability is high and positive, it suggests that the level of difficulty of the test items was consistent throughout the test. If it is not, the level of difficulty of items may vary too much to use them without revising some of them to reflect more similar levels of difficulty.

An even more accurate estimate of this indicator of reliability could be achieved using the related method that we will describe next, coefficient alpha. It is mathematically more complicated than the split half method, but this is no longer a major concern now that statistical software is so readily available to do the work for us.

Coefficient Alpha

If a measurement instrument can be split in half, it can also be further subdivided into as many parts as there are items contained within it. Coefficient alpha, a better estimate of the overall reliability of the instrument than split half reliability, may be obtained by securing the correlation between every pair of its items (the answers to questions about child abuse reporting laws in the previous example). Coefficient alpha is a statistic that summarizes the results of this kind of analysis. It provides an estimate of the reliability of a measurement instrument by generating the average correlation among all pairs of items. If a coefficient alpha analysis produces a high, positive correlation coefficient, it can be inferred that responses to individual items or questions are highly correlated. When this is the case, the instrument is strong in internal consistency, a hallmark of Coefficient Alpha. Most personal computers have available statistical software packages that can perform these statistics.

Some measurement instruments are designed to be multidimensional in nature—for example, occupational inventories or tests that measure different aspects or dimensions of personality, each with its own subscale. For these instruments, it would not be appropriate to estimate reliability of the instrument as a whole by using a measure of internal consistency such as coefficient alpha or split half reliability. For example, if a personality inventory is designed to measure both shyness and lack of social boundaries by asking participants how they would respond to various social situations, we would expect to get a low correlation coefficient if either method were used to evaluate the inventory as a whole. Some other method of reliability estimation (such as the test-retest method) might be more appropriate. However, either coefficient alpha or split half reliability could be used to assess reliability for only those items contained within a specific subscale.

Interobserver Agreement

When more than one person makes observations or reviews data such as DVD recordings, interobserver agreement can be used to estimate the reliability of the measurement process. Interobserver agreement is an estimate of the degree to which two or more researchers agree in their measurements of a variable. As is true with other types of reliability, the higher the positive correlation between the measurements of two observers or interviewers, the greater the indication of consistency in measurement.

When is interobserver agreement considered to be important to the quality measurement in a research study? Traditionally, it has been more important in quantitative research. That makes sense because findings about the relationship between variables (more common in quantitative studies) are worthless unless the variables were measured in a way that provides consistent measurements. But reliability is important for qualitative measurement as well. For example, a study using grounded theory (Chapter 6) may entail video recording in-depth interviews with research participants who recently experienced an event such as a tornado. Then two or more judges can review the recordings and log how they think each participant experienced the event or whether he or she expressed some emotion in discussing it. An estimate of the reliability of their measurements can be calculated (a correlation coefficient) using methods to estimate interobserver agreement. See Box 10.3 for a summary of the types of reliability discussed.

Which Type of Reliability Is Most Important?

The importance of any one type of reliability depends primarily on what variable is being measured, how it is measured, and how the measurement is to be used. The test-retest reliability of a data collection instrument or scale might be desirable in many studies (especially quantitative ones), but in some cases, it may be too costly or too big an imposition on research participants to ask them to measure the same variable twice using the same method of measurement. Demonstration of parallel forms reliability would be important and relevant (and possible) only in research that uses equivalent forms of the same measurement instrument. Split half reliability and coefficient alpha would be important for measurement of knowledge or attitudes where internal consistency of measurement is desirable. We might expect some demonstration of either or both if a new test or measurement instrument was being used. It would be important to demonstrate interobserver agreement if more than one interviewer or observer is used to collect or analyze data. Interobserver agreement would indicate that all of the interviewers or observers had been trained to observe and record the data in the same way.

Box 10.3   Different Types of Reliability Testing

Type of Reliability	Question(s) Addressed
Reliability	Does the measurement produce the same results under various conditions? Is the measurement consistent?
Test-retest reliability	Does the measurement produce the same results when the test is administered two times to the same group of participants?
Parallel forms reliability	Does the measurement produce the same results when participants complete two or more equivalent forms of the instrument?
Split half reliability	When the measurement is divided into two halves and completed by a group of participants, do their scores on one half correlate with their scores on the other half?
Coefficient alpha	Do all of the pairs of items correlate with one another? In other words, for each participant, are each of their answers on the instrument consistent with their other answers?
Interobserver agreement	When two observers record observations during the same period of time following the same instructions, how closely do their recordings agree?

Researchers can improve the overall reliability of measurement instruments by attending to a variety of factors. They include the following:

- **Standardizing environmental factors during measurement.** Many factors besides the measurement instrument used can negatively affect consistency of measurement of variables. When conducting cross-sectional research, data should be collected in similar settings, at similar times, under similar conditions, and in similar ways from all participants. These measures reduce measurement error, which will be discussed later in this chapter. In longitudinal studies, all measurements of the same variable should be conducted in similar settings.
- **Conducting a pilot study of the instrument.** In addition to its other uses (discussed in Chapter 12), the process of pilot-testing a measurement instrument with a few individuals who are similar to the research participants can help to make measurement more reliable. For example, if a previously developed measurement instrument is to be used, pilot-testing it can either confirm or refute the researcher's belief that the instrument is reliable when used with different research participants (i.e., those younger or from another culture than those on whom it was developed). If indicated, another measurement instrument can be substituted or revisions can be made in areas that appear to be unreliable. However, when using a standardized instrument with published validity and reliability statistics, if researchers add, delete, or change any items, this will likely affect the reliability and validity statistics presented. Therefore, they should reevaluate the validity and reliability of the revised instrument.
- **Increasing the number of items on a test or measurement instrument.** In general, for unidimensional measures (those measuring just one variable), adding items will improve the reliability estimate. This occurs because coefficient alpha

is a function of both the average correlation among items and the number of items on a test or other instrument. Even for instruments that are not unidimensional, adding additional, clear items can sometimes help to improve the reliability of measurement of their subscales.

Validity

When evaluating measurement, validity refers to the degree of fit between the construct we are trying to measure and the instrument or method we are using to measure it. Just to ensure we are on the same page, a definition of a construct might be useful here. A construct is something that is not tangible; it cannot be observed directly. It develops through a cognitive process, exists within human brains, and is defined by established theories. A construct might be an ability, a skill, an attribute, or (frequently in social work research) a problem or deficiency in one of these areas. We generally operationalize constructs as variables in a study.

The presence of one or more types of reliability is required for a measurement to be valid. But reliability is not in itself sufficient to guarantee that a measurement is valid.

The presence of one or more types of reliability is required for a measurement to be valid. But, as emphasized in Box 10.2, reliability is not in itself sufficient to guarantee that a measurement is valid. For example, a measurement instrument may claim to measure assertiveness among people, and it may produce consistent results (reliability). But it may, in fact, be measuring aggressiveness or anger, not assertiveness. A valid measurement is both reliable <u>and</u> it also measures what it claims to measure.

For example, suppose a researcher creates an instrument to measure the eating disorder, bulimia nervosa. The instrument contains items that measure binging behaviors only. While the instrument may consistently measure binging behaviors (good reliability), it would not be a valid measure of bulimia nervosa because it does not include other necessary symptoms of bulimia, such as purging behaviors and self-evaluation based on body shape and weight. It would also fail to distinguish between clients with bulimia nervosa, binge-eating disorder, and binge-eating/purging type of anorexia nervosa, all of which contain binging behaviors. Validity, like reliability, is not an all-or-nothing proposition. Validity is often a matter of degree and it too is estimated. We must be convinced (and be able to convince others) that a measurement possesses enough validity of the type most important to our research to produce an acceptable measurement of key variables within a given study.

Sometimes, it takes a long time before it is concluded that an instrument measures what it claims to measure. For example, the SAT examination was long held to provide a valid measurement of scholastic aptitude. Critics asserted that although it provided a reliable assessment of "something" (some said scholastic achievement), it was not a scholastic aptitude measure. The original name, Scholastic Aptitude Test, was changed to Scholastic Assessment Test in 1990, and then to SAT Reasoning Test (to distinguish it from the SAT subject tests) in 1993, to reflect this position. Currently, it is simply referred to as the SAT, and it is claimed (in concert with high school grades) to be a reasonably accurate predictor of success in higher education.

An instrument is said to be valid for a given use when data have been compiled and presented that provide evidence for the instrument's validity for a particular research purpose. Thus, the burden of proof is on us to show that an instrument may be appropriately used in our research study to measure the desired construct with the research sample being used. It is important to remember that an instrument may be valid with one sample, but may not be valid or appropriate for use with another sample. For example, a "feelings of hopelessness" scale shown to be valid when used with adolescents would probably not be valid or appropriate for use with people currently in hospice care. Responses that might suggest hopelessness for a teenager may simply suggest resignation or acceptance of reality (different constructs) among people in hospice care.

Evidence of the validity of a measuring instrument is developed in relation to its purpose. Instruments can be categorized as serving one or more of three purposes:

1. **To measure achievement in a content area.** Tests of knowledge (e.g., course examinations) have this purpose.

2. **To predict performance in regard to some criterion.** Examples would be aptitude tests or tests used to screen for admission into an educational program.

3. **To provide a measure of a construct to learn if it relates to some other construct.** Attitude scales or diagnostic instruments would be examples of instruments used for this purpose.

As with reliability, there are certain criteria that are commonly employed to provide an estimate of validity. They are content validity, criterion validity, and construct validity. They correspond roughly to the three purposes of measurement instruments.

Content Validity

Demonstrating content validity involves an assessment of whether a measurement adequately covers all aspects or components of a particular body of content. It also involves a determination as to whether irrelevant or inappropriate content is present in the measurement. Content validity is the indicator of validity that is of special concern to us when the purpose of a measuring instrument is to measure participants' learning or achievement in a content area. For example, to measure what participants learned in a workshop, seminar, or training session, tests need to be content validated.

Tests of knowledge that are believed to possess content validity pose questions that measure what was actually covered in a course, training session, or other educational program. They do not ask questions that do not relate to the curriculum's content. For example, an item on a test on this chapter that tested the reader's understanding of reliability in the context of measurement could be assumed to possess content validity; one that asked the names of the authors of this text (an old favorite among some professors) or one that required knowledge about content in Chapter 8 or about world history would not.

Tests are generally judged to possess content validity on the basis of how they were developed. Content validity is achieved by defining a real or hypothetical domain (or universe) of test items that fully cover the construct being measured. Items are then randomly selected so that they are believed to be representative of the domain. However, we may not actually develop a hypothetical domain of test items (sometimes called a *test bank*). Instead, we might simply define each content area, identify its major categories, and write items that correspond to the various categories or facets of the content area. This process is known as constructing a *blueprint* of the measure. When this is done well, it improves the likelihood that the measure will be content valid. When reporting on the content validity of a measure, we are expected to describe the procedures used in instrument development that support their claim of content validity.

The use of content experts is also extremely helpful in providing evidence of the content validity of an instrument. They may be used to help define the content area so that a useful blueprint will emerge. In addition, content experts might be asked to evaluate a draft of the instrument to assess the usefulness of specific test items. Or they may be used to examine the completed instrument to state how content valid the test appears to be.

In truth, this assessment really does not provide hard evidence of the content validity of the test. Content validity is better assessed by using other methods of analysis. What it often provides is information about the *face validity* of the measure, that is, that the test looks valid on the face (or surface). Face validity is measured on the basis of how valid the measure appears to be to content experts and/or the people (or the type of people) who will be asked to complete the instrument. Some authors do not include face validity in their discussions of validity, because having face validity does not mean that a measure *actually* measures what it is supposed to measure, but only that it *appears* to measure what it is supposed to measure.

Criterion Validity

Evidence of criterion validity is important when the purpose of an instrument is to predict behavior or measure a characteristic of research participants. Evidence of criterion validity is achieved by demonstrating that scores on the measuring instrument are consistent with some other accepted indicator of the same variable. The second indicator (which may or may not be a standardized measurement instrument per se) is known as the *criterion*. As with reliability, evidence of criterion validity is usually presented statistically as a correlation coefficient.

There are two subcategories of criterion validity: concurrent validity and predictive validity. *Concurrent validity* is demonstrated by producing a high, positive correlation between two measures—measurements using the measurement instrument and the criterion—both of which are made at approximately the same time. For example, we might correlate scores on a newly developed measurement of student test anxiety with scores on some other well-accepted measure of anxiety. If the new measure has concurrent validity, statistical correlation with the older measurement instrument should be high and positive. Or, if we develop an instrument presumed to measure charisma, we might demonstrate its concurrent validity by pilot-testing it with two groups: people generally acknowledged to possess charisma and those who are believed to lack it. If the instrument has concurrent validity, the first group should achieve high scores, whereas the latter group should achieve low measurements of the variable.

Predictive validity provides evidence of the correlation between a measure of what is believed to be a predictor and some future performance or behavior (the criterion). To develop evidence of predictive validity, follow-up data are gathered. For example, newly developed screening inventories to predict abusive behaviors might be correlated with the results of follow-up studies of research participants who completed the inventories to determine just how well the instruments were able to predict abusive behaviors.

One example of the concept of predictive validity that is well known to students is the use of standardized tests such as SATs or GREs to predict how students will perform

Behavior: Apply critical thinking to analyze, formulate, and advocate for policies that advance human rights and social, economic, and environmental justice.

Critical Thinking Question: Do you think that "personal statements," a component of many applications to Schools of Social Work, could be shown to have good predictive validity? Why or why not?

in college or graduate school. The measure of how students actually perform in school is the criterion. Educational researchers interested in providing evidence of criterion validity for standardized tests would attempt to demonstrate a high correlation between scores attained by students on these tests and their later performance in school (usually as measured by future grade point average or a similar indicator of academic success).

Construct Validity

As noted earlier, validity in measurement refers to the degree of fit between a construct and indicators of the construct. Then, isn't construct validity what validity is all about? Yes, in fact, it is. In some ways, it might be accurate to describe the other indicators of validity (content, criterion, and even face validity) as just different facets or components of construct validity.

A narrower definition of construct validity is the degree to which the measure of the construct of interest is related to other variables or constructs that are hypothesized to be either related or not related to our construct. It can be measured using *convergent validity*, *discriminant validity*, or both. Convergent validity is the degree to which the measure correlates highly to measures of other constructs or variables that researchers believe are related to the construct of interest. Discriminant validity is the degree to which the measure does <u>not</u> correlate to measures of other constructs or variables that are believed to be unrelated to the construct of interest. For example, the diagnosis of anorexia nervosa includes both disordered eating behaviors and unrealistic attitudes toward body and shape. Therefore, if we were testing the construct validity of a new scale believed to measure attitudes toward body and shape, we would look for a correlation between our scale and an established scale that measures disordered eating behaviors (evidence of convergent validity). Conversely, if there is no theoretical connection between disordered eating behaviors and, for example, conduct disorder, we would not expect to see a strong correlation between a scale measuring disordered eating behaviors and a scale that measures conduct disorder (evidence of discriminant validity).

Many of the variables that researchers seek to measure in social work research are really constructs. Psychiatric diagnostic categories, such as anorexia nervosa, bipolar disorder, attention deficit hyperactivity disorder, and schizophrenia, are constructs. Their presence is inferred when certain conditions exist. For example, schizophrenia is said to exist only when a certain group of symptoms or behaviors is identified as present (certain thought disorders, inappropriate affect, and so forth). Many other problems that social workers seek to address, such as unemployment, co-dependency, substance abuse, family violence, and homelessness, are also constructs. Thus, in many social work research studies, especially in single-system evaluation research (Chapter 8), these problems or constructs are usually defined as the dependent variable, the condition that we seek to alleviate or otherwise positively influence through our intervention. The intervention (i.e., an individual service or social program) is what we hope will alleviate or positively influence the dependent variable. Thus, the presence or absence of the intervention is often the independent variable. These interventions might be, for example, community empowerment programs, cognitive behavior therapy, family therapy, supportive treatment, confrontation treatment, and reality therapy.

It is important to note that each of these interventions (the independent variable) is also a construct. Construct validity requires that <u>all</u> variables are measured accurately. Thus, in many social work research studies, the construct that is the independent variable (the intervention or its absence) must also be understood and explained and appropriate indicators used to determine the degree to which it exists or does not exist as originally conceptualized. Why is this important for producing accurate and useful research findings? Suppose that our research study attempts to learn whether a new recreational program whose outcome objective was to reduce youth gang activity in a community was successful. Obviously, we would have to find a way to accurately operationalize and measure the variable "level of youth gang activity" (the dependent variable) in the community. However, before we could conclude whether the proposed program was effective in achieving its objective, we would also have to use appropriate indicators to learn if the program that was implemented was really the program that was supposed to be implemented, that is, it remained true to its original design. Our measurement of the independent variable will lack construct validity unless we do this, and any conclusions drawn from the research will be unlikely to be supportable. Suppose we did not do this (provide a valid measurement of the independent variable) and the program that was actually implemented drifted considerably from its original model (a fairly common occurrence). If youth gang activity declined following the onset of the program, we might erroneously conclude that the program (as originally conceptualized) was successful in reducing gang activity (a cause-effect relationship) and should thus be implemented in other communities. This conclusion would not be a valid one, since really a different program or other unknown factors may have produced changes in the dependent variable. What's more, our research would also lack *conclusion validity*; that is, the conclusion that the program that was designed and the level of gang activity are even related at all would be erroneous, because one of them wasn't even present!

If an instrument is to provide a valid measurement of a construct, it must measure the essential components of the construct. Thus, if we designed a data collection instrument to classify participants as homeless or not homeless, the instrument should include all items that cover all indicators of the construct "homelessness." If the instrument, for example, provides no indication of whether the participant has a permanent address accessible through the U.S. Postal Service it might suggest that the instrument is lacking in construct validity. Similarly, if the independent variable is the use or nonuse of a specific intervention, such as a new program designed to reduce homelessness, construct validity would require that we ensure that the program that was implemented is really the one described in its design or logic model.

There is no simple, direct way to assess the degree of construct validity that is present. It is assessed by accumulating a variety of evidence, usually in the form of the other indicators of validity. This involves the use of several related types of information. Construct validity demonstrates that the construct being measured exists within a theoretical framework, thereby explaining the construct itself and how it relates to other variables. In a sense, a test of construct validity becomes both a measure of the construct and a test of its underlying theory.

Concurrent validity data can help to provide evidence of the construct validity of a measurement instrument. For example, in the previous example we could determine if people who have been classified as homeless by The Salvation Army would also be classified as homeless using our measurement instrument. If the instrument shows a pattern of relationships with criterion measures (classifications that agree with the Salvation Army classification), then there is some evidence of construct validity. Face validity—for example, the fact that it is just logical to conclude that a person living in her car is probably homeless—could also help to support claims of construct validity. However, face validity cannot always be trusted. That individual living in her car could own a home, but has chosen to live in her car on a temporary basis in order to be closer to a terminally ill friend or relative.

What about the measurement of the independent variable? How would we demonstrate the construct validity of its measurement? Suppose the logic model or other description of the program to address the problem of homelessness contains services such as job training or substance abuse counseling. Concurrent validity data could be used to see if our methods of classifying these services are the same as or similar to those offered in other programs that claimed to offer job training or substance abuse counseling. Face validity might be implied by the fact that our measurement instrument was used to determine if participants in the program were given instruction in how to prepare a job application form or how to dress for a job interview.

As we have seen, some familiar words (e.g., *value, reliability, validity, true, normal*) have specific meanings in research and statistics, different from what they have in common speech or in social work practice. Sometimes, the same word even has different meanings within different research contexts. This can be especially confusing. In this chapter, we used the same word, *validity*, which we used in Chapter 5 to discuss the internal and external validity of research designs. Box 10.4 should be helpful in clearing up any confusion that this may have caused.

SOURCES OF MEASUREMENT ERROR

The validity of measurement in a research study can be negatively affected in many ways. When it is so affected, this is described as *measurement error*. In discussing reliability earlier in this chapter, we noted that virtually all methods of measurement and measurement instruments have their limits. For example, as mentioned before, a measurement instrument may be considered reliable for measuring a variable with males, but not with females. That may be because the data used to construct it was collected from only males and it is believed that females differ in some ways that relate to the variable. Caution should always be exercised when instruments are to be used with research participants who are different in important ways from groups with whom the existing instruments were developed and "normed." Before using an existing measurement instrument, we need to be familiar with how and on which population group(s) the measurement was constructed. It should never be assumed that established norms and benchmarks on which scoring is based apply uniformly to all individuals across all settings and cultural contexts. When conducting cross-cultural research, efforts should be made to find instruments normed on a variety of cultural groups or nationalities, or to look for instruments

Box 10.4   Different Types of Validity in Research

Type of Validity	Research Activity	Question(s) Addressed
Internal validity	Research design	If a relationship between variables was found, is it a causal one? Can I be certain that something else did not produce the measurements of the dependent variable?
External validity	Sampling	To what extent can I generalize the research findings beyond the research sample(s) in the current study?
Content validity	Measurement	Does the measurement instrument adequately cover all of the components of the construct being measured?
Face validity	Measurement	Does the measurement instrument appear to measure what it is supposed to measure?
Criterion validity	Measurement	Is the measure of the construct consistent with another accepted indicator of the same construct?
Concurrent validity	Measurement	Is the measure highly correlated with another indicator of the construct measured at approximately the same time?
Predictive validity	Measurement	Is the measure highly correlated with a future performance or behavior as measured by a second indicator or criterion of the construct?
Construct validity	Measurement	How well did I measure the variables/constructs that I claim to have measured? In particular, how does the measure of the variable correlate with other constructs that are theoretically related or unrelated to it?
Convergent validity	Measurement	Does the measure correlate highly with other variables theoretically related to it?
Discriminant validity	Measurement	Does the measure not correlate with other variables hypothesized to be unrelated to it?
Conclusion validity	Data analysis	Were the research conclusions correct? If hypotheses were tested, was an error made in determining whether or not there was found to be support for them?

developed in a variety of cultural contexts that attempt to measure the same underlying construct. Such instruments are sometimes difficult to find. Special concerns about reliability and validity arise when instruments are translated from one language to another for use with linguistically diverse study populations. The non-equivalence of research instruments can limit the usefulness of data obtained in cross-cultural research. There are many ways to increase the likelihood that both the reliability and validity of a measurement instrument will be maintained throughout the translation process. Five suggestions follow:

1. Attempt to understand one's own values and cultural perspectives and how they might influence one's definitions of key constructs that the instrument is designed to measure.

2. Consult with members of the group of interest to determine the cultural relevance of constructs of interest within the target population and assess the face validity of the instrument items for measuring constructs of interest in that culture.

3. Translate the instrument from the first language to the second language, using skilled, bilingually fluent translators working individually, sequentially, or as a team. (The translators should be aware of idiomatic subtleties related to geography or social class.)

4. Translate the instrument from the second language back into the first language, using skilled translators. The back-translation should then be compared to the original version to determine the accuracy of the original translation.

5. Field-test the translated instrument using bilingual participants, to establish equivalence through parallel forms reliability coefficients (compare scores on the translated version versus scores on the original version).

What we have just described is a way to avoid something called cultural bias, a form of *systematic measurement error* often seen in cross-cultural research. However, systematic measurement error can easily occur within research in one's own culture as well. When measurement lacks construct validity, systematic measurement error will almost certainly occur. We might, for example, believe that we are measuring a construct such as clinical depression, but if the only questions we ask relate to physical symptoms, we may really be measuring our research participants' physical health status instead. Or, if we asked participants how they would respond in a crisis situation such as a hurricane or flood, they might respond very differently than if we actually observed how they reacted in such a situation. If we used their responses as indicators of how they would act, we would likely get measurement error. Similarly, if we asked a group of social workers how they plan to vote in an upcoming election, they might be likely to say they would vote for candidates who are endorsed by NASW, yet many might do just the opposite when they got to the polls. Their responses would reflect what they think they should say (known as *social desirability bias*)—if we used them as an indicator of what they will do, we would again have systematic measurement error. Even the wording of questions can result in systematic measurement error if, for example, we word a question in such a way that virtually everyone feels they have to answer in a certain way.

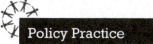

Policy Practice

Behavior: Assess how social welfare and economic policies impact the delivery of and access to social services.

Critical Thinking Question: How could a politician purposefully word a question about abortion in order to attempt to sway the participants to reflect a position in opposition to abortion?

Not all measurement errors are systematic and relatively easy to detect. There is also something called *random measurement error*, error that does not occur in any identifiable pattern or direction. If data are collected in a group setting, distractions such as cell phones ringing or the fact that the session is videotaped may affect some people's responses to questions, but not others. The problem is we have no way of knowing who was affected and who wasn't. Or, in a mailed survey, some people may just be tired and quit reading the items after a while. They complete the survey, just putting anything down to get finished. However, we will not know when this happened or with whom.

We have mentioned just a few ways that measurement error can occur—there are many more. As the reader has probably concluded, totally reliable and valid measurement may be unattainable. However, that does not relieve us of the responsibility to do the best we can to achieve it.

SUMMARY

Chapter 10 presented:

- The concepts basic to measurement of variables. Two early tasks of the measurement process were identified: conceptualization and operationalization.
- Other measurement tasks of the researcher involve deciding just how precisely a variable can or should be measured and determining the level of measurement. The four levels of measurement (nominal, ordinal, interval, and ratio) were differentiated.
- The criteria used to evaluate the quality of measurement were discussed. Reliability relates to the degree to which a measurement produces consistent results. Validity refers to the degree to which a measurement is successful in actually measuring what it has claimed to measure, that is, the construct that underlies a variable. A measurement that is reliable is not necessarily valid. However, a measurement that is valid will be both reliable and unbiased. We described the methods that researchers use to estimate the amount of various types of reliability and validity that a measurement instrument possesses. Their relative importance for different types of measurement and for different research objectives were identified and discussed.
- Finally, we examined a few ways in which reliability and validity of measurement may be influenced by cultural differences and other sources of measurement error.

MyEducationLab® for Research

Try the Topic 6 Assignments: Selecting Measuring Instruments and the Topic 6 Study Plan.

Chapter 10 Chapter Review Quiz.

Methods for Acquiring Research Data

One of the common characteristics of all types of research is that it seeks to increase our knowledge through the analysis of data. Data can come in many forms and have many origins. Some research designs (such as those used for evaluating social programs) require access to many data sources. Others rely on just a few or only a single source.

There is no one best data source. Each has advantages and limitations that are considered in answering the important research design question—what data source or sources would be most appropriate for my research study? In this chapter, we will examine the methods most frequently used in social work research (see Box 11.1 for overview of these methods).

SECONDARY DATA ANALYSIS

Sometimes, the time-consuming and expensive task of collecting original data for research studies proves unnecessary. Many research questions can be examined using data that already exist, often without leaving our place of employment. The reanalysis of selected data that were collected and stored for some other purpose is known as *secondary data analysis*. For reasons that will be self-evident, it is much more likely to be a viable option as a data source in quantitative studies than in qualitative ones.

Sources

Human service organizations store great amounts of information about their clients and programs, which can sometimes be used to examine research questions and test hypotheses using quantitative methods. Extensive data banks exist within public social agencies, both to meet government requirements and to facilitate service delivery to clients. Smaller private and sectarian organizations also store a substantial amount of information about clients and client functioning. Increasingly, information is stored and retrieved via computerized databases and information systems. However, in some smaller organizations, it is still maintained in the form of written files and records.

There are also many sources of research data within the public domain that can be useful to social workers for conducting research. For example, census data are a rich source of research-worthy information, collected at great expense to the taxpayer. However, they generally tend to be underused by researchers. The public documents section of a library stores a wide variety of statistical data such as labor and public health statistics. Federal grant reports and reports of demonstration projects are also available and frequently contain useful data.

More and more data, collected for a variety of purposes, are appearing on the Internet each year. They are often the product of well-funded research studies by governmental agencies or foundations and relate to human conditions and problems that are often the focus of social work research. Organizations such as the National Science Foundation, the National Institute on Alcohol and Alcoholism, the National Institute on Child Health and Human Development, and the National Institutes of Health now place their research data in the public domain and encourage others to use it for their own research. It has been suggested that this has occurred, in part, because of the recognition that the high cost of federal research studies can be better justified if the data they produce can be made available for "mining" to answer other research questions besides those originally addressed (Sales, Lichtenwalter, & Fevola, 2006). Trustworthy research data on the Internet presents some excellent opportunities for us as researchers. Data that are within the public domain may be used with appropriate citation from

There are many sources of research data within the public domain that can be useful to social workers for conducting research.

Box 11.1   Common Methods for Acquiring Research Data

Method	Definitions/Description
Secondary data analysis	Uses data previously collected for some other purpose
Oral histories	Recorded, firsthand descriptions of people who "were there" (Can be a source of secondary data or can be considered "original data")
Client logs	Data gathered by client regarding behaviors, thoughts, feelings, etc.
Systematic observation	Watching, observing, recording (may include participation)
Mailed surveys	Data collected via postal service
In-person interviews	One-on-one conversations; structure varies
Group interviews	Several individuals provide data simultaneously; structure varies
Telephone	Data collected via telephone
Electronic communication	Data collected via computer through e-mail, instant messaging, instant chats, etc.

their sources. We do not need permission to analyze census data or data published by the National Center for Health Statistics and other federal agencies. They can be used, for example, to chronicle social changes, such as the rise and decline of various occupations and urban migration or the increased presence of women in the workplace over the past century. However, as we noted in Chapter 4, it is worth remembering that not all data that appear on the Internet can be trusted. Thus, it is always wise to consider the source.

NASW, CSWE, and other professional organizations also annually collect data about their members. Social workers interested in conducting research using selected characteristics of professional social workers, as well as social work educators, schools, and students can obtain permission to reanalyze these data.

Different Uses

Secondary analysis is used in descriptive and some explanatory quantitative studies. It is not used in experiments because, by definition, they require that the independent variable is either introduced or manipulated by the researcher. In secondary analysis, this would be impossible because data used are typically those collected by someone else for some other purpose. Some examples of use of social agency data may help to demonstrate the wide variety of ways that secondary analysis can be used in research if ethical and legal requirements can be met:

- In a private psychiatric in-patient facility, a researcher may wish to describe the participation of institutionalized clients in making discharge plans. A secondary analysis of data drawn from available case records might be used.
- In a child protection agency, case record data could be used to compile a picture of the disposition of cases that are referred for investigation of possible child abuse. They could be used to create a composite picture of patterns of service delivery.
- As part of a program evaluation of a battered women's shelter, agency record data could be used to learn if clients served by the organization are representative of the community in age, income level, ethnicity, and so forth. Data could be compared statistically to county- or community-maintained data on the same social indicators.
- In an alcohol rehabilitation facility, secondary data analysis could be used to seek support for the hypothesis that there is a positive correlation between the level of clients' participation in a given program and positive changes in some aspect of their functioning.

When large databases can be accessed electronically, there may be a temptation to select most or even all variables and to simply see if there are relationships between or among any of them. We recommend caution in using this approach as a method of secondary analysis. For both ethical and statistical reasons (beyond our discussion here), relationships between or among variables should be analyzed only after the researcher has justified hypotheses about their relationships (on the basis of the literature review). Computers should be used to statistically analyze relationships believed to exist, not to engage in a "fishing expedition."

Tasks Required

There are many tasks that require special attention in research that employ secondary analysis of data. They include the following:

- **Operationalizing the variables.** Methods used to measure variables in the original data collection should be identified, and if at all possible, the same operational definitions should be applied in the current study. Also, an estimate of the degree of reliability and validity (Chapter 10) of the original measurement should be made.
- **Specifying the sampling plan used.** The source of data (case record, personnel file, monthly statistical report, and so on) and the strategy for selecting a sample of cases should be specified and justified.
- **Developing a data collection instrument and coding scheme for data collection.** Typically, this is accomplished by using a data collection instrument that has been developed specifically for the research. Data are drawn from the original documents and recorded on the instrument. It is a good idea to have more than one person read and record the same data from the original source. If this is done, an estimate of the interobserver reliability of the data gathering method can be made (Chapter 10).
- **Analyzing the data.** The appropriate level of measurement for each variable is determined (on the basis of information about how it was originally collected) before statistical analysis (Chapter 13) can be conducted.
- **Identifying the limitations of the study.** Although most research reports typically include a section describing limitations of the study, the inclusion of a limitations section is particularly important in secondary data analysis. Due to the nature of the data being analyzed (they were measured and recorded for some purpose other than the current study and usually by people other than the researcher), there is a greater-than-usual likelihood that they will have limitations regarding their application to the current study.

Advantages

Secondary data analysis is appealing to researchers for a number of reasons. First, the financial costs associated with it are often minimal compared with other data collection methods. Second, it may require less time than other forms of data collection and analysis. The data are already collected and recorded; we need only to develop a sampling method and an instrument for coding and recording them. If the data are already available in a form that is compatible with statistical analysis software, analysis can begin almost immediately following the literature review and the development of focused questions and/or hypotheses.

When ethically and legally feasible (under HIPAA, medical records are now generally inaccessible), secondary analyses are less intrusive than other methods that collect original data from participants. Permissions may not need to be secured, as people are not interviewed or observed in person by the researcher. However, when agency record data are used, clients' permission may be required because data were provided for use in receiving assistance, not for research. If data have been stored by case number or some other method that ensures that we cannot possibly know who provided which data (client anonymity) when it was originally collected, this may be less problematic.

Limitations

Given the many advantages of conducting secondary analysis, why is it not used more frequently? For one thing, even when data are available for secondary data analysis, they are often quite limited. When planning to collect original data, we generally learn from the literature review what variables need to be studied (Chapter 4). Then we collect whatever data are needed. In secondary analysis, the existing data may fall short of providing all that is required to answer a research question or providing support or non-support for a hypothesis. If measurements of a variable are not in the record or document, the variable generally cannot be examined (unless it is possible for the researcher to go back personally and measure it, or add another data collection instrument). Our plans for studying a question or testing a hypothesis may need to be modified to fit available data.

Another potential problem with the use of secondary analysis relates to the quality of the measurement that was conducted. If the data are lacking in credibility, no amount of secondary analysis will improve their quality. A thorough examination of the context in which data were originally collected can help us to determine whether they can be trusted. An assessment of their quality should be made. Questions might include, for example, Who gathered them, using what kind of recording method? Was there possibly a hidden agenda that may have influenced what was recorded and what was not? What assurances of confidentiality or anonymity were given? If the people who originally recorded the information are available to the researcher, they should be consulted on these and other issues.

Most secondary data that are in the public domain or otherwise available for research tend to focus on facts. Thus, they may offer limited opportunities for social work researchers to gain insight into human emotions, feelings, perceptions or what motivates certain human behaviors. Oral histories, the next data source that we will discuss, do provide these opportunities.

ORAL HISTORIES

One way to learn what it was like to experience some event or phenomenon is to ask people to describe it in their own words (and to preserve what was said). Oral histories are written, audio, and/or video recordings of people discussing an experience or life event from their own perspectives. These recordings are analyzed using a variety of research methods (e.g., content analysis as described in Chapter 6) to attempt to answer a variety of research questions.

Oral histories are firsthand accounts, which would seem to be, on the surface, trustworthy data sources. Who better to describe something than someone who "lived it"? However, when using oral histories as a data source, it should be remembered that what an oral history describes most accurately is how someone perceived or experienced something, not necessarily how it actually occurred. Even firsthand descriptions of an individual's perceptions and experiences may not be totally accurate if much time has lapsed, as memories tend to fade or become distorted over time.

Pre-research meetings with participants (sometimes called *narrators*) are often used to develop comfortable relationships and determine which questions might be most productive to ask when oral histories are compiled. Then, the interviews are conducted and recorded, often over many sessions. A relationship between the participant and the recorder will inevitably form. Consequently, the person compiling an oral history can unintentionally influence what the participant says.

Oral histories preserve history and the experiences that people had during a particular time. Thus, they enable us to learn from people who may no longer be with us or who are here now but will not always be around to tell their stories. For example, oral histories exist in which veterans of World Wars I and II, Holocaust survivors of Nazi concentration camps, participants in the American civil rights movement, early labor union organizers, and people who worked in President Franklin Roosevelt's New Deal programs describe what these events were like from their perspective. The Columbia University Oral History Research Office compiled oral histories of people who lived through the events of September 11, 2001, in New York and Washington, D.C. (Clark & Bearman, n.d.).

Oral histories preserve history. Thus, they enable us to learn from people who may no longer be with us or who are here now but will not always be around to tell their stories.

There are many examples of oral histories within the literature. Oral histories are sometimes used in ethnographic studies (described in Chapter 6). For example, the oral history data collection method was used in a study that examined life themes of native Hawaiian female elders (Mokuau & Browne, 1994). The elders, known as *kupunas* to native Hawaiians, play important roles in native Hawaiian culture. Three themes selected for emphasis in the study were relationships among people, peoples' relationships with nature, and their spiritual and religious beliefs. The data developed in interviews were transcribed and analyzed according to the themes and prepared in draft form for review by participants to aid in correcting any misinformation. Following the reviews, they were preserved by University of Hawaii's Center for Oral History.

In another study, Martin (1995) conducted in-depth interviews of elderly African Americans living in a community in the southeastern part of the United States. She gathered and recorded oral histories from members of fifteen families. The study evolved from Martin's concern with how the relative strengths of African-American families are portrayed. It documented African-American family adaptation systems.

Martin made extensive use of individual narratives to preserve the stories of her participants. All interviews were audiotaped and later transcribed. Themes related to adaptation, survival, and growth were identified in analyses of the transcriptions. The data were presented in both tabular form and thematically. Whenever possible, the respondents' own words were used to highlight important findings.

In the first phase of a more extensive project, Logan (2007) interviewed and recorded the experiences of ten African-American women who were involved in the civil rights movement in South Carolina. Each participant's life narrative was captured in both booklet form and DVD.

In these oral histories and in many others, participants were encouraged to *tell their story*, interpret what it meant to them, and to describe their emotions and feelings surrounding it. Oral histories can be used to create a historical record of almost any event where participants were present. For example, members of the original board of directors of a social agency can be asked to describe their recollections of the board's early meetings and discussions. Their oral histories can be used at a later time to provide insight into why the organization began, what it hoped to accomplish, and how its mission evolved.

The examples that we have cited help to illustrate the many uses of oral histories. They also suggest why it is difficult to say exactly what an oral history is. Is it a product that is compiled simply to preserve something for posterity? Is it data collected for immediate use by a researcher? Is it a secondary data source used by other researchers? It can be all three!

For many people whose work is simply compiling them, a collection of oral histories is often the end product of their work. It is a recorded description of how various people experienced a life event, preserved for posterity. It is potentially a valuable contribution to society, but compiling it does not require most of the skills of researchers.

If the person compiling a group of oral histories is more interested in answering research questions of immediate interest or, less frequently, determining if there is support for a research hypotheses (i.e., he or she is functioning more as a researcher), the histories can be regarded as an original or primary data source. For example, a researcher could compile oral histories in such a way as to seek answers to a question such as "Do recent legal immigrants from the Middle East perceive that they have been treated differently in North America following the terrorist acts of the early twenty-first century?" The histories that have been compiled would then be analyzed in search of an answer to the question, perhaps, through content analysis of them.

No matter why or by whom oral histories are compiled, once they are recorded they become a potential secondary data source for researchers who come along later. They can be used to seek answers to research questions that those who compiled them may have had little interest in or may have never even contemplated. Oral histories are often a good data resource for researchers. They can provide insights that other data sources cannot provide.

CLIENT LOGS

Client logs are a way of collecting data in written form directly from our clients. In qualitative research, these logs may involve journals that clients keep regarding a problem and the meanings they ascribe to the problem, descriptions of certain events, and thoughts regarding relationships, emotions, and mental health issues, among others. In quantitative research, client logs are generally used to give clients the ability to record behaviors, thoughts, and emotions on a continual basis. For example, they may count these activities, or they may record the length or the intensity of the activities.

It is also fairly common to mix quantitative and qualitative components within one client log. For example, a client may record each time they experience depressed feelings, log the intensity of the feeling, who they are with, where they are, and what activity they are involved in, all quantitative data. They may also enter into the journal qualitative data, such as a verbal description of the depressed feeling, the meaning they ascribe to the feeling, and what they think might be causing it.

Single-system evaluation (discussed in detail in Chapter 8) often uses client logs to gather the repeated measures necessary in single-system research. For example, the client may keep daily logs of disordered eating behaviors throughout the week between sessions, logging such behaviors as binging, purging, exercise, laxative use, etc. The complete logs would then be taken to the client's weekly therapeutic session and the data logged onto line graphs to show the client's progress.

Client logs are very versatile and can be created by the practitioner and client together to meet the unique needs of the client's situation. It is important to format the log so it is easy to understand and use, has plenty of room for necessary answers (particularly the qualitative descriptions), and has clear instructions so the instrument is used consistently by the client.

SYSTEMATIC OBSERVATION

When conducting either one-on-one interviews or group interviews such as focus groups, we frequently have the opportunity to observe research participants. These observations often yield additional, unanticipated data for our research. It my support, contradict, or supplement the other data collected.

Sometimes, we observe a behavior or phenomenon in a more planned way. When we make a plan to observe a behavior or phenomenon, then follow the plan by observing and recording the data in a systematic way, it is called *systematic observation*. It is used in both qualitative and quantitative studies, but it tends to be less structured in qualitative research than in predominantly quantitative studies.

Observation is sometimes made in a created or contrived situation. The Zimbardo studies (Stanford prison experiment) of college students assuming the role of prisoner or prison guard (Chapter 1) are an example of this type of research. The created situation may also involve deception, as in the ethically questionable Milgram electroshock studies discussed in Chapter 2. However, most observation is conducted in a natural setting, one that is not created specifically for the purposes of the research.

Unstructured Observation

There are many instances in social work research where we may use observation as a data source. For example, we may wish to know more about parent–child interaction, group process, or task completion. Or, as part of a program evaluation, we may wish to learn what it is like to be a client in the program by spending time observing how clients are treated in the waiting room when they arrive or while they are waiting to be seen. If so, systematic observation can constitute a valuable source of data.

Unstructured observation is characterized by a lack of formal data gathering instruments. Typically, in unstructured observation, the researcher is either a passive observer (observes but does not participate in the activity) or a participant observer (observes and takes part in the activity). These methods are appropriate when the phenomenon being studied cannot be clearly specified in advance and when it is important to observe participants in their own environments rather than in a laboratory setting. For example, we might be interested in studying the behavior of a group such as Weight-Watchers or Alcoholics Anonymous; we might choose to join the group and make observations over a period of time. Of course, in such situations, we would have to address certain ethical obligations since deception may be involved. We should also adhere to the rules of the group. For example, the identities of members of the groups should not be revealed to others, or social interaction with members outside the group setting may be prohibited. Researchers in anthropology and social psychology have used unstructured observational methods in their studies of street gangs, people who are homeless, and various non-Western cultures.

In areas of inquiry where knowledge is limited, it is often best to observe behavior in an unstructured manner. In so doing, we would not be constrained by categories or checklists and are open to viewing all behaviors (or components of behaviors) that are displayed. Unstructured observation really falls somewhere between exploratory and descriptive research. It is often used to begin to learn more about a behavior, culture, or environment of interest, often to lay the groundwork for subsequent studies that are more structured.

Unstructured observation requires maintaining field notes. These can consist of either mental notes for recording immediately afterward, or a written running account or description of behaviors during the observation period. Developing and maintaining field notes is crucial; otherwise, at the end of the observation, we would have to depend solely on our memory to recall what we observed.

Because unstructured observation tends to yield data that are primarily qualitative in nature, information collected is often presented in narrative rather than statistical form. Running accounts, case vignettes, and anecdotes are often used. Direct quotations from participants are frequently included.

We will use an example to demonstrate how unstructured observation might be used in social work research. Suppose that we are interested in developing an understanding of the psychosocial needs of family caregivers of older people. Unstructured observation might be used to study caregivers and the older people to whom they offer care in their homes. We could observe the needs and demands of older people as well as the responses of their caregivers. The interactions between the two would be observed and characterized. Particularly, the activities and emotional responses of the caregivers would be noted. The application of an unstructured observational method would allow certain kinds of questions to be addressed:

- Do caregivers seem able to perform the tasks required to provide needed care? If not, what are their emotional responses to not being able to meet the older peoples' needs?
- Do caregivers have opportunities to meet their own needs? What sacrifices do they appear to be making to care for the older person? How able are they to verbalize anger or frustration because of the demands of caregiving?
- What assistance is available to caregivers? Is it provided by other people who are part of the caregiving network? If so, which ones appear to be most helpful to caregivers, and why?

Advantages

Unstructured observation is characterized by flexibility. During the observation period, we would take note of behaviors, reactions, or environmental features that relate to the phenomenon being studied. Trained, sensitive observers are able to record data about many variables that may be impacting the phenomenon. During the course of an unstructured observation, we may become aware of the influence of other phenomena that were not originally identified or conceptualized. We may include observations of such phenomena in the findings of our study or make them the focus of a subsequent research study.

Findings from studies using systematic observation can often be generalized beyond those research participants who were studied. Especially in naturalistic observation— that is, in studies where data are gathered by observing large numbers of participants over an extended period of time in their own environments—the external validity of the research findings can be quite good. We can be relatively confident that the behavior observed is characteristic of what people (at least in that setting) actually say and do. Of course, as in any method of data collection, the external validity of the findings can also be quite limited if the sample of individuals studied lacks representativeness.

Limitations

In systematic observation, the validity of research findings may be affected by participants' *reactivity*, that is, the degree to which they modify their behavior in response to our presence. When possible, we should select an observer role that will at least minimize the impact of reactivity while still providing the needed access to data. For example, as an observer watching a child's behavior in the classroom we may choose to watch from behind a one-way mirror rather than from the back of the classroom in order to minimize reactivity.

Other disadvantages inherent in the use of unstructured observation (besides reactivity) relate to the consistency and objectivity of measurement procedures. Both can seriously damage the credibility of research findings. Consistency of data collection is a primary concern because, in unstructured observation, data collection is not standardized. When more than one observer collects data, variation in data collection procedures may be especially great. This is the issue of interobserver agreement (Chapter 10). The reliability of data can be enhanced by employing two or more observers to conduct the same measurement. Interobserver agreement can be assessed by using a form of statistical analysis that estimates the percentage of agreement between two observers.

Fatigue or boredom can also negatively affect the quality of the observations made, because observation generally occurs over an extended period of time. The potential for this problem can be reduced by using several observers, with each responsible for relatively short time segments of observation.

Because observers must be sensitized to a behavior before it is described and recorded, the likelihood exists that selective perception by observers will play a part in which behavior gets noted or the interpretation of what a behavior means. Training observers to increase sensitivity to the nature of the behavior of interest, use of appropriate observational techniques, and use of appropriate methods of recording data will minimize the major sources of measurement bias inherent in observation studies.

However, subjectivity must be assumed to exist in all data collected using unstructured observation. That is why it is generally more suitable for use in qualitative research than in quantitative studies.

Structured Observation

If our goal is to accurately describe a behavior or phenomenon, as is usually the case in a quantitative research study, structured observation is often used. Structured observation requires identifying a specific behavior or set of behaviors and systematically observing them over a given time period. A data collection instrument is used. Because of the structure imposed by this method, data are collected in the same format and therefore more easily sorted, coded, and analyzed than those collected using less structured observation methods.

In designing any form of observation, we would decide in advance the nature and degree of our involvement with the research participants. The most appropriate role for a given study depends on the purpose of the study, our assessment of how the most accurate data can be obtained, and legal and ethical issues. Observer roles may be understood as being located on a continuum from complete observer to participant observer. Possible observer roles follow:

- Concealed, nonparticipating (complete observer)
- Concealed, participating
- Observer role not concealed, nonparticipating
- Observer role not concealed, minimally participating
- Observer role not concealed, participating (participant observer)

The two variables, concealment of the role of observer and degree of participation, can affect the quality of the data collected. When the role as an observer is not concealed, participants may consciously or unconsciously alter their behavior (reactivity). However, when the role of observer is concealed, they are more likely to behave in their usual manner. Thus, if we wish to gather data without our presence affecting the participants, the role of observer should be concealed and we should be either participating or nonparticipating. If the data are unlikely to be adversely affected by the awareness that participants are being observed, the role of observer need not be concealed.

Concealing the fact that participants are being observed does not necessarily mean the participants are not told that they will be observed. As was noted in our discussion of research ethics in Chapter 2, not allowing participants to know that they will be observed may be considered unwarranted intrusion on their privacy. It might not be permitted by an IRB on ethical grounds because participants had not voluntarily agreed to be part of the research. Even if participants had agreed to participate in research but had not been told that it would entail being observed without their knowledge, it could be considered unethical. But if they voluntarily agreed to participate and were told that they would be observed but would not know exactly *where or when* they were being observed, this would not constitute deception and would probably be considered ethical.

How would the various roles be operationalized in social work research? Suppose a team of researchers is interested in studying the quality of interviewing skills of beginning social workers in a human service organization. If they observe the interview sessions of new workers from behind a one-way mirror, they would be considered to be "concealed, nonparticipating." If they observe from behind the mirror while using equipment that would enable them to prompt the interviewers, the observers would be "concealed, participating." They could also choose to observe a sample of client interviews conducted by beginning-level workers by actually sitting in on the interviews. If they only record behaviors and do not influence the direction of the interview in any way, they are "not concealed, nonparticipating." If they provide occasional suggestions to the workers, communicate approval or disapproval of the workers' interviewing methods through nonverbal communication, or otherwise subtly

Engagement

Behavior: Use empathy, reflection, and interpersonal skills to effectively engage diverse clients and constituencies.

Critical Thinking Question: What steps would you need to take before you observed a child's behavior in his classroom from behind a one-way mirror?

influence them to conduct the interview differently, they are "not concealed, minimally participating." However, if the interviews are conducted jointly by themselves and the workers, and the workers' skills are later evaluated, the researchers would be "not concealed, participating."

Following are seven steps that are generally used to implement a structured observational design:

1. **Define the behavior or list of behaviors to be studied.** In structured observation, the researcher decides what behaviors to study on the basis of the literature review. They are those behaviors considered critical to an understanding of the research problem and answering research questions and/or testing hypotheses. Operational definitions of the behaviors are developed and these definitions provide the basis for observation. Characteristics of the behaviors to be measured are also specified, for example, their frequency, duration, intensity, and so forth.

2. **Identify a time frame during which the behaviors will be observed.** The researcher has to know when specific behaviors are most likely to occur. This knowledge comes from a thorough understanding of the behavior under investigation derived from the review of literature, personal or professional experience, or an earlier research study. For example, if we are interested in studying verbal abuse of older people by caregivers, the researcher should have learned which times of day are most stressful for caregivers. This knowledge may have come from an earlier qualitative study that used unstructured observations to attempt to understand the caregivers' needs and problems. In addition to identifying a specific time during the day to observe (or week or month), the literature review might also suggest a time interval during which the observation should occur. Will the observer observe for one hour at a time, for three hours, or for five minutes each hour? A time sample should be selected on the basis of the nature of the behavior under study (when and how frequently it is likely to occur) and the physical and emotional capacities of observers to gather accurate data. If observers are required to gather data for long periods of time, the quality of the data may suffer (referred to as *measurement decay*). Observers may get tired or bored and may require breaks and relief from their work.

3. **Develop a data collection instrument.** In structured observation, instruments typically take the form of behavioral checklists or category schemes. They are designed so that, when a behavior is displayed, its characteristics can be easily recorded. The

instrument may also include demographic data on participants being observed, such as name, age, gender, or other identifying characteristics. As is true for new data collection instruments, the instrument should be pilot-tested before use. This is done to see how effective and accurate the instrument is in describing the behavior.

4. Select an observer role. The observer role most appropriate to the behavior being studied is selected. Logistical and ethical issues (as previously mentioned) are addressed.

5. Train observers. Structured observation requires the use of trained research personnel. Unless the researcher is conducting all observations personally (a potential source of bias), observers are usually recruited or hired to observe. They need to be trained by the researcher in the method of observation to be used and they need to gain experience with the use of the data collection instrument. Observers need to know what to look for, when to observe it, how to know if the behavior of interest is occurring, and how to record it using the instrument.

6. Conduct the observations. Observers observe participants' behavior, recording the data as they are obtained.

7. Verify the data. Data are checked for accuracy. One way to verify the data is to use two observers to observe and record the participants' behaviors. If the two observers generally agree on the behaviors observed, the researcher can be reasonably confident that the data are accurate.

Another way this is done is through the use of video recordings (with participant permission) to record behaviors. When recordings are made, an observer may or may not be present at the time the recordings are made. If an observer is present, then a second observer can watch the recordings later, and their findings can be compared to the original observer. In situations where it is more appropriate to not have an observer present during the recording, a team of trained reviewers can view the recordings later and arrive at a consensus as to what occurred. If such a consensus is not reached, a second review team may be used. If there is a serious discrepancy between the reviews of the two teams, the disputed data are generally discarded.

Advantages

A major advantage of structured observation is that the data acquired tend to be measured in a consistent manner and thus may be more accurate. They also tend to be better organized and in a more standardized format. It is easier to code them for data analysis, including statistical testing of research hypotheses.

Limitations

Observations tend to be somewhat limited in scope. Potentially valuable observations may not become part of the data if they were not planned for and included on the data collection instrument. Thus, structured observation is a more appropriate data source for quantitative studies, where the goal is to accurately measure a limited number of variables and examine possible relationships between and among them, rather than in qualitative studies, where we are more open to receiving and processing the unexpected.

SURVEYS

Surveys have always been an important part of social work research. In program evaluations, a client satisfaction survey in some form is almost always a requirement (even though, it should be remembered, client satisfaction is not always synonymous with program success). Most surveys are (1) cross-sectional, (2) used to collect both quantitative and more subjective data, and (3) descriptive. They are important tools in both basic and applied research, which are used to measure, for example, the demographic characteristics of people along with their opinions, preferences, and beliefs.

A good survey can answer many research questions. However, a poor one can lead to erroneous conclusions and actually be counterproductive toward attaining the goal of evidence-based social work practice. Planning to conduct a survey can be a painstaking process. It involves making many important decisions about, for example, sampling (see Chapter 9) and how data will be analyzed (see Chapter 13). It also requires an exacting process of word selection. Unless a previously developed, proven data collection instrument can be found that will generate the data required and offer valid measurements of key variables, a new instrument has to be developed and pilot-tested. Developing the instrument is not simply a matter of deciding what answers are sought and quickly writing a group of questions to elicit answers to them. The planning process entails considerable work and thought.

Even the best-planned surveys that rely on well-constructed data collection instruments can produce misleading findings. Because of their high potential for response bias (discussed later in this chapter), surveys that collect data by telephone or electronic data collection methods or rely heavily on mailed questionnaires are especially prone to producing misleading findings. This problem can also occur when acquiring data through in-person interviews, where reactivity can affect the validity of data. Next, we'll look at some of the challenges when conducting survey research.

Potential for Distortion

Distortion is likely to occur when any self-administered data collection instrument is used, but especially when data are collected by mail. When instruments are mailed to research participants, we do not know whether or not participants understood what was asked or if they responded honestly. A participant who does not need to face the researcher may be more likely to either inadvertently or deliberately misrepresent reality than one who participates in in-person interviews. That is why it is so important to word questions and statements well. For more information on constructing surveys, see Hutson and Kolbe (2010) or Rubin and Babbie (2014). Box 11.2 lists some of the common mistakes made when constructing surveys, along with examples of "how not to do it."

If inaccurate data are obtained because of poorly worded questions or statements, we cannot always detect it. For example, we would not know if a participant took an hour or two minutes to complete a survey. We would also have no way of knowing the state of mind of participants when the instruments were completed. They may well have been conscientious in completing them. However, they may also have "just put down

Box 11.2   What to Avoid When Constructing Survey Questions

Avoid	Examples of Poorly Worded Items*
Leading questions—a question that suggests an answer through the use of certain "loaded" words, or includes the information for the answer the researcher wants.	Should innocent children ever have to go without needed medical care?
Prestige bias—a question that could embarrass the respondent or encourage the respondent to give a false answer in order to look good.	Have you ever violated confidentiality in your handling of client data?
Vagueness—the inclusion of phrases that may mean different things to different people or the use of answer choices that are unclear or difficult to understand.	How often do you do things that are dangerous to others? (please circle) Frequently Sometimes Never
Double-barreled questions—a question that has two questions joined into one question making it hard for the respondent to answer accurately.	Do you favor national health care supported through tax increases and a cut in social security benefits?
Questions that are impossible to answer—questions that are impossible for the respondent to answer accurately.	If you had not entered military service, would you have finished college?
Jargon, acronyms—the use of slang or abbreviations that may not have the same meaning to everyone.	Do you think that ISIS has contributed to an increase in racial profiling?
Emotional language—the use of an emotional word or phrase that would bias the respondent toward one answer.	Have abuses by welfare cheats and deadbeat fathers contributed to skyrocketing Medicaid costs?
False beliefs—when a question assumes certain knowledge or belief held by the respondent.	When did you first learn that HIV is no longer a serious medical threat in your community?
"Loaded" responses—when the responses are loaded toward either a positive or negative response.	Would you rate your current health care provider as OK, inferior, or very inadequate?

*Some of the poorly worded items above may contain multiple problems.

anything," or even deliberately provided false information. Returned data collection instruments that contain clearly facetious or impossible responses can simply be discarded. But it is more difficult to determine what to do with a completed instrument that contains responses that are just a little unusual—it may contain valid data, or it may not.

Identity of the Participant

When using a mailed instrument, it may be impossible to know even if the person to whom it was sent completed it. Did it fall into the hands of a mischievous child? Or was it deliberately delegated to another for completion? The identity of the respondent is almost certain to be a problem with some groups of people. For example, if a mailed questionnaire is sent to physicians, research respondents are likely to be staff members who work for the doctors and complete all of their paperwork.

Return Rate

A common problem with data collection by mail is a low rate of return of completed instruments. It is just too easy for potential research participants to discard a request for data or, with all good intentions, to set it aside and forget about it. The researcher who uses mailed data collection asks much and offers little. There is no potential for a pleasant interpersonal exchange with the researcher, only a letter from a person who is most likely a stranger and whose motives for seeking participation in the research are likely to be viewed with suspicion.

Although some research naturally draws a higher rate of return (e.g., research on emotionally charged topics or requests for data sent to college alumni or people who are fellow members of religious or civic organizations), the typical return rate for data collection instruments mailed to strangers is quite low. Hager, Wilson, Pollak, and Rooney (2003) looked at seventeen studies using mailed surveys and found a median return rate of 52 percent, with a range from 10 to 100 percent. Paxson, Dillmon, and Tarnai (1995) summarized the return rates for 26 studies using mailed surveys, and found an average return rate of 51 percent, ranging from 26 to 95 percent. A response rate that is much higher than an average response rate should be viewed with suspicion. For example, a researcher may have first requested "interested volunteers" to complete a questionnaire and then mailed it out to only those who replied to the request. The implausibly high response rate reported may be misleading to the reader if this fact is not clearly stated in a research article or report. The research findings may be more biased than those of another survey with a more typical return rate in which a questionnaire was sent to a sample of possible participants in a single mailing.

One obvious implication is that if a sample of responses of a given size (often for purposes of statistical analysis) is needed, the researcher should either (1) send out at least two or three times that many instruments to ensure having enough completed ones for data analysis or (2) go to extraordinary lengths to attempt to increase the usual, expected rate of return. The latter method is the preferred one. Here are some ideas that seem to work:

- **Keep it short.** The potential value of a well-designed study can be quickly negated if the researcher cannot generate a sufficiently high response rate. Excessive length probably results in more discarded instruments than any other feature of the instrument. Few potential participants will complete a ten-page instrument, no matter what the topic or their interest in it. In addition, ten pages worth of questions jammed onto both sides of four or five pages, or use of a small font, will not fool anyone or fare any better. Such attempts at deception just make potential participants angry. Generally, if an instrument is longer than a few double spaced, easily read pages, it is probably trying to collect too much data at a single time. The researcher should also use as many fixed-alternative items (see Chapter 12) as possible. People are more likely to make a check mark or an X than to write one or more words.

- **Avoid bad times.** Although there is no ideal time to ask research participants to complete an instrument, some times of the year have been found to be worse than others. The December holidays should be avoided. Among student participants, midterm and final examination times (and spring break) are not likely to result in a high response rate.

- **Provide incentives.** A small cash payment or a small gift as payment for participation will almost always result in more instruments being completed and returned. However, a promise of a reward after a completed instrument is received will be less effective in improving the response rate than an incentive mailed out with the instrument and cover letter. Why, then, are incentives not used more frequently? The costs of providing them may be great, and the costs may be more than just monetary. They may influence the responses received. Are participants who are paid for their responses more likely to provide (either consciously or unconsciously) those responses that they think are being sought by the researcher? The answer to this question is almost impossible to determine. Another type of incentive that can increase the response rate is an offer to share an outline or summary of the major research findings. If it is used, any requests for the summary (there are usually relatively few) must be honored, despite the cost of the additional correspondence. Not to do so would be unethical.

- **Provide postage-paid, preaddressed return envelopes.** People are unlikely to return an instrument unless they can do it simply and with no cost to them. Given the usual rate of return for mailed instruments, it is generally more economical to use metered envelopes than to affix a stamp to the return envelope. The postage for each response will be a little higher than if a stamp were provided, but it is charged only for those that are mailed back. Postage also affects return rate in another way. Generally, more expensive mailing methods yield higher rates of response. First-class mail is more likely to result in completed instruments than third-class mail. High-priority methods, such as overnight delivery, yield relatively high rates of response, but their cost can be prohibitive.

- **Use a carefully worded cover letter.** The cover letter should tell potential participants how they were selected to receive the instrument and that their response is important to the success of the research. Especially, if the research deals with sensitive matters (e.g., sexuality, religious or political beliefs, or behaviors that are either illegal or not socially approved), potential respondents will want to know how the researcher got their names and how data will be used, and they will need to be assured that any confidentiality or anonymity promises will be kept.

The cover letter should reflect the researcher's genuine interest in the research problem and the assumption that potential participants may share that interest. Potential respondents will also need to be convinced that the instrument is not just being sent to millions of people and that their responses are important to the success of the research. Personally signing each cover letter can reinforce this impression.

Like the survey itself, careful wording of the cover letter is important. The wrong type of appeal for participation can actually reduce the rate of response. For example, a statement such as "I am a social work student who needs to collect data to meet my research course requirement" suggests that (1) the researcher is probably not really interested in the problem; (2) the researcher would not be conducting the research if it were not required; and (3) the findings are unlikely to ever be used for anything other than helping a professor assign a course grade. Why would anyone want to take the time to respond favorably to such an appeal?

- **Use return addresses and letterheads.** The return address on an envelope used to mail out a data collection instrument and the inside address on the cover letter can affect the rate of return of mailed instruments. A home or business address can lend credibility to a research study; generally, a post office box number can harm it.
- **Use an organization or agency address when it is likely to be beneficial.** The use of some organization or agency addresses can help to increase the return rate; the use of others can decrease it. When an organizational affiliation is likely to increase the response rate, permission to use agency letterhead can be helpful; they suggest written endorsement of and support for the research. However, some organizations, such as state departments of social services, mental health, or corrections, evoke certain emotional responses. Using their envelopes and stationery might negatively affect return rate and can even bias the data that are received.

Response Bias

It can be easily determined if a researcher has received a satisfactory return rate. A second and more difficult issue to be addressed is whether the data that are available for analysis were collected from a representative sample of participants. Although a relatively high percentage of responses to an instrument mailing (e.g., 50 percent) is likely to produce a representative sample of those who were requested to participate, there is no guarantee that it will. The 50 percent who failed to respond may differ from the 50 percent who did respond in an important way that could have produced a biased sample. Conversely, although not likely, even a very low rate of return (e.g., 25 percent) could theoretically have produced a sample that is representative of the population being studied. The problem with using mailed instruments is that it is difficult to know whether those who did not return the instrument are similar to or different in an important way from those who did. Some follow-up calls to determine why the former group did not respond are sometimes informative. They can provide at least some insight into whether or not a response bias exists. However, the calls can also be perceived as harassment by those people who already

Engagement

Behavior: Apply knowledge of human behavior and the social environment, person-in-environment, and other multi-disciplinary theoretical frameworks to engage with clients and constituencies.

Critical Thinking Question: If you wanted the parents of third grade elementary students to complete a survey and return it to their child's teacher, what are five things you would do to encourage the parents to respond?

indicated their unwillingness to be research participants when they did not return their data collection instruments.

In some research situations, a response bias is quite predictable. For example, a follow-up survey to assess the vocational success of people denied admission to a job-training program would be expected to prompt a disproportionately high rate of return from three groups: (1) those who have been successful and wish to boast about their success; (2) those who are still unemployed and wish to blame the denial of admission to the program for their failures; and (3) those who receive the instrument, perceive that it means that they are still being considered for admission to the program, and therefore are careful to complete and return it. A lower rate of return might be expected from other people who are employed but have not been especially successful in their careers or otherwise have less extreme views regarding the program being evaluated.

A descriptive study (McQueen, 2000) of hazing rituals (emotional and physical abuse of students attempting to be admitted to membership in a group or an organization) among high school and college students provides a good example of how response bias can operate. In August 2000, many major newspapers reported that a large percentage of students had been victims of hazing. Although this conclusion was based on a study in which mailed questionnaires were completed and anonymously returned by a large number of students, the questionnaires only had a 12 percent return rate; that is, only 12 percent of the questionnaires mailed out were returned. The low return rate should be reason enough for us to question the external validity of any findings drawn from returned questionnaires. However, we should also ask who was most likely to return the questionnaires and who was not. Wouldn't students who had experienced hazing be more likely to take the trouble to complete and return the questionnaires than students who had not experienced hazing and thus had no particular interest in it? It would probably be safe to assume that generalizations from this sample (at least any about incidence of hazing) were very suspect. In situations in which the use of the mail for data collection would likely result in response bias, other methods of data collection, such as in-person interviews, should be considered. A smaller (but more representative) sample of participants is almost always preferable to a larger, biased one.

While there are certainly weaknesses to acquiring data using mailed surveys, they are likely to remain popular for conducting certain types of research. What is a desirable stance to take in regard to them? We can recognize their limitations (primarily questions about the external validity of their findings), not assume that their findings are 100 percent accurate, and acknowledge their many contributions to our knowledge base.

A while back there was discussion of how traditional methods of conducting large-scale national surveys could be revised to yield high response rates and better data. One researcher (Trei, 2006) proposed that a carefully selected, representative sample of 1,000 American households might be identified and provided with laptop computers and high-speed Internet access to allow them to participate in a thirty-minute secure survey every month. The time blocks with these "professional research participants" could then be sold to researchers such as political pollsters or others who seek to measure American opinions and trends. Undoubtedly, the twenty-first century will see other innovative approaches to survey research as the full capacity of the Internet is realized.

INTERVIEWS

There are a variety of methods of interviewing clients and research participants to obtain research data, including in-personal interviews, group interviews, and telephone interviews. We will look briefly at some of the strengths and weaknesses of each method.

In-Person Interviews

In-person interviews with research participants have always been an especially popular method of data collection among social work researchers. They are likely to remain so. Interviews are essential to almost all qualitative research, but often perform a valuable function in quantitative studies as well. However, quantitative and qualitative research interviews differ in several important ways. Box 11.3 summarizes some of the most important ones.

Goal and Objective

Of course, the primary purpose of all social work research interviewing is to collect data about a human phenomenon. In quantitative research, we use the interview most often to attempt to accurately describe a behavior, attitude, belief, or knowledge level by measuring one or more variables that are indicators of them. We want to get accurate, factual information that will allow for the testing of research hypotheses.

In predominantly qualitative studies, we are likely to be attempting to learn more about, for example, how research participants experienced an event, how they perceived it at the time, and what it currently means to them.

Reason for Use

In quantitative studies, interviews are often not the primary method of data collection. They are often used to verify the accuracy of data acquired in some other way, such as through a mailed questionnaire. The interview may just be a follow-up to verify, explain, or elaborate on information provided by the primary data collection method. In quantitative research, interviews are also used to collect data that can only be obtained through

---

Box 11.3   In-Person Interviews in Quantitative and Qualitative Research

	Quantitative Studies	Qualitative Studies
Goal	Test hypotheses	Elicit perceptions, subjective meanings
Immediate objective	Accurate measurement	Insight, understanding
Reason for use	Verification, necessity	Method of choice
Relationship: participants	Detached, objective	Close, supportive, even therapeutic
Emotionality	Discouraged	Encouraged, supported
Structure	Highly structured	Unstructured, conversational, responsive
Discussion of sensitive issues	Avoided or delayed	Sought, encouraged early, supported

oral communication or a combination of oral communication and first-person observation. Characteristics of research participants sometimes suggest that research interviews are the best way to obtain data. For example, very young children, some older people, people with learning disabilities, or people with minimal or no literacy skills may all require the use of an in-person interview.

Aspects of specific cultures may also favor the use of the in-person interview. Because cooperation in interpersonal interactions is important in cultures that are more collectivistic, research participants from such cultures who adhere to these values may respond more favorably to in-person data collection approaches than to less personal data collection approaches, such as questionnaires or Internet surveys. In many Hispanic cultures, *personalismo* is valued, that is, time is taken for people to get to know one another and trust is established before information (especially that of a sensitive nature) is shared. The in-person interview is more conducive to this type of interaction and may increase rate of compliance with research protocols among people who hold this cultural perspective.

In qualitative research, interviewing is often the primary or even the only method of data collection. Through it (and the observations that accompany it), we hope to find out how people experienced a phenomenon or an event and learn its meaning or essence for them. The data that are provided are thus subjective. In addition, there is also a second layer of subjectivity present—our *interpretation* of its meaning. Consequently, since there is little pretense of objectivity, richness rather than factual information is sought, often through development of relationships of candor and trust with the participant. There is no pretense that our presence did not influence the data; it was unavoidable.

Relationship with Research Participants

In a research interview in a predominantly quantitative study, we would not seek to form a close or supportive relationship with research participants and may consciously try to avoid one. Thus, in a quantitative research interview, we would strive to not influence the responses of research participants by our choice of words, behaviors, facial expressions, and so forth. When a participant responds to questions, there is no indication provided in the form of either positive or negative reinforcement that would suggest that one response is preferable to another. Special attention is even paid to our dress, mode of communication, manner of presentation, and overall demeanor. We would work to eliminate personal characteristics that may offend, intimidate, or otherwise influence the responses of participants. Of course, we cannot alter certain personal characteristics, such as age, gender, or ethnicity. However, we would remain sensitive to them and attempt to determine how they may have influenced data collection.

In quantitative interviews, only necessary data are sought; any additional exchange of information is viewed as unnecessary and even undesirable. One common problem encountered is that requests for advice or other forms of assistance often occur, especially since the research participant would often know that we are a social worker. For example, it is difficult to collect factual data about participants' methods of child rearing without advice being sought at some point during the interview. To a quantitative researcher, promptly responding to such requests could compromise the role of "objective researcher"—it can affect the participant's subsequent responses. It can also disrupt the flow of data collection, making it difficult to get the interview back on track.

We may feel a professional obligation to provide assistance, if able, but probably would not do so during data collection. A reply that "I will be happy to talk about that with you after we complete our interview" is appropriate and is usually accepted by the participant. Naturally, such promises should be remembered and kept. Assistance may entail actually giving advice or, more commonly, making a referral to an appropriate organization or helping professional.

In contrast, in a qualitative research interview, the relationship with participants is likely to be close and even supportive, when needed. This represents no particular problem because, as previously noted, there are few pretenses to objectivity in data collection and therefore little concern that it might be compromised. Interpersonal exchanges, such as questions about our family or educational background or requests for assistance, are considered natural and expected. So we would usually respond to them when they occur. Providing requested help on the spot is viewed as both an ethical responsibility and desirable from a research perspective, since it will increase the likelihood that a participant will trust us and thus be more open and candid in the conversation that follows.

Attitudes Toward Emotionality

Emotionality by the participant in a predominantly quantitative interview represents a problem for the researcher. Even when measurements of attitudes and feelings are sought, emotional responses are assumed to provide unreliable indicators of them. Besides, emotionality in a quantitative research interview can seriously interfere with the collection of other needed data.

In contrast, in qualitative research, displays of emotion by participants are not uncommon. In fact, sometimes, we might encourage emotionality to help better understand how the participant is experiencing or has experienced an event and its current impact on him or her. They may be helpful in achieving the researcher's objectives.

Structure

In predominantly quantitative research interviews, major digressions by the participant are generally viewed as undesirable. We would exert fairly tight control over the flow of the interview because too long or too frequent digressions can interfere with the completion of data collection. Research interviews that run overtime can result in fatigue for participants or us and may threaten the quality of the data acquired. Unnecessarily long interviews can also cause other appointments to be missed or delayed and thus jeopardize interviews with other potential research participants.

Usually, qualitative research interviews tend to involve relatively little structure and control. Digressions by participants are expected and generally regarded as useful because they can lead into topics that may prove to be more productive than those that we might have introduced. Getting participants back on track is required only if it becomes apparent that they are avoiding topics that both need to be discussed and seem to be within their emotional tolerance for discussion.

Discussion of Sensitive Issues

Both quantitative and qualitative interviews may include discussion of behaviors or feelings of a personal or sensitive nature. Because this can provoke discomfort for participants, judicious placement of such content within the interview is important. In predominantly quantitative research, discussion of sensitive matters occurs only if necessary; that is, only if it relates to the research question and/or hypothesis. In such instances, it is usually planned for near the end of the interview. Placed too early, there is a risk of losing potential participants who may decide that they have had enough, terminating the interview before much data have been collected. But if placed near the end of the interview, there is sufficient time for debriefing and the interview to end on a less emotionally charged note.

In a qualitative research interview, sensitive content is often introduced and encouraged early in the interview. This allows plenty of time to explore it and to provide support, if needed.

Advantages

Besides the fact that they allow us to collect data from participants who might be unable to complete written data collection instruments, there are a number of other important advantages to collecting data using in-person interviews. As should be obvious from our previous discussion, they are generally more relevant to qualitative studies than to predominantly quantitative ones.

- **Opportunity to probe.** While talking with research participants, we are able to initiate clarification about their responses by making such comments as "I wonder if you could tell me more about that" or "What led you to that conclusion?" These comments provide participants with the opportunity to expand on responses more fully, thereby allowing us to acquire more in-depth, accurate data. It may thus be possible to understand and measure an individual's attitude about an issue and perhaps even determine the origins of that attitude. This type of insight is less likely to occur if a mailed data collection instrument or other method that does not allow for person-to-person interaction between us and the participant is used.
- **High completion rate.** In-person interviews usually permit us to acquire complete data. If participants agree to be interviewed, they will usually complete the interview.
- **Access to supplementary data.** We are able to observe participants while they are responding to questions. Nonverbal communications may provide important supplemental data. They can indicate the participant's ease in responding, evasiveness in answering questions, or how seriously the participant seems to be taking the interview. These can be carefully observed, recorded, and used as part of later data analysis.
- **Opportunity to individualize data collection.** Interviews can be individualized as needed to facilitate data collection or aid in obtaining complete data from participants. Of course, the more interviews differ, the more difficult it becomes to compare responses of participants.
- **Use of interviewing and relationship-building skills.** Interviewing is natural for those of us whose professional education prepares us to conduct interviews about a wide range of topics, including some very personal ones. We should also have learned how to build a variety of in-person relationships with clients and

client groups. This can be very useful, especially in qualitative research studies and, to a lesser degree, in more quantitative ones. Thus, in-person interviewing takes advantage of our strengths as social workers.

Disadvantages

If in-person interviews were the perfect data source, no other methods of data collection would be needed. But there are some major problems inherent in research interviews, especially in quantitative research. Although good preparation can minimize them, they cannot be totally eliminated.

- **Influence of the interviewer.** As we observed in discussion of other data collection methods, the fact that the researcher is present and posing questions directly to the participant may influence the responses of participants (reactivity). In some cases, participants may choose a response that they believe is the one we are seeking. This type of distortion in responses is known as an *expectancy effect*. Participants may also choose a socially desirable response rather than provide their true response, leading to erroneous conclusions by the interviewer. Qualitative researchers regard such influence as inevitable, but quantitative researchers generally try to minimize this type of influence.
- **Potential for recording errors.** The accuracy of data collected in an interview may also be negatively affected by the manner in which we record responses. Participants may provide truthful and accurate data, but if they are forgotten, distorted, misinterpreted, or recorded in error by us, data quality will still be low. Careful preparation for data collection, which addresses how data are to be gathered and recorded, can reduce the potential for recording errors. If interviewers other than ourselves are to be used, they will need to be carefully trained so that they have a thorough understanding of their expected role and demeanor and the overall design and purpose of the study. They should be given supervised practice in the use of any interview schedule that is to be used and the correct manner of recording data.

  Interviewer training can be expensive, but its cost is justified. If two or more interviewers are to be used, consistency in recording is enhanced if interviewers are trained together. They should be provided with the opportunity to ask any questions about the study that they may have. Interviewing simulations and role play can be part of the training package.

  When research participants will agree to it, audio- or video-recording of interviews can greatly reduce recording errors and is a common practice in qualitative research studies. The recordings can be reviewed later, as many times as necessary, until we are reasonably certain about what was said or what emotions were expressed. Others can also listen to or view the recordings (while respecting confidentiality) to verify or refute what was believed to have transpired. Recording of interviews is generally more feasible in qualitative studies than in quantitative ones, in which there may be more reluctance by research participants to allow it (less of a trust relationship) and researchers may have greater concern about how it might affect the truthfulness of responses.

- **Errors caused by demographic differences.** When interviewers and research participants are from different language, racial, cultural, or even socioeconomic groups, the possibility of inaccurate data may be increased due to either participants giving socially desirable responses or their unwillingness or fear of providing honest answers. This is especially likely to occur when the research topic touches on areas related to the nature of differences between investigator and participant (e.g., racial profiling or attitudes toward law enforcement). Under certain conditions, it may be preferable to match interviewers and participants by language, culture, and/or socioeconomic status. Use of same-ethnic data collectors can increase rapport and trust. Communication is also enhanced when bilingual interviewers are used for participants who are not native English speakers. Bilingual and bicultural interviewers are more likely to be aware of idiomatic variations among particular ethnic or nationality groups, as well as subtle differences in meaning for the same or similar words. They are also more likely to recognize and understand nonverbal forms of communication, which may be more critical than what participants actually say (Marin & Marin, 1991).

Butler (1992) cautions that simply matching interviewer and participant by race or ethnicity may be insufficient to guard against problems relating to demographics of the researcher and research participants. She notes, for example, that many African-American researchers are from the upper and middle classes and trained in mainstream educational settings, which may have removed them from the realities of African-Americans from lower socioeconomic groups.

Interviewing Protocol

Whenever in-person interviews are to be used for data collection, we would first contact potential participants and acquire their permission to be interviewed. Then the interview is conducted at a time and place mutually agreeable to both us and the participant.

Interviews can be conducted in a human service organization, a public place, or the participant's home. If participants are interviewed in their home, additional data can be collected and later analyzed. For example, observations can be made about the home environment and their interaction with significant others. These kinds of data can provide us with additional (in some cases, serendipitous) information which may help to explain the participant's other responses more fully.

There are other practices that can be used to ensure that data received through interviewing are as complete and usable as possible. They include the following:

- **Provide complete identification.** We should appropriately identify ourselves and remind the participant of the purpose of the study and their agreement to be interviewed. An appropriate introduction helps to confirm that the study is legitimate and thus helps to make the participant more willing to provide all requested data.
- **Promote pleasant interaction.** Respect and courtesy, of course, are appropriate in all research interviews. They are especially essential when interviews are conducted in the participant's home, where we are guests. Research participants often give much more than they receive in turn; our demeanor should reflect an appreciation of this fact.

- **Use data collection instruments.** Because quantitative research interviewing tends to be more structured than interviewing used in qualitative research, data collection instruments (sometimes referred to as *interview schedules*) are generally used. In interviews in which a high percentage of items are designed to be read to participants, the specific wording of an item and the sequence in which items are covered take on great importance. Any deviation from the wording or sequencing of items could influence the responses received and invalidate any comparisons made between research participants. In less structured research, such as many qualitative studies, a schedule serves only as a general outline of topics to be introduced; wording and sequencing of items are less critical.
- **Record unobtrusively.** The method of recording research data and observations will vary from one study to another. The interviewer may be required to circle the appropriate responses on a data collection instrument or record verbatim what the participant says. If data are recorded, it should be done as unobtrusively as possible in order to not disrupt the flow of the interview.
- **Specify the progress of the interview.** As the interview progresses, it is helpful to periodically let the participant know about what percentage of the interview remains to be completed. This may help participants avoid becoming frustrated about the time required, help them remain focused, and give them a more positive feeling about the interview process. We could say something like "Now we have reached the halfway point," "We have just two more questions to go," or "We're nearly through now."

Group Interviews

Another useful method for acquiring research data is the *group interview*. It can occur in person, in a conference call, or online and can be an efficient and economical way of collecting research data.

Focus Groups

A common form of in-person group data collection in social work research (and one that is especially well suited to the skills of social workers) is the *focus group*. Focus groups are more likely to be used in qualitative studies than quantitative ones. They are used to gain insights from clients, staff, and others who have formed opinions about certain experiences, problems, or social programs.

How does a focus group work? People who share a similar problem or have experienced a similar life experience may be invited to participate in a group discussion that we lead. For example, a focus group of openly gay teenagers could be formed to discuss how they experienced the attitudes of teachers and other high school students, or a group of Native American students might meet with a researcher to describe their perceptions of how they have been treated in a school in which students are predominantly white.

Focus groups are sometimes intentionally formed that consist of individuals who do not share the same experiences, beliefs, values, or demographic characteristics. For example, a researcher might lead a focus group of diverse people (ethnically, socioeconomically, educationally, and so forth) to assess the degree of support in a community for a proposed group home for people with developmental disabilities.

Focus groups are sometimes intentionally formed of individuals who do not share the same experiences, beliefs, values, or demographic characteristics.

It is believed that a focus group has certain advantages over one-on-one interviews. Particularly, if the experience is one that is difficult to talk about, the group can be a source of emotional support. Members are especially likely to be candid among others who have had similar experiences or have similar values or opinions. The group can also be a stimulus for individual participants in another way. Members may think about and respond to issues brought up by other members that they might not otherwise have considered.

Are there negatives associated with collecting data in a group of research participants? Yes. A major one is that the influence of the group can easily produce data of questionable validity. It is difficult to know when participants are speaking honestly about their own experiences and perceptions. In focus groups of members who are similar to each other, participants may be just joining in and revealing what they think the other group members expect them to offer. In diverse focus groups, they may just be so outraged by what others say that they may overreact and say things that may not be correct or reflective of their true opinions, or they may refuse to speak up at all. Because of the possibility of group influences on individuals, data collected in focus groups must be used cautiously.

The role of the leader (often called a facilitator) in a focus group is a little different from the role that the leader plays in other types of groups in which social workers participate (such as treatment groups). It is also different from the role we would play in either qualitative or quantitative one-on-one in-person interviews. Leading a focus group to collect research data entails providing some degree of structure and direction to the discussion to acquire the data that are sought. At the same time, we would not want to limit discussion excessively or lead it too much, thus missing out on unanticipated, valuable insights that participants might otherwise have provided. This requires a difficult balancing act.

Other Group Data Collection Methods

While focus groups are a common method of acquiring data in groups, they are not the only one. Other types of groups (e.g., social groups, committee meetings) are potential data sources as well, through interviewing, observation, or (most often) a combination of the two. Even treatment groups have this potential, but if they are to be used, additional ethical obstacles, such as the presence of dual relationships (Chapter 2), must be overcome.

Finally, not all group data collection involves interviewing. In studies that rely on standardized instruments or questionnaires for data collection, we may simply use a group setting for their completion. When it is logistically feasible to gather a number of research participants in one place (e.g., in a social agency or at a college or university), group administration can be a cost-efficient way to collect data. In addition, there is the advantage of our presence—if any questions or items are unclear, participants can receive clarification and the clarification is then provided to everyone else in the room.

Telephone Interviews

The telephone can sometimes still be used for collecting data, even though this type of data collection now seems to have more limitations than advantages. If the amount of data required is small and not too personal and if the research participants have some connection or positive association with us or a group that we represent, telephone calls can be an economical way (the primary advantage) to collect data from a large number of participants.

Two common examples of research that often use telephone interview surveys are client satisfaction surveys in human service organizations and alumni follow-up surveys in schools of social work. If an administrator is interested in determining to what degree a sample of clients is satisfied with services recently received, the phone can be used to contact former clients (at least those whose phone number in agency records remains current). Securing their responses to five or six questions can be performed quickly and inexpensively. Similarly, current students or faculty members can conduct a survey of a sample of a school's recent graduates to learn, for example, if they had difficulty in finding employment, what courses they found most useful in their practice, what curriculum changes they might recommend, and so forth. Notice that in both of these cases, the potential participants have an established relationship with the organization making the calls.

When should telephone interviews be conducted? Common sense and experience would suggest that it is a poor idea to call between 5:00 P.M. and, say, 7:00 P.M., when many people are returning from work or having dinner. Similarly, calling either late in the evening or very early in the morning is often resented by potential participants. Although these times are especially inconvenient for people to provide data over the phone, almost any time that we might call is likely to find potential participants doing something that they would prefer to do. Perhaps in earlier times, people enjoyed unanticipated phone calls, but few do today. Finding a time that is convenient is a difficult but important task in telephone interviewing. Therefore, it is prudent to schedule telephone interviews with participants in advance whenever possible.

Even if a phone call comes at an ideal time, any simple requests for information are now suspect. Recent years have witnessed a plethora of robo-calls, attempted scams from distant places, and other unsolicited calls. Telephone interviewers must overcome the annoyance and normal suspicions that people display when they receive a call, even from someone purporting to conduct legitimate research. We now would almost expect to hear "I don't have time for this!" or an obscenity, or just a hang-up, unless our credibility has been previously established.

Unfortunately, pseudo-research has been used as a device to make a sale, to gain support of a position on some political issue or, even worse, to collect personal information to be used by the researcher for some self-serving (or even illicit) purpose. Telephone requests for information, even from a known reputable source such as a university or social agency, now often meet with suspicion. Although virtually anyone can memorize a few questions to collect telephone data, overcoming resistance to providing information over the phone is the hardest part of telephone interviewing.

Most of the same principles that apply to in-person interviews apply to the telephone interview as well. However, because participants may be naturally suspicious of why they have been called and of the true purpose of the caller, when conducting

Diversity and Difference in Practice

Behavior: Apply and communicate understanding of the importance of diversity and difference in shaping life experiences in practice at the micro, mezzo, and macro levels.

Critical Thinking Question: If we were to complete a survey using telephone interviews between 10 A.M. and 2 P.M. on Mondays and Wednesdays during the month of February, what are two populations that might be over-represented? Two populations that might be underrepresented?

Telephone requests for information, even from a known reputable source such as a university or social agency, now often meet with suspicion.

telephone surveys we have an especially hard sell. We would need to quickly identify ourselves and tell what organization is supporting or endorsing our research. We should also ask permission to conduct the interview, even if it has been previously obtained through previous contact. If a participant indicates that the call has come at an inconvenient time, a request to reschedule the interview should be made.

A serious limitation of data gathered through telephone interviews is the difficulty of obtaining a sample of participants who are representative of the group being studied. Therefore, as we suggested earlier, the external validity of research that uses this type of data collection is often regarded as poor.

Any time of day when telephone interviews are conducted has the potential to interfere with sample representativeness because of response bias. For example, people employed outside the home tend to be unavailable during daytime hours. The representativeness of the sample can be hindered in other ways, too. An organization administrator might have access to all case records (containing phone numbers) to conduct a follow-up client satisfaction survey. But some former clients may have moved or had their phones disconnected or changed phone numbers and would thus be unavailable to be contacted. These people may disproportionately be the very people who are either doing very well and have moved out of state or are having the most problems and are most dissatisfied with their services. Similarly, an alumni follow-up survey might get the participation of only those alumni who are most satisfied with their education (and want to express their appreciation) and those who are most dissatisfied (and want to take the opportunity to vent about it). The alumni who are more neutral may have little interest in providing data. They are more likely to refuse to provide it and therefore will be underrepresented in the data collected.

Often, the researcher who lacks access to current agency or university records is even less fortunate. If numbers are chosen at random or selected randomly from a phone directory (and they are rapidly disappearing) a biased sample is almost certain to result. A telephone directory is not a good sampling frame from which to draw a research sample. It automatically excludes people who use only their cellular phones, do not have phones, or do not have listed numbers. In addition, the widespread use of voice mail has made it difficult to get through to many of those who have even listed home phone numbers. All of these factors can severely bias a sample in relation to age, occupation, gender, ethnicity, socioeconomic class, and other related variables that may be important to the research.

Despite the likelihood of response bias, telephone interviews continue to be used for research data collection. "Unlimited minutes" for long-distance calls have made them a more economical alternative than most other methods. When they are used, certain rules can be applied (e.g., asking the person in a household who most recently celebrated a birthday to provide data) to at least minimize sampling bias and even to calculate the true response rate (Risley-Curtiss, Holley, & Wolf, 2006).

ELECTRONIC COMMUNICATION

The widespread use of electronic communication (e-mail, voice-over IP, instant chats, online groups, and instant messaging) has made it a tempting alternative as a method for data collection. There is software available, such as Survey Monkey, that makes it relatively easy to create online surveys (after the survey itself is developed). After the online survey is created, a link is sent to the intended participants through their email accounts. Data can be collected quickly and at minimal cost. Many people (especially younger ones) rely heavily on the use of electronic communication and would rather communicate by e-mail or texting than by, for example, completing a written questionnaire on paper and mailing it back to the researcher.

Like the land telephone, electronic communication has a major problem relating to response bias and the external validity of findings. Some people still do not have regular access to a computer or cell phone, or if they do, they may not use e-mail or instant messaging. Differences in relation to gender, ethnicity, and age are not as pronounced as they once were, but they still exist. Thus, the likelihood of acquiring a representative sample in relation to such variables is likely to be reduced when using electronic communication as opposed to some other methods. Of course, as suggested earlier, some people's preference for communicating electronically may leave them disinclined to participate in research that requests data in any other way.

Because of obvious limitations, electronic communication is used most effectively as a method for data collection only when certain conditions exist:

1. A reasonably complete list of potential research participants is available, along with their e-mail addresses.

2. The majority of potential participants are likely to be people who regularly use electronic communication as their primary method of daily communication (such as students or young people).

3. Variables that are believed to relate to differences in ownership and usage are unlikely to be relevant to the research questions that are being examined.

4. The data sought are such that they lend themselves to a questionnaire format and are not personal (do not arouse suspicions about viruses or spoof mail).

5. The research is primarily quantitative.

Of course, electronic communication (like the other methods for acquiring data that were discussed in this chapter) can also be used in conjunction with other methods, as preliminary to one or more of them, or as a follow-up to them. For example, an e-mail or text message survey can be used to identify potential participants who have certain characteristics and are willing to participate in an in-person interview or to seek bits of data that may have not been previously collected for some reason during a prior interview.

SUMMARY

This chapter presented:

- Some of the most common ways that social work researchers acquire the research data that they hope will provide answers to their research questions and/or allow them to test their hypotheses. It should be obvious by now that some of these methods are more suited to some types of research design (e.g., quantitative or qualitative; exploratory, descriptive, or explanatory; and so forth) than others.

Box 11.4 Common Methods for Acquiring Research Data: Primary Advantages and Disadvantages

Source	Primary Advantage	Primary Limitation
Secondary data analysis	Cost	Validity issues
Oral histories	Access to firsthand observations	Subjectivity, bias
Client Logs	Access to firsthand information	Subjectivity, bias
Systematic observation	Less reliance on others	Distortion
Mailed surveys	Accessibility of participants	Low response rate, response bias
In-person interviews	High response rate, researcher presence	Cost, measurement bias
Group interviews	Efficiency, group support	Group pressure
Telephone interviews	Cost	Response bias, suspicion
Electronic communication	Cost	Response bias, suspicion

- The primary advantages and disadvantages of each method that make them better suited for a particular type of research are summarized in Box 11.4.
- Each option presented in this chapter should be viewed as a data source to be considered. Together, they form a kind of menu from which to select one or more. Each method can be used alone to acquire data or the methods can be used in combination.

MyEducationLab® for Research

Try the Topic 7 Assignments: Survey Research and the Topic 7 Study Plan.

Chapter 11 Chapter Review Quiz.

12

Data Collection Instruments

In Chapter 11, we discussed data collection methods. Sometimes we rely on secondary analysis of sources, such as crime records, census data, or social agency records. Other times we gather the data ourselves, using in-person or group interviews or surveys completed through either the mail, telephone, or via electronic communications such as Survey Monkey or Qualtrics. Systematic observation of people's behaviors is another unobtrusive way to gather data from our research participants. Other methods of measurement, called *indirect measurement*, require no direct contact between a researcher and research participants. For example, we might get permission to check public recycling bins to attempt to learn which electronic items are considered obsolete or not worth repairing, or count the number of people running red lights at a busy intersection as a measure of reckless driving.

Whether we take measurements directly or indirectly, we generally use some form of data collection instrument to record the measurements of variables and organize the data into a more or less standard format. As we shall see, data collection instruments vary widely in length, structure, and content. In this chapter, we will focus on the creation, selection, and use of data collection instruments.

As Box 12.1 suggests, data collection instruments usually consist of (1) individual items, each of which provides a measurement of a

---

Box 12.1 Components of Data Collection Instruments

1. One item; one variable
   A. Fixed-alternative items, simple indexes
   B. Open-ended items

2. Two or more items; one variable
   A. Composite indexes
   B. Scales* (e.g., Likert, semantic differential)

---
*A scale may contain subscales, each of which contains two or more items. Each subscale may measure a different variable or construct.

Whether we take measurements directly or indirectly, we generally use some form of data collection instrument to record the measurements of variables and organize the data into a more or less standard format.

single variable, (2) a group of items that together provide a measurement of a single variable, or (3) a combination of both of these. We will look at the least intricate of these—one item, one variable—first.

FIXED-ALTERNATIVE AND OPEN-ENDED ITEMS

When variables or constructs can be measured using a single item or question, the items may be classified as either fixed-alternative (also called *closed-ended*) or open-ended. A fixed-alternative or closed-ended item is an item that has a fixed number of choices from which the research participant can select. The open-ended item allows the respondent to answer in his or her own words. An example of a fixed-alternative item is:

> Please indicate your current legal marital status by circling the letter of one response below:
>
> a. Married
> b. Single, never married
> c. Separated
> d. Divorced
> e. Widowed
> f. Other

A slightly different form of a fixed-alternative item, a *simple composite index*, is sometimes used for collecting data that are a little less factual, that is, more of a subjective judgment on the part of the person providing the data. An example of a simple composite index is:

How would you rate your marriage overall? (Circle one number.)

Very Good		Good		Fair		Poor		Very Poor
1	2	3	4	5	6	7	8	9

The following is an example of an open-ended item:

In your own words, please briefly describe your experience with marriage and your current attitudes toward it.

_____

_____

_____

Fixed-alternative items are usually used when the range of responses to the item can be anticipated, that is, when we are quite sure what the variety and range of different responses will be. They are also used when we want the research participants to consider certain responses that they might otherwise fail to consider.

In contrast, open-ended items are used when the range of responses is likely to be great and we cannot possibly anticipate all of them, or when the research topic is one that has not been studied extensively and we simply do not know how the participants are likely to respond. We may also select an open-ended item format to avoid suggesting possible responses to research participants. Open-ended items also allow us to collect data in the form of direct quotations that can add richness to the data when describing participants' perceptions, attitudes, or opinions in our research report. Thus, they can be especially useful in qualitative research studies.

Sometimes, we might develop the first draft of a data collection instrument using an open-ended item. However, after pilot-testing the instrument (discussed later in this chapter) we observe that most responses to the item tend to fall within a small number of values or value categories. Then, a fixed-alternative item containing those responses would be substituted in the next (perhaps, the final) draft of the instrument. Conversely, a pilot-testing of a data collection instrument that contains a fixed-alternative item may produce a larger number and range of responses to the item than anticipated. Many of them may fall in the "other" value category that is frequently offered as an alternative response. Then we would probably decide to revise the instrument, substituting an open-ended item for the fixed-alternative item.

Open-ended items can provide a more in-depth understanding of attitudes or feelings than fixed-alternative items. They are especially useful in qualitative studies because we cannot anticipate what an individual participant's response might be. It may be different from those of any other participant. Open-ended items allow research participants to personalize their responses in a way that fixed-alternative items do not. However, especially when used in self-administered data collection instruments (discussed later in this chapter), this advantage may be offset by a number of potential disadvantages:

Assessment

Behavior: Apply knowledge of human behavior and the social environment, person-in-environment, and other multi-disciplinary theoretical frameworks in the analysis of assessment data from clients and constituencies.

Critical Thinking Questions: Write a fixed-alternative item and an open-ended question regarding attitudes toward people who are homeless.

- Participants are less likely to complete items that require them to develop and write their responses. Thus, the overall return rate may be lower.
- We cannot precode response categories for computer data entry as it is impossible to anticipate responses by participants.
- We may experience difficulty in analyzing data that reflect a wide variation and are not readily amenable to quantitative analysis. There are data analysis software programs for analyzing qualitative data, however. (See Chapter 13.)

COMPOSITE INDEXES AND SCALES

Although it is possible to measure a variable such as age, gender, or marital status by using a single fixed-alternative or open-ended item, there are many other variables that are not so easily measured. For example, many attitudes, beliefs, and behavioral patterns cannot be accurately measured by a response to a single fixed-alternative or open-ended item. They may be constructs that, by definition, possess multiple indicators such as clinical depression or anxiety. Or they may reflect an attitude or belief that individuals may not readily acknowledge through a response to a single direct item, such as attitudes toward recent immigrants or people with a disabling condition. More subtlety may be needed. In either case, to accurately measure the variable, multiple items may be required. The items are generally organized in a format referred to as a *composite index* or *scale*. In a composite index or scale, the response to each item makes a contribution to our understanding of the participant in relation to the variable that we are measuring. Ultimately, all the relevant responses viewed as a whole make it possible for us to assign a value or value category to represent the participant's measurement of the variable.

Composite indexes and scales (especially the latter) tend to be highly structured and refined. They can be used as independent data collection instruments or as a component of a larger instrument. Although composite indexes and scales both perform measurements of complex variables, they do so in different ways.

Composite Indexes

A composite index consists of a number of items that are believed to be important indicators of the construct being measured. In general terms, the more items that participants indicate as applying to them, the greater the quantity of the construct or variable they are presumed to possess. An example of a composite index to measure "clinical depression" might be the following:

> Place a check mark in front of each feeling that you have experienced during the past week:
>
> _____ Sadness
> _____ Hopelessness
> _____ Powerlessness
> _____ Just not caring
> _____ Wanting to be alone
> _____ Anxiety

A composite index requires a research participant to respond to each item in a dichotomous manner, often by simply checking or circling those items that apply (as in the preceding example) or by indicating "yes" or "no" for each. The number of check marks or "yes" answers then becomes the participant's measurement of the variable. The measurement thus produced is at best ordinal level data, since it is not assumed that all items are weighted equally. In other words, some of the items on the above list are stronger indicators of the construct "clinical depression" than others. Although measurements produced by composite indexes are sometimes adequate, often they are not. In many cases, we must turn to scales to get the measurements we need.

Scales

A scale is based on one or (less frequently) both of the following assumptions that are not true of composite index measurements:

- The degree or intensity of an indicator is an important factor. For example, the amount of agreement that a person feels with a statement or how frequently a behavior occurs should be a factor in the measurement of a variable or construct.

- Not all indicators of a variable or construct are equal in importance. Thus, they should not carry the same weight in the overall measurement of the variable.

Linear or Summated Scales

One common form of scale, known as a *linear* or *summated scale*, is similar to a composite index in that it allows us to derive a measurement of the variable for each participant by adding up the responses to individual scale items. Unlike the composite index, however, it considers the intensity or level of each of the indicators listed in the scale. It is, therefore, based on the first of the two assumptions listed above. An example of a linear or summated scale to measure clinical depression follows:

Indicate how often you experienced each of these symptoms during the past week by circling the appropriate number.

	Never				*Often*
1. Sad/down	0	1	2	3	4
2. Hopeless	0	1	2	3	4
3. Powerless	0	1	2	3	4
4. Apathetic	0	1	2	3	4
5. Withdrawn	0	1	2	3	4
6. Anxious	0	1	2	3	4

In this example, participants would be asked to circle a number for each item indicating the frequency of the feelings they have experienced during the past week. The numbers for each of their responses would then be totaled. Thus, the highest possible score would be 24 (a score of 4 on each item) and the lowest possible score would be 0 (a score of 0 on each item). On this type of scale, lower scores are operationalized to mean a lower level of the variable being measured (clinical depression) and relatively higher scores on the scale indicate a higher level of the variable.

Linear or summated scaling is popular among social science researchers. Many variables (especially constructs) that we are interested in studying can be scaled using this model. The best known type of a summated scale is the *Likert scale*. In a Likert scale, a number of items are listed and participants are asked to indicate their level of agreement with each item to indicate the intensity of their feelings toward that item. For example, the following Likert scale might be used to measure client satisfaction with worker services:

Indicate your level of agreement with each of the items listed below by circling the appropriate number: 1 = strongly disagree; 2 = somewhat disagree; 3 = undecided or neutral; 4 = somewhat agree; 5 = strongly agree

	Strongly Disagree				Strongly Agree
1. My worker seemed prepared for sessions.	1	2	3	4	5
2. My worker was considerate of my schedule.	1	2	3	4	5
3. My worker seemed preoccupied.	1	2	3	4	5
4. My worker acted professionally.	1	2	3	4	5
5. My worker did not care about me as a person.	1	2	3	4	5
6. My worker tried to understand me.	1	2	3	4	5
7. My worker really wanted to help me.	1	2	3	4	5

Likert scales generally contain a combination of items, some of which are worded positively and some that are called "reversal" items. *Positive items* are those where a higher level of agreement with the item reflects a high quantity of the variable being measured and a lower level of agreement with the item reflects a low quantity of the variable (such as items 1, 2, 4, 6, and 7 in the preceding example). *Reversal items* (such as items 3 and 5) are worded in such a way that a higher level of agreement with the item reflects a lower quantity of the variable being measured, and a lower level of agreement reflects a higher quantity of the variable. In scoring reversal items, we reverse the scores given by the respondent so that responses of "strongly agree" (usually scored as a 5) are scored as a 1, responses of "strongly disagree" (usually scored as a 1) are scored as a 5, and so forth. In the above example, if the participant responds with "strongly agree" to the item "My worker seemed preoccupied," less satisfaction is reflected rather than more. Therefore, an answer of 5 is converted to a 1 to reflect the least amount of satisfaction.

Why do we include reversal items in a scale? They are included primarily to determine whether the participant has answered honestly. When reversal items are included, an individual completing the scale is less likely to determine what is being measured, gauge about where they fall in relation to the variable, and simply circle the same number for all items. To further ensure honesty, we would not want simply to alternate positive and reversal items, a pattern that could soon be identified by the participant. A random mixture of positive and reversal items allows us to determine whether participants really read and carefully considered each item before responding to it. If they did, a relatively consistent pattern of responses (reflecting a higher or lower measurement of the variable) should be evident in both types of item.

In a Likert scale, all items contribute equally to the measurement of a variable. Although this characteristic makes scoring simple, it is also the scale's greatest weakness. Invariably, no matter how much time and effort has gone into the construction of a Likert scale, some items continue to reflect "more" of the variable than others or are a stronger indicator of it than other items. Yet this is not reflected in the scoring of the scale—the items are not weighted in any way. Thus, measurements are less precise than they might be. For this reason, Likert scales are generally considered to produce ordinal-level rather than interval-level data. Nevertheless, it is common in research reports and professional journal articles to see measurements produced by a Likert scale that are treated as if they were interval-level for purposes of statistical analysis. This is a practice that is often used but is really not necessary. There are plenty of good statistical tests available that can be used to examine the relationship between variables when the measurements of one or both variables are only ordinal level.

Semantic Differential Scales

Some variables of interest require an indirect, more subtle type of measurement. To simply come out and ask straightforward questions (e.g., "How homophobic are you?" or "Do you consider yourself racist?") might produce only politically correct or socially desirable responses, not a true measurement. In these cases, a semantic differential scale might be appropriate. A scale of this type is characterized by the following:

- It is used to measure variables when direct questions might not produce honest answers.
- It provides a subtle, indirect measurement of the variable.
- It is "projective" and often seeks to measure unconscious feelings or attitudes.
- Respondents are instructed to respond quickly and not think too long or look for the "right" answer.

A semantic differential scale provides a list of word opposites (e.g., slow / fast, simple / complicated, old / new, and so forth). They may seem to have only a vague or indirect relevance to the construct being measured. The words may be placed on opposite ends of equal-length lines or a row of numbers may be placed between the pair of words. In the first instance, the research participant is instructed to place an X on each line to indicate his or her response in relation to the construct being measured. In the second instance, the respondent is asked to circle one number for each pair of words to indicate his or her feeling or attitude toward the words in relation to the construct. The numbers are then added up to determine the respondent's score, using reverse scoring where appropriate.

A semantic differential scale is a kind of word association game. The assumption underlying it is that, in completing it, the participant will unintentionally reveal something about himself or herself in their responses to the pairs of word opposites—often his or her true attitudes. For example, suppose that our research required us to measure two variables, attitudes toward corporal punishment and attitudes about old age among social work students. To be successful, we would have to avoid responses that reflect the attitudes that the participants think they, as social workers, *should* have. We might use two semantic differential scales that look something like these:

Attitudes about Corporal Punishment:

Good	1 2 3 4 5 6 7 8 9	Evil
Pleasant	1 2 3 4 5 6 7 8 9	Unpleasant
Sour	1 2 3 4 5 6 7 8 9	Sweet
Happy	1 2 3 4 5 6 7 8 9	Sad
Healthy	1 2 3 4 5 6 7 8 9	Sick
Love	1 2 3 4 5 6 7 8 9	Hate
Fair	1 2 3 4 5 6 7 8 9	Unfair

Attitudes about Old Age:

Pleasant	1 2 3 4 5 6 7 8 9	Unpleasant
Sour	1 2 3 4 5 6 7 8 9	Sweet
Happy	1 2 3 4 5 6 7 8 9	Sad
Healthy	1 2 3 4 5 6 7 8 9	Sick
Love	1 2 3 4 5 6 7 8 9	Hate
Fair	1 2 3 4 5 6 7 8 9	Unfair

Like composite indexes and Likert scales, semantic differential scales do not provide very precise measurements. Thus, they produce what is generally regarded as ordinal level data. Not surprisingly, semantic differential scales are most often designed by psychologists. After all, they are just a variation of the projective testing methods clinical psychologists often use for diagnostic purposes. Of course, psychologists are not the only professionals to use various forms of composite indexes and scales in their professional practice. Social workers are likely to encounter different forms of them, especially in clinical work with individuals, families, or groups. They are used for diagnostic purposes with clients, treatment planning, and even to evaluate how effective we are in our interventions. We described one type of semantic differential scale that can be used to evaluate our own practice, goal attainment scaling (GAS), in Chapter 8.

We have included examples of the scales that we as social workers are most likely to develop or encounter in conducting research. The reader will note that they all meet the first assumption mentioned earlier in this chapter (the degree or intensity of an indicator is an important factor in measurement of a variable). However, they do not address the second assumption (not all indicators of a variable or construct are equal in importance), since each item is given equal weighting in all of these types of scales in the measurement of a variable. That is why we have said that they produce no more than ordinal level measurement. Do any scales address both assumptions? Yes. For example, Guttman (e.g., Keller & Wagner-Steh, 2005; Lindemann & Brigham, 2003; Tractenberg, Yumoto, Aisen, Kaye, & Mislevy, 2012) and Thurstone (e.g., Krabbe, 2008; Shafer, 2001) scales do. Through a long and tedious process, these types of scales assign various weights to each indicator included in the calculation of the measurement of a variable. We have not included a discussion of them here because social workers are generally not involved in their construction, which can take years. However, in those rare instances when we encounter one of these scales that meets the measurement needs of our research study, they can be most useful.

USING EXISTING DATA COLLECTION INSTRUMENTS

The generic term, *data collection instruments*, is used to describe documents (paper and pencil, electronic, or in other formats) used to assist a researcher in acquiring necessary data and recording them. As we noted at the beginning of this chapter, data collection instruments vary widely in length, structure, and content. In many qualitative exploratory studies, instruments may consist of only a group of topics or a list of questions to be covered in an unstructured interview in no particular order. At the other extreme, perhaps in a quantitative study designed to discover if there is support for several research hypotheses, a long, carefully worded data collection instrument or group of instruments may be used. They are likely to contain a mixture of fixed-alternative items, open-ended items, and/or composite indices and scales.

When we discussed data collection methods in the previous chapter, we suggested that secondary analysis of data that were collected for some other purpose (such as oral histories) can be a real time- and effort-saver when trying to answer some current research questions. Similarly, if it is possible to use a data measurement instrument or even part of one that was developed by another researcher, a great deal of time and effort can be saved. The process of developing new instruments often represents a major research project in and of itself. Thus, where appropriate, we should always first consider using instruments or portions of instruments that have already been developed.

Another major advantage of using existing data collection instruments is that their validity and reliability may have been assessed and reported in previous research studies. In addition, *norms* (the range and distribution of scores that can be expected for members of specific populations) and *cutting scores* (the score that separates two levels of a condition, such as having or not having a certain condition) may have been identified for the instrument. When data collection instruments possess established validity and reliability (and frequently norms and cutting scores), they are called *standardized questionnaires*. Some standardized questionnaires are designed to be self-reports and are completed by the research participants; others are completed by the researcher. Many of these instruments are in the public domain.

In determining if an existing measurement instrument would be appropriate to use in a given research study, a number of issues need to be examined. First, we need to determine if the instrument can appropriately be used with the population of interest. Is it likely to provide reliable measurement with <u>our</u> participants? Measures are developed for specific uses with specific research populations. Are our proposed research participants similar enough to the participants on whom the instrument was developed and tested that the instrument will yield reliable data? Cultural differences, especially the meaning of words within and across cultures or within different ethnic groups, should be given special attention.

> *Another major advantage of using existing data collection instruments is that their validity and reliability may have been assessed and reported in previous research studies.*

The question of validity requires a comparison of conceptual definitions. Before using an instrument developed as part of another study, we would want to be sure that what the instrument purports to measure is the variable that we need to measure. To use an existing measure, we would have to (1) find one that was developed using the same (or similar) conceptual definition of the variable we are interested in or (2) adapt our conceptual definition to the definition that was used in the development of the existing instrument. For example, if we are planning to measure parenting skills we could try to find a measurement instrument that was developed using a conceptual definition of parenting skills that is the same as the conceptual definition suggested by our review of the literature. If this proves to be impossible, it may still be possible to find another instrument that seems to measure most aspects of parenting skills of interest to us, and then conceptually redefine the variable in our study to be consistent with the conceptual definition of parenting skills used by the developer of the instrument. Fortunately, reference material regarding specific measures often includes the conceptual definition of the variable that was used by the author of the instrument. Information about the instrument may also include how to contact the author of the measure and how to obtain a copy of

Box 12.2   References for Scales, Tests, and Other Types of Measurement Instruments

Carlson, J. F., Geisinger, K. F., & Johnson, J. S. (Eds). (2014). *The nineteenth mental measurement yearbook*. Lincoln, NE: Buros Center for Testing.

Fischer, J., & Corcoran, K. (2013). *Measures for clinical practice and research: A sourcebook* (5th ed., 2 Vol set.). New York: Oxford University Press.

Fisher, T. D., Davis, C. M., Yarber, W. E. and Davis, S. L. (Eds). (2011). Handbook of sexuality-related measures. (3rd ed.). New York: Routledge.

Hudson, W. W. (1982). *The clinical measurement package*. Homewood, IL: The Dorsey Press.

Miller, D. C., & Salkind, N. J. (2002). *Handbook of research design and social measurement* (6th ed.). Newbury Park, CA: Sage Publications.

Rauch, J. B. (1994). *Assessment: A sourcebook for social work practice*. Milwaukee: Families International Incorporated.

Touliatos, J., Perlmutter, B. F., & Straus, M. A. (2001). *Handbook of family measurement techniques* (3 volume set). Newbury Park, CA: Sage Publications.

the instrument. If the instrument is copyrighted (most composite indexes and scales are), it may have to be purchased from the publisher or directly from the author. If it is not copyrighted, it can usually be used with the author's written permission. Of course, if the instrument is in the public domain, it may be used without permission of the author.

There are many data collection instruments available for use by social work researchers. Box 12.2 lists some reference volumes that contain and/or describe scales and other data collection instruments that might be appropriate for use in social work research. A specific type of standardized instrument, called a *rapid assessment instrument* (*RAI*), is particularly useful for evaluation of social work practice. RAIs are instruments that can be completed and scored quickly and easily and are designed so that they can be completed multiple times, making them applicable for single-system research designs (Chapter 8).

REVISING EXISTING DATA COLLECTION INSTRUMENTS

If we are unable to locate an existing measure that is appropriate for use without revision, we may still be able to find an existing instrument that could be modified

Research-informed Practice or Practice-informed Research

Behavior: Use and translate research evidence to inform and improve practice, policy, and service delivery.

Critical Thinking Behavior: Complete and score a Rapid Assessment Inventory and determine if the score is above or below the available cutting score.

and used. For example, an instrument may be available that measures client satisfaction with services received from an out-patient mental health clinic. If we are interested in measuring client satisfaction with services received within an in-patient mental health setting, the existing instrument may possibly be modified for use. Several items may be borrowed from the instrument exactly as written and others reworded for use in our study. The revised instrument should then be pilot-tested with a sample of participants who are similar to the intended study group to see if measurement problems have been introduced by the revision.

If the research study is exploratory or if the instrument is to be used only as a guideline for the researcher (e.g., in a qualitative study in which data collection is conducted using unstructured interviews), modifications of existing instruments can be made with little concern about the effects of the changes. When these data collection methods are used, parts of different instruments may be freely borrowed and changed as deemed appropriate. There is little reason to be concerned about how a change in wording might affect the validity of measurement. Instead, an assessment of the quality of measurement is often based on the researcher's judgment of the degree of candor and truthfulness that participants seemed to display in response to its use.

In predominantly quantitative studies, which rely heavily on accurate measurement of variables to test hypotheses, rewording of existing instruments or changing them in any way should be undertaken with extreme caution. When using revised instruments, advice regarding the possible effects of the modifications of individual items on the quality of the measurement can sometimes be obtained by contacting the author of the original instrument. If large sections of a data collection instrument are borrowed from an existing instrument (especially if it is copyrighted), we must gain permission to use the instrument from the author or publisher. If only a few items are used, and if the original wording is substantially altered, permission is usually not necessary.

When borrowing items from an existing instrument, we should remember that assessments of its reliability and validity were based on the instrument as a whole. Thus, it would not be correct to alter items and assume that the reliability and validity assessments would be accurate for the revised instrument as well. Composite indexes and scales are especially sensitive to revision. If any items are changed, added, or deleted, previous assessments of reliability or validity for the original instrument may no longer be accurate and should not be claimed in reference to the revised instrument.

CONSTRUCTING NEW DATA COLLECTION INSTRUMENTS

If it is not possible to use an existing data collection instrument, a new instrument will have to be developed. In those predominantly qualitative studies that rely on a data collection instrument to ensure only that certain topics will be addressed, but do not seek to standardize data collection methods, it is often simplest to create a new instrument from scratch rather than to try to revise an existing one that is likely to have been developed to study some other question with some other group of research participants. The process of developing such an instrument may be relatively simple. It may consist primarily of thinking through and discussing with others what areas should be explored within the context of an in-person interview, focus group, etc., as well as, perhaps, the best sequence in which to explore them.

In predominantly quantitative studies, which rely more on careful, standardized measurement of variables, construction of a new data collection instrument is an exacting and demanding task (Nunnaly & Bernstein, 1994). Whichever formats and methods are selected, the task requires careful attention if we are to have reliable and valid measurements.

Scales are generally developed by researchers following rigorous rules and procedures. Many scales have been developed, tested, and repeatedly revised and honed over decades. Up to this point, we have described only some of the general methods employed in constructing the various types of scales mentioned in this chapter. However, scale building is an exact science. It is the focus of graduate courses in statistics and measurement. Only rarely would a social worker attempt to construct a new scale as part of a research study. But to gain an appreciation of the effort that goes into their construction, we will mention briefly the usual sequence of events in constructing a scale.

1. **The variable to be measured is operationally defined.** The definition should refer to all relevant indicators of the variable. A clear definition enables us to write an *item pool*, a preliminary set of items (ideally 80–100) that may be included in the scale. The item pool should be as exhaustive as possible so that less relevant items can later be eliminated while leaving enough items to constitute the scale. The items are then reviewed by people believed to have expertise in measurement of the construct or variable. Their role is to evaluate the items for clarity, relevance, appropriateness, and ease in responding. The items are then revised as needed. A draft instrument is produced, and a pilot test of the instrument is conducted. Pilot-test participants are asked to respond to the items and provide a critique of them. They are encouraged to make comments about the items themselves, for example, which items are not clear, which contain words they do not understand, and so on.

2. **Data from the pilot test are analyzed.** This is accomplished using statistical analyses known as *item analyses*. The process typically involves the calculation of two statistics by computer: item-to-total-scale correlations (for each item) and a reliability coefficient that provides a measure of the internal reliability of the scale (such as coefficient alpha, described in Chapter 10). They are calculated to ensure that all of the items that are to comprise the scale are measuring the same construct and that the items, when taken together, represent the unidimensional measure that is sought.

    The item-to-total-scale analysis determines how responses to each item correlate with how participants responded overall to the scale. (It is similar to the item analysis that professors sometimes use on multiple-choice or true/false tests to eliminate bad test items—those that were missed by students who did well on the test overall and/or were answered correctly by students who did poorly.) We would want to retain only items with the highest positive item to total correlations. Items with low or negative item to total correlations are usually deleted. The analysis required for item to total correlations is conducted using statistical software packages, specifically designed for social science data that assist us in deciding which items to keep and which ones to delete.

    Coefficient alpha, we recall, reflects the degree to which responses to individual items correlate with each other. Scales that are designed to measure a unidimensional construct should reflect a high degree of internal consistency. Scales that are multidimensional (including multiple subscales) in nature (e.g., the Minnesota Multiphasic Personality Inventory [MMPI]) would not be expected to have a high degree of internal consistency overall, but each of their various subscales would be expected to have high internal consistency.

3. **The scale is modified as needed.** Items are deleted or revised, often as a result of a statistical procedure known as factor analysis. If items are added at this stage, they should be subjected to additional pilot-testing and further statistical analysis. Once the scale is fully developed, data about its individual items and the scale's reliability and validity are retained for reporting and for future analysis.

When a scale (or at least a portion of it) is published in a book of data collection instruments or a professional journal, the process of its development is described along with a description of the people who contributed data for its development. Conclusions about the scale's reliability and validity (based on statistical analyses) as well as its limitations are noted. For example, we might read that "The scale was found to have a test-retest reliability of 0.89 among a sample of Latin Americans under age 65 who reside in the United States and Canada for whom Spanish is a first language. However, its reliability among other Spanish-speaking people was only 0.45."

Issues in Development

There are many issues that should be considered in developing a new data collection instrument. They relate to its intent, formatting, and sequencing of questions, as well as to its length, clarity, wording, and presentation. Although these issues are most relevant to participant-completed instruments, most of them are equally relevant to data collection in which participant responses are recorded by the researcher.

There are many issues that should be considered in developing a new data collection instrument. They relate to its intent, formatting, and sequencing of questions, as well as to its length, clarity, wording, and presentation.

Intent of Items

One issue relates to the nature of what is being measured: Is an item or series of items designed to measure (1) knowledge, (2) attitudes or beliefs, or (3) behaviors of participants? The intent of the measurement determines the way in which a question or series of items is worded. Often, when measuring complicated constructs, we require a composite index or a scale consisting of several items. However, it is sometimes possible to measure even knowledge, attitudes, beliefs, or behaviors using one question:

- Can a friend call the hospital to learn your room number so that he or she can visit you (knowledge)?

  _____ Yes _____ No

- How helpful was your social worker during your hospitalization (attitude or belief)?

  _____ *Very helpful*
  _____ *Somewhat helpful*
  _____ *Not helpful*

- During your hospitalization, how many times did you meet with your social worker (behavior)?

  _____ Never _____ Once or twice _____ Three times or more

Of course, for reasons discussed earlier in this chapter, it is sometimes preferable to use an open-ended question to measure knowledge, attitudes or beliefs, or behaviors. Then the items might look more like this:

- Please describe your understanding of the HIPAA laws and how they affect visitors to the hospital (knowledge).
- Do you think that your social worker was helpful to you during your hospitalization? Why or why not (attitude or belief)?
- What were some of the questions that you asked your social worker (behavior)?

Clarity of Items

If items are not clearly understood by participants, their responses may not provide an accurate measurement of a variable. The best items are generally those that ask participants for a simple response, are unambiguous, and are phrased positively rather than negatively. People do not always notice a qualifying word in a question (e.g., words such as *hardly, never, not,* or *barely*); therefore, it is best to avoid them.

Use of Contingency Instructions

When using self-administered data collection instruments, contingency instructions are sometimes appropriate. They are used to direct the participant through the instrument in an efficient manner (or, if it is administered by an interviewer, to assist him or her). They also provide a way to reduce the number of items that participants are asked to respond to and to avoid asking participants to answer items that are not applicable to them. They reflect consideration on the part of the researcher and help to organize the data that are collected. An example of a contingency instruction follows:

If you answered "yes" to question 2 above, please respond to questions 3 through 7; if you answered "no" to question 2, please skip down to question 8 on page 3.

Sequencing of Items

In developing new instruments, there are two perspectives on the sequencing of items. Some researchers prefer general-to-specific sequencing—begin with the most general (and least controversial or personal) items and then move to the more specific ones. Placing demographic and/or less threatening items first may help to gain the trust and confidence of the participant. Of course, we would need to have some understanding of the participants beforehand, and have an idea what items might be perceived as personal or most threatening to them. Then, the more personal or more threatening items can be placed near the end of the instrument.

If we are not concerned that some items in the instrument might be threatening to or might otherwise alienate participants, the specific-to-general sequence may be preferable. Then, the most important and the most specific (to the study) items are placed first. The more general data (often, demographic information) can be secured at the end. An advantage of this sequencing pattern is that if the instrument is not fully completed, some of the most important data will still be available to the researcher.

Instructions for Responding

In securing useful data, especially if the instrument is to be self-administered, the wording of instructions is equally as important as the wording of the items themselves.

Participants must understand how they are expected to respond to items. This seems self-evident; however, researchers frequently assume that the correct method to respond to items is as obvious to the participant as it is to them. Consequently, they fail to provide complete instructions for responding. If there are two or more distinct sections and/or question types used, separate instructions should be included directly above each section or question type. For example, if the respondent is supposed to mark on a clinical depression scale what feelings he or she has experienced, such as helplessness and sadness, it is important to specify the time period to be considered. On a composite scale, we might include the instruction, "Place a mark in front of each of the following feelings you have experience during the past week."

Length of the Instrument

Length is perhaps best addressed through use of common sense. As we suggested in the previous chapter, the longer the instrument, the less likely people are to complete it. However, it is also true that longer instruments, particularly scales, tend to be more reliable than shorter instruments. We need to collect enough data to be able to answer our research questions and/or test our hypotheses. Necessary items must be included, but unnecessary ones should be omitted. Frequently, the length of an instrument can be reduced through the elimination of demographic items that are not relevant to the focus of the research. As we have stated previously, there is no such thing as a "usual" or standard group of demographic variables that must be included within every study. The collection of demographic data should always be consistent with the purpose of the study and the specific research questions being addressed.

Presentation

A self-administered data collection instrument should not appear crowded. Leaving adequate space for participants to respond to items and not crowding questions helps them to complete it. In addition, instruments should be free of errors in spelling, grammar, sentence structure, paragraphing, etc. The goal is to make their completion a pleasant (or at least a non-stressful) experience, so that a high percentage of fully completed responses will be received.

The Importance of Pilot-Testing

Even though we may think that all of the preceding issues have been addressed, newly developed data collection instruments almost always produce some surprises. Even experienced researchers are not able to anticipate just how items on a data collection instrument will be perceived or interpreted by the participant or how a participant might respond overall to the instrument. A "panel of experts," perhaps consisting of people knowledgeable about instrument construction and/or those very familiar with the culture of potential research participants, can provide good advice and suggestions. But what these individuals can contribute may be no substitute for the feedback provided by people similar to the research participants themselves. A pilot-testing of an instrument provides information on many factors that relate to the quality of a data collection instrument. Feedback is likely to provide insights about the following:

- Clarity/misinterpretation of wording of items
- Errors in grammar and spelling

- Juxtaposition of items that may bias measurement
- Potential offensiveness of items
- Redundancy that may annoy participants
- Indication that more structure (such as subheadings) is needed
- Indication that less structure is needed
- Time required to complete the instrument

Some of the preceding feedback areas can be gleaned from the way that the pilot-study participants complete the instrument. Some of it may require one or more additional broad questions that are not a part of the measurement instrument per se. For example, we might add a concluding question, such as "What parts of the instrument were difficult for you to complete and why?" Another good question would be, "Do you feel that the instrument gave you an opportunity to represent yourself or your experiences accurately and, if not, why not?" Such questions reflect an awareness of the possibility that the newly developed instrument may somehow lead participants to answer in certain unanticipated ways, or that questions or items that should have been included as part of the instrument may have been inadvertently omitted. A good pilot test and the thoughtful revisions that it generates can result in fewer problems and better measurement when data are subsequently collected from research participants.

There is an ethical issue that often comes up when using people as participants in the pilot-testing of a data collection instrument. If no concluding questions about the instrument are added to it (that is usually a "giveaway"), participants might not be aware that they are not "real participants" unless they are told so by the researchers. Should they be told the true reason why they are being asked to complete the data collection instrument, or should we allow them to misunderstand their role? Not to tell them seems dishonest and deceptive, but to tell them may influence the seriousness with which they approach the task. In many instances, the pilot test includes giving participants the same introduction or cover letter that will be given to other participants, to see how effective it is. Such an introduction is almost certain to mislead them about why they were selected to complete the instrument. If no changes are made to the instrument on the basis of the pilot test, the data that pilot study participants provide can be aggregated along with that of other participants, thus avoiding the issue. But in other situations, when changes are made to the instrument based on the findings of the pilot study, the data given by the participants in the pilot study will not be included in the actual study. We must decide the most ethical way to approach the issue. It may entail telling participants in general terms what their role is, stressing the importance of their unique contribution to the research effort, and asking them if they still wish to participate.

USE OF SELF-ADMINISTERED DATA COLLECTION INSTRUMENTS

Many of the issues we have discussed relate most directly to data collection instruments that are self-administered, that is, they are completed without the presence of the researcher. Self-administered data collection instruments are commonly associated with surveys in which we are interested in aggregating data about the characteristics, behaviors, feelings, attitudes, or opinions of a given population.

Other types of knowledge building (besides surveys) also use self-administered instruments. Many composite indices and scales are completed by the participant without the guidance of the researcher. Social work practitioners might also use self-administered instruments to secure a measurement of an aspect of client functioning in their practice. For example, a clinician may wish to get an objective measure of the level of grief that clients are experiencing following the recent death of a family member, and may either find or develop a data collection instrument that clients can complete without any in-person instructions or supervision.

Ethical and Professional Behavior

Behavior: Make ethical decisions by applying the standards of the NASW Code of Ethics, relevant laws and regulations, models for ethical decision-making, ethical conduct of research, and additional codes of ethics as appropriate to context.

Critical Thinking Question: Do you think participants who are really just pilot-testing an instrument should be told that they are not actually participating in the research study? Why or why not?

Advantages

Because they are highly structured, self-administered instruments have several advantages:

- **Presence of the researcher is not required.** Once the instruments have been developed and distributed, we are free to work on other research tasks while awaiting their return.
- **Responses and response categories can be precoded.** Analysis of the data is greatly facilitated when we collect data that are pre-sorted into data entry codes.
- **Data can be collected using fixed stimuli.** All participants are asked to respond to the same questions, worded in the same way. Thus, at least one aspect of data collection is standardized. This is especially important in quantitative studies.
- **There is the perception of anonymity.** Even though instruments may be numbered with identifying information kept on file, generally participants do not write their names anywhere on the instrument. The appearance of anonymity (if not the reality of it) is thus maintained. This may increase participants' willingness to provide honest data. Most researchers that use self-administered instruments for data collection report data in aggregate form, enhancing confidentiality of responses. When the participants are informed of this, they can be confident that their individual responses cannot be attributed to them. This is an advantage to us, both for securing truthful information and by increasing the likelihood of a larger percentage of completed questionnaires.

Supervised Administration

A major reason for supervising data collection either individually or in a group situation is to secure a high rate of completion. If we are present and distribute and collect the data collection instrument from participants, more fully completed instruments will be received than if the instruments were mailed out, thus yielding a higher return rate. There are other reasons we might wish to be present during data collection, for example, to clarify the meaning of items, or to observe whether the instruments were completed conscientiously or in a haphazard way. This latter determination would be impossible if a mailed questionnaire were used.

Supervised individual completion of instruments (perhaps in the research participant's home, office, or a neutral site—whatever is most appropriate) can produce a high completion rate. But if comparisons of participants and their responses or hypothesis testing is part of the research design (as in most quantitative research), too much individualized data collection arrangements may not be desirable. It can introduce potentially confounding variables. Thus, whenever possible, the same setting should be used for data collection with all research participants.

A useful alternative to the one-on-one, supervised method of data collection is instrument completion in a group setting. For example, we might supervise the completion of an instrument by all members of a focus group or by all participants in a social program. Or a group meeting consisting of the research participants might be constituted specifically for the purpose of data collection. When group supervision of data collection is used, instruments are distributed, participants complete them at their own pace or within a prescribed time limit, and they are collected. We are then available for clarification and to address questions related to the data collection instrument.

The major benefit of this kind of administration is efficiency—a large amount of data can be collected in a relatively short amount of time. Its relatively low cost and high rate of return are advantages that we should consider when selecting a data-gathering method. However, like individually supervised completion of data collection instruments, our presence can have the potential to influence the data received. In addition, responses may be influenced by the reactions (e.g., anger, embarrassment, boredom) of others in the room.

SUMMARY

In this chapter, we

- looked at data collection instruments as tools for use in data collection. Some variables and constructs can be measured with a single item or question, using either a fixed-alternative or an open-ended item, depending on the specific data needs of the researcher.
- discussed the use of other instruments that require many items to measure complex variables: composite indexes and scales. An overview of some of the most common types of scales was presented.
- described the construction of scales as a highly complex process; it generally is beyond the scope of a social work research study. The pros and cons of using existing data collection instruments or modifying existing instruments were discussed. We examined many of the issues that are of concern when constructing new instruments.
- discussed the option of individual or group-supervised completion of data collection instruments (as opposed to self-administered ones). Group administration is more cost efficient than individual supervised data collection, but when using either method, the researcher's presence can have the effect of biasing data that are collected.

MyEducationLab® for Research

Try the Topic 6 Assignments: Selecting Measuring Instruments and the Topic 6 Study Plan.

Chapter 12 Chapter Review Quiz.

Analyzing Data

Data can take many forms. In predominantly qualitative studies, they may take the form of audio or video recording of interviews, field notes of interaction with participants, or pictures of individuals engaged in particular activities. In secondary analysis, they consist of completed data collection schedules compiled from case records or census data. In meta-analysis, they may be the reports of many studies that examined a similar problem or question. When a mailed survey method of data collection is used, they may consist of a stack or file of completed questionnaires. In a quantitative explanatory study, they may be pretest and posttest scores of a scale measuring some problem or experience.

No matter what form data assume, they must be organized, summarized, and analyzed, often with the help of statistical analysis software packages. Generally, we associate statistical analysis of data with quantitative research methods; however, methods for statistical analysis of qualitative findings have also been developed. A number of computer software packages are now available to assist researchers in the tasks of classifying, ordering, and analyzing both quantitative and qualitative data.

THE DATA IN PERSPECTIVE

In order to begin to make sense of the data collected, it helps to first understand the source of the data by asking certain questions. The answers to these questions help us put research findings in perspective. For example, if original data were collected from research participants,

- Who were the participants?
- Under what conditions did they provide data?
- What assurances about anonymity or confidentiality were given?
- What understanding did they have about how data would be used?
- What prior relationship, if any, did they have with the researcher?
- As a research sample, do they appear to be representative of the sampling frame or accessible population from which they were drawn?

- Was the sample biased in some way?
- How might any possible bias affect the quality of the data?
- Given the size of the sample, how much might sampling error have affected the quality of the data?

When appropriate, a good place to start is to calculate the percentage of completed responses, also called the *response rate*. This is done by dividing the actual number of cases for which there are reasonably complete data by the total number of cases that we sought to include in the sample. A high percentage of completed responses are more likely to produce a representative sample than a low response rate, but certainly does not guarantee representativeness. Participants who do not provide the data requested (and could account for a low response rate) may include:

- People who agree to participate in an intervention, but drop out during the course of the study and do not complete the posttest.
- People who agree to participate in a control group, complete the pretest, but fail to return to complete the posttest.
- People who agree to complete a survey or who simply receive the survey in the mail or via email, but do not return the completed survey, or return it without completing it correctly.
- People who agree to participate in a longitudinal study using telephone interview, but after the first interview, the phone number is no longer a working number.

There are many ways during a research study that participants fail to provide the necessary data to be included in the data analysis. It is important, particularly if the response rate is low, to try to identify patterns of response and non-response that may suggest the presence of response bias. Certain questions can be helpful in this regard, for example:

- Among the potential cases within the sample, which ones contain complete data and which do not?
- Do they differ in any meaningful way?
- If so, should this be reported and discussed, or is the difference one that is probably unrelated to any research findings?

Most researchers summarize the most relevant characteristics of their data sources in a separate section of their reports. The summary helps both researchers and the readers of their reports to estimate whether their data sources were representative of the accessible population or sampling frame from which they were drawn. A description of the sample is presented in group form as a broad demographic profile. It might include such variables as age, race, gender identity, educational level, marital status, or employment status. However, as we noted in Chapter 4, there are no "standard demographic variables" that must be measured in all research studies. Only those that are relevant to the research problem and/or that can be useful to the reader of a research report in deciding how to use the research findings are appropriate. To collect data on other variables that do not meet either of these criteria could risk creating suspicion or risk antagonizing research participants and result in a lower response rate.

A limited demographic profile of research participants can help the researcher put the findings of a research study into perspective. It can suggest the degree of the study's external validity. For readers of a research report to be able to assess the relevance of the research findings to their own specific practice situations, a clear picture of those who provided data is necessary. For example, a report of a study based on a sample of low-income mothers needing assistance in developing parenting skills might include a demographic summary of the research participants in relation to the variables age, presence of a father or father figure, number of children, and degree of support from extended family. Readers of such a report can assess how closely the participants resemble their own clients and thus can determine whether the findings and any recommendations might be useful for their own practice.

In more qualitative research, data are less likely to be aggregated. Instead, the demographic characteristics of each individual research participant may be included in a narrative description of our interaction with him or her. For example, it might look like this:

> Lucretia W. is a 62-year-old Caucasian woman with three adult children, all of whom live out of state. Her husband (who was ten years older) passed away six months ago from advanced stage Alzheimer's disease. She has a high school education and worked as a cook in various restaurants until she decided to quit work about one year ago to care for her husband. She is an active church member and states that "my faith got me through it all." Her first explanation for her husband's illness was "it was God trying to make me stronger," but the longer that she and I talked over coffee in her kitchen, I began to detect that . . .

In addition to describing the relevant demographic characteristics of participants, when conducting either quantitative or qualitative research we describe the setting in which the research was conducted. It allows readers of our report (1) to judge to what degree the setting in which data were collected might have influenced findings and (2) in the case of organization-based research, to assess whether the nature of the organization and its services are similar enough to their own that the findings of the research may be helpful in informing their own practice decision-making. For example, a social worker who works at an outpatient clinic where federal reimbursement usually limits services to only four individual treatment sessions may quickly conclude that a research finding that a 10-week individualized treatment program is more effective than the standard 4-week group treatment is of little relevance to her.

PREPARING FOR DATA ANALYSIS

Prior to conducting data analysis and attempting to draw conclusions and findings, it is helpful to revisit the purpose of the study. It suggests the general type of analysis that would be appropriate. For example, was the research designed to assess the relative effectiveness of various treatment interventions for addressing a problem that clients were experiencing? Or was it designed to describe the effects that the problem has on specific client groups? In the first instance, we would be expected to conduct and report on statistical analysis that would provide evidence of the relative effectiveness of the various intervention methods. The second would require analysis that provides a clear description of the range of effects of the problems observed and some indication of their distribution within the people in our research sample.

The presence of other research purposes would suggest other approaches to analysis of the data. For example, if the purpose of a study was to describe group performance before and after exposure to an independent variable, or compare two or more groups in relation to a behavior or an attitude, the method of data analysis used would be different from that of a study whose purpose was to determine to what degree several variables, viewed together, may explain or predict a problem or phenomenon. If the purpose was to assess how effective an individual's or a program's intervention was, still another method of analysis might be appropriate.

A review of how research questions and/or hypotheses were stated can help in selecting the most appropriate method of data analysis. Sometimes questions are posed in such a way that it is clear that differences between or among groups are being sought; other times, it is clear that the degree of association or correlation between or among variables is the primary focus of the research. There are other interrelated issues associated with the choice of methods used to answer research questions and/or seek statistical support for hypotheses. They require that we recall and review many aspects of the research design that produced the research data. Once again, certain questions can be helpful, for example:

- Were the research methods used primarily quantitative or qualitative?
- What general category of sampling was used (probability or nonprobability)?
- How many samples or subsamples were used?
- How large was each sample?
- Are the variables of interest believed to be normally distributed (their values would approximate a "normal curve" within the population) or is their distribution badly skewed?
- What level of measurement was generated for each variable that will be used in statistical analysis?

Research-informed Practice or Practice-informed Research

Behavior: Use practice theory and experience to inform scientific inquiry and research.

Critical Thinking Question: How does the purpose of the research study affect the data analysis methods selected?

QUALITATIVE AND QUANTITATIVE DATA ANALYSIS

An in-depth discussion of methods of data analysis is beyond the scope of this book. However, we will examine the conceptual underpinnings that are critical to understanding how statistical analysis is conducted and how it assists us in drawing conclusions on the basis of research data. Determining whether a research study will utilize primarily quantitative or qualitative analysis is often one of the initial decisions we make.

Qualitative Analysis

If we employed primarily qualitative research methods, the data are also primarily qualitative in nature, perhaps in the form of summaries of in-depth interviews, participant observations, video recordings, or something similar. Qualitative data analysis tends to be less standardized than that used in more quantitative designs. While it may rely on some widely practiced methods, it may also be highly creative and even unique to a given research study.

Qualitative data analysis seeks to make sense out of the data—to learn what actually occurred during the data collection process and what it might all mean. Even verbal qualitative data, such as recordings of in-person interviews, can have meaningful values or value categories assigned to certain variables. From the outset, the process of assigning values or value categories may be a little more subjective and a little less precise than when quantitative data are present. However, once assignment is finished, the values and value categories can be manipulated and sometimes even analyzed using statistical analysis. However, the design of most qualitative studies (e.g., use of non-probability samples, lack of control groups, reliance on interviewing or observation for data collection, completeness of data that vary from case to case, lack of emphasis on measurement of variables) seriously limits the number and type of statistical analyses that can be used.

Assignment of values or value categories often entails a certain amount of counting (quantification) of behaviors, use of certain words, or emotional responses—content analysis (Chapter 6). Content analysis can be performed with the assistance of software packages that have been developed for this purpose. Or, it may entail more "human" methods, such as the use of two or more judges independently examining the same data and drawing their own conclusions as to what they observed. Afterward, the judges may meet to attempt to arrive at a consensus as to what they observed, or the researcher may attempt to reconcile any differences in the judges' observations. Sometimes, a "majority rules" method is used. For example, if two out of three judges perceived that in a videotape a person seemed anxious but a third judge did not, it would be concluded that the research participant was indeed anxious. Alternately, the decision may be made beforehand that an emotion or behavior will not be reported as a research finding unless all judges reported it—it must be a unanimous observation.

A wide variety of computer software packages, such as NVivo, XSight, MAXQDA, EZ-Test, ATLAS.ti, and Ethnograph, are now available to help analyze qualitative data. There are many books that identify and describe computer software to aid in the analysis of qualitative data (e.g., Gahan & Hannibal, 1998; Gibbs, 2002; Kuckartz, 2004; Weitzman & Miles, 1995). In addition, there are books that offer more general information on the analysis of qualitative data (e.g., Auerbach & Silverstein, 2003; Marshall & Rossman, 2016; Merrium, 2014; Patton, 2014; Saldana, 2015; Warren & Karner, 2014).

Quantitative Analysis

In research studies that are more quantitative in nature, statistical analysis plays an important part in answering research questions and concluding whether there is adequate support for research hypotheses. It is often the final step in the process to determine whether a relationship between or among variables within a research sample is likely to be a real one that exists beyond the sample, or whether the relationships can be explained by sampling error or by one or more confounding variables.

If the amount of data being analyzed is small and the type of statistical analysis that is to be performed is relatively simple, we might choose to not use a computer to assist in data analysis. However, because of the many user-friendly statistical software packages now available for use with personal computers and other handheld electronic devices, statistical analysis is now almost always conducted electronically.

Complex statistical computations are performed flawlessly when electronic methods are used for data analysis, assuming that the data have been entered accurately and the appropriate method of statistical analysis has been selected. The most time-consuming step in statistical analysis has probably always been coding and data entry. However, even this tedious operation may soon be eliminated as technology allows us to scan the data from surveys and questionnaires directly into a computer for analysis. Once data are entered into a computer software package, a wide variety of statistical analyses can be performed, each in just a matter of seconds. Some of the more widely used computer software packages for the analysis of quantitative data include Statistical Package for the Social Sciences (SPSS), Statistical Analysis System (SAS), Stata, Minitab, Systat, and Excel. There are several books that offer help to researchers using these and other statistical software packages (e.g., Bryman & Cramer, 2011; Bryman & Cramer, 2003; Greasley, 2008; Norusis, 2011).

Complex statistical computations are performed flawlessly when electronic methods are used for data analysis, assuming that the data have been entered accurately and the appropriate method of statistical analysis has been selected.

The ease with which statistical analysis can be performed by a computer represents both a blessing and a danger for the researcher. Statistical tests that would have been outside the mathematical competence of many of us just a few years ago are now possible for anyone with even average statistical analysis skills. However, because hundreds of statistical analyses can be performed easily and quickly, there is a real danger that, if we do not have a clear understanding of the statistical tests being used, findings may be interpreted incorrectly and the results will be misleading to readers of research reports. We must remember that computer programs simply take the data and compute the findings. Statistical software packages do not:

- know if, based on the characteristics of the data, the appropriate statistical test has been selected to analyze the data.
- know whether we have even a beginning understanding of how the results of statistical analysis should be interpreted in light of a research question or hypothesis.
- know how the sample that provided the data was selected and how sampling bias may have affected results.
- know whether the measurement instruments used were reliable and valid.
- alert the reader of the report that we may have stumbled on a spurious (i.e., not real) relationship between variables simply by trying an almost infinite number of combinations of variables—something that is now quite easy to do because of the ease with which computer analysis of data can be performed.

Policy Practice

Behavior: Apply critical thinking to analyze, formulate, and advocate for policies that advance human rights and social, economic, and environmental justice.

Critical Thinking Question: Think of an instance when a politician used statistics to support his or her platform. Can you think of a way the statistics could have been "slanted" to serve the politician's needs?

USES OF STATISTICAL ANALYSES

Statistical analyses are versatile and can be used at several points in the research process to assist in decision-making. Statistical analysis plays an important role (1) in the design of research, (2) in summarizing the distribution of variables within research data, (3) in estimating the characteristics of the population from which a sample was drawn, and (4) in drawing conclusions and interpretations about answers to research questions and the presence or absence of support for hypotheses. In this chapter, we will discuss only briefly the first and third of these uses, focusing most of our discussion on the second and fourth.

Designing Research

Some statistical methods help us make decisions related to the design of research. For example, statistical analyses can tell us when a simple random sample is sufficiently large that the impact of sampling error is acceptably low, or they can tell us the mathematical probability that a sample is sufficiently representative of a known population in relation to a given variable. As we noted in earlier chapters, statistical analyses are used to:

- help design and refine data collection instruments, such as scales and indexes.
- perform operations to help assess the overall reliability and validity of a data collection instrument.
- identify items in the instrument that appear to be redundant or unnecessary.
- identify items that appear to not measure the construct of interest at all.
- help in constructing parallel forms of an instrument, shortened versions of an instrument, and versions of the instrument for different populations, such as populations with different ages, reading level, ethnic backgrounds, etc.

Summarizing the Distribution of Variables

Descriptive statistical analysis is used to provide a concise summary of the data accumulated about and from those persons or cases that were studied. We use descriptive statistical analyses (sometimes referred to as *data reduction*) to reduce large amounts of data to a manageable size so that both we and the reader of our report will be able to visualize the major characteristics of the participants and the data they provided.

Frequency Distributions

Descriptive statistical analyses may involve the construction of frequency distributions. A *frequency distribution* is a table displaying how many participants or cases fell in each value or value category (measurement) of a variable. The frequencies are displayed alongside the various values or value categories of the variable. Also, if the variable is at least ordinal level, frequency distributions may include additional columns for *cumulative frequencies* (how many cases had a measurement larger or smaller than a given value). Another column may reflect percentages of all cases represented by the cases in a given value category and, in some cases, what percentage of all cases had a measurement above or below a given value (*cumulative percentages*). Sometimes, values are grouped, that is, ranges of values are used instead of individual values, to make a frequency distribution table smaller. For example, in a table that displays the participants' ages, we may group the ages into ranges of 10 years (0–10 years, 11–20 years, 21–30 years, etc.), making the data easier to interpret when looking at the frequency table. See Figure 13.1 for an example of a frequency distribution table (including frequencies, cumulative frequencies, percentages, and cumulative percentages) showing the results of a client satisfaction survey. The cumulative percentage allows us to easily see that 62 percent of the clients were either satisfied or extremely satisfied.

We use descriptive statistical analyses (sometimes referred to as data reduction) to reduce large amounts of data to a manageable size so that both we and the reader of our report will be able to visualize the major characteristics of the participants and the data they provided.

**Behavior: Apply critical thinking to engage
in analysis of quantitative and qualitative
research methods and research findings.**

Critical Thinking Question: Create a
frequency table to show the number,
percentage, and cumulative percentage
of students' undergraduate classification
(i.e., freshman, sophomore, junior, senior)
for all the students in your research class.
Why can we use cumulative percentages
with a variable measured at the ordinal
level but not with one measured at the
nominal level?

Graphs

Graphs are also frequently used to describe the distribution of variables within a sample or population. Simple graphs are used to portray the same data that are contained in frequency distributions, that is, the distribution of values or value categories of a single variable in pictorial form, usually at the expense of detail. Some commonly used examples are bar charts, column charts, histograms, and pie charts. Bar charts and column charts use bars or columns of lengths that are proportional to the number of cases that possess a given measurement of a variable. Column charts use vertical columns, while bar charts can use either vertical or horizontal bars to represent the data. Figure 13.2 provides an example of the data from Figure 13.1 displayed in a bar chart. For the variable "client satisfaction," notice that twice as many clients were dissatisfied as were extremely dissatisfied; therefore, the bar is twice as tall for the value category "dissatisfied."

Histograms are graphs that portray the shape of the distribution of a variable. They can be created simply by connecting the midpoint of the tops of the bars or columns in a bar chart to form a shape (a polygon). Then the overall distribution can be described in summary form. For example, if the shape thus created is essentially bell-shaped with most values clustering around the middle and then tailing off similarly to the right and left, the variable is regarded as normally distributed within the sample or population that provided the data.

Pie charts use areas of a circle or other enclosed figure to correspond to the percentage of all cases that were found to have a given measurement of a variable. Figure 13.3 shows a pie chart based on the data from Figure 13.1. In our example, 24 percent of participants in the study were extremely satisfied; therefore, the pie chart for the variable "client satisfaction" is constructed with a slice labeled "extremely satisfied" that is 24 percent or 86.4 degrees (360 degrees 0.24 = 86.4 degrees) of the pie.

Bar charts, histograms, and pie charts can all display the distribution of measurements of a variable among cases made at or around the same time. A different graph is used to display the repeated measurements of a single variable over time for an individual or some other system to see if change seemed to occur. It is the line graph, and it is used extensively in single-system evaluation. We introduced and provided several

	N	Cumulative N	Percentage	Cumulative %
Extremely satisfied	12	12	24%	24%
Satisfied	19	31	38%	62%
Neutral	7	38	14%	76%
Dissatisfied	8	46	16%	92%
Extremely dissatisfied	4	50	8%	100%
TOTAL	50		100%	

Figure 13.1   Example Client Satisfaction Frequency Distribution Table

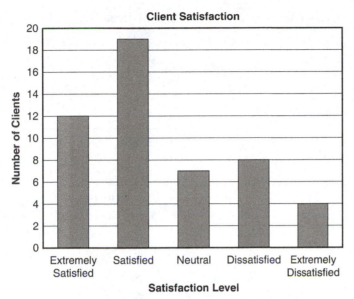

Figure 13.2 Example Client Satisfaction Bar Chart

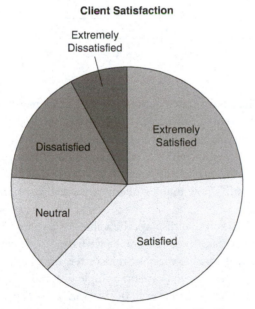

Figure 13.3 Example Client Satisfaction Pie Chart

examples of the line graph in Chapter 8 when we described how measurements of the target problem for a single client or client system are recorded.

Frequency Distributions and Graphs for Multiple Variables

Distribution tables and graphs can also be created to display the relationship between two or more variables. For example, one distribution table can be used to display the measurements of two nominal level variables among cases. It shows the value categories of one variable along the x-axis and the value categories of a second variable

Student Class/Gender	Male	Female	Total
Freshman	7	11	18
Sophomore	12	24	36
Junior	18	32	50
Senior	23	33	56
TOTAL	60	100	160

Figure 13.4   Example Cross-tabulation Table showing Gender by Student Classification

Student Class/Gender	Male Social Work Major		Female Social Work Major		Total Social Work Major	
	Yes	No	Yes	No	Yes	No
Freshman	5	2	8	3	13	5
Sophomore	9	3	19	5	28	8
Junior	16	2	28	4	44	6
Senior	19	4	28	5	47	9
TOTAL	49	11	83	17	132	28
TOTAL by Gender	60		100		160	

Figure 13.5   Example Cross-tabulation Table showing Gender, Student Classification, and Major

along the y-axis and is called a contingency table or a cross-tabulation table. Figure 13.4 shows an example of one that portrays the distribution of participants' *gender* by their *undergraduate student classification*. We can include additional variables in the same table by creating additional columns within each of the columns or additional rows within each of the rows. Figure 13.5 shows an example of a table that also includes the variable *social work major* to identify how many students are social work majors and how many are in other programs.

A commonly used graph that displays the values of two interval or ratio level variables is the scattergram. Unlike the other graphs we have described that all portray aggregate data for the values of a single variable, the scattergram shows the individual values for each of of two variables for each case on a single graph. Each dot on the graph represents a case and its measurement for each of two variables. The values of the first variable are displayed on the x-axis and the values of the second category are displayed on the y-axis. You simply move to the right on the x-axis (or to the left if the value is negative) to the measurement of the first variable for each case, and then move up (or down if the value is negative) on the y-axis to the value of the second variable. The scattergram is used to create a visual representation of the correlation between two variables. The overall pattern of dots can be used to suggest whether measurements of the two variables are positively or negatively correlated and, somewhat crudely, how strong a linear correlation they possess. The more clearly the dots move in a clear upward direction (approximate a straight line) from left to right, the stronger the positive correlation, and the more clearly they move down from left to right, the stronger the negative correlation.

Measures of Central Tendency

Another way of describing the distribution of a single variable within a data set is to report what was found to be a typical value category or value among its measurements in one of several ways. They are referred to collectively as *measures of central tendency*. One or more measures of central tendency for variables of interest may be computed and included in the research report. The most common ones are the mode, median, and mean:

- **Mode.** The value category or value that has the largest frequency (occurs most often) within the data. Calculate by creating a frequency distribution, and identifying the value or value category that occurs the most often.
- **Median.** The midpoint in a rank-ordered distribution of an ordinal-, interval-, or ratio-level variable. Calculate by putting all the values (or value categories if ordinal variable) in order from least to greatest, then finding the central value. If there are an even number of values, then the median is equal to the average of the two central values.
- **Mean.** The arithmetic average of the values of all cases for an interval- or ratio-level variable. Calculate by summing all of the values and dividing by the number of cases.

Measures of Variability or Dispersion

In describing the distribution of a data set, it is also helpful to describe to what degree cases were *homogeneous* (similar) in relationship to a variable and to what degree their value categories or values reflected *heterogeneity* (difference). In other words, we look at how spread out or close together the values of a variable are within a sample. Descriptive statistics (referred to as parameters when describing populations) that do this are referred to as *measures of variability* (also known as measures of dispersion or spread). The larger a measure of variability is calculated to be, the more variation there is among values, and vice versa. When reported along with one or more measures of central tendency, measures of variability offer a fairly complete summary description of the distribution of a variable among cases in a research sample or population. Some of the more commonly used measures of variability are:

- **Minimum and maximum.** The smallest and the largest values in a distribution.
- **Range.** The distance between the minimum value and the maximum value, encompassing both values. Sometimes you can simply state the minimum and maximum values. To calculate the range, you subtract the minimum value from the maximum value and add one (so that both the minimum and the maximum values are included in the range).
- **Interquartile range.** The distance between the 75th percentile (where three quarters of values are smaller) and the 25th percentile (where one quarter of values are smaller) in a rank-ordering of values. In other words, how spread out is the middle 50 percent of the values? This is used when there are extreme values at either the lowest end, the highest end, or possibly at both ends of the distribution.
- **Mean or absolute deviation.** The mean deviation is, simply speaking, the average distance from the mean of all the values in a distribution.
- **Variance.** Variance is obtained by subtracting the mean from each case value, squaring the difference, adding all the squared differences together to obtain the

sum of squares, and then dividing it by the number of cases (for population data) or the number of cases minus one (for sample data).

- **Standard deviation.** The square root of the variance.

Statistics books provide more details on how to calculate measures of central tendency and variability, how they differ, and criteria for determining when each should be used (Weinbach & Grinnell, 2015).

Estimating the Characteristics of a Population

Although descriptive statistics such as measures of central tendency and measures of variability can be ends in themselves, they are also used in calculating other, more complex, statistical analyses. In studies (primarily quantitative) in which random samples have been drawn, it can be useful to estimate (within a certain range) what the true mean of a variable would have been if the researcher had studied the entire population. For example, if a random sample of clients of a given size is drawn, and the clients' mean clinical depression level is calculated using a standardized instrument, statistical analysis could tell us with different degrees of confidence the range in which the true mean depression level of all clients would lie. This is known as constructing *confidence intervals*. Reporting a confidence interval in a research report can help the reader of the report understand how much sampling error the measurement of a variable may contain. Generally, we calculate either the 95 percent confidence interval (i.e., the interval or range of values in which we are 95% confident that the true population mean lies) or the 99 percent confidence interval (i.e., the interval or range of values in which we are 99% confident that the true population mean lies). The calculations of the confidence intervals are based on the mean and standard deviation of the sample data drawn from the population of interest.

Answering Questions and Testing Hypotheses

In some descriptive research studies, and in most explanatory research studies, we are looking for support for an hypothesis about the association, correlation, or even causation between variables. We want to do more than simply describe the characteristics of the participants in the study. For example, suppose that the existence of a relationship between variables has been predicted and stated as a hypothesis. A sample of research participants has been selected using methods designed to maximize the likelihood that they accurately represent members of the population, and they have been studied with the goal of determining if there is support for the hypothesized relationship.

Perhaps, on first blush, there is an apparent relationship between variables—it can be seen within the data collected from the research sample. Is that sufficient proof of the relationship? No. Before we can conclude that a relationship is a real one that probably exists within the population from which the sample was drawn, we must be reasonably certain that something else did not cause the apparent relationship.

Consider a rather typical scenario in which there appears to be support for our hypothesis that an experimental intervention method is more effective than the treatment generally used. Within the data collected from a sample of clients, the experimental intervention method seems to have produced better results than the usual treatment. For example, we might have observed that one group of ten randomly selected clients with a diagnosis of alcoholism receiving an experimental counseling method reflected a

Before we can conclude that a relationship is a real one that probably exists within the population from which the sample was drawn, we must be reasonably certain that something else did not cause the apparent relationship.

60 percent rate of treatment success (operationally defined as alcohol abstinence for one month) as compared with members of a control group who received the usual treatment and reflected only a 40 percent success rate.

Inferential Statistical Analysis

Suppose that the research was well designed (using a classic experimental design or most of the elements of one) and implemented. We can be reasonably confident that our design has good internal validity. In other words, we are reasonably certain that the different values of the independent variable (i.e., the two different interventions) caused the different measurements of the dependent variable (percent of alcohol abstinence). Another way of saying the same thing would be to say that "all threats to internal validity were adequately controlled." Does that mean that the relationship between the variables is a real one that exists beyond the sample? Not necessarily. What about sampling error? Wouldn't we expect to have some difference in success rates with any two relatively small groups of clients selected randomly, even if the two treatment methods were really equally effective? Yes. Remember, only sampling bias, not sampling error, was controlled by random selection and random assignment to the two treatments.

We must ask the question, "Is the difference in the success rates of the two groups of research participants (the experimental and control groups) large enough that it can safely be assumed that it is not simply the result of sampling error?" Statistical analysis can determine how safe it would be to make generalizations about the relative effectiveness of the two treatments that would go beyond the participants in the current research. This use of statistical analysis employs methods that are broadly referred to as *inferential statistical analysis*. Some of the more commonly-used bivariate statistical tests (tests involving two variables) used to analyze the relationship between variables include:

- **Chi-square**—compares the distribution of value categories between nominal-level variables to determine if there is an association between the variables. For example, we can look at the distribution of ethnicity of our experimental group members compared to the distribution of ethnicity of our control group to ensure that they are basically equivalent before starting the intervention. Or, we can use chi-square to attempt to learn if an apparent relationship between religious affiliation and political party affiliation is likely to be a real one.
- **Correlation**—looks at the relationship between the pairs of values of two variables for each participant within a research sample. A positive correlation indicates that when the values of one variable increases, the values of the second variable increases, and vice versa. A negative correlation indicates that when the values of one variable increases, the values of the second variable decreases, and vice versa. For example, we can determine if age appears to be correlated to grade point average among college undergraduate students and, if so, how strongly.
- **T-test for dependent samples**—looks at the difference between two measures of the same variable within a single sample of individuals, for example, we can determine if there is a statistically significant difference between the pretests and posttests for our experimental group. The *t*-test for dependent samples can also compare measures of the same variable in a sample in which pairs of participants have been matched together on some characteristic, for example, we may

compare the IQ score for a matched set of biological twins to see if the differences between the twins' IQ scores differ significantly.

- **T-test for independent samples**—looks at the difference between the mean of a variable for one sample compared to the mean of the same variable for a second sample that is independent from the first sample. For example, we could determine if there is a statistically significant difference between the posttest measurements of certain variables within our experimental and control groups.

- **Analysis of variance**—a collection of statistical tests used to compare more than two groups or measures. For example, we could determine if there are statistically significant differences among the posttest measurements of certain variables among one research group receiving an experimental intervention, one group receiving the usual intervention, and a third group receiving no intervention.

There are many more bivariate statistical tests, as well as multivariate tests (tests involving more than two variables), that are used in social work research. For a more thorough explanation of these tests, see Weinbach and Grinnell (2015) and Randolph and Myers (2013).

Statistical Significance

Using a theoretical concept called a *sampling distribution*, inferential statistical tests can tell us the mathematical probability that the apparent relationship between or among variables that can be seen in the research data is the work of sampling error (or chance). The statistical tests are based on probability theory and, in our previous example, could determine the mathematical probability that the difference between a 60 percent success rate using one intervention and a 40 percent success rate using another intervention with a second group (each group consisting of 10 members) could exist because of sampling error. Thus, inferential statistical analysis can be used to help us draw conclusions about the relative effectiveness of the two treatment methods being evaluated. Any one of several statistical tests (there is usually one that is most appropriate) could be used to determine the exact probability that a 20 percent difference in success rate would occur with two subsamples of ten cases drawn at random just because of sampling error. If that probability is very low, and since the usual threats to internal validity are believed to have been controlled, we would be able to "reject the null hypothesis" (that any apparent relationship is just the result of sampling error) and conclude that the relationship between the type of treatment received and success rate is probably a real one.

> *Using a theoretical concept called a sampling distribution, inferential statistical tests can tell us the mathematical probability that the apparent relationship between or among variables that can be seen in the research data is the work of sampling error.*

Most of the time, being more than 95 percent certain that an apparent relationship within a research sample is not the work of sampling error is good enough for researchers to claim support for a relationship between variables. (As we noted in Chapter 1, all scientific knowledge is tentative anyway.) Of course, as in our example, we must also be reasonably certain that threats to internal validity have been adequately controlled by the research design.

When inferential statistical analysis demonstrates that the probability of sampling error having produced an apparent relationship between variables is less than 5 percent or one time in twenty (referred to as $p < 0.05$), researchers customarily describe the relationship between variables as *statistically significant* (see Box 13.1). Of course, we may set the level of statistical significance at some other level (referred to as a *rejection level* or *alpha level*), such as 0.01, or even as small as 0.001, if we want to be even more certain that sampling error did not produce the apparent relationship between variables before we reject the null hypothesis. If we do select one of these less commonly used alpha levels,

Box 13.1   Statistical Significance: What It Is and What It Is Not

- It is mathematical evidence, based on probability theory, that the relationship between or among variables within a sample is very unlikely to be the work of sampling error (chance).

- It is not evidence that the strength of the relationship in the sample is the same as that within the population.

- It is not 100 percent proof that the relationship within the sample was not the work of sampling error.

- It is not 100 percent proof that the variables are related at all.

- It is not proof that something else (a threat to internal validity) did not cause the relationship.

- It is not proof that the relationship is necessarily a strong one.

- It is not proof that the relationship is necessarily a meaningful one.

we generally are expected to provide justification as to why we selected that particular alpha level.

As we have noted, *statistically significant* has a very specific meaning in research and statistics. "Significant" is not used the same as the way that we use it in every day speech, and that can be confusing. For example, we might say, "He made a significant improvement in his grades," or "Her contribution to the program was a significant one," but statistical significance is definitely not implied. Because it can lead to misunderstanding, we might want to consider avoiding the term completely in a research report. It is possible to imply that a statistically significant relationship was found to exist without actually using the words *statistically significant*. For example, in a report, we might summarize the findings of a study simply by stating, "Among low-income women without extended family support, women who used casework services were more likely to possess a higher level of awareness of the medical needs of infants than those who did not use casework services. However, clients who used casework services were no more likely to use outpatient medical facilities for their babies' treatment than those participants who did not receive casework services."

It is important that we not make too much of a finding of statistical significance. First of all, as we have suggested, a finding of statistical significance, like all of the findings of scientific inquiry, is only a tentative conclusion based on reasonable certainty that is based on the laws of probability. It says only that sampling error is a very unlikely explanation of the apparent relationship between or among variables that occurred among cases that were studied. It never totally rules it out.

Statistical Significance versus Meaningfulness

Sometimes statistically significant relationships between or among variables that may not be the work of sampling bias or any of the threats to internal validity, are real. But they are still not terribly valuable! They reflect real relationships, but they are relationships between or among variables that are virtually worthless because they are not very strong (Weinbach & Grinnell, 2015). Statistical significance is achieved quite easily, even if the relationship between variables is a weak one, if very large samples are used. But statistical significance thus achieved may be of limited or no practical value to the social work practitioner. For example, suppose several hundred students participated in an SAT preparation course and their average scores increased by 15 points, while the average scores of the students who did not participate in the course did not increase. Because of the large samples used, this relatively small difference in scores would be statistically significant. A manager in charge of finding continued funding for the course could safely conclude that there almost certainly is a relationship between the scores on the SAT and participation in the class. However, the same manager might also conclude that the difference in scores, while statistically significant, is not large enough to warrant the cost (in time and dollars) of continuing to offer the course.

We can minimize the likelihood of achieving statistical significance when the relationship between variables is so weak as to be meaningless if we use a sample that does not exceed the size recommended for the statistical test that we use. However, even if the appropriate sample size is used and statistical significance is achieved, interpretations of conclusions regarding the value of the results may still require a dose of common sense. A good question to ask prior to statistical analysis is, if a statistically significant relationship between variables is found, how strong would the relationship have to be in order to be considered meaningful? While a statistically significant relationship says that the variables are probably related beyond the sample, it says nothing about the strength of the relationship. Fortunately, there are types of statistical analyses that produce something called *measures of association* that are indicators of the strength of the relationship. They can be helpful in putting a finding of statistical significance in perspective.

There is still another reason why meaningless statistical significance is sometimes found even when the recommended sample size is used and the analysis is performed correctly. The problem is that the research finding is simply nothing new or unexpected! This occurs fairly frequently when statistical tests are used to determine if a correlation between two variables is probably a real one. Some correlations are valuable; but many others are not, even if they are real. For example, among a group of human service organization clients, we could almost certainly demonstrate a statistically significant positive correlation between income and the amount of money spent on groceries. But would such a finding be valuable? It is highly predictable, because one generally has to have money (or at least good credit) to spend it. Besides, would the finding help us to be more effective in our intervention with human service organization clients? Probably not. These types of findings are more common with the advent of computer statistical software. Statistical tests can be run so quickly and easily that we can be tempted to conduct numerous analyses that may reveal a few relationships between variables that are statistical significant, but they are unlikely to offer us any new or useful knowledge.

Selecting a Statistical Test

All statistical tests have assumptions (requirements) that underlie their use. However, there are also certain situations in which it is acceptable to ignore one or more of the usual assumptions for the use of a statistical test—the results will still be quite accurate. Even the selection of a frequency distribution, graph, or other descriptive statistic to report central tendency or variability is not always simple. Statistical analysis requires that we be knowledgeable about rules and conditions that must be met. It also requires an ethical commitment to report the findings of research as accurately as possible. As we all know, it is easy to lie with statistics by selecting a type of analysis that portrays the data the way we want them to look.

Intervention

Behavior: Apply knowledge of human behavior and the social environment, person-in-environment, and other multidisciplinary theoretical frameworks in interventions with clients and constituencies.

Critical Thinking Question: How might the difference between statistical significance and the true importance of the relationship between variables affect your practice decision-making?

Fortunately, even the process of identifying the correct statistical test to use is becoming easier thanks to advances in computer technology. Software packages and websites are now available that use a series of questions (sometimes in the form of something called a *decision tree*) that can help us to narrow the list of tests that might be appropriate. However, they still require a good basic understanding of research design. For example, to use them correctly, we have to understand factors specific to our research study, such as the sampling methods that were used, the level of measurement that was produced, and how certain variables tend to be distributed within a population.

Finally, while it should be obvious, we would be remiss if we did not remind the reader again that findings of statistically significant relationships between and among variables are not the only findings that are valuable. A lack of statistical significance (a *null finding*) may be just as valuable or even more valuable! For example, learning that the difference in success rate between group counseling and individual treatment for a particular client problem was not statistically significant could be helpful to a social work administrator in attempting to adjust to budget cuts without reducing the quality of services.

INTERPRETING AND REPORTING THE RESULTS

Once data have been analyzed and, where appropriate, statistical tests have been performed, the results must still be interpreted and summarized. Any limitations of the methods of data analysis used should be identified and interpreted as to their possible effects.

The results are first examined in relation to the focus of the research. What do the results suggest about the answer to the research question or questions? What do they tell us about any hypotheses? Were they supported or not? If so, what does that mean for social work practice? How can the results of data analyses be used to better understand the research problem or to suggest effective prevention or intervention methods for alleviating it? What are the implications for the social practitioners who are seeking to provide better social work services? How will any findings make them better evidence-based practitioners?

Data analysis generates many findings. Often, they can be interpreted in a variety of ways. The specific meaning of each individual finding must be determined. Often, individual findings may need to be reinterpreted in light of other findings from the current research study or from the findings in other studies. This often requires us to make use of our practice experience, and also may require us to look again at the relevant literature in an attempt to reconcile our findings with those of other researchers. Eventually, we must use our best judgment, knowing that we can always be wrong in our interpretations.

In predominantly qualitative studies, we may ask for feedback of our study results from our research participants and others in their communities. We share our major tentative study findings with them, and enlist their help in interpreting the meaning of the results. This can be especially important since our own biases and life experiences can lead us to erroneous conclusions. This "checking and verifying" should occur before publication of the results in formal reports or scholarly journals. There are several advantages to doing this, especially in cross-cultural research (Chapter 6). First, people who know the community well offer a unique perspective on a study's findings, and may suggest differences in interpretation that might never occur to us. They can also help determine how best to use the study findings to address community concerns and problems. Finally, sharing the data prior to dissemination reinforces the notion of partnership in the research enterprise and communicates respect for study participants and the communities they represent.

Interpreting research findings is not easy. For example, how do we interpret the descriptive finding that adolescents have widely differing attitudes toward the use of contraception to prevent unwanted pregnancies? Or that the staff perceives a program to be highly successful while community leaders express resentment about it? Or that a software program used to perform content analysis of transcribed conversations with college students shows that anti-Semitic attitudes still persist among them? Or that a test of statistical significance fails to support a hypothesis that an intervention is effective, when it has been assumed for years to be effective? Or that another statistical finding suggests that one variable is positively correlated with another variable? Does it suggest that one variable is contributing to variations in the other variable? Or is it the other way around? Is the strength of the correlation really all that strong?

Because of the difficulty of drawing definitive conclusions from research data, we sometimes simply report findings, suggest several possible interpretations, and let the readers of our report draw their own conclusions. If we have used a particular theory to guide us, including the development and measurement of constructs consistent with that theory, we may be able to interpret the findings in light of what the theory is designed to explain. When inferential statistical analysis has been used, both findings of statistically significant relationships between variables and findings of non-significance (null findings) are reported. All research findings from soundly designed and implemented research are potentially valuable to others, helping them make better decisions and become better evidence-based practitioners.

SUMMARY

In this chapter:

- We looked at the general processes involved in analyzing research data so that they can be used to inform practice.
- Some of the more commonly used methods of data analysis (frequency distributions and graphs, measures of central tendency, and measures of variability) were described. It was emphasized that the researcher has an obligation to accurately describe the research sample or population from which data were collected.
- Results of descriptive statistical analysis are usually reported to portray participants' relevant demographic characteristics.
- If hypothesis testing is undertaken, inferential statistical analysis of data is performed to determine the likelihood that sampling error may have produced an apparent relationship between or among variables within a research sample.
- It was explained how, in some situations, a finding of a statistically significant relationship between variables may be of little practical value or a lack of statistical significance may still be valuable.
- All statistical tests of significance have assumptions—conditions relating to sampling methods, level of measurement, etc., that are requirements for their use.

MyEducationLab® for Research

Start with the Topic 17 Assignments: Descriptive Statistics and the Topic 17 Study Plan and then try the Topic 18 Assignments: Inferential Statistics and the Topic 18 Study Plan. Try the Topic 20 Assignments: Qualitative Research, Data Analysis, and Application and the Topic 20 Study Plan.

Chapter 13 Chapter Review Quiz.

Writing the Research Report and Disseminating Research Findings

A major reason for conducting research is to contribute to the social work knowledge base. For this to occur, research findings must be analyzed, summarized, written up, and communicated to interested audiences in the research and practice communities. This chapter focuses on the last of these steps: writing the research report and disseminating the research findings.

MAIN SECTIONS OF THE RESEARCH REPORT

Most research reports follow the same general format. The report describes the problem that precipitated the study, the logical progression that we followed in designing and implementing it, and the rationale behind our findings and recommendations. It makes it possible for a reader of the report to critically evaluate the credibility of our findings in light of the methods that we used to arrive at them. Each of the following areas is included in a research report, generally in the same sequence:

Title

Developing a title for your study can be challenging. A good title reflects the main purpose of the study and, where applicable, information about the intervention employed and the research population that was studied. Titles often include a subtitle, which allows us to share even more information for readers to determine if the report is of interest to them. For example, Louden-Gerber's (2009) dissertation title, "A Group Forgiveness Intervention for Adult Male Homeless Individuals: Effects on Forgiveness, Rumination, and Social Connectedness," informs the reader of the study's

LEARNING OUTCOMES

- Describe the main sections of the research report.
- Compare and contrast the writing requirements of quantitative and qualitative research reports.
- Summarize the guidelines for referencing various sources in a research report.
- Describe the role of the researcher within the research report.
- Compare the strengths and weaknesses of the various ways of disseminating research findings.

CHAPTER OUTLINE

intervention, population, and outcome variables. When looking through a long list of article titles to select articles of interest, titles like this can quickly draw the reader's attention.

Abstract

Most research reports, including journal articles and dissertations, include an abstract, which summarizes the research study. Thyer (2008) points out that the abstract will probably be read far more times than the complete article, and should include (a) the issue or problem under investigation; (b) information about the participants, listing age race, gender, and other pertinent features; (c) the research method, the intervention(s), and the outcome measures; (d) the results, including statistical significance and effect sizes; and (e) the conclusions and any applications to practice (p. 40–41). The sixth edition of the *Publication Manual of the American Psychological Association* (2009) recommends that abstracts be 150 to 250 words long.

Introduction

In the introduction section of a research report, we describe the historical background of the study and the origin of our interest in the topic. We specify the research problem and describe its importance and scope. We state the broad research question that is the focus of the study.

Review of the Literature

This section is a summary and synthesis of literature relevant to the research question. In general, the literature is used to summarize what was already known about the research question and to explain how the research study promises to build on and extend knowledge previously available. It also provides the rationale for the specific research questions that were addressed, for any research hypotheses, and for the research methods that were employed. (See Chapter 4 for a more in-depth discussion of the functions that the literature review performs).

How do we go about conducting a review of the literature and summarizing the review as a section of a research report? After a search of existing knowledge, we usually find ourselves with a great deal of information. It may consist of a stack of file cards (or some computer-assisted variation) with useful quotations on one side and the full citation (including all page numbers, volume numbers, and other necessary specifics) on the back. A good first step in making sense out of all this knowledge is to sort it into several broad topic areas. These may have been identified prior to embarking on the literature review, or they may simply suggest themselves during the sorting process.

Organizing the products of a literature review into an outline containing broad topic areas can serve a number of useful purposes. Some knowledge that we have collected may not fit perfectly within any of the broad topic areas. We may conclude that it is not as relevant to the research problem or questions as we had originally assumed. Thus, it may be discarded and not included in the literature review section of the research report.

Or, if it seems to stand alone but clearly does enlighten some aspect of our research problem or questions, we may decide to incorporate it as a new topic area. If we decide that it is an important contribution, we may need to seek additional related literature to further expand upon the topic area.

If it appears that there is no logical link between the topics when a broad outline is constructed, additional topics and/or references may be required to link the topics already included. When all topic areas and subtopics have been included, they should reflect a logical flow, usually from the more general areas related to the current research question to the topics most closely related to the research question. The topics are frequently used as headings and subheadings in the literature review section of our research report.

An example will help to illustrate how this is done. Suppose that we had conducted a literature review on the broad research question, "How has the increasingly chronic nature of HIV affected the role of caregivers and the demands made upon them?" The variety of relevant knowledge collected could have been sorted and organized using the following outline format:

I. Terminal and chronic illnesses
   A. Definitions and examples
   B. Interventions
   C. Caregiver roles
      1. Terminal illness
      2. Chronic illnesses

II. HIV/AIDS: The early years
   A. Confusion, fear, and misunderstanding
   B. Beginning insights
      1. Diagnosis
      2. Symptoms
      3. Course of the disease
      4. Methods of transmission
      5. Those most at risk
      6. Prevention options
      7. Treatment options
      8. Role of the caregiver
   C. Judgments and accusations
   D. Social and political responses

III. Changes and developments
   A. Increased social acceptance
   B. Pharmacological advances
      1. Ethical issues
      2. Economic issues
   C. Incidence
      1. Traditional populations
      2. Third world
      3. Nontraditional groups
   D. Longevity

IV. HIV as a chronic disease
    A. Perceptions of those who are HIV-positive
        1. Self
        2. The community
        3. Friends and relatives
    B. Current services
        1. Hospital
        2. Outpatient
        3. Hospice
    C. Caregiver requirements
        1. New stressors
        2. Relationship issues
        3. Economic impact

If we were to use this outline for the literature review section of our research report, it would begin with the general topics of terminal and chronic illnesses and caregiver issues involved with them. It would then move to the history of the HIV / AIDS epidemic and the social and political responses, changes and incidence of the epidemic, and, finally, up to our current understanding of HIV as a potentially chronic disease. This last topic included discussions of perceptions of people who are HIV-positive, current interventions available, and finally caregiver requirements for this population. It should lead the reader of our research report to better understand the focus of our study on the role of caregivers in today's population of people who are HIV-positive, and why we used the research methods that we did.

What are the characteristics of a good literature review section of a research report? How can our compilation of existing knowledge be organized and presented so that it will be of maximum benefit to the reader? This is a fairly complex topic, and entire books have been written on it (see Galvin, 2006; Hart, 1998). We will address only the major issues here.

In the literature review section of the report of a research study that is primarily quantitative, the reader should expect to find topics (identified by subheadings) of general relevance to the research questions near its beginning. For example, consider a research study seeking an answer to the broad research question, "Is there a relationship between use of party drugs such as ecstasy and adolescent suicide?" Early sections of the literature review might be devoted to a historical overview of substance abuse, a summary of what is known about adolescent drug usage, and a description of statistical trends in the incidence of adolescent suicide in North America. Knowledge that is more directly related to the research question—for example, a summary of the results of suicide autopsies conducted on recent cases of adolescent suicide, or results of other studies that examined the relationship between substance abuse and adolescent suicide—should appear later. Reports of research that studied the use of ecstasy and adolescent suicide would be summarized and discussed near the end of the review, so that the current research will appear to be a logical extension of previous scientific inquiries.

Thus, the flow of the literature review is reflective of deductive logic, a characteristic of quantitative studies in general. It reflects both direction and a logical progression from the general to the specific. It demonstrates how the quantitative researcher used existing knowledge to refine his or her thinking about research problems and questions, and how more specific questions and, often hypotheses, evolved from it.

In reports of qualitative research studies, there is also a review of literature section in which the researcher describes how existing knowledge relates to the current study. By convention (since that is the way it is done in quantitative studies), this section is often found early in the report, just before the methodology section. However, some qualitative reports place it after a description of the data, and some have two literature reviews, a brief one before the methodology section and another after the presentation of the data. This would be more consistent with the ways that the literature is used in qualitative research. An early review is often completed to learn just enough to move forward with the data collection, and then later a more in-depth review is completed to help interpret the data in light of existing knowledge.

Statement of Research Questions and Hypotheses

Related to the purpose of the study and following logically from the review of the literature, the specific set of research questions and/or hypotheses that were examined in the study are specified. Operational definitions of key terms (also derived from the review of literature) may be included here, or may appear early in the next (methodology) section.

Methodology

In the methodology section of a research report, a detailed description of the research design is presented. It generally includes subsections that describe the setting of the research, the research participants, the treatment or program being evaluated (if applicable), the outcome measures, and the statistical analyses that were used. The subsection on participants should include a description (size, characteristics) of the research sample or samples, as well as the method used for sample selection and the rationale for it. A data collection subsection should include a description of the methods used for obtaining measurements of key variables (how, when, where, and by whom the data were collected). There should also be a discussion of the selection and/or development of any data collection instruments that were used. When describing previously published measurement instruments, there should be at least one reference in which the psychometric properties (reliability, validity, norms, cutting scores, etc.) are described.

The methodology section describes in detail the research design [what was done, to whom or what, and by what method(s)]. The rationale for all major methodological decisions is presented (sampling, measurement, data collection methods, and choice of methods for statistical analysis). The section enables the reader of the report to assess the credibility of both the research methods used and the research findings and, if desired, it enables the reader to replicate the research.

Findings

In this section, we would list the principal findings derived from our research methods. In quantitative reports, results of the statistical analyses are summarized. Tables, graphs, or other methods of summarizing the results of analyses help the reader better visualize what was found. In qualitative reports, there are generally direct quotations from the research participants and descriptions of observations made by the researchers.

The findings section of a research report is limited to a description of the data collected and the results of any statistical analysis of it—just the facts. The discussion of their possible meaning and importance occurs in the next section.

Discussion

In this section, the findings are discussed in relation to the research questions and/or hypotheses. Answers to questions are proposed, and, if applicable, evidence of support or nonsupport for hypotheses is presented. Findings are also discussed in relation to the findings of others as reported in the literature. Findings that corroborate those of other researchers and theoreticians are identified and findings that conflict with what has been reported elsewhere are discussed and, where appropriate, reconciled.

Limitations

In this section we list and discuss the study's methodological shortcomings of which we are aware. No research design is perfect—all research tends to be limited somewhat by one or more inherent design constraints or obstacles encountered in attempting to implement the design. For example, an explanatory design may contain inherent problems because of an inability to use a true control group or because of our need to draw a sample from an available sampling frame rather than from the accessible population. Limitations can also result as a function of other methodological difficulties, such as the need to use a data collection instrument that had not yet been demonstrated to be reliable with the participants used in the research, or because of constraints on the kinds of data that were allowed to be collected. There are many issues in research that prevent studies from being designed and/or executed flawlessly. The reader requires an honest description of these limitations to know how to interpret and evaluate findings. A useful format for the discussion of each major limitation consists of (a) a specific description of the nature and scope of the limitation; (b) an explanation of why the limitation was unavoidable; (c) the researcher's speculation on how the limitation may have negatively affected the research and its findings; (d) a description of what, if anything, was done to minimize the potential negative effects of the limitation on the research; and (e) an assessment of how successful the effort was.

> **Research-Informed Practice or Practice-Informed Research**
>
> **Behavior: Apply critical thinking to engage in analysis of quantitative and qualitative research methods and research findings.**
>
> **Critical Thinking Question:** If you conduct a pretest posttest study with 15 of your adolescent clients with bulimia nervosa that you are seeing at your agency, list three limitations you would want to discuss in a research report describing the study.

Recommendations for Future Research, Implications for Social Work, and Conclusions

In this section, we include a description of how the study is believed to have advanced knowledge in the problem area. We also recommend further research that is needed and suggest ways additional studies might be designed and implemented to both build on the achievements of the current research and to avoid its shortcomings. The implications of the findings for social work practice are an especially important component of this section of the research report. Generally, we make specific suggestions as to how the findings might be implemented to improve the delivery of services to social work clients, that is, what changes in intervention methods appear to be indicated on the basis of the findings of the study.

References and Appendices

The reference list is placed immediately after the body of the manuscript in most research reports. We should ensure that the references in the text of the report as well as the references in the reference list follow the appropriate formatting style. Every publication referenced in the body of the report should be included in the reference list, and every publication in the reference list should be referenced at least once in the text of the report.

Appendices, which may be of interest to only a few readers, may also be included in the report. These might include, for example, copies of data collection instruments that were used, complete results of statistical testing that were only summarized in tabular form in the findings section or, in the report of a program evaluation, materials developed by agency personnel to describe or publicize the program.

QUANTITATIVE VERSUS QUALITATIVE RESEARCH REPORTS

Most quantitative research reports, including journal articles (discussed later in this chapter), follow the general format described above. We are expected to address each of the sections, although sometimes two or more can be combined under one heading. If the research is primarily qualitative, the same general format may be used. However, there are likely to be several important differences in the report:

- The introduction section is likely to be briefer and contain fewer facts and numbers, since less is generally known about the problem than in predominantly quantitative studies.
- The review of literature section early in the report is shorter, because (a) there often is relatively little known about the problem and (b) the literature may have been reviewed less thoroughly prior to data collection to avoid biasing the collection and interpretation of the data.
- There are research questions but, very rarely, research hypotheses.
- The methodology section is likely to be shorter than in a report of a quantitative study. Since replication of a qualitative study is not likely to occur, there is generally less need to describe the research design in great detail. A notable exception might be if the design employed grounded theory (see Chapter 6), which prescribes certain tasks and a specific sequence of events. The reader may want to know whether they were adhered to in order to evaluate the credibility of the research findings.

- The results section may be quite long, often containing case vignettes or extended narrative descriptions with verbatim quotations from research participants. It may contain some descriptive statistics and, rarely, inferential statistics. In a qualitative study, we are often looking for the deeper meaning of the phenomenon being studied, something that cannot be condensed into statistics, which are more characteristic of a report of a predominantly quantitative study.

- The discussion section may be quite long and contain numerous references to the literature as we attempt to relate our observations and conclusions to what was previously known about the problem. It may contain one or more story lines, theories, or hypotheses that have evolved from the research and are now proposed for testing by other researchers.

- The limitations section may be shorter than in the report of a quantitative study, or even nonexistent. Since there are usually no claims to objectivity, sample representativeness, or control of confounding variables in most qualitative studies, there is no need to speculate on their likely effects.

- While there are conclusions and recommendations, they may be more tentative and cautious than in reports of quantitative studies. They often contain ideas for future research, both qualitative and quantitative, and suggestions as to how the insights achieved during the study might help to inform social work practice.

REFERENCING IN A RESEARCH REPORT

As we have suggested, the reader of a research report should receive a clear picture of what the research was designed to accomplish, how it was conducted, and what was learned from it. A research report reveals both our communication skills and our knowledge of research methods.

The technical aspects of research report writing, such as footnoting and referencing style, use of certain terminology, whether or not to include data collection instruments in the appendices, and so forth, are beyond the scope of this book. However, there are entire books devoted to these topics (e.g., Pyrczak & Bruce, 2014; Thyer, 2008). The most common formatting style used in social work research reports is the American Psychological Association (APA) format. For a detailed description of this formatting style, we can turn to the manual of the American Psychological Association (2009). Several other books have been written in an effort to present the APA formatting style in an easier-to-use format (see, for example, Houghton & Houghton, 2009; Rossiter, 2009). One APA formatting book (Szuchman & Thomlison, 2010) was written specifically for social work researchers.

In addition, several websites are now available to answer our APA formatting questions, for example,

- http://owl.english.purdue.edu/owl
- http://www.apastyle.org
- http://www.writinghelp-central.com/apa.html

There are also computer software programs to assist us in creating documents following the APA formatting style. Some of these are Scholarword, PERRLA, Dr. Paper,

StyleEase, FormatEase, and Reference Point Templates. Sometimes these software packages lag one or even two editions behind the most current APA manual. Therefore, when using software to format a manuscript, it may be necessary to make additional changes to it in order to comply with the newest formatting rules.

Both direct quotations and references appear most frequently in the literature review section of a research report. While sometimes useful, quotations should be used sparingly. It is the substance of what others have to say rather than their specific words that are important to the researcher. Excessive use of quotations may mislead the reader because quotations are always taken out of context. In addition, because all writers have their own style, quotations can make the flow of the text uneven while providing more detail than the reader requires (Pyrczak & Bruce, 2014).

If factual reports, such as statistical results, are included from previous research, it is always appropriate to provide citations. They allow the reader to verify the accuracy of what was included. But, like quotations, they should be included only if the work cited contributes a unique understanding of a topic, not simply as evidence that we missed little in reviewing the literature.

There may be a natural tendency to want to include every bit of knowledge that has been discovered. After all, finding it took a considerable amount of effort! But, if ten articles present essentially the same position, there is no reason to cite them all—that would be overkill. One or two will make the point and be less likely to disrupt the flow of the text.

How relevant should knowledge be in order to be cited? How much detail of another researcher's work is needed or desirable? Bem (2004) has provided some useful guidelines:

- Only cite articles that are pertinent to your specific research question
- Emphasize major findings and conclusions, avoiding unnecessary detail
- If another review article surveys the literature relevant to your research question, simply refer the reader to the review
- When you do want to describe an entire research study, condense it as much as possible while still communicating the relevant details

Are some types of citations better than others? Yes. But a good mix is often desirable. The best citations to use (all other factors being equal) are those that refer to recent, well-designed research, as opposed to those that may be dated or methodologically flawed. But it is perfectly acceptable to include some older citations, especially if the contribution was a major influence on subsequent thought on a topic or issue. Older citations can also be useful for providing a historical perspective on a problem or event. They reflect the state of the art of knowledge, beliefs, and attitudes at a point in history.

Whether in the literature section or in the discussion of our research findings, the quotations and citations included are there to help explain how we went from point A to point B. They are not there to impress others with how much relevant information was examined. If anything will impress the reader of a good research report, it is our objectivity and open-mindedness.

Objectivity can be demonstrated in a number of ways. For example, it can be seen in a willingness to include the conflicting opinions and conclusions of other researchers, which almost invariably exist. It is not unusual for two scholars to express beliefs and

The inclusion of references that reflect both sides of an argument suggests that we have been both thorough and objective in conducting the literature review and in deciding what is important to include in a research report.

conclusions that are diametrically opposite. The inclusion of references that reflect both sides of an argument suggests that we have been both thorough and objective in deciding what is important to include in a research report. Open-mindedness can be demonstrated by including the ideas and opinions of others that are controversial, may not agree with our own findings, or are generally not consistent with mainstream beliefs and the reasoning behind them.

ROLE OF RESEARCHER IN THE RESEARCH REPORT

By encouraging open-mindedness, we do not mean to suggest that the researcher should always remain behind the scenes in a research report or express no opinions or conclusions. In fact, the opposite is true. Although our biases should not be evident, our thought processes should be both obvious and open to critique. The reader should be able to sense the presence of the researcher in the text.

The role of the researcher in a research report has some similarities to that of a travel guide. (This is especially true in the review of literature section.) What do we mean by this? Suppose you are visiting a city like San Francisco for the first time and you only have one full day to take in the sights. You could spend hours or days surfing the Internet before you travel, plan an itinerary on the basis of what interests you, and then rent a car to get around when you arrive. Or, you could simply sign up for a city tour in a van or bus with a travel guide to take you to the most commonly visited tourist attractions and give you some background on each attraction. The latter choice might cost a little more and some of what you see may not interest you too much, but the savings in time and effort will be well worth it. Like a travel guide, as the writer of a research report, we have identified and organized what we believe is of interest and is most relevant to the research problems and questions that we addressed. This is a real time and effort saver for readers—relevant knowledge acquired from others has been distilled down into an organized, well-written narrative. But there is more to the analogy. A travel guide would not tell you that you must be very impressed by the Golden Gate Bridge or that Coit Tower is really disappointing. He or she would simply provide access to a number of potentially interesting sights and let you decide for yourself if you share his or her opinion of them. Similarly, we as researchers simply share what we learned from our research and how it may relate to existing knowledge. We do not tell the readers of the review of literature section or the research findings or implications sections in a research report what to conclude or how to interpret them. We merely summarize what <u>we</u> derived from them and, of course, readers are free to agree or disagree with our conclusions and recommendations.

In a well-written literature review, we help the reader navigate through existing, relevant knowledge, stopping along the way to pull together conclusions and evaluate where—in our opinion—the literature seems to be leading. We try not to exert too much influence on the reader, whenever possible letting the literature speak for itself. In a well-written literature review, the reader will generally come to the same or similar conclusions as we have and will agree about what the literature has to say about the research questions and how best to study them. Our conclusions should contain no surprises. They will have been anticipated by the reader on the basis of the evidence that has been presented in the literature.

If we perceive our role as similar to that of a travel guide, neither of the two problems that frequently characterize literature reviews is likely to occur. One fairly common problem occurs when our own thinking appears to dominate the literature review and appears to be invulnerable to influence by it. The reader is left with the suspicion that existing knowledge had little influence on the conclusions that we drew. Even if a fair number of citations are present, they do not reflect balance. It appears that we selectively used only literature that would support our existing biases and beliefs. We emerged from the literature review with our beliefs unchanged (something that rarely, if ever, happens in a good review of literature). The reader, sensing this, is likely to doubt whether other stages of the research process were not compromised in the same biased manner.

The second problem occurs when the development of our thinking is not evident in the literature review section of a research report. It seems to be little more than a long series of quotations, perhaps only because they are expected. They lend a scholarly appearance, but seem to have no other apparent purpose. There is no way for the reader to evaluate our thought processes and the literature does not seem to lead logically to our research questions and/or hypotheses or to the research design that we used.

In the two preceding scenarios, we would not have made productive use of the accumulated literature and may have damaged the credibility of our research findings and recommendations. But if we assume the role of guide, the proper mix of quotations reflecting relevant knowledge and the use of that knowledge to refine thinking about the research topic will be evident. The literature review will be a unified whole that seems to take the reader somewhere—from Point A to Point B.

Similarly, it should be obvious to the reader of a research report than any references to existing knowledge in the research findings or conclusions and recommendations sections were used to clarify our thinking about what we observed, not to simply confirm our pre-existing beliefs or biases. Thus, the related findings and conclusions of others, both those that seem to agree with what we learned, but also those that do not, are referenced. The former may lend support to what we believe we found or help us to better understand it. But the latter are equally important. They can lead us to challenge our interpretation of it or to qualify or modify it. References to knowledge acquired by others is an integral part of a research report. It is included to put our research, all components of it, in perspective.

DISSEMINATING RESEARCH FINDINGS

There are many vehicles that can be used to share research findings. We will describe some of the more commonly used ones.

Internal Correspondence and In-Service Training

There are many reasons why we may choose to disseminate research findings through internal correspondence or in-service training sessions. Research studies with limited external validity, research on unique client populations, or unreplicated evaluation studies all may be appropriately disseminated through venues internal to the organization.

Research studies with limited external validity, research on unique client populations, or unreplicated evaluation studies all may be appropriately disseminated through venues internal to the organization.

Some organizations have monthly or quarterly newsletters, often available on-line, and their editors are looking for materials to publish. As vehicles to disseminate research findings, these outlets have several advantages. When we submit a summary of our research (emphasizing its findings) to the editor of such a publication, it is almost certain to be published, especially if an inquiry to see what form it should take has been made in advance. If published, the summary is likely to be read, because staff members generally like to read about what is going on in their work setting. In addition, any recommendations will be put to use with only minimal time lag following completion of the research.

If the researcher's organization has a regular in-service training or staff development program, it can be used to disseminate research findings. Some organizations prefer to do this informally, for example, in a brown bag lunch program, where staff members take turns leading discussions about various work-related issues. This type of program attracts those who have a genuine interest in our findings and increases the likelihood that they will be disseminated quickly and put to use.

Professional Conferences

Research findings of a more general interest can be disseminated through presentations at professional conferences and symposia. Many national and international social work organizations—for example, NASW, SSWR, American Public Welfare Association, Child Welfare League of America, CSWE, the International Federation of Social Workers, and the Human Services Information Technology Applications—hold conferences at various locations throughout the United States and (in some instances) the world. Some of them sponsor conferences that may be more geographically limited, such as state conferences, or that may be more narrowly focused on a topic or population, such as conferences relating to services to people with HIV, family support and preservation programs, long-term care, family violence, or homelessness. In addition, there are many other major conferences in fields related to social work, such as psychology, sociology, public health, public administration, or education, that often include presentations that are of multidisciplinary interest.

The largest and most prestigious conferences usually solicit proposals and abstracts for presentations about a wide range of topics that are loosely related to a theme. A "call for abstracts" or "call for proposals" and a deadline for their receipt is published in professional journals or newsletters, or mailed to the organization's members along with advertisements for the conference. Typically, a prospective presenter is asked to write an overview or abstract of what is to be presented and indicate the area of the program in which it would best fit. Many major conferences now have a separate grouping for proposals for presentations that are empirically based and another for those that are more conceptual or theoretical in nature. Proposals for presentations of research are generally expected to follow a specified outline—usually a mini version of a traditional research report—plus descriptions of the methods for presentation. The author may be asked to indicate those individuals who would most likely benefit from and be interested in the presentation. The presentation overview or abstract itself generally does not include

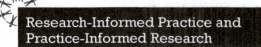

Research-Informed Practice and Practice-Informed Research

Behavior: Use and translate research evidence to inform and improve practice, policy, and service delivery.

Critical Thinking Question: Look up NASW and CSWE on the Internet. When will the next national conferences of these two organizations be held and what are the themes of each of the conferences?

any identifying information, allowing it to be reviewed anonymously. A separate or detachable cover page includes the proposed presenter's name and affiliation, phone number, e-mail address, and other identifying information.

Generally, the major conference planning committees receive many more proposals for presentations than there are places on the program. It is not unusual for a major conference to accept only 10 or 20 percent of all proposals received. The review process takes time. Often, there is a lag time of several months between the proposal's receipt (typically acknowledged through e-mail) and notification of a decision by the planning committee.

The major conferences tend to use a large number of volunteer reviewers who are generally accomplished professionals and/or researchers. A proposal may be read anonymously by two or three reviewers who provide a numerical rating on a scale devised by the conference planning committee. The system is likely to give points for such criteria as the proposal's relevance to the conference theme, the potential interest of conference participants in the topic, the quality of the research described, and how well the proposal is written and conforms to guidelines. The review criteria to be used are usually listed in the call for abstracts.

The system is likely to give points for such criteria as the proposal's relevance to the conference theme, the potential interest of conference participants in the topic, the quality of the research described, and how well the proposal is written and conforms to guidelines.

All people who submit proposals are notified at the same time of the decisions of the planning committee. Those who are invited to present are asked to respond in writing whether or not they can commit to attend. Presentations can take different forms. A researcher may be asked to write and present a formal paper, leaving time for discussion and questions from those in attendance. Although it is possible to simply read the paper, this is not very enjoyable for anyone involved and is now rarely done. The single-paper presentation is less popular today than it once was. Now it is more common to group two or three related papers in one session (perhaps lasting 1 or 1½ hours), where each individual has an allotted period of time to present an overview of his or her research. A moderator introduces the presenters, monitors the time, and generally makes sure all presenters are treated equitably. Presenters often use PowerPoint slide presentations or other methods to help those in attendance visualize what they are describing. Handouts summarizing major findings are sometimes given out to those in attendance.

Another presentation format is the poster session. (It is similar to how junior high and high school students showcase their research at science fairs). The presenter is located in a large hall with many others who are also there to present and discuss their work. Typically, presenters are provided with a mobile display board to exhibit their research visually and a table and a few chairs to discuss informally their research methods and findings with conference attendees interested enough to stop by. It can be intellectually stimulating to discuss our research with colleagues, some of whom invariably challenge some aspect of the research design and/or question our findings and recommendations.

Those who choose to attend our conference presentation (where there are many available options running concurrently) generally have shared interests and may even be doing research in the same problem area. Opportunities to share findings and to collaborate on future research projects can develop. In addition, we can learn a great deal about research from attending other presentations that interest us at the conference.

The presentation of research at a prestigious conference can also enhance a social work career. This is especially true for academicians or those who work for research-oriented organizations such as teaching hospitals. In addition, continuing education units (CEUs) can be obtained to help meet state licensure requirements. Because major conferences also tend to be held in interesting places, there are also opportunities for sightseeing and recreation. Attending them can be just plain enjoyable.

Many larger conferences help with the dissemination of research knowledge in another way. Presentations or a summary of them are often put together in electronic or monograph form and are sold (or sometimes distributed at no charge) to members who either attended the conference or were unable to attend. If the sponsoring organization has its own professional journal or journals, presenters may be asked to submit (for publication consideration) a paper based on their presentation.

There are many other smaller conferences—for example, local and regional meetings—where researchers can disseminate their research findings. Getting on the program of, for example, a state NASW symposium or regional conference may be a less prestigious achievement than presenting at a major national or international conference. However, especially if the findings are primarily of local interest, a local or regional conference may be the best venue to share newly acquired knowledge.

Presenting our research at local and regional meetings has certain advantages. Costs associated with presentation (travel, registration fees, lodging, and so forth) tend to be lower at smaller conferences, which have fewer attendees and are often held in less exotic locales. Opportunities to meet and network with fellow professionals may be better in some respects. At local and regional conferences, we can interact with those individuals whose help may be valuable for meeting daily job responsibilities or for acquiring needed support for future research projects.

Professional Journals

The most traditional and potentially the most effective way to disseminate research knowledge is through publication in a professional journal. Journals can be purchased by individual subscribers. Some journals are given as a benefit to the members of a social work organization and thus tend to reach more potential readers.

Professional journals are also purchased by libraries, where they are increasingly available to students, scholars, and researchers to use in their research literature reviews and thus in their own research. Journal articles now are also available on-line. They remain available for use indefinitely, long after a conference presentation has been forgotten.

When writing a manuscript for possible publication in a professional journal, we would follow the general report outline presented earlier. However, research reports in a professional journal are much shorter, usually between twelve and twenty printed pages.

A potential journal article should be sent to only one journal at a time. Anything else is considered unethical. Most journals use volunteer, unpaid reviewers who give their time as a service to their profession. It would be a major imposition for an author to send a manuscript to several journals simultaneously, perhaps getting it accepted by two or more. Because only one can ultimately publish it, the reviewers from the other journals would have wasted their time reviewing and critiquing it. However, once one journal has rejected a manuscript, it is perfectly okay to send it elsewhere. Sometimes reviewers reject an article but offer the author an opportunity to resubmit with changes. It is not unusual for a manuscript to be rejected by several journals until finally being accepted.

Getting an article published in a professional journal can be a tedious, time-consuming, and sometimes frustrating experience. Among the most prestigious journals, many more manuscripts are submitted than are accepted for publication. Many people want to publish in them; academicians want and sometimes need to be published in them to maintain or advance their careers. While the best-known journals publish only a small percentage of manuscripts submitted for publication, in contrast, some of the more narrowly focused and less well-known ones may accept up to 50 percent of the manuscripts submitted, or even more.

There are books available to help prospective authors prepare manuscripts and find the scholarly journals most likely to publish a report of their work (Beebe, 1993; NASW Press, 2009; Thyer, 1994). Colleagues who have been published (especially academicians) are often another good resource. Most journals describe the procedure for submission of a manuscript in each issue of the journal and on their websites. The procedures tend to be fairly similar across journals.

Journals that use a *blind review procedure* use a group of consulting editors, usually relatively accomplished academicians and other professionals who serve limited terms. They have agreed to anonymously read and review manuscripts that have been submitted for publication. Two or three reviewers, selected by the editor on the basis of their expertise or interest in the topic, read and critique the manuscript and make an assessment of its publication potential. The final decision, however, generally remains with the editor, a small committee, or an editorial board.

Ethical and Professional Behavior

Behavior: Use supervision and consultation to guide professional judgment and behavior.

Critical Thinking Question: Why does the blind review process help ensure the quality and integrity of the articles published in professional journals?

What can happen when a manuscript is submitted to a professional journal? Usually, the author can expect one of three possible responses:

1. The manuscript is accepted for publication without revision. This rarely happens, especially among the best-known, most prestigious journals.

2. The manuscript is rejected by the journal. This can happen in one of three ways. Depending upon the journal, the length of time between submission and rejection may suggest which one occurred.

    i.   The editor, in a cursory reading, may have concluded that the manuscript is either simply not publishable at all or not appropriate for the journal. Thus, the decision was made to not send it out to reviewers. If the author gets a rejection letter in a very short time, say, just a few weeks, this is most likely what happened.

    ii. If rejection takes longer, the editor may have decided that the manuscript might have publication potential and sent it out to reviewers, but a majority of them decided that the manuscript should not be published.

    iii. If an even longer period between submission and rejection occurs, it generally means that the initial reviewers may have read the manuscript but disagreed as to whether it should be published. It was then sent to another reviewer who cast the deciding vote to not publish it.

3. The manuscript is not accepted in its present form but the author is provided with suggestions for revisions. He or she is encouraged to make

the requested revisions and then resubmit it. The author can then choose to (a) seek publication elsewhere or (b) inform the editor that he or she will make all or most of the required revisions. As a general rule, the latter alternative is the better choice. While not a guarantee of publication, if the author is conscientious in responding to suggestions by either making revisions as suggested or (occasionally) explaining why they should not be made, the manuscript will usually be accepted for publication. The research findings will be disseminated sooner than if the manuscript were to be submitted to another journal where the review process would begin anew. However, if the author believes that the suggestions for revision are incorrect or otherwise unacceptable, it makes more sense to seek publication elsewhere than to refuse to make many of the requested changes and resubmit the manuscript to the same journal. This stonewalling generally just results in rejection.

Even in instances in which a manuscript is rejected outright, it has become common practice to provide the author with limited feedback and, sometimes, suggestions for other methods for dissemination. This is both a professional courtesy and a useful service. It acknowledges that (1) a considerable amount of work went into preparing a manuscript for possible publication and (2) it may still be possible to find another venue (such as those we have discussed) where at least some of the author's efforts will be rewarded. For example, it may be tactfully suggested that, while the manuscript may not be publishable, the research findings might be better suited for a poster presentation at a professional conference.

Although the quality of the research methods employed, the importance of the findings, and the quality of writing displayed are major considerations in whether a manuscript is accepted for publication, luck and timing also play roles. For example, assuming that the manuscript meets all these criteria, its acceptance for publication may still depend in part on <u>when</u> it is submitted to a journal. Its chances are enhanced if it arrives when the journal needs another good article to complete an upcoming issue. A situation wherein the journal has already accepted but not yet published another manuscript on a similar topic or problem area could prove fortuitous or it could work against the author. The journal may decide to accept the manuscript along with the previously accepted one, to complement it or make the topic the focus of a special issue on the problem area. But the other, already accepted manuscript on the topic may also work to the author's detriment. The editor may decide that the manuscript that the author submitted, although otherwise publishable, is simply not needed. The editor may reject the manuscript or possibly publish it in a later edition of the journal.

There are intangible rewards for having a published article in a professional journal. There is something gratifying about seeing the results of our research in print and perhaps cited in someone else's work, and hoping that it is being read, appreciated, and used by others. But journals do not pay authors for their articles when they publish them; in fact, publishing an article can be expensive in terms of the time and effort entailed.

Unfortunately, publication in journals also does not result in rapid dissemination of research findings. Getting a manuscript accepted can take a year or more. Once accepted, it may not be published for another year or two. Despite this disadvantage, publication of our research methods and findings in a professional journal probably remains the most generally accepted acknowledgment that we have met an obligation to the scientific community.

Monographs, Dissertations, and Theses

If research is sponsored (funded) by an organization or designed to meet a graduate degree requirement, it is usually written (and often bound) using a standardized format developed by the organization or university involved. The report is generally quite lengthy. In the case of funded research, it may be distributed to interested parties as a research monograph. If the research was a degree requirement, it may be called a thesis (master's degree) or a dissertation (doctorate). The report is placed in the library of the university where the student completed the degree. It is also made available to others through interlibrary loan systems in either hard copy or via electronic communication. A complete research report provides a detailed description of all aspects of the research study discussed earlier in this chapter, including the participants, research design, outcome measures, findings, and conclusions. Sufficient information is offered so that readers can replicate the research and/or evaluate whether the researcher's conclusions appear to be justified and the recommendations seem appropriate for implementation in their own practice.

Sufficient information is offered so that readers can replicate the research and/ or evaluate whether the researcher's conclusions appear to be justified and the recommendations seem appropriate for implementation in their own practice.

SUMMARY

In this chapter:

- The sections of the research report were described.
- We looked at some of the differences between qualitative and quantitative reports.
- Practical suggestions were given for organizing a wide array of knowledge into a logical and coherent report of what is known relative to the research problem and the questions chosen for study.
- We considered some of the issues involved in referencing other sources in a research report.
- We proposed the analogy that the writer of a research report functions much like a tour guide. The writer compiles relevant knowledge and presents it to the reader along with his or her interpretations and conclusions drawn from it. The writer encourages the reader to critique these conclusions and the thought processes that produced them and agree or disagree with them.
- Alternatives for disseminating research findings were discussed, including internal correspondence and in-service training, conference presentations, publication in professional journals, and publication of monographs, dissertations, and theses.

MyEducationLab® for Research

Start with the Topic 21 Assignments: Preparing a Research Report and the Topic 21 Study Plan, and then Topic 22 Assignments: Evaluating a Research Report and the Topic 22 Study Plan.

Chapter 14 Chapter Review Quiz.

References

Chapter 1

Anderson, R. C. (2000). *We are all casualties of friendly fire in the war on drugs*. Retrieved from http://rockyanderson.org/?page_id=8269

Begun, A. L., Berger, L. K., Otto-Salaj, L. L., & Rose, S. J. (2010). Developing effective social work university-community research collaborations. *Social Work, 55*, 54–62.

Bronson, D. E. (2009). Critically appraising studies for evidence-based practice. In A. R. Roberts (Ed.), *Social worker's desk reference* (2nd ed., pp. 1137–1141). New York: Oxford University Press.

Corcoran, J., & Littell, J. H. (2009). Meta-analysis and evidence-based practice. In A. R. Roberts (Ed.), *Social worker's desk reference* (2nd ed., pp. 1149–1152). New York: Oxford University Press.

Council on Social Work Education. (2015). *Educational policy and accreditation standards*. Alexandria, VA: CSWE.

Denzin, N. K., & Lincoln, Y. S. (Eds.). (1994). *Handbook of qualitative research*. Thousand Oaks, CA: Sage Publications, Inc.

Gambrill, E. (2009). Integrating information from diverse sources in evidence-based practice. In A. R. Roberts (Ed.), *Social worker's desk reference* (2nd ed., pp. 1120–1126). New York: Oxford University Press.

Gambrill, E., & Gibbs, L. (2009). Developing well-structured questions for evidence-informed practice. In A. R. Roberts (Ed.), *Social worker's desk reference* (2nd ed., pp. 1120–1126). New York: Oxford University Press.

Garvin, C. (1981). Research-related roles for social workers. In R. Grinnell, Jr. (Ed.), *Social work research and evaluation* (pp. 547–552). Itasca, IL: F. E. Peacock.

Gelso, C. J., & Lent, R. W. (2000). Scientific training and scholarly productivity: The person, the training environment, and their interaction. In S. D. Brown & R. W. Lent (Eds.), *Handbook of counselling psychology* (3rd ed., pp. 109–139). New York: Wiley.

Glasser, M., Kolvin, I., Campbell, D., Glasser, A., Leitch, I., & Farrelly, S. (2001). Cycle of child sexual abuse: Links between being a victim and becoming a perpetrator. *British Journal of Psychiatry, 79*, 482–494.

Grinnell, R., Jr., & Siegel, D. (1988). The place of research in social work. In R. Grinnell, Jr. (Ed.), *Social work research and evaluation*. Itasca, IL: F. E. Peacock.

Guyatt, G., & Rennie, D. (2002). *Users' guides to the medical literature: Essentials of evidence-based clinical practice*. Chicago: American Medical Association.

Hamilton, S., Nelson Goff, B. S., Crow, J. R., & Reisbig, A. M. J. (2009). Primary trauma of female partners in a military sample: Individual symptoms and relationship satisfaction. *American Journal of Family Therapy, 37*, 336–346.

Howard, M. O., Perron, B. E., & Vaughn, M. G. (2009). Practice-guidelines and evidence-based practice. In A. R. Roberts (Ed.), *Social worker's desk reference* (2nd ed., pp. 1157–1162). New York: Oxford University Press.

Israel, N., & Jozefowicz-Simbeni, D. M. H. (2009). Perceived strengths of urban girls and boys experiencing homelessness. *Journal of Community & Applied Social Psychology, 19*, 156–164.

Levin, J. (2013). *The welfare queen*. Retrieved from http://www.slate.com/articles/news_and_politics/history/2013/12/linda_taylor_welfare_queen_ronald_reagan_made_her_a_notorious_american_villain.html

Littell, J. H., & Corcoran, J. (2009). Systematic reviews and evidence-based practice. In A. R. Roberts (Ed.), *Social worker's desk reference* (2nd ed., pp. 1152–1156). New York: Oxford University Press.

Lynam, D. R., Milich, R., Zimmerman, R., Novak, S. P., Logan, T. K., Martin, C., Leukefeld, C., & Clayton, R. (1999). Project DARE: No effects at 10-year follow-up. *Journal of Consulting and Clinical Psychology, 67*, 590–593.

Mears, S. L., Yaffe, J., & Harris, N. J. (2009). Evaluation of wraparound services for severely emotionally disturbed youths. *Research on Social Work Practice, 19*, 678–685.

Montgomery, P., & Mayo-Wilson, E. (2009). Randomized controlled trials and evidence-based practice. In A. R. Roberts (Ed.), *Social worker's desk reference* (2nd ed., pp. 1142–1148). New York: Oxford University Press.

National Association of Social Workers. (2015). Retrieved from http://www.socialworkpolicy.org/research/evidence-based-practice-2.html

O'Neill, J. (2000). Practice-research sync "crucial for survival." *NASW News, 45*, 3.

Parish, S. L., Rose, R. A., & Andrews, M. E. (2010). TANF's impact on low-income mothers raising children with disabilities. *Exceptional Children, 76*, 234–253.

Petrosino, A., Turpin-Petrosino, C., & Buehler, J. (2005). Scared straight and other juvenile awareness program for preventing juvenile delinquency. *The Scientific Review of Mental Health Practice, 4*(1), 48–54.

Prentky, R. A., Nien-Chen, L., Righthand, S. Schuler, A., Cavanaugh, D., & Lee, A. F. (2010). Assessing risk of sexually abusive behavior among youth in a child welfare sample. *Behavioral Sciences & the Law, 28*, 24–45.

Proctor, E. (2003). Evidence for practice: Challenges, opportunities, and access. *Social Work Research*, 27, 195.

Rank, M. R. (1994). *Living on the edge: The realities of welfare in America*. New York: Columbia University Press.

Roberts, A. R. (2009). *Social worker's desk reference* (2nd ed.). New York: Oxford University Press.

Rosen, A. (2003). Evidence-based social work practice: Challenges and promise. *Social Work Research*, 27, 197–208.

Rotheram-Borus, M. J., Desmond, K., Comulada, W. S., Arnold, E. M., & Johnson, M. (2009). Reducing risky sexual behavior and substance use among currently and formerly homeless adults living with HIV. *American Journal of Public Health*, 99, 1100–1107.

Rubin, A., & Parrish, D. (2009). Locating credible studies for evidence-based practice. In A. R. Roberts (Ed.), *Social worker's desk reference* (2nd ed., pp. 1127–1136). New York: Oxford University Press.

Simpson, R. (1979). Understanding the utilization of research and other applied professions. In A. Rubin & A. Rosenblatt (Eds.), *Sourcebook on research utilization* (pp. 16–28). New York: Council on Social Work Education.

Strauss, S. E., Richardson, W. S., Glasziou, P., & Haynes, R. B. (2005). *Evidence-based medicine: How to practice and teach EBM* (3rd ed.). New York: Elsevier.

Thyer, B. A., & Myers, L. L. (2007). *A social worker's guide to evaluating practice outcomes*. Alexandria, VA: Council on Social Work Education.

Thyer, B. A., & Myers, L. L. (2009). N=1 experiments and their role in evidence-based practice. In A. R. Roberts (Ed.), *Social worker's desk reference* (2nd ed., pp. 1176–1182). New York: Oxford University Press.

Thyer, B. A., & Myers, L. L. (2010). Cultural diversity and social work practice: An evidenced based approach. In B. A. Thyer, J. S. Wodarski, L. L. Myers, & D. F. Harrison (Eds.), *Human diversity and social work practice: An evidenced-based approach* (3rd ed., pp. 3–28).Springfield, IL: Charles C. Thomas.

The United States Conference of Mayors. (2005). *A status report on hunger and homelessness in American cities*. Retrieved from http://www.usmayors.org/hungersurvey/2005/HH2005FINAL.pdf

Van Burgh, J., Redner, G., & Moon, C. (1995). *A report of project DARE with eighth grade students*. Retrieved from http://files.eric.ed.gov/fulltext/ED423454.pdf

Wakefield, J., & Kirk, S. (1996). Unscientific thinking about scientific practice: Evaluating the scientist-practitioner model. *Social Work Research*, 20, 83–95.

Zimbardo, P. (2010). *Stanford prison experiment*. Retrieved from www.prisonexp.org.

Chapter 2

Anastas, J. W. (2010). Quality in qualitative evaluation: Issues and possible answers. *Research on Social Work Practice*, 14, 57–65.

Annas, G. (1992). *The Nazi doctors and the Nuremberg Code: Human rights in human experimentation*. New York: Oxford University Press.

Associated Press Report. (1997, September 18). Experts blast AIDS studies that endanger poor subjects. *The State*, A14.

Council on Social Work Education. (2007). *National statement on research integrity in social work*. Alexandria, VA: CSWE Publications.

Day, N. L., & Richardson, G. A. (1993). Cocaine use and crack babies: Science, the media, and miscommunications. *Neurotoxicology and Teratology*, 15, 293–294.

Deer, B. (22 February 2004). Revealed: MMR research scandal. *The Sunday Times* (London).

Deer, B. (8 February 2009). MMR doctor Andrew Wakefield fixed data on autism. *The Sunday Times* (London).

Deer, B. (2011). How the case against the MMR vaccine was fixed. *British Medical Journal*, 342, c5347.

Delva, J. (2007). The human subjects review process: A subjective view. *Social Work*, 52, 2, 101–102.

Drug Policy Alliance. (2004). *Cocaine and pregnancy*. Retrieved from www.lindesmith.org/library/research/cocaine.cfm

Education Development Center, Inc. (2009). *Willowbrook hepatitis experiments*. Retrieved from https://science.education.nih.gov/supplements/nih9/bioethics/guide/pdf/master_5-4.pdf

Eisner, R., Vasgird, D., & Hyman-Browne, E. (n.d.). *RCR responsible authorship and peer review*. Retrieved from http://ccnmtl.columbia.edu/projects/rcr/rcr_authorship/

Ellenberg, S. S. (2009). The use of placebo-control groups in clinical trials. In V. Ravitsky, A. Fiester, & A. L. Caplan (Eds.), *The Penn Center guide to bioethics* (pp. 259–270). New York: Springer Publishing Company.

Falit, B. P., & Gross, C. P. (2008). Access to experimental drugs for terminally ill patients. *Journal of the American Medical Association*, 300, 2793–2795.

Florida State University. (2010). *Human Subjects Committee*. Retrieved from http://www.research.fsu.edu/humansubjects/

Griggs, R. A. (2014). Coverage of the Stanford Prison Experiment in introductory psychology textbooks. *Teaching of Psychology*, 41, 195-203.

Haney, C., Banks, C., & Zimbardo, P. (1973). *A Study of Prisoners and Guards in a Simulated Prison*. Washington DC: Office of Naval Research.

Health and Medicine. (1994). UCLA didn't ask schizophrenic patients' consent for experiment. *New York Times*, pp. B9–B10.

Humphreys, L. (1970). *Tearoom trade: Impersonal sex in public places*. Chicago: Aldine Press.

Jones, J. H. (1982). *Bad blood: The Tuskegee syphilis experiment*. New York: Free Press.

Milgram, S. (1963). Behavioral study of obedience. *Journal of Abnormal and Social Psychology*, 67, 371–378.

National Association of Social Workers. (2008). *Code of Ethics*. Retrieved from http://www.socialworkers.org/pubs/code/code.asp

National Commission for the Protection of Human Subjects of Biomedical and Behavioral Research. (1978). *The Belmont Report*. Retrieved from http://www.hhs.gov/ohrp/humansubjects/guidance/belmont.html.

Office for Human Research Protections. (2009). *Protection of Human Subjects*. Retrieved from http://www.hhs.gov/ohrp/humansubjects/regbook2013.pdf.pdf

Office of Research Integrity, Department of Health and Human Services. (2006). *Responsible conduct of research*. Retrieved from http://ori.dhhs.gov/education/

Pittenger, D. J. (2002). Deception in research: Distinctions and solutions from the perspective of utilitarianism. *Ethics and Behavior, 12*(2), 117–142.

Pryce, N. (1995). *A heuristic study using an evolutionary perspective of the experience of adolescents adapting to the head injury of a parent.* Unpublished dissertation, Columbia, SC: University of South Carolina.

Sieber, J. E. (1992). *Planning ethically responsible research.* Newbury Park, CA: Sage Publications.

Taylor, L. (1998). Parents who lost an adult child to AIDS. In A. Godenzi (Ed.), *Abenteuer forschung* (pp. 189–258). Freiburg, Switzerland: University of Freiburg.

U.S. Food and Drug Administration. (2014). *Institutional Review Boards Frequently Asked Questions – Information Sheet.* Retrieved from http://www.fda.gov/RegulatoryInformation/Guidances/ucm126420.htm

Vasgird, D., & Hyman-Browne, E. (n.d.). *RCR mentoring.* Retrieved from http://ori.dhhs.gov/education/products/columbia_wbt/rcr_ mentoring/

Wakefield, A. J., Murch, S. H., Anthony, A., Linnell, J., Casson, D. M., Malik, M., Berelowitz, M., Dhillon, A. P., Thomson, M. A., Harvey, P., Valentine, A., Davies, S. E., & Walker-Smith, J. A. (1998). Ileal-lymphoid-nodular hyperplasia, non-specific colitis, and pervasive developmental disorder in children. *The Lancet, 351,* 637–41. (Retracted February 2010 by the Editors of *The Lancet*)

Rortveit, K., Astrom, S., & Severinsson, E. (2009). The feeling of being trapped in and ashamed of one's own body: A qualitative study of women who suffer from eating difficulties. *International Journal of Mental Health Nursing, 18*(2), 91–99.

Rothery, M. (1993). Problems, questions, and hypotheses. In R. M. Grinnell, Jr. (Ed.), *Social work research and evaluation* (4th ed., pp. 17–37). Itasca, IL: F. E. Peacock.

Rubin, A., & Babbie, E. (2008). *Research methods for social work* (6th ed.). Belmont, CA: Brooks Cole.

Shields, J. J., Broome, K. M., Delany, P. J., Fletcher, B. W., & Flynn, B. M. (2007). Religion and substance abuse treatment: Individual and program effects. *Journal for the Scientific Study of Religion, 46,* 355–371.

Shontz, F. (1986). *Fundamentals of research in the behavioral sciences.* Washington, DC: American Psychiatric Press.

Smith, C. (2007). Support services for students with Asperger's Syndrome in higher education. *College Student Journal, 41,* 515–531.

Vrabel, K. R., Ro, O., Martinsen, E. W., Hoffart, A. & Rosenvinge, J. H. (2010). Five-year prospective study of personality disorders in adults with longstanding eating disorders. *International Journal of Eating Disorders, 43,* 22–28.

Walsh, R. A, & Tzelepis, F. (2007). Adolescents and tobacco use: Systematic review of qualitative research methodologies and partial synthesis of findings. *Substance Use and Misuse, 42,* 1269–1321.

Chapter 3

Agee, J. (2009). Developing qualitative research questions: A reflexive process. *International Journal of Qualitative Studies in Education, 22,* 431–447.

Anastas, J. W. (2010). Quality in qualitative evaluation: Issues and possible answers. *Research on Social Work Practice, 14,* 57–65.

Bellomy, P., Berstein, H., & Bickley, S., et al. (1989). *Factors affecting child protection workers' decision-making in Sumter County.* Unpublished MSW research project. Columbia, SC: University of South Carolina, College of Social Work.

Creswell, J. W. (1998). *Qualitative inquiry and research design: Choosing from among five traditions.* Thousand Oaks, CA: Sage Publications, Inc.

Creswell, J. W. (2007). *Qualitative inquiry and research design* (2nd ed.). Thousand Oaks, CA: Sage Publications, Inc.

Denzin, N. K. (1989). *The research act: Theoretical introduction to sociological methods* (3rd ed.). Englewood Cliffs, NJ: Prentice Hall.

Fennig, S., & Hadas, A. (2010). Suicidal behavior and depression in adolescents with eating disorders. *Nordic Journal of Psychiatry, 64,* 32–39.

Frankfort-Nachmias, C., & Nachmias, D. (1992). *Research methods in the social sciences* (4th ed.). New York: St. Martin's Press.

Kartalova-O'Doherty, Y., & Doherty, D. T. (2008). Coping strategies and styles of family carers of persons with enduring mental illness: A mixed methods analysis. *Scandinavian Journal of Caring Services, 22,* 19–28.

Ramos-Lira, L, Gonzalez-Forteza, C., & Wagner, F. A. (2006). Violent victimization and drug involvement among Mexican middle school students. *Addiction, 101,* 850–856.

Chapter 4

Acker, G. M. (2010). The influence of managed care on job-related attitudes of social workers. *Social Work in Mental Health, 8,* 174–189.

Beck, A. T., Steer, R. A., Ball, R., & Ranier, W. (1996). Comparison of Beck Depression Inventories –IA and –II in psychiatric outpatients. *Journal of Personality Assessment, 67,* 588–597.

Bellomy, P., Berstein, H., Bickley, S., et al. (1989). *Factors affecting child protection workers' decision-making in Sumter County.* Unpublished MSW research project. Columbia, SC: University of South Carolina, College of Social Work.

Bonewell, K. J. (2009). Intrinsic and extrinsic religiosity and sexual compulsivity with Christian males: Understanding concepts and correlations based on race, age, socioeconomic status, and marital status. *Dissertation Abstracts International, 69,* 7802. Doctoral dissertation, Capella University, 2009.

Donate-Lopez, C., Espigares-Rodriguez, E., Jimenez-Moleon, J. J., Luna-del-Castillo, J. D., Bueno-Cavanillas, A., & Lardelli-Claret, P. (2010). The association of age, sex and helmet use with the risk of death for occupants of two-wheeled motor vehicles involved in traffic crashes in Spain. *Accident Analysis and Prevention, 42,* 297–306.

Goldstein, H. (1969). *Research standards and methods for social workers.* Northbrook, IL: Whitehall Company.

Hogan, T. P., Awad, A. G., & Eastwood, R. (1983). A self-report scale predictive of drug compliance in schizophrenics: Reliability and discriminative validity. *Psychological Medicine, 13,* 177–183.

LaGuardia, C. (Ed.). (2003). *Magazines for libraries* (12th ed.). New York: Bowker.

Leung, A. W. (2007). Shyness and social anxiety: Causal modeling of developmental antecedents. *Dissertation Abstracts International, 68*, 626. Doctoral dissertation, State University of New York at Albany, 2007.

Marmorstein, N. R. (2010). Longitudinal associations between depressive symptoms and alcohol problems: The influence of comorbid delinquent behavior. *Addictive Behaviors, 35*, 564–571.

National Association of Social Workers. (2009). *An author's guide to social work journals* (5th ed.). Silver Spring, MD: NASW Press.

Smith, B. C. S. (2009). Job burnout, spirituality and social support in women who are perinatal social workers: A quantitative and qualitative study. *Dissertation Abstracts International, 70*, 1035. Doctoral dissertation, Tulane University, 2009.

Sowers, K. M., Ellis, R., & Dessel, A. (2010). Literature reviews. In B. Thyer (Ed.), *The handbook of social work research methods* (2nd ed., pp. 504–516). Thousand Oaks, CA: Sage Publications, Inc.

Townsend, L., Floersch, J., & Findling, R. L. (2009). Adolescent attitudes toward psychiatric medication: The utility of the Drug Attitude Inventory. *Journal of Child Psychiatry and Psychology, 50*, 1523–1531.

Weinbach, R. W., & Grinnell, R. M., Jr. (2015). *Statistics for social workers* (9th ed.). Boston: Allyn & Bacon.

Chapter 5

Benoliel, J. (1985). Loss and adaptation: Circumstances, contingencies, and consequences. *Death Studies, 9*, 217–233.

Campbell, D., & Stanley, J. (1963). *Experimental and quasi-experimental designs for research*. Chicago: Rand.

Gonzales-Prendes, A. A., & Jozefowicz-Simbeni, D. M. H. (2009). The effects of cognitive-behavioral treatment on trait anger and paranoid ideation. *Research on Social Work Practice, 19*, 686–693.

Kübler-Ross, E. (1989). *On death and dying*. New York: Macmillan.

McMillen, J. C., & Raghaven, R. (2009). Pediatric to adult mental health service use of young people leaving the foster care system. *Journal of Adolescent Health, 44*, 7–13.

Plow, M. A., Mathiowetz, V., & Lowe, D. A. (2009). Comparing individualized rehabilitation to a group wellness intervention for persons with multiple sclerosis. *American Journal of Health Promotion, 24*, 23–26.

Rubin, A, & Babbie, E. (2012). *Essential research methods for social work* (3rd ed.). Belmont, CA: Thompson Brooks/Cole.

Schwinn, T. M., Schinke, S. P., & Trent, D. N. (2010). Substance use among late adolescent urban youths: Mental health and gender influences. *Addictive Behaviors, 35*, 30–34.

Singleton, R., & Straits, B. (2005). *Approaches to social research*. New York: Oxford University Press.

Chapter 6

Anastas, J. W. (2004). Quality in qualitative evaluation: Issues and possible answers. *Research on Social Work Practice, 14*, 57–65.

Ayon, C. (2009). Shorter time lines, yet higher hurdles: Mexican families' access to child welfare mandated services. *Children and Youth Services Review, 31*, 609–616.

Beauvais, F., & Trimble, J. E. (1992). The role of the researcher in evaluating American–Indian alcohol and other drug abuse prevention programs. In OSAP, *Cultural competence for evaluators* (pp. 173–202). Washington, DC: U.S. Department of Health and Human Services.

Bengtsson-Tops, A., Saveman, B-L., Tops, D. (2009). Staff experience and understanding of working with abused women suffering from mental illness. *Health and Social Care in the Community, 17*, 459–465.

Bergen, H. A., & Ezzy, D. (2009). Mass media and religious identity: A case study of young witches. *Journal of the Scientific Study of Religion, 48*, 501–514.

Blum, E., Heinonen, T., & White, J. (2010). Participatory action research studies. In B. Thyer (Ed.), *The handbook of social work research methods* (2nd ed., pp. 449–465). Thousand Oaks, CA: Sage Publications, Inc.

Brown, C. G., Weber, S., & Ali, S. (2008). Women's body talk: A feminist narrative approach. *Journal of Systemic Therapies, 27*(2), 92–104.

Butler, J. P. (1992). Of kindred minds: The ties that bind. In OSAP, *Cultural competence for evaluators* (pp. 23–54). Washington, DC: U.S. Department of Health and Human Services.

Dauz Williams, P., Piamjariyakul, U., Graff, C. J., Stanton, A., Guthrie, A., Hafeman, C., & Williams, A. R. (2010). Developmental disabilities: Effects on well siblings. *Issues in Comprehensive Pediatric Nursing, 33*, 39–55.

Dwairy, M., Achoui, M., Filus, A., Rezvannia, P., Casullo, M. M., & Vohra, N. (2010). Parenting, mental health, and culture: A fifth cross-cultural research on parenting and psychological adjustment of children. *Journal of Child and Family Studies, 19*, 36–41.

Gagne, P. (1992). Appalachian women: Violence and social control. *Journal of Contemporary Ethnography, 20*, 387–415.

Garcia, A. C., Standlee, A. I., Bechkoff, J., & Cui, Y. (2009). Ethnographic approaches to the internet and computer mediated communication. *Journal of Contemporary Ethnography, 38*, 52–84.

Gold, R. L. (1969). Roles in sociological field observation. In G. J. McCall and J. L. Simmonds (Eds.), *Issues in participant observation* (pp. 30–39). Reading, MA: Addison-Wesley.

Haight, W. L. (2002). *African American children at church: A sociocultural perspective*. Cambridge, England: Cambridge University Press.

Happell, B., Moxham, L., Reid-Searl, K., Dwyer, T., Kahl, J., Morris, J., & Wheatland, N. (2009). Promoting mental health care in a rural pediatric unit through participatory action research. *The Australian Journal of Rural Health, 17*, 155–160.

Harding, R., & Hamilton, P. (2009). Working girls: Abuse or choice in street-level sex work? A study of homeless women in Nottingham. *British Journal of Social Work, 39*, 1118–1137.

Harmon, V. (2010). Experiences of racism and the changing nature of White privilege among lone White mothers of mixed parentage children in the UK. *Ethnic and Racial Studies, 33*, 176–194.

Holosko, M. J. (2010). An overview of qualitative research methods. In B. Thyer (Ed.), *The handbook of social work research methods* (pp. 340–354). Thousand Oaks, CA: Sage Publication, Inc.

Kim, S., McLeod, J. H., & Shantzis, C. (1992). Cultural competence for evaluators working with Asian American communities: Some practical considerations. In OSAP, *Cultural competence for evaluators* (pp. 203–260). Washington, DC: U.S. Department of Health and Human Services.

Krippendorf, K. (2004). *Content analysis: An introduction to its methodology.* Thousand Oaks, CA: Sage Publications, Inc.

Leenaars, A. A., Sayin, A. Candansayar, S., Leenaars, L., Akar, T., & Demirel, B. (2010). Suicide in different cultures: A thematic comparison of suicide notes from Turkey and the United States. *Journal of Cross-Cultural Psychology, 41,* 253–263.

Lipman, J. J. (2002). A qualitative analysis of women's relational and sexual functioning following date rape. *Dissertation Abstracts International: Section B: Sciences and Engineering, 63,* 1567.

Lowery, C. T. (2010). Ethnographic research methods. In B. Thyer (Ed.), *The handbook of social work research methods* (2nd ed., pp. 435–448). Thousand Oaks, CA: Sage Publications, Inc.

Malson, H., & Burns, M. (2009). *Critical feminist approaches to eating disorders.* New York: Routledge.

Marin, G., & Marin, B. (1991). *Research with Hispanic populations.* Newbury Park, CA: Sage Publications, Inc.

Moncrieff, J., Cohen, D., & Mason, J. P. (2009). The subjective experience of taking antipsychotic medication: A content analysis of Internet data. *Acta Psychiatrica Scandinavica, 120,* 102–111.

Neuendorf, K. (2002). *The content analysis guidebook.* Thousand Oaks, CA: Sage Publications, Inc.

Reid, A. H. (2009). The garden of eves: Non-kin social support among low-income African American single mothers in a public housing community. *Dissertations Abstracts International: Section B: Sciences and Engineering, 70,* 3830.

Reinharz, S. (1992). *Feminist methods in social research.* New York: Oxford University Press.

Shek, D. T. L., Tang, V. M. Y., & Han, X. Y. (2005). Evaluation of evaluation studies using qualitative research methods in the social work literature (1990–2003): Evidence that constitutes a wake-up call. *Research on Social Work Practice, 15,* 180–194.

Smith, V. (2009). Ethical and effective ethnographic research methods: A case study with Afghan refugees in California. *Journal of Empirical Research on Human Research Ethics, 4,* 59–72.

Takahashi, Y., Ushida, C., Miyaki, K., Sakai, M., Shimbo, T., & Nakayama, T. (2009). Potential benefits and harms of a peer support social network service on the internet for people with depressive tendencies: Qualitative content analysis and social network analysis. *Journal of Medical Internet Research, 11,* 1–14.

Taylor, L. (1998). Parents who lost an adult child to AIDS. In A. Godenzi (Ed.), *Abenteuer forschung* (pp. 189–258). Freiburg, Switzerland, University of Freiburg.

Timmerman, G. M. (2006). Restaurant eating in non-purge binge-eating women. *Western Journal of Nursing Research, 28,* 811–824.

Trinidad, A. M. O. (2009). Toward kuleana (responsibility): A case study of a contextually grounded intervention for Native Hawaiian youth and young adults. *Aggression and Violent Behavior, 14,* 488–498.

Van de Vijver, F., & Leung, K. (1997). *Methods and data analysis for cross-cultural research.* Thousand Oaks, CA: Sage Publications, Inc.

Van der Velde, J., Williamson, D. L., & Ogilvie, L. D. (2009). Participatory action research: Practical strategies for actively engaging and maintaining participation in immigrant and refugee communities. *Qualitative Health Research, 19,* 1293–1302.

Weinbach, R. (1989). Sudden death and secret survivors: Helping those who grieve alone. *Social Work, 34,* 57–60.

Chapter 7

Corcoran, J., & Littell, J. H. (2010). Meta-analyses. In B. Thyer (Ed.), *The handbook of social work research methods* (2nd ed., pp. 299–312). Thousand Oaks, CA: Sage Publications, Inc.

Fetterman, D. M., Kaftarian, S. J., & Wandersman, A. (Eds.) (1996). *Empowerment evaluation: Knowledge and tools for self-assessment and accountability.* Thousand Oaks, CA: Sage Publications.

Franklin, C., Kim, J. S., & Tripodi, S. J. (2009). A meta-analysis of published school social work practice studies. *Research on Social Work Practice, 19,* 667–677.

Greaves, J. & Salloun, A. (2015). Evaluation of a youth with sexual behavior problems (YSBP) outpatient treatment program. *Child and Adolescent Social Work Journal, 32(2),* 177–185.

Kemp, K., Signal, T., Botros, H., Taylor, N., & Prentice, K. (2014). Equine facilitated therapy with children and adolescents who have been sexually abused: A program evaluation study. *Journal of Child and Family Studies, 23,* 558–566.

Littell, J. H., & Corcoran, J. (2010). *Systematic reviews.* In B. Thyer (Ed.), *The handbook of social work research methods* (2nd ed., pp. 313–337). Thousand Oaks, CA: Sage Publications, Inc.

Litschge, C. M., Vaughn, M. G., & McCrea, C. (2010). The empirical status of treatments for children and youth with conduct problems. *Research on Social Work Practice, 20,* 21–35.

Nugent, W., Sieppert, J., & Hudson, W. (2001). *Practice evaluation for the 21st century.* Belmont, CA: Brooks Cole.

Pignotti, M., & Thyer, B. A. (2009). Why randomized clinical trials are important and necessary to social work practice. In H-W. Otto, A. Polutta, & H. Ziegler (Eds.), *Evidence-based practice: Modernizing the knowledge base of social work* (pp. 99–109). Farmington Hills, MI and Opladen, Germany: Barbara Burdich.

Rossi, P.H., Lipsey, M.W., & Freeman, H.E. (2003). *Evaluation: A systematic approach* (7th ed.). Thousand Oaks, CA: Sage Publications.

Royse, D., Thyer, B.A., & Padgett, D.K. (2009). *Program evaluation: An introduction* (5th ed.). Chicago: Nelson-Hall Publishers.

Thyer, B. A. (1989). First principles of practice research. *British Journal of Social Work, 19,* 309–323.

Thyer, B. A. (1991). Guidelines for evaluating outcome studies on social work practice. *Research on Social Work Practice, 1,* 76–91.

Thyer, B. A., & Myers, L. L. (2007). *A social workers' guide to evaluating practice outcomes.* Alexandria, VA: Council on Social Work Education.

Thyer, B. A., & Myers, L. L. (2010). Cultural diversity and social work practice: An evidenced based approach. In B. A. Thyer,

J. S. Wodarski, L. L. Myers, & D. F. Harrison (Eds.), *Human diversity and social work practice: An evidenced-based approach.* (3rd ed., pp. 3–28). Springfield, IL: Charles C. Thomas.

Unrau, Y., Gabor, P., & Grinnell, R. Jr. (2015). *Program Evaluation for Social Workers: Foundations of Evidence-Based Practice.* New York: Oxford University Press.

Weinbach, R. (2005). *Evaluating social work services and programs.* Boston: Allyn and Bacon.

Chapter 8

Bloom, M., Fischer, J., & Orme, J. (1999). *Evaluating practice: Guidelines for the accountable professional.* Boston: Allyn & Bacon.

Compton, B., Galaway, B., & Cournoyer, B. (2005). *Social work processes* (7th ed.). Pacific Grove, CA: Brooks Cole.

Corcoran, K., & Fischer, J. (2013a). *Measures for clinical practice: A sourcebook. Volume 1: Couples, families, and children* (5th ed.). New York: The Free Press.

Corcoran, K. & Fischer, J. (2013b). *Measures for clinical practice: A sourcebook. Volume 2: Adults* (5th ed.). New York: The Free Press.

Mattaini, M. A. (2010). Single-system studies. In B. A. Thyer (Ed.). *Handbook of social work research methods* (2nd ed., pp. 241–273). Thousand Oaks, CA: Sage Publications, Inc.

Weinbach, R. (2005). *Evaluating social work services and programs.* Boston: Allyn & Bacon.

Chapter 9

Cohen, J. (1988). *Statistical power analysis for the behavioral sciences* (2nd ed.). New York: Lawrence Erlbaum Associates.

Levy, P., & Lemeshow, S. (2008). *Sampling of populations: Methods and applications* (4th ed.). New York: Wiley-Interscience Publishing. Wiley Series in Survey Methodology.

Rosenthal, J. (2001). *Statistics and data interpretation for the helping professions.* Belmont, CA: Wadsworth/Thomson Learning.

Rubin, A., & Babbie, E. (2007). *Essential research methods for social work.* Belmont, CA: Thomson Brooks/Cole.

Thompson, S. (2012). *Sampling* (3rd ed.). New York: Wiley-Interscience Publishing.

Weinbach, R., & Grinnell, R., Jr. (2015). *Statistics for social workers* (9th ed.). Boston: Allyn & Bacon.

Chapter 10

Corcoran, K., & Fischer, J. (2013a). *Measures for clinical practice: A sourcebook. Volume 1: Couples, families, and children* (5th ed.). New York: The Free Press.

Corcoran, K. & Fischer, J. (2013b). *Measures for clinical practice: A sourcebook. Volume 2: Adults* (5th ed.). New York: The Free Press.

Hudson, W. (1988). *CAS: The clinical assessment system.* Tallahassee, FL: WALMYR.

Neuman, W. L. (1997). *Social research methods: Qualitative and quantitative approaches* (3rd ed.). Boston: Allyn & Bacon.

Rubin, A., & Babbie, E. (2014). *Research methods for social work* (8th ed.). Belmont, CA: Brooks/Cole, Cengage Learning.

Chapter 11

Butler, J. P. (1992). Of kindred minds: The ties that bind. In OSAP, *Cultural competence for evaluators* (pp. 23–54). Washington, DC: U.S. Department of Health and Human Services.

Clark, M. M., & Bearman, P. (ongoing). *The September 11th, 2001 oral history narrative and memory project.* Columbia University Oral History Research Office. Retrieved from www.columbia.edu/cu/lweb/indiv/oral/sept11.html.

Hager, M. A., Wilson, S., Pollak, T. H., & Rooney, P. M. (2003). Response rates for mail surveys of nonprofit organizations: A review and empirical test. *Nonprofit and Voluntary Sector Quarterly, 32,* 252–267.

Hutson, R. A., & Kolbe, A. R. (2010). Survey studies. In B. Thyer (Ed.), *The handbook of social work research methods* (pp. 131–148). Thousand Oaks, CA: Sage Publications, Inc.

Logan, S. (2007). *In their own voices. (10 voices: Ten African American women who made a difference).* Columbia, SC: University of South Carolina College of Social Work.

Marin, G., & Marin, B. (1991). *Research with Hispanic populations.* Newbury Park, CA: Sage Publications, Inc.

Martin, R. (1995). *Oral history in social work: Research, assessment, and intervention.* Thousand Oaks, CA: Sage Publications, Inc.

McQueen, A. (2000, August 29). Students humiliated by hazing. *The State,* p. A1.

Mokuau, N., & Browne, C. (1994). Life themes of native Hawaiian female elders: Resources for cultural preservation. *Social Work, 39,* 43–49.

Paxson, M. C., Dillman, D. A., Tarnai, J. (1995). Improving response to business mail surveys. In B. G. Cox, D. A. Binder, B. N. Chinnappa, A. Christianson, M. J. Colledge, & P. S. Kott (Eds.), *Business survey methods* (pp. 303–315). New York: Wiley-Interscience.

Risley-Curtiss, C., Holley, L., & Wolf, S. (2006). The animal–human bond and ethnic diversity. *Social Work, 51,* 257–268.

Rubin, A., & Babbie, E. R. (2014). *Research methods for social work* (8th ed.). Belmont, CA: Brooks/Cole Publishing.

Sales, E., Lichtenwalter, S., & Fevola, A. (2006). Secondary analysis in social work research education: Past, present, and future promise. *Journal of Social Work Education, 42,* 543–558.

Trei, L. (2006, September 27). Social science researcher to overhaul survey methodology with $2 million grant. *Stanford Education News.*

Chapter 12

Keller, J., & Wagner-Steh, K. (2005). A Guttman Scale for empirical prediction of level of domestic violence. *Journal of Forensic Psychology Practice, 5,* 37–48.

Krabbe, P. F. M. (2008). Thurstone scaling as a measurement method to quantify subjective health outcomes. *Medical Care, 46,* 357–365.

Lindemann, D. F., & Brigham, T. A. (2003). A Guttman Scale for assessing condom use skills among college students. *AIDS and Behavior, 7,* 23–27.

Nunnally, J., & Bernstein, I. (1994). *Psychometric theory.* New York: McGraw-Hill.

Shafer, A. B. (2001). Relation of the Big Five to the EASI scales and the Thurstone Temperament Schedule. *Personality and Individual Differences, 31*(2), 193–204.

Tractenberg, R. E., Yomoto, F., Aisen, P. S., Kaye, J. A., & Mislevy, R. J. (2012). Using the Guttman Scale to define and estimate measurement error in items over time: The case of cognitive decline and the meaning of 'points lost.' *PLoS ONE*, 7(2), ArtID: e30019.

Chapter 13

Auerbach, C. F., & Silverstein, L. B. (2003). *Qualitative data: An introduction to coding and analysis.* New York: New York University Press.

Bryman, A., & Cramer, D. (2003). *Quantitative data analysis with Minitab: A guide for social scientists.* New York: Routledge.

Bryman, A., & Cramer, D. (2011). *Quantitative data analysis with IBM SPSS 17, 18 & 19: A guide for social scientists.* New York: Routledge.

Gahan, C., & Hannibal, M. (1998). *Doing qualitative research using QSR NUD*IST.* Thousand Oaks, CA: Sage Publications, Inc.

Gibbs, G. R. (2002). *Qualitative data analysis: Explorations with NVivo.* Philadelphia, PA: Open University Press.

Greasley, P. (2008). *Quantitative data analysis with SPSS: An introduction for health and social science.* New York: Open University Press.

Kuckartz, U. (2004). *An introduction to the computer analysis of qualitative data.* Thousand Oaks, CA: Sage Publications, Inc.

Marshall, C., & Rossman, G. B. (2016). *Designing qualitative research* (6th ed.). Thousand Oaks, CA: Sage Publications, Inc.

Merrium, S. B. (2014). *Qualitative research: A guide to design and implementation* (3rd ed.). New York: John Wiley & Sons.

Norusis, M. (2011). *IBM SPSS statistics 19 guide to data analysis.* Englewood Cliffs, NJ: Prentice Hall.

Patton, M. (2014). *Qualitative research and evaluation methods: Integrating theory and practice* (4th ed.). Thousand Oaks, CA: Sage Publications.

Randolph, K. A., & Myers, L. L. (2013). *Basic statistics in multivariate analysis.* New York: Oxford University Press.

Saldana, J. (2015). *The coding manual for qualitative researchers* (3rd ed.). Thousand Oaks, CA: Sage Publications, Inc.

Warren, C. A. B., & Karner, T. X. (2014). *Discovering qualitative methods: Field research, interviews, and analysis* (3rd ed.). New York: Oxford University Press.

Weinbach, R., & Grinnell, R., Jr. (2015). *Statistics for social workers* (9th ed.). Boston: Allyn & Bacon.

Weitzman, E. A., & Miles, M. B. (1995). *Computer programs for qualitative data analysis: A software sourcebook.* Thousand Oaks, CA: Sage Publications, Inc.

Chapter 14

American Psychological Association. (2009). *Publication manual of the American Psychological Association* (6th ed.). Washington, DC: Author.

Beebe, L. (1993). *Professional writing for the human services.* Washington, DC: NASW Press.

Bem, D. J. (2004). Writing the empirical journal article. In J. M. Darley, M. P. Zanna, & H. L. Roediger III, (Eds., 2nd ed.), *The Compleat Academic: A Career Guide.* Washington DC: American Psychological Association Press.

Galvin, J. (2006). *Writing literature reviews: A guide for students of the social and behavioral sciences* (3rd ed.). Los Angeles: Pyrczak Publishing.

Hart, C. (1998). *Doing a literature review.* Thousand Oaks, CA: Sage Publications, Inc.

Houghton, P. M., & Houghton, T. J. (2009). *APA: The easy way!* (2nd ed.). Flint, MI: Baker College.

Louden-Gerber, G. M. (2009). A group forgiveness intervention for adult male homeless individuals: Effects on forgiveness, rumination, and social connectedness. *Dissertation Abstracts International Section A: Humanities and Social Sciences*, 69, 4640.

NASW Press. (2009). *An author's guide to social work journals* (5th ed.). Washington, DC: NASW Press.

Pyrczak, F., & Bruce, R. (2014). *Writing empirical research reports: A basic guide for students of the social and behavioral sciences* (8th ed.). Glendale, CA: Pyrczak Publishing.

Rossiter, J. (2009). *The APA pocket handbook: Rules for format and documentation.* London: Daryl Willcox Publishing Company.

Szuchman, L. T., & Thomlison, B. (2010). *Writing with style: APA style for social work* (4th ed.). Belmont, CA: Brooks/Cole.

Thyer, B. A. (1994). *Successful publishing in scholarly journals.* Thousand Oaks, CA: Sage Publications, Inc.

Thyer, B. A. (2008). *Preparing research articles.* New York: Oxford University Press.

Text Credits

Chapter 1

p. 1: From "Educational Policy And Accredition Standards for Baccalaureate and Master's Social Work Programs". Published by Council on Social Work Education © 2015; p. 2: From "Evidence-based medicine: How to practice and teach EBM (3rd ed.)" Published by Elsevier © 2005; p. 2: From "Users' Guides to the Medical Literature: A Manual for Evidence-Based Clinical Practice." Published by American Medical Association © 2002; p. 2: From "Social Work Policy Institue from "EVIDENCE-BASED Practice". Published by Social Work Policy Institute © 2010; p. 5: From "Evidence-based Medicine: How to Practice and Teach EBM." Published by Elsevier/Churchill Livingstone © 2005; p. 7: From "Handbook of counselling psychology (3rd ed.)." Published by John Wiley & Sons, Inc © 2000; p. 7: From "Social Work." Published by National Association of Social Workers © 2010; pp. 8–9: From "The Scientific Review of Mental Health Practice." Published by Center for Inquiry © 2005; p. 10: From "Living on the Edge: The Realities of Welfare in America." Published by Columbia University Press © 1994; p. 16: From "Social Work." Published by American Psychological Association (APA) © 2005; p. 19: From "Handbook of Qualitative Research." Published by Sage Publications, Inc. (US) © 1994.

Chapter 2

p. 37: From "Research on Social Work Practice." Published by Sage Publications, Inc. (US) © 2010; pp. 42–43: From "Ethics and Behavior." Published by Lawrence Erlbaum Associates © 2002; p. 43: From "The Penn Center Guide to Bioethics." Published by Springer Publishing Company © 2009; p. 48: From "The Belmont Report." Published by Office for Human Research Protections © 1979.

Chapter 3

p. 52: From "Research Methods for Social Work." Published by Cengage Learning © 2008; p. 52: From "Research Methods in the Social Sciences (4th ed.)." Published by St. Martin's Press © 1992; p. 52: From "Social Work Research and Evaluation." Published by Peacock Publisher © 1993; p. 66: From "Addiction." Published by John Wiley & Sons, Inc © 2006; p. 66: From "Journal for the Scientific Study of Religion." Published by John Wiley & Sons, Inc © 2007; p. 66: From "International Journal of Qualitative Studies in Education." Published by Taylor and Francis © 2009; p. 67: From "International Journal of Mental Health Nursing." Published by John Wiley and Sons © 2009; p. 67: From "College Student Journal." Published by Project Innovation © 2007; p. 67: From "Scandinavian Journal of Caring Sciences." Published by Blackwell Publishing Inc © 2008; p. 68: From "Qualitative Inquiry and Research Design (2nd ed.)." Published by Sage Publications, Inc. (US) © 2007; p. 68: From "The research act: Theoretical introduction to sociological methods (3rd ed.)." Published by Pearson Education © 1989; p. 68: From "Research on Social Work Practice." Published by Sage Publications, Inc. (US) © 2010.

Chapter 4

p. 73: From "The Handbook of Social Work Research Methods." Published by Sage Publications, Inc © 2010.

Chapter 6

p. 126: From "Quality in Qualitative Evaluation: Issues and Possible Answers" by Jeane W. Anastas. Published by SAGE Publications © 2004; p. 127: From "The Handbook of Social Work Research

Methods" by Bruce Thyer. Published by SAGE Publications © 2010; p. 135: From "Abenteuer forschung" by Godenzi Alberto. Published by Freiburg, Switzerland, University of Freiburg © 2005; p. 144: From "Evaluation of Evaluation Studies Using Qualitative Research Methods in the Social Work Literature (1990-2003): Evidence That Constitutes a Wake-Up Call" by Daniel T. L. Shek, Vera M. Y. Tang, X. Y. Han. Published by "SAGE Publications" © 2005; p. 145: From "Evaluation of Evaluation Studies Using Qualitative Research Methods in the Social Work Literature (1990–2003): Evidence That Constitutes a Wake-Up Call" by Daniel T. L. Shek, Vera M. Y. Tang, X. Y. Han. Published by "SAGE Publications" © 2005.

Chapter 7

p. 148: From "The Handbook of Social Work Research Methods" by Bruce Thyer. Published by Sage Publications © 2010; p. 150: From "Evaluating Social Work Services and Programs" by Robert W. Weinbach. Published by Pearson © 2005.

Chapter 8

p. 179: From "The Handbook of Social Work Research Methods" by Bruce Thyer. Published by Sage Publications © 2010; p. 185: Robert W. Weinbach; Laura L. Myers; Bonnie L. Yegidis, Research Methods for Social Workers, 8 Ed., © 2018. Pearson Education, Inc., New York, NY; p. 187: Robert W. Weinbach; Laura L. Myers; Bonnie L. Yegidis, Research Methods for Social Workers, 8 Ed., © 2018. Pearson Education, Inc., New York, NY; p. 189: Robert W. Weinbach; Laura L. Myers; Bonnie L. Yegidis, Research Methods for Social Workers, 8 Ed., © 2018. Pearson Education, Inc., New York, NY. p. 190: Robert W. Weinbach; Laura L. Myers; Bonnie L. Yegidis, Research Methods for Social Workers, 8 Ed., © 2018. Pearson Education, Inc., New York, NY; p. 193: Robert W. Weinbach; Laura L. Myers; Bonnie L. Yegidis, Research Methods for Social Workers, 8 Ed., © 2018. Pearson Education, Inc., New York, NY; p. 194: Robert W. Weinbach; Laura L. Myers; Bonnie L. Yegidis, Research Methods for Social Workers, 8 Ed., © 2018. Pearson Education, Inc., New York, NY; p. 195: Robert W. Weinbach; Laura L. Myers; Bonnie L. Yegidis, Research Methods for Social Workers, 8 Ed., © 2018. Pearson Education, Inc., New York, NY; p. 197: Robert W. Weinbach; Laura L. Myers; Bonnie L. Yegidis, Research Methods for Social Workers, 8 Ed., © 2018. Pearson Education, Inc., New York, NY; p. 198: Robert W. Weinbach; Laura L. Myers; Bonnie L. Yegidis, Research Methods for Social Workers, 8 Ed., © 2018. Pearson Education, Inc., New York, NY.

Chapter 9

p. 208: Robert W. Weinbach; Laura L. Myers; Bonnie L. Yegidis, Research Methods for Social Workers, 8 Ed., © 2018. Pearson Education, Inc., New York, NY.

Chapter 10

p. 225: From "Social research methods: Qualitative and quantitative approaches " by W. Lawrence Neuman. Published by Pearson © 1997.

Chapter 13

p. 302: Robert W. Weinbach; Laura L. Myers; Bonnie L. Yegidis, Research Methods for Social Workers, 8 Ed., © 2018. Pearson Education, Inc., New York, NY; p. 303: Robert W. Weinbach; Laura L. Myers; Bonnie L. Yegidis, Research Methods for Social Workers, 8 Ed., © 2018. Pearson Education, Inc., New York, NY; p. 304: Robert W. Weinbach; Laura L. Myers; Bonnie L. Yegidis, Research Methods for Social Workers, 8 Ed., © 2018. Pearson Education, Inc., New York, NY.

Chapter 14

p. 314: From "Preparing Research Articles" by Bruce Thyer. Published by Oxford University Press © 2008.

Index